LANGUAGE BEYOND POSTMODERNISM

Northwestern University
Studies in Phenomenology
and
Existential Philosophy

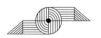

LANGUAGE
BEYOND
POSTMODERNISM

Saying and Thinking in Gendlin's Philosophy

Edited by David Michael Levin

Northwestern University Press
Evanston, Illinois

Northwestern University Press
Evanston, Illinois 60208-4210

ISBN cloth 0-8101-1358-9
    paper 0-8101-1359-7

Library of Congress Cataloging-in-Publication Data

Language beyond postmodernism : saying and thinking in Gendlin's
    philosophy / edited by David Michael Levin.
        p.   cm. — (Northwestern University studies in phenomenology
    and existential philosophy)
        "A collection of critical studies . . . Following each of the
    studies, there is a reply by Gendlin"—Introd.
        Includes bibliographical references and index.
        ISBN 0-8101-1358-9 (alk. paper).—ISBN 0-8101-1359-7 (pbk. :
    alk. paper)
        1. Gendlin, Eugene T., 1926–   —Contributions in philosophy of
    language.   2. Language and languages—Philosophy.   I. Gendlin,
    Eugene T., 1926–   .   II. Levin, David Michael, 1939–   .
    III. Series: Northwestern University studies in phenomenology &
    existential philosophy.
    P85.G455L36   1997
    149'.94—dc21   97-19492
                                                                    CIP

The paper used in this publication meets the minimum requirements of the
American National Standard for Information Sciences—Permanence of Paper
for Printed Library Materials, ANSI Z39.48-1984.

We must distinguish between the existing system of language forms, on the one hand, and the power of language, on the other. . . . Language escapes the old forms of language, although the forms are never absent.

If we *dwell* in anything explicitly formed, we attend to *more* than that form. This "more" is what fresh thought-steps can "follow" from. We can call it "implicit" only if we allow that word to "open" to this kind of "following."

A fresh step of thought must "follow"; we must be able to come with the old word-uses and *follow* the new one. This word brings the old logical type of following, which meant: What follows was already implicit in the logical form that preceded. Now we "open" this so that the old "following" enables the new one to *follow*. What now follows "was" already there . . . but not as a logical form.

If we dwell, we dwell *with* how anything is both already formed, shaped, cut, present, representable, and yet *also* implicit and being-for further moves. What is implied-from-the-form can be gotten directly, but anything *is* also "implicit," which means, if we dwell, that it is for poetizing. "Implicit" does not convert into explicit, ever, as if it were merely a form we did not notice.

Eugene T. Gendlin, "Dwelling"

Contents

Introduction: David Michael Levin   1

1 Eugene Gendlin   3
   How Philosophy Cannot Appeal to Experience, and How It Can

2 David Michael Levin   42
   Gendlin's Use of Language: Historical Connections, Contemporary
   Implications

3 David Kolb   65
   Filling in the Blanks
   Eugene Gendlin: A Reply

4 William James Earle   84
   Tacit Knowledge and Implicit Intricacy
   Eugene Gendlin: A Reply

5 Hans Julius Schneider   97
   The Situatedness of Thinking, Knowing, and Speaking: Wittgenstein
   and Gendlin
   Eugene Gendlin: A Reply

6 Meredith Williams   120
   The Implicit Intricacy of Mind and Situation
   Eugene Gendlin: A Reply

7 Mark Johnson   148
   Embodied Meaning and Cognitive Science
   Eugene Gendlin: A Reply

8 J. N. Mohanty   176
   Experience and Meaning
   Eugene Gendlin: A Reply

9 Robert C. Scharff   190
   After Dilthey and Heidegger: Gendlin's Experiential Hermeneutics
   Eugene Gendlin: A Reply

10 Lawrence J. Hatab   234
    Language and Human Nature
    Eugene Gendlin: A Reply

11 Kenneth Liberman   252
    Meaning Reflexivity: Gendlin's Contribution to Ethnomethodology
    Eugene Gendlin: A Reply

12 Jerald Wallulis   270
    Carrying Forward: Gadamer and Gendlin on History, Language, and
    the Body
    Eugene Gendlin: A Reply

13 Graeme Nicholson   288
    Intricacy: A Metaphysical Idea
    Eugene Gendlin: A Reply

14 Véronique M. Fóti   305
    Alterity and the Dynamics of Metaphor
    Eugene Gendlin: A Reply

15 Joseph Margolis   321
    Language as Lingual
    Eugene Gendlin: A Reply

Works Cited   339

Notes   343

Contributors   375

Introduction

David Michael Levin

When it comes to the practice and theory of language, Eugene Gendlin offers a radically different approach—an approach that not only challenges other philosophies of language at a theoretical level, but demonstrates its own merit in a way of using words, a reflexive practice of extraordinary intricacy and subtlety, which enables us to attend very carefully to the *events* of language that are taking place at a micrological level and involve the body of felt experiencing.

Dancing on the ruins of representation, the remains of the modern philosophies of language that have held us under their spell since the beginning of the modern age, the advocates of postmodernism have been dreaming a language of excess and endlessly deconstructive reflexivity, a language that could never be held captive in any conceptual forms, a language released from the logic of identity and the grammar of the same. But, surprising as it may seem, this dream is not nearly radical enough. For this language of excess, of endless difference, is actually arrested and frozen, unable to move beyond the dilemma of a persistent structuralism, either caught inside finished conceptual structures or lost outside them in utter indeterminacy. Because he is able to carry meaning forward and show how this practice works, Gendlin goes beyond both alternatives. Thus, what he contributes to the current debates is indeed a language that "exceeds," a language that moves with great agility— beyond postmodernism.

This book is a collection of critical studies on the Gendlin work in the philosophy of language. Following each of the studies, there is a reply by Gendlin. In addition, Gendlin himself has contributed a chapter—a major new formulation of his practice and theory of language. All of

1

DAVID MICHAEL LEVIN

the chapters were written especially for this collection and involved their authors in some fruitful collaboration or exchange of ideas with both Gendlin and the editor. The essays gathered together in this collection identify problems of general and timely significance and raise difficult critical questions. I do not doubt that they will provoke thoughtful debate.

1

How Philosophy Cannot Appeal to Experience, and How It Can

Eugene Gendlin

1. Why the Project Seems Impossible

We can develop a new mode of language and thinking which enters, and speaks from, what is *more than* conceptual patterns (distinctions, differences, comparisons, similarities, generalities, schemes, figures, categories, cognitions, cultural and social forms . . . . .), although these are always inseparably at work as well. For example, "more than" is a pattern, but here it says more than the pattern.

Language brings patterns and distinctions, but *what it says* exceeds them. A new mode of language can turn to advantage what has long seemed a problem: *the incapacity of the conceptual patterns* to control, contain, or capture an unavoidable so-called "excess." I agree that all patterns and distinctions can break down, but what exceeds them can be found performing many roles that go far beyond the breakdown of concepts and distinctions.

It is now widely recognized that every person speaks from somewhere, *situated* in midst of life and situations. But this has been understood only as limiting and disappointing the wish for a so-called "objectivity" which would apply to everyone, be a pure pattern, and require no person at all.

In the current postmodern impasse there are calls for some new way to philosophize from *experience (the more, practice, situations, situatedness, wisdom, the body, thickness, the open . . . . .),* but this has to be done in a very new way.

I will first present the reasons why it seems impossible for philosophy to enter into experience (. . . . .). Then I will show how these very reasons enable us to speak from it in a new way.

We cannot *speak* of experience (situations, ...) *apart from* the distinctions and concepts that each word brings. All speaking involves them, and they are implicit also in any silent experience and wordless situation. So we can speak of *more* only *with* some conceptual patterns or distinctions. Conversely, the distinctions are never pure or separate either. In seemingly pure logic one's situatedness plays many implicit roles. The problem is that since neither is ever separate, and we always already have both, how could we possibly do more with the *more*, than we already always do?

I will show that we can distinguish quite different ways of speaking from *more*. We can distinguish logical ways from more-than-logical ways, and use both. We can employ all that logical thought can give us and also move beyond it. This can be distinguished from what is merely arbitrary and less than logical. But today this distinction seems to hinge on unexaminable assumptions.

Another problem is that experience is largely implicit; it seems foolish to want to explicate the implicit. The explication will be another *explicit* version, not the implicit which functions implicitly.

It also seems to be a problem that no exhaustive examination of experience (. . . . .) is possible, since it is never completely in view, never only an object presented in front of us, never totally present to us. Experience is always also dispersed *in* our situations; we are *in it*, and there is always more of it *in us* (*with*, *under*, and *behind* us, and *out there* . . . . .). These little prepositions mean not only their spatial meaning, but also *more*, as they say what they are saying here. How words can work in this way will be important to us.

What words mean is not presented before us either. They mean their effects in the situations in which we say them. Therefore, Wittgenstein thought that no theory of language is possible at all, since it would present something called "language" in front of us—and be false even to the very language being used to tell about language.

Philosophy is said to be at an end today. People recognize that logical arguments can be devised for mutually exclusive positions on any question. Nothing seems capable of adjudicating between them, except just such arguments again. Arguments are not only various; each ends in contradictions if pursued. There is no longer any belief in the power of argument to criticize and found itself.

People debate whether relativism (philosophical or cultural) is a tenable position, although to *argue* about it presumes the value of argument. Moreover, relativism consists of a menu of just the kind of arguments and positions which seem to have lost their power. Nor is relativism avoided if we consider ourselves locked into one point in the historical sequence of successive approaches. Historicism only locks us into one spot in the sequence.

The traditional concepts inhere in all the words, and cannot be removed. Even when we have criticized and rejected them, they are still implicit in our words.

People recognize at last that every standpoint centers; every argument organizes (differentiates, synthesizes, entitizes . . . . .) in a way that could be otherwise. Various traditional schemes can be recognized in my string, ending in . . . . . I will show that this variety is not a problem to be solved. It is not an obstacle to be removed. That there are many schemes and centers, and that the organization from each can break down, is a central insight without which philosophy would be naive.

I was helped to this insight long before it became the new center of philosophical attention. I have been trying to establish a philosophy that begins with it. I am now ready with several decades of work on these problems. With McKeon we became able to recognize one or another strand of the tradition in any sentence. At that time only a few of us kept pointing this out. I am glad that many people now turn to notice the traditional concepts in the words they just used. Let us not fall back from this recognition. But the question is: What sort of thinking is possible *with* and *after* it?

No matter how we proceed, there are always other ways. We have some choice among alternatives, but much more would be different if we were differently situated in history, social class, culture, circumstances, and personal uniqueness, if we were burglars or farmers, or specialized differently. It can seem that whatever we assert is contradicted and canceled by equally arbitrary alternatives. There are other ways to structure anything—including ways that would not be in terms of "ways" and "structuring," as if by an assumed operator. So we cannot even say *that*. This is ironic but not a joke, since consequences follow not only from positive assertions. It is well known that they follow equally from how one unitizes and organizes the problem to show why nothing can be asserted.

These insights are very valuable, and not negative. They will enable us to go on in a new way. *The choice today is not between remaining mired, or falling back and ignoring these problems.* The choice is not between pretending to lose logic and science, or upholding logic and science by ignoring their implicit assumptions. We need not pretend to be blind, in order to find a way to go on. Philosophy can go on in a new way—not without these insights, but through them.

The dead end of postmodernism arises when one discounts the role of experience because it is never pure, never without conceptual forms and distinctions already implicit in it, and then discounts those because they are never purely logical but always involve experience. They are said to obscure each other, as if distinctions *ought to* work purely alone, and as if situations (experience) *ought to* consist of finished givens that we could simply observe and represent. These assumptions are still honored by the current contention that if they are false, we are at an end.

Supposedly, we cannot say anything because *saying* is taken to be an innocent and hopeless attempt to make the statement *be* what we want to say. But why consider ongoing speech futile because it fails to fit an old model, especially one we reject? Why speak of speaking as if it were what it is evidently not, and never could have been?

The time has come to reverse this: We can let "saying" say what happens when we say it, and when we say any other words. Saying does not enclose in patterns, nor does it seek to do so. The saying that we do is not impossible. We can develop a way to speak from *this* saying.

Instead of the impossible purity of each alone, we find that distinctions *work-in* situations. It is true that situatedness (the more, the . . . . .) is not separable from language, nor from distinctions. This insight corrects the old assumption of meanings apart from words and concepts. But it is an overcorrection of this error to take "*not separable from*" as if it meant that situations and language *have no order other than* distinctions (concepts . . . . .). We will find that the capacities of language are greater and different from concepts and distinctions, and that situations are always wider than the existing language. What is more than distinctions shows itself not only as their contradictions and breakdowns; it functions in many *orderly* ways. (These can also let the word "orderly" work in their way.) But since distinctions, language, and situatedness cannot be had separately, they seem merged. It is true that we always speak from more than distinctions, but not always in the same way. My first task will be to show that we can distinguish between very different ways of speaking from more.

We will find that experience (situatedness, more, the excess . . . . .) *plays many different distinguishable roles* which a new mode of language can employ *deliberately*. I will show that we can speak from these roles when they are happening.

We need not wish for convenient givens, and then despair. *We can recognize from the start that experience (. . . . .) is not given in already-formed units which cognition could simply observe, represent, or approximate.* Experience is "non-numerical and multischematic," as I phrased it in *Experiencing and the Creation of Meaning. It* does not come in cleanly shaped units. When we speak of *an* experience, or call *it* "it," those little words exceed their grammar of delimited things. We can recognize that experience is never just equal to patterns or entitized units. What we say may seem right, but if we go further, we soon change what we said. Anything experienced is further differentiable, and in various ways. Some people consider it a desperate problem that this drives the cognitive forms into contradictions.

Not only does experience (. . . . .) not come in cognitive units; we will also recognize that it is always open for further living and action. And, not just open; it often *demands* further steps; then we are not at liberty to invent them as we please, and yet they are not already determined. *Experiencing offers neither the convenience of finished givens, nor the convenience of indeterminacy.* It does not permit us to say whatever we wish, and yet it is not finally determined. Therefore, its articulation cannot be representation nor can it be construction; its articulation is itself a further experiencing.

The word "experience" (situation, excess, practice . . . . .) comes with a string of quite different words, and with a . . . . . after them. Once we know the variety, the other words are implicit even when only one is written. Each word also adds something different, if it makes sense in that spot. The . . . . . is not their combination; it is rather a situation (an experience, a slot in a sentence . . . . .). *We can let a . . . . . come in any spot where we pause, and we can think from it, even if we don't write it.* This way of using words will soon explain itself (and augment what "explain" can mean). To think from such a . . . . . , rather than only from some *concept of* experience is one way in which our appeal to experience differs from the old appeals.

But can we move beyond the old distinctions and concepts? Must we not always fall back? For example, my friend says he wants to speak of "the body as subject," but isn't his project already lost? The word "subject" brings the old distinction between an external objectivity and a (leftover) subjective realm. The word brings the assumption that reality is the objects. In that reality the body is an externally perceived *object.* The subject seems "subjective," already depreciated and segregated from "objective reality." In the object-language it seems we cannot speak of *the body from which we are speaking,* and yet—didn't my last phrase do just that?

Wittgenstein helps us to get past the old concepts. He showed that a word says (means) *what it does* in a situation. He could give a series of twenty or more quite precise, yet different meanings for the same word. The different uses have "no feature in common," he showed. No concept determines what a word means. (I discuss him further in section 3.) We can take it from Wittgenstein that the uses of words are not bound by (old) concepts and schemes.

We can go on from this. We can let words acquire new uses in our situation here, the one in which we are discussing how words and situations interact. We can say that the situation *gives the word a new life.* A situation *changes itself* in response to the words, and this change is their meaning. The situation *absorbs* the words that are spoken in it. The situation *gives birth* to the words that *change* it. Situation and words *cross,* so that each becomes part of the meaning of the other. As word after word *comes,* the situation *reads* (. . . . .) the words in its own way.

What these words say is also happening to them here; they say what they make happen. They say how they work.

This reading of language opens many paths. Words that speak from how they work can tell about language. They can enable us speak from *ourselves* and from how words *come* in our *bodies.* But "ourselves" and "bodies"—indeed all such words—will develop further meanings in new uses. *Thereby they can move beyond the traditional schemes they bring.* Today all this is on the verge of becoming widely understandable, but may still seem impossible. I will show it gradually.

Let me say a little more about the supposed "end of philosophy." The phrase comes from Heidegger who used (or misused) the word "philosophy" to name certain traditional Western assumptions, especially two of them: the subject/object distinction, and the assumption that fundamental truths can be *stated.* He said that every assertion hides more than it reveals. He convinced many philosophers to reject the subject/object distinction, but now there seems to be no way to talk about ourselves. And the topic we seem unable to discuss is still called "the human subject." He convincingly rejected many other concepts, but because they inhere in the language there seems to be no way to go on.

The Heideggerians speak of "the new beginning which cannot begin." They mean that the tradition stands in the way, and yet we cannot begin outside of it. They are not wrong to guard against simplistic "solutions." But Heidegger pointed to a way to go on. In the very act of recognizing the old forms he found an "openness" beyond the forms. He said that poetry and philosophy both take their rise from this openness. But he said he could only "point" to the openness. And we could wonder how he could even *point,* since that word seems to speak of the openness as if it were a thing in space, over there.

Derrida says he finds no openness; the old distinctions always reen-close fresh thinking. And new ones would not be better. He finds a flow of inconsistent distinctions, new ones displacing the old which continue underneath as well. At best one can keep both sides of the contradictions.

Not all of this is new. In Greek times it was known that there is no neutral way to observe and report. Nature and nurture were said to be inseparable in humans, and nurture (education, culture) varies greatly.

It was widely held that there is no way to adjudicate among the variety. It was known that one can argue for and against any position. The ancient dialecticians knew that concepts easily turn into their opposites. Plato's *Parmenides* showed how all terms can contradict themselves; Aristotle wrote a book of strategies which he claimed could undermine *any* definition. All this was old even then. We can say with some justice that these insights are the *beginning* of philosophy, since philosophy always seeks to examine assumptions. But every examination brings its own assumptions. This too has long been recognized. It has led to skepticism, or to a new philosophy with some special claim to be not just one more. Most major philosophers, for example Plato, Aristotle, Kant, and Hegel did make such special claims. Their philosophies break down too, but first they go a long way. Their breakdown could be seen only at the edge, if they are pursued far enough.

What is new today about all concepts and distinctions breaking down is that this insight is already at the center. One can *begin* with it. But now all formulations are rejected in advance, and there seems to be no way forward. No philosophical projects seem possible. For example, Hilary Putnam concludes a long discussion by asking: "Is there something left for philosophers to do?" And he answers: "Yes and No." He has the courage to refrain from the common retort that all this cannot be so, since we cannot go on philosophizing if it is (and surely we must go on philosophizing). Instead he bravely says that we can still work on small questions, not for the sake of results, but to have a satisfying time. He now favors giving "practical wisdom" some major role. (See *Realism with a Human Face.*)

Bernard Williams (*Ethics and the Limits of Philosophy*) says that practice is "thicker" than theory, especially in ethics. My word "thickness" comes from him.

Those who call for some sort of practical wisdom or experience recognize that we can appeal to experience only in some new way. We are well aware of the failures of previous ways. But the postmodern impasse does show a remarkable loss of the contributions of certain philosophies. The problem of the twentieth century has been to move beyond conceptual forms, and some important openings *were* achieved.

Of course, I did not find a new way alone. It comes out of Wittgenstein, Husserl, Heidegger, Sartre, Merleau-Ponty, and before them Dilthey and the American pragmatists, including McKeon (whose main works are just now being published). But we have to move past the usual way of reading them. It is customary to read back into their works just those assumptions which they most questioned. In section 3 I offer a reading that shows how they point the way.

Meanwhile we can recall where these philosophers stand, when they speak: (1) they speak *neither just logically from concepts and distinctions, nor apart from them*; (2) they speak *neither from the objective, nor the subjective,* neither from an external nor an internal standpoint. Let me show how these two standpoints are restored in my philosophy, and discuss what I owe my predecessors at the end.

The purely logical side of philosophy has made beautiful advances, going from strength to strength. But on the more-than-logical side, the subtlety has been lost today. Logic is now only denigrated by the recognition that it always involves implicit assumptions that remain unexamined.

Of course, logic has only a limited validity. We notice this when we see that lifting out even just one additional detail from a situation utterly changes the logically necessary conclusions we had before. Logic does not begin until after the terms (the units, the variables) have been generated, and this always involves most of the assumptions we would need to examine.

As I have already said, if we insist that logical structures and situatedness are always simply mixed, we lose both. But, if we enter even a short way into what implicitly happens in logical inference, we find that in logic and most scientific thinking one *takes* a distinction or conceptual pattern *alone* (that is to say *as if it were alone*), which requires *the implicit effort* to set aside all of the inseparable *more* (all one has there, knows, feels, experiences, is . . . . .), including the genesis and social context that is assumed in the conceptual pattern and its applications. This setting aside is real in that it actually occurs; one actually does it, but of course this does not in any way avoid the unexamined assumptions and consequences inherent in all that, to which one is not attending.

This is what the phrase "taking the distinction *alone* . . . . ." says, if we let "alone" speak from what happens when we use it logically. (Yes, the word "alone" here *does* this here, as well as saying it about itself and all other logical uses.) It might seem that "alone" really says its opposite here, but that isn't so. Its scheme of something separate does still work here, but now it says how its scheme (and any scheme) *does* work *in this kind* of alone . . . . . , as in logic.

Let the italicized words say how they work: To *take* patterns as patterns *alone* . . . . . , *purely logically*, is a vital human power, but the great advances of logic and science have been poorly controlled because logic has not yet been well understood either by the logical or by the more-than-logical side of philosophy.

The power of logical implications can be employed more knowingly, if (a minute later) we also articulate (carry forward, differentiate, synthesize, enter, speak from . . . . .) its situated context. To know how to do this would open avenues for thought and reevaluation in every scientific context, ways which do not now exist.

Our society has not yet developed a known and expected way to enter the crucial implicit contexts which logical reasoning always involves. But to use this fact only to denigrate it provides no bridge, no relation to logic and science. They march on and leave the philosophical critique of science simplistic and helpless. Instead, we can come to understand and control it, if we enter into what happens implicitly in a logical or scientific move. As we find throughout my philosophy, if we enter this even a short way, we can move past the old issues. Here we will establish logic, and then also what is less than logic, and what is more.

Conceptual patterns are never just alone without all sorts of assumptions, but when one draws logical implications from a conceptual scheme or distinction *alone* . . . . . , let us allow *this* "alone" to say how it *does* work (even if we don't write the . . . . . every time). Then it says how its own scheme works, and how concepts work alone . . . . . in logic and science.

When it is said that *logic and situatedness are always simply mixed*, logic is disqualified altogether. Instead we need to distinguish: Yes, indeed, logic and more than logic are always together, but they can be together in *many* different ways. What is usually called logic is one characteristic and distinguishable way, as I just tried to show. Here is one other: We can fail to enter into the implicit context at all even quite without logic. That is what everyone does most of the time. We say the next thing without taking any conceptual pattern alone, or at all. Not attending to the implicit context from which we speak is the most common way in which both are together. This is less than logic.

I will soon turn to progressions that involve more than logic.

2. How Some Roles of Experiencing Can Be Deliberately Employed in Our Thinking

The distinction between objective and subjective still dominates current discussion, as Thomas Nagel has recently pointed out:

> The problem of bringing together subjective and objective *views of the world* . . . is how to accommodate in a world that simply exists and has *no perspectival center* any of the following things: a) oneself [the first person "I"]; b) one's *point of view*; c) *the point of view* of other selves, similar or dissimilar; and d) the objects of various kinds of judgments that seem to emanate from these *perspectives*." (*VFN*, 27)

> The real problem stems from a clash between the view of action from inside and *any* view of it from outside. Any external view . . . seems to omit the doing of it. (*MQ,* 198–99)

> There is something deeply suspect about the whole enterprise of fitting subjective *points of view* into a spatiotemporal world of things and processes. (*VFN,* 31; my italics)

> I am trying to invoke a sharp *intuitive puzzle* and to convince you that there is something real in it, even if *its verbal expression is faulty.* . . . We can feel the question (about "I") *apart from its verbal expression,* and the difficulty is to pose it without . . . inviting answers that may seem adequate to its verbal form but that don't really meet the problem beneath the surface. *In philosophy* the question is never just what we shall say. We can reach that point only after considerable effort has been made to express and deal with *inchoate perplexity.* (*VFN,* 55–56; my italics)

Nagel says something important about ourselves (first persons) and about the role of inchoate perplexity in philosophy. I agree, of course, but he just assumes the old scheme according to which a meaning exists "apart from its verbal expression." Many current philosophers would see only a mistake here. If we miss Nagel's point and consider only his distinction, we would reject it. Meaning is not something separate that could be poured into different expressive bottles without changing. It *follows logically* that what he asks us to do is impossible. We would ignore the fact that his puzzle has already reached us in some puzzling way. Instead, we would insist that the puzzle he speaks *about* need not have anything to do with us, the readers to whom he appeals.

Instead of moving only logically, let us now enter into how Nagel's phrase "even if its verbal expression is faulty" *does* work here. This is more intricate, but still obvious: We cannot do it *while* it tells the puzzle (the meaning, the point, the more . . . . .) but we are invited *afterwards to go on from* the more (from the point . . . . .), in another way, a way that might not follow from the verbal expression alone.

The Noticeable Role of the More . . . . .

We begin to see the role of the more (the meaning, the point, the experience . . . . .) *when we go on from it,* rather than from the distinction alone . . . . . Let me go on from it here by telling a story.

In my yearly class on Aristotle's *De Anima* I ask students who don't know Greek to use two translations. "Read only one" I say, "but when it doesn't make sense, turn to the same spot in the other one." Each translation knocks out misimpressions created by the phrases of the other. But what did Aristotle say? One comes closer by assuming that it was something that could give rise to both of these two different English sentences. The students understand Aristotle best when they think with— *that* . . . . . What they say next shows whether or not they thought further from *that* . . . . .

My stories about Nagel and the Aristotle class give the reader two versions of our question: How can *the more* be distinguished from concepts and distinctions? The point is not separable from the stories; nevertheless it is neither story. *In moving from one version to another the different roles of the more can be discerned.*

Suppose another person says something that you don't understand. Then you cannot even *try* to paraphrase it. You can only repeat the words.

When you make a point and someone doesn't get it, you rephrase your point. You may do it spontaneously, without a pause. But if new words do not come easily, you lean back and let your point come home to you again. It comes as *that*, as a . . . . .

Now it is important to recognize that *that* is not an unsymbolized experience without concepts and distinctions. The word "that," and our direct attention entitize (unitize, distinguish, symbolize, set up . . . . .) *that* sense (see *ECM*). The . . . . . implicitly contains the concepts and distinctions that made the point, and many others as well. There is no experience without words and distinctions, but *the different possible transitions* enable us to recognize the various roles of the more. What can *follow* from . . . . . is markedly different from what can *follow* from distinctions *alone* . . . . .

When we rephrase a point, we *carry* the point *forward* into other words and distinctions; thereby we also find out more of what the point *was*. I will soon say more about this "carrying forward" and the intricate time pattern of this word "was." I will also show how a . . . . . is more exact and exacting than a statement's scheme alone . . . . . can be. Here I want to show only that one can rephrase *that exact point*, not a different one. *R*ephrasing is going *on*, of course. But going on, even disagreeing, can move from *that* exact point, or fail to do so. How can you tell whether someone got your point exactly? You can tell only from how they go on from it. Any vocabulary can be made to make the point, because the words will augment their meanings—from the point they make.

The role of the *more* . . . . . is noticeable in all these ways. Obviously, speaking does not consist just of distinctions, and is not stopped or made contradictory when the distinctions break. Speaking is sense-making (point-making, experiencing . . . . .) and it goes on in more ways than can follow from schemes or distinctions alone. I must still show that these ways can be more exact, more precise, than the distinctions. The *very* point that is made by certain distinctions can lead on to further steps of thought that could not follow from those distinctions alone. Nor could it follow just from contradicting them. In such transitions the *role of the more* is quite noticeable.

More-than-logical transitions can happen spontaneously, but we can also let a . . . . . come at any juncture, and think from it deliberately. We often want to do this, not just to rephrase, but to think further. We can do it from any spot; we need not always write the " . . . . ." there. From the . . . . . *new phrases* and *new steps* can carry a point further. But how could we *explain* this power of a . . . . . ?

Perception Is Not Primary

How can someting seemingly so subjective lead to steps of thought that have objective validity? To answer this, we must move beyond the subject/object distinction.

Objective and subjective cannot be put together. They exclude each other. Nagel discusses them as conflicting "perspectives" or "views." We can recall that Husserl, Wittgenstein, and Heidegger rejected the "spectator view." They thought they could do this because they were speaking from a place that is not a perspective, not an observation or view. Wittgenstein spoke from what we do and say in our situations. This is not a perspective. But he said he could only "show" it, much as Heidegger said that one can only "point" beyond the schemes in the language. But where they stood so as to be able to do this has been lost. To reestablish where they spoke from, we must go further. It is not just the *conflicting* (subjective or objective) perspectives we must question, but *perspectives* as such. Perspectives (and views) come from perception. I think we have to recognize that the subject/object approach comes from perception. *Philosophy must not begin with perception.*

Perception always divides what is seemingly over there from a perceiver here. I have written about this more elaborately (see "PB" and "RO"). Science presents the world as something observed, something external, consisting of percepts. But this depends on an idealized observer who supplies the connections. It brings the familiar cluster of problems about "appearance" and "reality," the relativity of observers, and the subject/object scheme. This problematic is still involved when people say that there are only appearances, only interpretations, only constructions, or that whatever is other than those shows itself only in contradictions.

The objects are there; we are dropped out of the universe. We are elevated to be its "constructors," disembodied, floating beside the universe. *Within* the universe presented by science we seem impossible. But we know something is wrong with this, since we are here. Let us see if we can think from here . . . . .

Any starting point is questioned today, but perception as the traditional starting point of philosophy has great implicit effects which still remain with us. It is an old but false assumption that experience begins with perception. Perception is never first, and never alone. It is not the main way we are in our situations. Perception divides your perception of me from mine of you. But interaction is more than two perceptions. And interaction is not inherently divided. Between two people there is *one* interaction.

We will move beyond the subject/object distinction if we become able to speak from how we interact bodily in our situations. Let me show that this is a bodily interaction, and not primarily perception.

Even the simplest situation (experience . . . . .) cannot be reduced to colors, sounds, and smells. People and things exist in terms of living and interacting. We are observable, yes, but we don't begin as observations. We are never just things lying around, over there, waiting to be observed. Nor do we live just as observers. Our interactions involve long stories that do not consist chiefly of externalities that can be photographed. Speaking is interaction; it is a change in a situation. It changes how the story will ensue.

We *speak from* being here . . . . . , from being bodily in our situations, not from something presented before someone, whether in our own perspective or the ideal observer's. Both perspectives are with us, but we are always also here in that way in which "we" and "bodily" and "are" and "here" say more . . . . .

Merleau-Ponty pointed out that we can sense the space behind our backs. Please check that now. You can; isn't that so? And it is not a seeing or a hearing. Our bodies sense more than the five senses.

Now I will add that we do not only sense the physical, Euclidian space; we sense *our situation* there. We sense what might happen to us from there, and what we will and won't do there. In the apartment behind the wall in back of me are people whom I could now disturb, but I won't, because . . . . . Of course I sense my situation also in front and all around me. It is much more than the space and the things around me. A situation is not a view of things over there. My . . . . . is my *bodily* sense of living (planning, feeling, being about to act . . . . .) in my situation.

Let me tell another story to go further into how the body functions in situations. You see someone you know coming down the other side of the street, but you don't remember who it is. This is totally different from seeing a stranger. The person gives you a very familiar feeling. You cannot place the person, but there is a gnawing feeling in your body. That gnawing feeling does know. Your body *knows* who it is. That knowing is a . . . . . , a whole sense in your body.

Your body also knows how you feel about the person. Although you don't remember who it is, the . . . . . has a very distinct quality. If you had to describe it, you might say, for example: "It is a sense of something messy. I feel a little as if I'd rather not have much to do with that person, but there is also mixed in with it some odd curiosity that doesn't feel too sound, and uh . . . . . " You may not like this, but you are not free to make it something nicer! If you try, you will notice keenly that you are no longer thinking from the . . . . .

A . . . . . is very exact and precise, more precise than the common phrases and distinctions. But it is not given in convenient cognitive units. It does not come as three aspects or five. To think from it, you have to separate and entitize this and that. You must also let new phrases come from it. Furthermore, all of the . . . . . is not present before you. You have to go *into* a murky sort of *down* or *in*, or allow some sort of coming *from* it. (These little words speak beyond their simple schemes as they say this.) Nor is all of it implicit at the start. As you *carry* some of it *forward* into words, the . . . . . comes to imply more and more. And even if you don't go far into it, you sense that you could find more and more, both about the person and about yourself. It includes a great many potentially separable strands, but it is an *unseparated multiplicity*, a single . . . . . , *that* one. It is uniquely your sense of that person. Any other person gives you a different body-sense.

What you *now* say you always "felt" about the person cannot be equated to your feeling in the past. There was no . . . . . before, per-haps not in all the years you knew the person. You have also carried the . . . . . further by thinking from it just now. And, you cannot equate the murky . . . . . with the phrases that *carry* it *forward*.

By focusing your attention on the . . . . . , you may suddenly remem-ber who the person is. Now you might be surprised. You might say "I didn't know that I felt that way about the person!"

How can we understand this? Does your body have its own opinions of the people you know? And if it has, why does it keep its opinions to itself, instead of telling you right along?

In such *funny sentences* the words ("body," "know," and "your") all change, and "change" changes to say this change in the words. In these sentences person and body are not the same thing, nor two things, nor just the contradiction of same-and-different. What the words say exceeds conceptualized entities such as a body that contains a person who contains a self which has experiences. The changed way in which these words work here can lead to much better concepts, but even so we know *in advance* that we will put the . . . . . after anything we say. We have to take it along and always *return* to it. We can employ the . . . . . to let *any* theory speak from our being here. Without this return, every theory is destructive.

Let me tell a story I have told before, to show how language works implicitly in a . . . . .

Consider a poet, stuck in midst of writing a poem. The poem is unfinished. How to go on? The already written lines want something more, but what? The poet rereads the written lines. The poem goes on, there, where the lines end. The poet senses what that edge there needs (wants, demands, projects, *entwirft*, implies . . . . .). But there are no words for *that*. It is ah, uh, ... The poet's hand rotates in the air. The gesture says *that*.

Many good lines offer themselves; they try to say, but do not say— *that*. The blank still *hangs there*, still implying something *more precise*. Or worse, the proposed line makes the . . . . . shrivel and nearly disappear. Quick, get that line out of the way. The poet rereads the written lines and ah . . . . . , there it is again. Rather than that line, the poet prefers to stay stuck.

The . . . . . seems to lack words, but no. It knows the language, since it understands and rejects—the lines that came. *So it is not preverbal*; Rather, it knows what must be said, and knows that these lines don't say that.

Speech is inherent in all human experience even without words. The implicit *implies* action and speech. When we cannot find words, we poignantly feel the insufficiency of the available phrases. We feel the implicit language unable to come, struggling, trying to come. In such a . . . . . the language is . . . . . —in pain in it. To so describe it is a case in point. In a . . . . . the language is reworking, rearranging, recreating itself, so that phrases to carry it forward may then come.

The . . . . . knows what we want to say. It knows with a bodily gnawing, very much like something forgotten, but now we can add something quite striking: *what it knows may be new in the history of the world!*

Now I need to intrude on your privacy in a personal way. I need to ask you: Doesn't this happen when you write? Isn't it so, that in order to go on, you must often use (directly refer to, focus on, experience, find yourself in, think from, physically sense, feel, have, be . . . . .) a . . . . . which comes there, where the writing stops, but what you want to say continues?

When you think, you may think the beginning steps clearly, but their cumulative effect can lead beyond them. Sometimes, don't you find that something continues where the words stop? You reach an edge where there is more. You don't just pass by there. You could say something familiar, but no; you *prefer* to stay stuck at that edge. You even glory in it—you say "I'm onto something! Something *new* can come here!"

Also, in your everyday situations, when the usual routines won't do, isn't there often a . . . . . that implies a novel course of action so finely shaped, that you cannot immediately devise it? Doesn't that finer sense of the situation *function* much like the poet's . . . . . in my story? You reject one possible action after another because they do not *carry* the . . . . . *forward.*

As you check my assertions, you directly refer (you find yourself in, you have, you are . . . . .) *this,* which you are doing. Now "find," "have," "are," "referring," and "doing" all change to say this (and "change" changes in this way to say *this* change). For example, "referring" says more than the old scheme of a referring that does not change what it points at. Here *this* "referring" speaks from how you find it, and *this* "finding" says however you are doing it, being it . . . . . Here "referring" *says* how the word manages to exceed its old scheme—namely by the referring you are doing.

Something similar had to happen when Heidegger said he could only "point" to the openness. The word had to take its meaning newly from the doing from which it spoke, else he could not have said even that, since the old scheme of the thing in space would have hidden the openness to which he pointed.

We can *take* most any statement in this way, whether it was written to be so taken or not. We can let the words mean what they do and what happens to them. We can let them say and mean the saying they are doing. Let me give some examples of this mode of language, and then turn to its use in a philosophy of language.

The Continuing Function of the Implicit

For example, suppose you and a friend see a powerful film together, and then discuss it. We often find that the analysis makes the film's impact shrink and die away. Then we are sorry we analyzed. But sometimes the analysis will maximize the impact; it will open dimensions we had not yet felt as such, and lead to implications and effects that greatly maximize the impact. Then we are glad we analyzed. What makes the difference?

We need not wait till the end of a long sequence of thinking. *We can know whether silencing or maximizing is happening, by sensing how each little step affects the unarticulated experience . . . . . with which we began.* If it shrivels, we can quickly discard the thought and remain with . . . . . , waiting for a step of thought that will carry it forward and maximize it.

A . . . . . opens into an intricacy of many potentially separable strands. *If we articulate even just a few of those, we move beyond the traditional schemes and alternatives. This will of course also involve alternatives, but it need not be the same ones! This is a major feature of experiential differentiation.* The next step is more demanding and precise than can be derived from the conceptual forms and distinctions we had at the previous step. Even one small experiential detail can overarch and overthrow the very distinctions that have led to it. I only sketch this here. I have shown it elaborately elsewhere (See *ECM*, chap. 4B, nos. 7, 8).

For example, my friend tells me he argued with another philosopher who held that "natural kinds" are "structurally inherent." A whole philosophy would seem to be involved in this assertion. But I asked what instances the man had given. Was he thinking that pregnant cats never have puppies? (Genetic engineering has changed this.) Perhaps he was celebrating the difference between males and females. What "natural" kinds was he thinking of? If I heard his instances and especially how he went on from them, I might let "natural" say how his kinds differ from other kinds of kinds, of which he should also give us examples, perhaps "classical" versus "romantic," or even less stable kinds. There are many fascinating kinds of kinds. Or, perhaps he was after something else. *If we enter into the intricacy, we can move in many further ways that do not involve what his general assumption would seem to require.* Why argue about the floating, empty, unresolvable, schematic issue of natural kinds? I want to hear from the much more precise . . . . . From it we could go on. But my friend didn't ask the man.

Wittgenstein was right that language does not consist of universals; the sense we make with words is unique in each case, and not forced into one pattern. That is why thinking is exciting, and why discussion expands it. The insights of postmodernism are vital, but they are upside down. It is not the concepts and distinctions that give our speech their *order.* Their inevitable breakdown does not kill what we want to say. Only the pretended universals have broken down. The experiential *order of sense-making* . . . . . is revealed in all our speaking, and not just in terms of contradictions and breakdown of concepts and distinctions.

But we do not respect all illogical thought equally. We must often retrace our transitions, and let distinctions come, to reveal both the sense and the gaps and errors. But how do we decide what is sense and what is gap and error? Certainly not by invoking existing distinctions, because our new thinking might *rightly* overthrow them. So we must let our distinction come out of the sense we are making. Thereby we usually rediscover old distinctions, but when we find them carrying our sense-making forward, then we are glad we knew them. Even so, at the very next step they may break. They may carry forward or not; they are not alone the order of the world.

When we have retroactively filled in the logical steps, we have done very much more than might appear. Each logical interpolation is actually a further development of the whole mesh, and a sequence of them can vastly expand the sense we are making. Not only can we then communicate and build the world. Before that stage, the expansion enables us to sense anything soggy, dishonest, or too easy. We can also sense anything that is still opaque, or merely avoided. The process of thinking has these and many other *internal criteria* which we employ all the time, and can employ freshly when logical steps expand the sense we made.

Logical patterns and distinctions are indeed inseparable from experiential sense-making, but in many different ways, among them this indispensable role of finding error. Notice that logical interpolation and tracing cannot point to error alone; we must sense what carrying forward freshly makes at that spot, whether a change in our sense-making comes there, or only the need to cut the units in a different way.

This mode of language requires that we enter the . . . . . and constantly check, not for correspondence, but for carrying forward. "Checking" now says *this* checking which is familiar to any thinker who has spent time (minutes or months) preferring to stay stuck with a . . . . . , rather than settle for good statements that do not carry it forward. How exciting it is at the edge, to get even one statement that does!

How is speaking even possible without carrying forward? How do words even form, when they don't speak from there? People use a phrase from the common store, without noticing whether it speaks from what they are living in their situations.

The commonly used phrases come easily in each situation. Most people assume that one of those *must* be what they are experiencing, even if they keenly lack the carrying forward. As one person said: "Where I grew up, *whatever* I may have felt, it *had to be* one of two or three things." He went on to say with some intensity: "If there is another way to think, I *want* it."

He can have it, if he will let experience (. . . . .) play its roles. This mode of language also has major political implications, because it can free people to speak from how they are living, instead of being silenced by the common categories.

Philosophy of Language

A philosophy of language becomes possible if language can employ its ongoing capacities to speak from them. We cannot present language in terms of the artificial scheme of signifying, symbolizing, reference, denotation, an *external relation* between words and what they "stand for." We cannot *present* language as something before us, even though words do bring patterns and pictures. But we can let how language works and moves tell us about how language works and moves.

In most any context, we can deliberately let words say and mean how they work. Then they say how their patterns are exceeded by what functions implicitly.

If the words also happen to be about how words work, then they say not only how they work, but thereby also something from how all words work.

Throughout the twentieth century words were not permitted to say how they work. A long history made it seem that an explication of what language does would claim to equal the implicit activity of language. No, implicit and explicit are never equal. Speaking from the intricacy *carries it forward*. What is implicit *continues to function implicitly*. It is what enables words to speak from it, and so also of it.

A philosophy of language is possible because words can say how they work.

Functions of the Implicit

Let me list some implicit functions we have already mentioned. Of course there are many more, and many ways of entitizing and naming them. Just from my stories and what we said, I can list the following:

1. Something implicit lets us *know* . . . . . that we forgot something.
2. It also lets us know . . . . . when we have remembered.
3. It lets us know when a new step of thought is implied.
4. It functions to reject otherwise good proposals if they leave the . . . . . hanging there, still implying something more precise.
5. Something implicit *knows* our situation directly.
6. What we want to say forms implicitly, and words *come*.
7. Something new can implicitly rearrange the language, so that
8. quite new phrases form, and come.
9. It lets us know when "the right" phrases have come.
10. The cumulative effect of a chain of thought is implicit.
11. To understand is an implicit function. We say "Oh . . . . . , yes, I see what you mean."
12. The point is implicit.
13. To rephrase what we said, we go on from the implicit sense of it.
14. The new use of a word makes new sense—implicitly.

15. Words say how the implicit functions, if we *take* the way the words make sense in and about that.
16. *Taking* the same word or sentence in various ways is made possible by the implicit. How do we know which way we took it? The difference does not lie in the sentence; it lies in how we think on from having taken the sentence this way, rather than that way. Logical taking depends on this function.

These functions are so ubiquitous, and each is so orderly and precise; why did people ever think of them as contradictions, ambiguities, or indeterminacy in an otherwise form-distinguished universe?

A New Kind of Concept

If the usual concepts about cognition, speaking, and the body were right, the *instances* in my stories would be impossible. Since they happen, they are possible. What changes in the usual concepts do they *instance*? The word "instance" changes; instead of instantiating a preexisting concept, an experience (any . . . . .) can become a *first instance* of new concepts to which it can lead (see "IOFI" in *ECM*, chap. 5). Such new concepts do not replace—they require—the implicit functions that happen in them.

I have already used the phrases "unseparated multiplicity" and "carrying forward." Let me now set them up as concepts, and add a few more.

"Implying"

From poetry and from what happens in new thinking we can say that a . . . . . can *imply* what has never existed before in the history of the world.

In the usual scheme something "implied" is already there, only hidden, folded under. But when we say a . . . . . "implies" a next step, we *know implicitly* that the next step is not already there. Nor is it simply not there. Nor is it the contradiction of both. Rather, "imply" says how the . . . . . does it. Let us allow *that* to inform the concept; that is more intricate than there or not there. From this intricacy we can say more.

"Carrying Forward"

When the right phrases come, they don't copy the blank. A set of words looks different—it cannot be the copy of a blank. When we say that the right phrases "*were* impli*ed*," we tell about a special relation, not a correspondence. It is the relation of which I said that we notice its absence keenly, when we try to tell ourselves a nice story about a bad event. We saw this relation also when I said that rephrasing a point *carries* the point *forward* so that we discover more of what it "was." It happens also when a special step of thought excites us because it has the carrying-forward relation to the . . . . . at the edge of our thinking.

When phrases or actions *carry forward*, they neither lose the . . . . . , nor leave it hanging, still demanding and implying. They carry it along, and—they do more. They are a further continuation.

What about when there is no . . . . . , when the moves come smoothly as in ordinary speech? A great deal functions *implicitly* also without a . . . . . We encounter some of what it *was*, if we let a . . . . . come, but of course that is not how it functioned without one. We cannot impute a . . . . . where there isn't one, but neither can we deny that a great deal functions implicitly then too. Our concept "carrying forward" can say this: the very coming of a . . . . . is a kind of carrying forward. Then to speak (entitize, differentiate, synthesize . . . . .) from it is a further carrying forward.

"Unseparated Multiplicity"

When you remember the person on the street, the . . . . . opens, and all about the person comes to you. That carries the . . . . . forward so that it no longer hangs there, no longer implying as before. Now your whole history with the person has returned, what you hope for, and worry about. You don't need to take the time to lift out this and that. They are *too many* to think each one. The usual quantitative scheme *does* work here, but it is exceeded *by this way in which* they are many. Most of them have never been separate. To speak of them as *them* (as *many*) alters the usual scheme of multiplicity. In our new concept, "unseparated multiplicity," how are they many and yet unseparated? Well, in this way, like a . . . . . is unseparatedly many.

"Implicit Governing"; "Crossing"; "Always Already Crossed"

An unseparated multiplicity is not a merger, nor does it function like separated things. To say more from how it does function, let us enter into how it can shape one's next move. On the street, when you remember the person, you go over and say an appropriate hello, not too warm, not cold, not long but not too short, your slight smile *implicitly governed* by that whole multiplicity. But it won't come out that way if you say to yourself "Now smile, smile."

As formed determinants, one of these factors would make you smile broadly, another frown, and another hit the person. But when they function implicitly, they are *always already crossed*, so that all are implicit in how each functions (See "PB," "CD," and *PM*, chap. 4). But our concept includes not only this pattern, but also the implicit formation of the right smile.

With this concept we can say how it is possible that many mutually exclusive concepts and distinctions can *function implicitly* together. Such schemes cannot be added together; they would cancel each other. But they do not do so when they are implicit. None of them works as it would do alone. Rather, they *cross*, so that each becomes implicit in what the others are. The result is not their addition or the subtraction of each from the others, as would have to be the case if each worked as if it were alone. *Implicit determinants do not work as if alone.* Rather, each unseparated factor has the others implicit in what it is, and so it makes a unique contribution in a much more finely shaped result (*ECM*).

The many unseparated factors would be contradictory if they worked like logical premises. They cross in one *focal* implying which shapes a next step that is more intricate than any existing shape.

We can use the concept of "crossing" to think about how words acquire new meaning in a new situation or slot in a sentence. The situation *crosses* with the words. I said that the situation *reads* the words. We could say it *sings* the words. It *colors* them. It *cooks* them. Any word that makes sense here will say *this* cooking which happens to it here, but each word carries the slot forward differently. Each makes a new taste (which we can *then* carry further by making new comparisons and distinctions).

Technical words are more likely to trap us in old schemes. For example, if we say that word and situation are *superimposed*, we might think of two unchanging patterns, as Black thought. But if we let "superimpose" say what it makes happen, we find that we do not imagine the situation as a pattern. Indeed, we cannot begin to try to do that! Once we find that we cannot, then "superimposing" words and situation *can* say what it (and any word) does in the slot.

So also, if we take "crossing" as a familiar technical term, say in animal breeding. We would assume that the horse and the donkey must first exist separately, in order to make the mule. But when words and situations cross, only the immediate new meaning happens, not first what the words and situation would have been without each other.

I can apply the concept of "crossing" to correct an old error: It is not true that concepts are abstractions that drop out the specific intricacy (*ECM*). The meaning of a concept is the crossed multiplicity of its applications. When we apply the concept, how it works now *crosses* with its other applications, so that the new one becomes implicit in them. Each further application lets a concept make more sense. It does not drop out its instances; it brings their crossed multiplicity to each new crossing.

Let us trace how this happens here with the several applications of this concept, "crossing." Let the instance of your smile cross with the instance of words and situation crossing to give a word its meaning in that situation. How the many factors shape your smile is also how the many uses of a word are an *already crossed* multiplicity (see "CD"). The uses are not next to each other; they form one *knowing*—the "native speaker's knowing how to use the word," as the Oxford philosophers called it. If we think of this *already crossed* knowing as a bodily knowing (like your sense of that person which forms your smile), then we can understand how the right words *come* in our bodies, like your smile *comes*.

Conversely, we can understand how one smile can be so exactly expressive, if we think of it as coming from the same situational crossing from which the fine shadings of our phrases come.

"Restored Implicit Governing"

The crossed implicit governing can be upset, for example if you concentrate on smiling, or in a sport, say golf, if an instructor tells you to keep your right arm stiff. You didn't know whether it *was* loose or stiff. Now you realize that it *was* loose. Your arm becomes salient for a while. Your game is thrown off, which shows that there was an implicit governing that is now disturbed.

After some time the stiff arm becomes "natural." *The implicit governing is restored.* The arm rejoins all the other factors that are mutually implicit in how they shape and imply the next move. Now your score is even better than before.

That also happens in the history of civilization. Language elaborates (it does not create) human living. First we separate and elaborate something; then it is *restored to a higher level of implicit governing.*

We do this also in philosophy. Our thinking never replaces, but must always return, to be restored to the implicit governing. Then it is available *both* as distinct and as implicitly crossed. For example, we are helped by separating and explicating the metaphysical forms that trap us—but not if we end with nothing but those. A string of conflicting schemes would just be relativism. We gain the advantage only if we also restore them to the slot, the situation, the *already-crossed, implicit governing* that can shape our further moves (as in a string of words with a . . . . . after them).

Science vitally needs the concepts I propose. Machines enact our purposes quite well, but notice: a machine is a logical system of defined units that has been transferred into copper and steel. The metal can corrode, but the *crossing and governing* of the original situation can no longer happen. For example, a few living cells are made to produce life-saving chemicals in a dish. We want this, but we need to remain aware that the whole body's crossing and *implicit governing* can no longer happen there. We need to give scientists the concepts with which to find and study implicit governing, so that we can retain it.

The concepts I propose make sense about the implicit functions which they explicate, and which continue to function in them. These concepts restore themselves to what they are about. So there *is* a way to say—we have been saying—*how* the implicit functions. The attempt to say is not foolish.

How the Word "Body" Works in the . . . . .

When words change their meaning in use, we can formulate new and better concepts from the implicit intricacy. Let us do that with the word "body." I need only say that the implicit functions I listed are supplied by the *body*, and the word "body" changes. In a longer work I have formulated logically interlocking theoretical concepts that have *both* logical *and* more-than-logical connections (*PM*). Those concepts have all the powers of theoretical constructs to generate logical inferences, yet they also retain the implicit functions that exceed them. There are four kinds of body-environment interaction, a derivation of behavior, perception, and patterns, which makes it understandable how patterns can carry a body-environment process forward. Concepts of that kind require many steps of development.

Here I will sketch four broad generative assertions that are only one step removed from how the word "body" has worked here.

1. From the bodily knowing of the forgotten we can say that the body *knows* people and situations directly. Human situations are built with language. So we do not consider the body as if it were before language. It is obvious that the body knows the language and how it applies in a situation, since it can deny sentences that we try out.

Usually we don't say *the body* knows the situation; we say that *we* know it, and our bodies only *react* to what we know. Of course they do react to what we know, but not only to that. *Our bodies know (feel, project, entwerfen, are, imply . . . . .) our situations directly.*

Since our bodies do perform this implicit knowing function, we can let this function change our concept of the living body. It changes how animal and plant bodies are usually conceived. We have to rethink the simpler organisms too. How shall we think of *living bodies*, such that one of those can be ours and perform this kind of knowing?

What sense might it make, if we try out saying that the bodies of animals and plants *know* their situations? Aha, yes! A plant lives in and with soil, air, and water, and it also makes itself of soil, air, and water. Now the word "is" also changes if we say: a living body *is* its environment.

Similarly, the word "knows" changes if we say a living body *knows* its environment *by being it.* Its environment is not just something perceived, waiting to be photographed. The body is (part of, made of, ongoingly emergent from . . . . .) the environment. Environment and body are one interaction; the body knows the environment by being the interaction.

Our environment is elaborated by languaged situations. Living bodies have the intentionality that Heidegger worked out between *Dasein* (the human mode of being) and world. As *Dasein* knows the world, the plant-body knows the air, soil, and water implied and *crossed* in its life process. *Now we can understand how we understand by being our bodily living-in our situations.* The body knows (feels, is . . . . .) the implicitly crossed, unseparated multiplicities of all the many factors.

We have situational bodies . . . . . The body knows the situation directly.

2. The body's being-knowing is not something spread out before the body. It is not a percept. This knowing is not perception, not something here that indicates something else over there. It does not involve the traditional problematic of appearance, and of "signifier and signified." Knowing by being is of course another traditional problematic, but that one can help us to carry this forward. Situational meanings are not additions to objective things in space.

If a plant-body could sense itself, it would sense its environment in sensing itself, *quite without the five senses.* It would sense itself expanding as water came in, and it would sense itself implying water when it is lacking. It would sense itself absorbing the light in the photosynthesis that the plant-body is.

I speak of a plant because it doesn't have our five external senses. Those only elaborate how a living body *is* environmental interaction. The body is not behind a wall, as if it could know the environment only through five peep holes.

We humans have plant-bodies . . . . . , *but ours sense the ongoing interaction they are.*

3. In Western science everything is passive, organized by externally imposed relations. A formalized "observer" connects and interrelates it all. But if we want to study the actual observers, we cannot attribute the interrelating to still another observer. Somewhere there is a *self-organizing* process. Let us say that a living body is a self-organizing process.

We can take how a . . . . . *implies* and use that as a concept. We can apply this implying to (i.e., we can cross it with) how living bodies *imply* their next bit of life-process. The body of a plant or an animal projects (*entwirft,* structures, organizes, enacts, expects, is ready to go into, implies . . . . .) its own next step.

A living body implies its own next step . . . . .

4. The next bodily-implied bit of human living is often something that we want to *say*. Speaking is a special case of bodily interaction. If we let "speaking" mean the speaking we do, then the subtleties of language no longer seem to float, as they do in much of current philosophy. Humans expedite food-search partly by speaking. The plant absorbs from the ground; animals interpose food-search between hunger and feeding. Behavior is a special case of body-process: each bit of food-search is a special version of hunger implying the eventual consummation of feeding. But in animals the plant-body is elaborated; now it needs far more than food. Animals need each other, groom each other, pick each other's fleas—and not only because the flees bite, but to comfort each other. Animal bodies imply many more bodily consummations than plants do, and we humans even more. Our interposed behavior, no less than the animal's, carries forward a bodily implying. The body implies what we want to do *and say*.

Therefore sophisticated linguistic and philosophical details can make *our bodies* uncomfortable. From such a discomfort the body can project (imply . . . . .) finely shaped new steps to deal with such a situation. Such a . . . . . can exceed and rearrange the common phrases until we can speak from it. The body is not just an inferred precondition as Merleau-Ponty is sometimes understood to have said (see "PB"). Rather, our bodies shape the next thing we say, and perform many other implicit functions essential to language.

That is how our next words "come" from the body, just as hunger, orgasm, and sleep *come* in a bodily way, and just as food-search comes in an animal. It is familiar that after inhaling the body implies exhaling, and when in danger it totals up the situation and its muscles and blood circulation imply fighting, or quite differently, may imply running, or again differently, it may paralyze itself and freeze. Many factors function in an *implicit governing* of a specific next step. These situations are familiar, but when an animal finds itself in a new situation, still the body will shape, imply, and if possible enact a next step, only this might be a new and more intricate step. Animals act in new ways very often. With linguistic and cultural elaborations, our bodies imply *what we want to say*, which can be typical or something very new. It can surprise us.

Our bodies imply the next words and actions to carry our situations forward.

Explaining

Do these rough concepts explain how the body performs the implicit functions? But it was from these functions that we made the concepts. We retain them in the concepts. They *cross* and inform each other. And that remains so when we develop concepts with logical interrelations in the conceptual model (*PM*).

How is our next step of thought shaped by the . . . . . that comes after a string of words? It is by the crossed implicit governing in which a great many factors shape just the right smile. But, conversely, we now understand better how the smile is shaped by many factors, like a single next step from the . . . . . after the many words.

Crossing is an understanding, a sense of many implications at once. The crossing is what makes us say "Aha, *that's* how it goes." The concept of "crossing" explains this kind of explaining.

This philosophy of language does of course involve schemes and distinctions, but also more. Its explanatory power employs both.

A Summary

Let us look back to see how far we have come. We have allowed many words to say and mean how they worked. Thereby they sometimes also said something about how words work. This happened, for example, with alone, an, apart, are, be, behind, body, carry, change, checking, come, do, down, exceed, experience, explain, expression, figure, find, follow, from, ground, have, here, implicit, imply, in, instance, intricacy, is, it, know, more, move, multiplicity, one, order, ourselves, point, precise, refer, reversal, same, said, say, speaking, superimpose, stating, subject, that, thinking, together, two, under, was, we, work, and your.

These words changed when *they said more than the schemes* they brought, and we went on from the more (the effect they had, the point they made . . . . . .). By going on from them in this way, we could let them say how they *exceeded* the schemes. For example, in this sentence the quantitative pattern "exceeded" *does* play a role, but *this* exceeding which happens here *says and is* how it exceeds the quantitative pattern. Now my word "says" also *says* the saying it is doing, and "doing" says what it *does* here.

The possibility of new meanings showed that language has an order that cannot be equated with distinctions. We grasp a new use immediately; only *from* this grasp, and only later, with plenty of time, and only if we need to, do we compare and *make* distinctions to explicate the sense we have already made, how our saying has changed the situation. It is a mistake to consider a new meaning as a set of new distinctions, differences, or commonalities. Those do not yet exist as such. We also saw that endlessly many differences and similarities can be formulated from *one* precise new meaning or situational change (see "CD").

What I called "funny sentences" led us to some new concepts. From how the body *knows* your situation, we also developed some rudimentary concepts about the body (more in *PM*).

The listed "implicit functions" were roles played by something implicit in speaking and thinking. There are many more.

We formulated the concepts of "intricacy," "carrying forward," "unseparated multiplicity," "crossing," "always already crossed" and "implicit governing." *Such concepts enable us to make sense in a vast arena for which simplistic schemes have usually been used.*

When people discover how to enter, they prefer to let words mean *what they make happen* in the intricacy.

We can move past the unresolvable old philosophical problems by entering into the . . . . . from the point being made, and from how someone goes on from the point.

We also let the traditional systems work implicitly, as when I say that words create (find, differentiate, synthesize . . . . .) what they say. They move beyond their schemes. Each says what happens to it here (and to any word when it comes into a slot). But each also carries this forward differently. Now "create" does not say that it makes something from nothing, but it does emphasize the novelty. And, "finds" does not find something that was already there, but it does say that what we find is not arbitrary. "Synthesize" does not put something together out of preexisting bits, but it does say that a complex unity can result. And, "differentiate" does not say that we first see an undifferentiated grainy surface in which we then separate something out, but it does say that anything can be thought of as differing from other things. Not only are these not contradictory, but we gain a lot if they are all implicit wherever any one of these words is written.

Once we know these traditional schemes, we are not at all inclined to force our further thoughts into one of those old diagrams. We go on from . . . . . . , so that our next step is implicitly governed by how each crosses with the slot in the sentence and the situation. A situation is always an already-crossed multiplicity.

Not the End of Philosophy

It is not a calamity that thinking does not enclose, and is always situated. It is well that we cannot think only with conceptual patterns, nor without them. That is not the end of philosophy. Nor is it relativism. The different systems and cultures do not constrain and exclude each other unless they are taken as distinctions and schemes, and even those do not constrain and exclude when they function implicitly. If we make ourselves able to speak and form concepts from the implicit functioning, a whole arena opens.

How We Dealt with What Seemed Impossible

Let us recall the insights that seemed so negative at the start. Our appeal to experience (. . . . .) takes account of—actually employs and requires—just those insights which have seemed to make any such appeal impossible.

1. We reverse the old order of priority in which conceptual criteria, rules, or distinctions were considered prior determinants of speech or action (see *ECM*, chap. 4A, "Reversal of the usual philosophical procedure").

We can *follow* how new meanings make sense. Rules and distinctions are formulated in retrospect, but they are not arbitrary; they are *a further* step of making sense.

2. Old schemes and distinctions are always implicit, but they are not the only order, nor the only way another order shows itself. Experience (. . . . .) is a more intricate order which functions differently. Words reposition themselves in it in new ways that let us speak and think beyond the schemes.

No scheme can prevent words from immediately crossing with a situation (a context, a discourse, a practice, a circumstance . . . . .) in a new way. We can speak with and from them in philosophy, on these very questions.

3. In any one moment, experience (. . . . .) is not separable from distinctions and concepts, but we can distinguish its roles in different transitions, different ways of going on.

We worry about the inseparable old schemes only because we do not wish always to be led on by them, and prevented from moving in other ways. *What counts is how we go on. And it is just in this respect, that we can distinguish!* At the next step we can ask and come to know whether we have spoken from the scheme alone (and held the more aside), or if we moved on from the wider . . . . . (in which the scheme did also inseparably function).

From new moves we can formulate new kinds (and kinds of kinds) of moving, and of following. We can do that from how we moved, rather than from distinctions alone . . . . . (and not only from distinctions between kinds of moves, but from the moves).

4. Experiences (situations, people, practices . . . . .) do not consist of fully formed givens that our articulations could just represent. *Speaking from* situations does not make copies or approximations. Speaking is like

living and acting; what we say changes and develops what we say it "was." (This leads to a more intricate model of time [see *PM*, chap. 4B]).

Anything, however small, is further differentiable in many different ways. When words (ordinary or philosophical) are repositioned in the intricacy, we see that it responds with unsuspected meanings that are more precise than conceptual forms and distinctions can be.

Every philosophy repositions major words in the intricacy (see "TWRP"). This is a hallmark of philosophy. It is possible because the intricacy does not consist of forms or distinctions. It is more exact and demanding, imperious in instantly making us feel and live the new meanings as soon as words are said in it.

We can think anything *in advance* as differentiable in many ways that have not happened, and need not actually happen (see "Fans" in "TBP," and *ECM*, chap. 6).

5. How you are (feel, act, speak, live in your situations . . . . .) is never arbitrary. You can try to say whatever you wish, but do you find that you become whatever you wish? Obviously a situation is not just putty or limbo; we cannot make of it whatever we like. That is why we are so often wrong. A situation is so finely ordered that almost anything we say about it is too simple. And yet it is not finished happening.

There is no unsymbolized experience which we would be at liberty (or just at a loss) to interpret. Experiencing is inherently a sense-making, always implicitly "symbolized" at least by interactional events with other people (see *ECM*). Such events are elaborated by at least implicit language and distinctions. Experiencing is this eventing; we cannot represent or construct it. We can only carry it forward.

Heidegger said that your mood understands more about what you are doing, and why, than your cognition can reach. Situatedness is how you are (living in, enacting, being, feeling, knowing, finding, making . . . . .) your situations. Your how-you-are . . . . . is never arbitrarily whatever you wish. But it can be carried forward.

6. A philosophy of language is possible if we let the words say how they work in the language from which we speak. Then they say more than their schemes and distinctions.

7. What we say and think is more than what is presented in front of us as perceptual objects and diagrams. Those may be before us, but they need not be what guides us to our next thought, speech, or action.

8. *Logical taking* involves implicit functions. If we enter the implicit context of any scientific move, we can differentiate and open choices that are now impossible. Our society badly needs officially recognized ways to do that.

The units on which logic depends have to be generated; they are not the constituent parts of nature or the world. Scientists are currently losing the *crossing and implicit governing* of living processes, without even being aware of it. This is dangerous.

9. A new use of words is a change in the *public* language, and in the culture. When we let implicit meaning play its roles, this new *mode* of language can enter the culture.

In saying this, the word "public" says something more intricate than the old distinction between two kinds of issues, with the public ones already cut and defined, often obscuring what really affects us.

Language is *always* the public one, but that does not mean that we must silence and deny what is not yet in "the common storehouse" of shared meanings. The social and public nature of language consists rather in this: when what we are living is carried forward into words, what an individual says cannot help but be significant to others.

10. The polyphony of many voices and ways of life does not invalidate any one of them. We can discard not only the assumption that there is one true way, but also the assumption that if there is not, then each is invalid.

The variety does not invalidate the variants. The variety would be a problem, if all order depended on cognitive forms, because those *can* contradict each other. Experiences do not contradict each other. Two experiences may invite contradictory conclusions, but they do not cancel each other. They interaffect and cross. Similarly, when two people interact, their situatednesses (. . . . .) do not contradict; rather *they cross.* In crossing, some of each becomes part of what is already implicit in the other.

When determinants of any kind work implicitly, they do not confine; they are part of *a crossed implicit governing* into which more and more can always be brought.

Humans have no universal content in common. But there are practices (*FOP, F*) by which we can understand (carry forward, differentiate, synthesize, cross-affect, cross-continue . . . . .) anything human. Thereby more becomes implicit also in how we understand ourselves.

Ethics, Politics, and Psychotherapy

I must refer my reader to other works which show the implications of this philosophy for psychology, ethics and politics, writing, physics, and biology. In those fields the entry into the intricacy provides a road forward between the locked alternatives of either having to know what one cannot know, or mere relativism and construction. This philosophy makes for a different ethics ("PEP") and it has led to a different psychotherapy.

It was Carl Rogers who invited this philosopher into his group, and first employed *Experiencing and the Creation of Meaning* in his research.

He wanted to measure a correspondence between awareness and experience; instead of this impossibility, we could measure the role of experiencing (. . . . .) in distinguishably different kinds of talking during therapy interviews (see "What Comes after Traditional Psychotheraphy Research"). That began a series of research studies resulting in one of the best replicated findings in the field.

Therapists long thought they had to know the right interpretations of the clients' experience. Then they shifted to the opposite, claiming mere construction, devising a better "narrative" of the clients' past. But these alternatives are easily left behind by the demanding precision of the . . . . . , which leads to steps that are neither invented, nor repetitions of the past, but more intricate steps of further experiencing. This practice (see *FOP*) is now no longer limited to psychotherapy. It is available to the public (see *F* and "The Politics of Giving Therapy Away").

Elsewhere, for example, in "Thinking beyond Patterns," I have traced the long-standing assumption that nature and living bodies are mechanistic and mathematical. Social patterns were thought to be imposed on mechanical bodies. An escape from determinism and socialization was long looked for only in art—but art was understood as illusion. Something similar is still assumed today, when it is said that we live only in liminal and ephemeral moments between the last dead form and the next dead form, tragic for having no real existence. This view of ourselves is a newer version of the old surrender to scientized forms, as if they are "real" and we are the illusion, an excess, indicated only by their breakdown.

It is still widely maintained that the individual is autistic except for externally imposed common meanings. We find just the contrary: it is the most developed individual who can stand the constant surprise of the otherness of another person, and can interact more intricately than would be determined by the social roles.

We can carry postmodernism forward also in this regard: overthrowing hierarchies is freeing, but let us change the reactionary teaching that experience is created by the public language. People's lives include a great deal that they cannot say in the existing language, but can become able to say. As philosophers, let us stop telling people that they cannot possibly have anything to say that is not already in the public language. We can study the social and political circumstances (Mark Warren) that maximize such articulation, in contrast to silencing people.

In recent decades many social situations have come to include a distinct role for the individual to restructure the situation. Room is made (even the demand) to articulate unique experience. In some respects people are form*ing* their social patterns, rather than only being form*ed* by them. It is a mistake to assume that social change must *always* move from the social level to the individuals. But individual development does not usually change the social structure. We need a whole new branch of social science to study the *more rare* conditions under which social change moves *from* the articulation of experience *to* structural change.

I have tried to show that a new arena opens when we speak deliberately from the implicit functions of experiencing (situatedness, interaction . . . . .) which has a more intricate order than concepts, distinctions, and social patterns alone . . . . .

3. The New Way Expressed in Terms of Other Philosophers

Let me express some of this in terms of Derrida, Wittgenstein, Heidegger, and Husserl, McKeon, the Pragmatists, and Dilthey. What I have said could come in many versions and could be organized on many maps.

Derrida has (at last) brought home to people that there is no way to avoid ungrounded assumptions (distinctions, conceptual patterns), even when we only say that there is no way to avoid them. We want more than the postmodern impasse, of course, but not at the price of falling back. Derrida has greatly strengthened the negative side of Heidegger's middle period with its emphasis on inescapable assumptions in the Western languages. Derrida moves on with great metaphorical richness. He could be read as making an opening, but he denies such a reading (see his comment against Caputo's reading of him, Loyola Conference, Chicago).

People have wondered why I am at times both so positive and so critical of Derrida. Before him only few people grasped the need for a critique of *all* the words. I am so positive about Derrida because he has cleared the way to go on. I am so critical because of where he seems to tell people to stop: without the openness, with contradiction, undecidability, and aporia. Those terms do not say even what Derrida himself does. His wonderful ongoing probing and metaphorizing is much more than an is-and-is-not. I understand the strategy of not asserting anything, but it seems to deny that words can work in new ways even as it happens in front of us. This happening is not contradiction, not aporia, not two sides saved. Although affirmed *and* denied, he still makes the old forms cover up the intricacy from which something new is actually being said.

If all order consisted only of distinctions and concepts, they could not generate their own contradictions. They do this because they *are* a *working-in* another order. Implicitly they bring the situations in which they work and make sense. Making sense does not consist in contradictions of distinctions ("TBP," "PB," *PM*).

If words were only discursive forms, then they could not say something new, nor something that does not follow from their established patterns. Then what words *newly say* has to be considered only a contradiction and a rupture.

For example, Derrida criticizes Levinas for saying that the other person is "not just my other," not just *the other of* me, not just other than *me*. The other is "other" in a more independent sense. Derrida understands that Levinas is saying more than "other" says as a discursive form, but he argues that Levinas has not established a mode of language in which "other" would not have to mean the other-of. Levinas has not done that, but Derrida's own metaphorizing constantly and deliberately exceeds the discursive forms while overtly denying that this is possible.

To move past this we can cite Bordo's call for "recognizing wherever one goes that the other's perspective is fully realized, not a bit of exotic 'difference' to be incorporated within one's own world . . . by sight-seeing." She is clear that resources are not all borrowed from the established language of the texts but "happen in the reading of the text." I agree. Whenever we enter the experiencing of anything that is being talked about, we immediately find an intricacy with vast and obvious *resources* that go beyond the existing public language.

If we enter the intricacy we can establish the mode of language in which Levinas and Bordo are speaking: I can say that in my human relations I am often frustrated (and worse) because other people do not fit my needs. They do not fit me. I berate them for it, but I recognize that they are *other than* me. I see the difference clearly enough. It is easy to see that *the other person is not what would fit me.* But only after a lot of living do I come to the deeper recognition that others do not live in terms of what does not fit me. They live in their own terms: of course they are not what would fit me, but they are also not what does not fit me. Another person is not alive in terms of my issues, and does not consist of what is other than *me.* Each person is another life altogether. Only thereby do I sense the other as "really" other, as Levinas said.

As a discursive form, "other" has only one meaning, but in language-use in the context of situations we find at least two. But the distinction between them did not exist when I was only puzzled by my troubles with other people. I did not just find the distinction already there, nor did I just make it up. It has a very compelling but more-than-logical continuity with what was there before. It neither represents nor imposes. It *carries forward* how things were.

To say all this I dipped into the intricacy. From it I could speak in new ways. That can be done again and again. It does not depend on the few poor discursive distinctions we have. In our intricate situations the word "other" has many, many uses—right now—not only after we compare and differentiate them.

Words *can* say something from the more-than-discursive intricacy, and *thereby* they can also *say how* they can. Both have been badly lacking.

There is no way to show *abstractly* (in discursive forms, in kept-same patterns . . . . .) that "other" can mean anything other than "other than." But we can carry forward what Levinas said, if we enter the intricacy of life with people.

Wittgenstein, Husserl, and Heidegger rejected the split between "outer" and "inner." They were critical of the scientific construction of reality from outside.

I have already mentioned how Wittgenstein speaks from living and acting in situations. Let me say a little more. Wittgenstein is often read as if he denied the existence of our obvious so-called "inner" experiences, for example, pains, images, and felt meanings, as if philosophy should not concern itself with those. Even Malcolm read him this way, to Wittgenstein's annoyance. Of course Wittgenstein did not deny those obvious events; he constantly appeals to them to show that they are more various and intricate than the simplistic packaged entities imputed by the grammar: "What gives the impression that we want to deny anything?" (*PI*, 305). "Why should I deny that there is an inner process?" (*PI*, 306). " 'Are you not really a behaviourist in disguise? Aren't you at bottom really saying that everything except human behaviour is a fiction?'—If I do speak of a fiction, then it is of a *grammatical* fiction" (*PI*, 307; his italics).

Instead of these fictions, Wittgenstein appeals to us to attend to what we find. He asks several thousand questions that begin with "What happens when we . . . ?" He constantly asks us to refer directly, to convince ourselves that the entities imputed by the grammar are *not* what happens. What we find is "more intricate" (*verwickelter*: *PI*, 182).

For example, he shows that there is not a wordless meaning-object for a word to "refer" to. Instead, he *refers directly* to the intricacy:

> *What happens* when we make an effort, say in writing a letter, to find the right expression for our thoughts? . . . But cannot all sorts of things happen here? I surrender to a mood and the expression *comes*. Or a picture occurs to me and I try to describe it. Or an English expression occurs to me and I try to hit on the corresponding German one. Or I make a gesture, and I ask myself: What words correspond to this gesture? And so on. (*PI*, 335; his italics)

Wittgenstein found the intricacy! He asks us to attend directly to it, so that we can deny the simplistic schematic packages in favor of the intricacy we do find.

For example, Wittgenstein argues that there is not a single univocal inner process that would be the referent of "to expect." He asks us to notice, for example, that "I expect him" may mean simply that I think he will come. Then there is no process at all. But, differently, it might mean that I cannot keep my mind on my work today because I keep thinking of him. Then there is a process, but it is that one. Or, again, it might mean that I am surprised to find that after all that happened, I still expect him (*PI*, 575–77). None of these are the simple supposed process of expecting.

Wittgenstein left words to their ordinary uses. He did not do what I do. He did not develop a mode of language in which words mean how they work. But sometimes he comes very close to this. For example, he said that a word's uses have no concept in common, only a "family resemblance." He might have pointed out that this phrase *works by* a family resemblance between its usual use and his new use. In his use of it, "family resemblance" says how it works, and how words work. This term of his does indeed work in the way my main terms do.

Wittgenstein refers directly to feelings and so-called inner processes, but he understands them as part of the situational matrix, *just as words are.* When we enter into a . . . . . we find all about our situations, what we did and hope to do with other people, and our work and thought, for example right now your reaction to reading what I have written, and your sense of the philosophical situation (see "What Happens When Wittgenstein Asks 'What Happens When . . . ?' ").

Heidegger (*Being and Time*) speaks from "being-in-the-world," how we are in situations. If I ask "How *are* you?" the answer is neither a description by an external observer, nor something purely inner. Suppose I ask: "How are you?" and you take a moment to find out . . . . . The quality of your well-being (or whatever came) is from *how your life is going,* isn't it? Your *how you are* is how you feel yourself in your situations, what you are trying to achieve or avoid, and the whole history and intricacy of how you came into these situations. There is a situated kind of understanding which "*goes further than cognition can reach,*" Heidegger said. I think we must not deprive philosophy of this more than cognitive mode of thinking.

Husserl denied that we see colors and hear sounds. He pointed out that we see trees and hear motorcycles or a door slamming. He found the lifeworld in our immediate experience. He could show that it was vastly richer than the constructs that are usually meant by "experience." He discovered the intricacy and showed that it enables us to move past simplistic schemes and theories. But where Wittgenstein said he could only show it, Husserl thought he could describe it—*purely*—without imposing any assumptions on it. But all descriptions involve variable assumptions and these interact with anything we describe.

The phenomenologists (Husserl, the early Heidegger, Sartre, Merleau-Ponty) *did* enter into the intricacy (experience, "phenomena") directly, but they used different conceptual categories. As a result they differed among themselves just as much as philosophers always do. Phenomenology was in style for a while, but eventually the claim merely to describe phenomena was laughed at and dropped out of philosophy.

I warned about the differing and questionable categories in an early paper, but I do not laugh at the phenomenologists. They rejected other philosophies as consisting of "free-floating" notions. But ask yourself in what respect their "descriptions" were indeed more than free-floating notions. In what way did they give phenomena (experience) a role that other philosophers did not?

I find that experience did play a new role in their philosophies. They did *begin* from experience in a way others did not. What they called "phenomena" are *directly accessible*, whereas most philosophies consider "experience" to be a cognitively organized system.

I set up a first criterion: it is phenomenology if the sentence has a different or lesser meaning for someone who reads it without starting from the experience. For example, many of Heidegger's statements satisfied my criterion. They cannot have their full meaning *alone*; one has to employ direct access to that which they are about ("WCS").

But I want more than that from phenomenologists. I want them *also to return* to the directly accessible experience *after* each step of thought, to notice what effect their (very various) conceptualizations have had. They never return. They move from experience to what they say, and then on and on. Their explications seem designed to replace experience, to make it no longer necessary. They give experience no *continuing* role.

I set up a second criterion, a "zig-zag" (see my "Human Nature and Concepts"), a continual return to what remains implicit and continues to function implicitly.

If these philosophers had checked back to the experience with which they began, they could not have said some of what they said. If they had not only taken off from experience, if they had often *returned*, what they called "phenomena" would have opened into many, many further steps for them. They would have noticed that it is always again there, and capable of further steps we can follow, but which overthrow the distinctions or categories of the previous step.

The critics rejected the results of the phenomenologists as being entirely dependent on their distinctions and conceptual forms. But that isn't so. Although their different assumptions brought out different results, each of them found more intricacy in experience than could ever have followed from the assumptions with which they approached it.

I am interested in the kind of *order* which cannot be had apart from variable assumptions, and yet always responds with something more precise than could possibly have followed just from the assumptions.

In this respect I also moved further than my great teacher, Richard McKeon. Since much of his work is not yet published, I must characterize it in relation to Heidegger. Where Heidegger makes one set of frequent assumptions visible, McKeon shows us four very different recognizable strands of the tradition. Where Heidegger sees always only one dominant set, McKeon makes us familiar with four recurring alternatives, each in several kinds of recognizable variants. In the Western tradition they were always contemporary and implicit, no matter which one was overtly employed. But once they become familiar to us, we are ready to think with powerful alternatives at any point. In this respect we become more sophisticated than almost any author.

For example, I say that I went *further*, but "further" is dialectical progress. An alternative is the *articulation* of a context in which action and thinking are already functioning. Or shall we pursue another alternative: *analyzing* into parts? We might also use all methods, depending upon our (unexamined?) purpose. The effect of McKeon is often a kind of paralysis. One cannot avoid thinking several powerful alternatives of whatever one thinks or reads. It does protect one from falling into a typical pattern, but it can seem to make further thinking impossible.

But the greatness of McKeon is realized not in the impasse, but in the way one can think further (. . . . .) *with* one's knowledge of the variants implicitly at work, shaping one's next step, and protecting it from the pitfalls of any one variant. The . . . . . provides an *implicit governing* by and of all systems one knows, and even more by the intricacy of the implicit situations (experiencing, what we study, practice, the thicker . . . . .). Any text or theory becomes more valuable when it is taken experientially in this way, taken for what it *can* show, even when we reject or are noncommittal in regard to its formal assumptions (see *ECM,* chap. 6).

McKeon was the inheritor of American pragmatism, which claimed to be able to use many approaches and methods—many mansions. Pragmatism is now misunderstood as determining everything by unexamined assumptions and purposes. But the Pragmatists understood how doubtful all external criteria are. Instead, they pointed to *internally arising criteria* which develop within ongoing practices, including scientific inquiry. They did not enter into the experiential intricacy of these, which is why this insight has been lost. To entitize and state such criteria involves their ongoing role, of course, but when words can say how they work, we can speak from them. They do not enclose or determine in a fixed way, but they are superior to arbitrariness or assumed external criteria.

Perhaps the most radical impact of my philosophy today stems from Wilhelm Dilthey. It is something Heidegger approached but lacked. This vital part of Dilthey's works (vol. 7) was published later, when Heidegger was no longer reading Dilthey. Many others have written about Dilthey without seeing it there.

Dilthey had three terms: "experiencing," "expression," and "understanding." Taken in the usual way, an author (artist, social creator) first has some experience, then expresses it in a concrete work, and then we understand the work. But Dilthey says that experiencing *is* inherently always also an understanding already, and also an expression. Each is a case of the other two.

As I would explain this, say a bug runs away from you, or a spider plays dead. They need no *separate* thought to understand what they do. Their living experiencing *is* itself the understanding of danger, and also the expression of wishing to avoid danger. Experiencing and understanding are not private just inside the bug. This experiencing and understanding is also an expression in the world.

These links yield further steps. Now an "expression" is not the copy of an experiencing; it is itself a *further* experiencing. Or, take understanding: it is always an experiencing in its own right, a bit of further living in the world, and so it is also an expression there.

Why is this so radical? It overthrows the whole system according to which something first exists and is only then interpreted. Dilthey has not only the negative recognition that expression and understanding *are not* representations or copies. He also has a positive assertion: they *are* a further experiencing. Dilthey pointed to characteristic *kinds of continuity* (*Zusammenhang*) of the three.

In understanding a text or another person we neither impose our meanings nor just receive theirs: Dilthey said that we can understand the authors only if we understand them *better* than they understood themselves, and this happens only if we carry their experiencing forward with our understanding (our further experiencing), when the author's experiencing is reconstituted as our experiencing—accurately but enriched by ours, as ours is enriched by theirs. Or, as I would say it: these *cross*, so that each becomes *implicit* in the other. Then our statements about the author's work will be accurate, but implicitly governed by the richer crossing, and so they will be a better understanding than the author could have managed.

"In principle any human expression is understandable," Dilthey said, and I add: the more unique it is, the more significant it will be to us when it implicitly crosses with ours.

2

Gendlin's Use of Language: Historical Connections, Contemporary Implications

David Michael Levin

1

In August 1924, the German poet Rainer Maria Rilke wrote these deceptively plain words about words: "*Nach so langer Erfahrung sei 'Haus,'/'Baum' oder 'Brücke' anders gewagt.*"[1] Rendered in English, these lines say "After such long experience let 'house,' 'tree' or 'bridge' be dared differently." Gendlin, I believe, is one of those philosophers who, *with* words and *for the sake of* words, has dared differently.

Gilles Deleuze and Félix Guattari have argued that "philosophy is the art of forming, inventing, and fabricating concepts."[2] Nothing could describe Gendlin's contribution to philosophy better than this. One example of this art is his concept of "carrying forward." The beauty of this new concept is that, among other things, it gives us a way to think beyond both the traditional logic of concepts of change and also the postmodern deconstruction of this logic—beyond the metaphysically saturated concepts of progressive development and beyond the teleological conception of potentiality, but without losing what we need to salvage and keep. Gendlin's new concept gives us, beyond the seemingly "unavoidable" dilemmas of postmodernism, a reformulation of the Hegelian *Aufhebung*, the Hegelian "sublation" that both transforms and preserves. It is, then, a major contribution to a use of language *beyond* postmodernism.

At the beginning of a recently published text, Derrida put these words: *"Dès qu'il est saisi par l'écriture, le concept est cuit."*[3] In Gendlin's chapter and the studies that follow, we shall perhaps begin to understand why Derrida's words could be read as an expression of uncertainty about how to go beyond the postmodern dilemmas, beyond the concepts and concept-forming processes of modern thought, beyond a history in which, on the one hand, there has been an increasing awareness of the ways, often exceedingly subtle and contrary to even the noblest of intentions, that language serves the forces of domination, but also, on the other hand, there has been great difficulty in thinking any alternative practices with language.

Perhaps, as Derrida suggests, one cannot entirely avoid doing violence while living in this world and on this earth. Perhaps most uses of language are violent, for a "speech produced without the least violence would determine nothing, would say nothing, would offer nothing to the other. . . . There is no phrase which is indeterminate, that is, which does not pass through the violence of the concept. Violence appears with [every] articulation," and "only a language of pure invocation, pure adoration, proferring only proper nouns in order to call the other from afar," could avoid all violence.[4] Still, it is necessary, and possible, as Derrida points out, to distinguish different degrees, and perhaps different kinds, of violence, fighting greater violence with lesser, "in order to avoid the worst evil."[5] To his credit, Derrida owns up to his own violence: the violence of the philosopher, one who recognizes a responsibility to make the discourse of philosophy somehow responsive to the force of events—and more open to the voices of those who have not been heard, or have been silenced. Derrida's textual and subtextual strategies are ways he invented that enable him to fight the forces of repression at work within language and, in particular, within the discourse of philosophy. Derrida's strategies are ethical gestures, gestures of respect for the voices of the other, gestures designed to resist normalization, institutional appropriation, instrumentalization, and commodification. They are designed to break out of the rhetorical norms that have, for centuries, regulated our cultural discourse, opening up our language to new possibilities for conceptualization. And yet, as the remark about concepts getting "cooked" implies, Derrida finds it difficult to think past the design.

In the course of many years, Eugene Gendlin has worked out a major new philosophical theory and employment of language, equal in its originality, boldness, and power to the theories of Husserl, Heidegger, Wittgenstein, and Derrida. Although he draws on those familiar resources, he gives them an original use, introducing theoretical terms of an entirely new kind, to illuminate and employ what is involved in the formation of meaning. No theory of language has seemed possible, because the actual working of language always exceeds it. Theory cannot encompass language; it exists only within language. Gendlin can overcome these and other philosophical problems because he devises a mode of language in which *what* he says about the formation of meaning also *happens* in the sentences that tell about it. Now, as always, the working of language exceeds the concepts; but now, instead of pretending to represent what language does, concepts have a different, nonrepresentational relationship to the process of meaning-formation which is at work in the very sentences that tell about it.

This theory and practice of meaning-formation also leads to a broader philosophical concern: How can we think once again about maximizing the flourishing of the individual in our social and cultural life, perhaps conceived and practiced in a new way, but still in keeping with the spirit of the Enlightenment? Gendlin remains neither with the Enlightenment conception of the individual as a self-contained, self-sufficient monad whose essence is a purified rationality, nor with the conception of the individual as a mere product of culture, the current view that there is no human nature, but only a variety of culturally constructed natures. Although he grants that the cultural conception went deeper than rationalism, a still deeper understanding of the individual emerges in his work. Individual experience is not derived just from the existing patterns, concepts, or social and cultural arrangements. The existing patterns do not enclose us.[6] Language is not an interpretive screen between us and others. Language is always a newly forming *bodily* interaction with others in situations. But, in order to show that the existing conceptual and social forms do not enclose us, that they need not predetermine and limit our further formations, that our next steps in language are not constrained to be consistent with the old forms, it is of crucial importance to him to show exactly how the existing forms *do* function both explicitly and implicitly, and especially what role they play in the formation of new meanings and interactions.

Gendlin is in agreement with Wittgenstein's dictum that the meaning of a word consists in its uses and effects—how it functions in a situation. But his emphasis is on the creation of new meanings. He writes that Wittgenstein "would bring up not two or three, but sometimes twenty-three examples of using the [same] word, each quite precise—and different."[7] The new meanings are not mere details that could be subsumed under a definition. Wittgenstein showed that no concept can *define* the uses of a word. But what lies beyond definition is not indeterminate. Since the word generates *just that* new meaning, and *a quite precise* new meaning each time, we see, according to Gendlin, that "our situations are far more intricately ordered than the conceptual patterns" ("TBP," 27–28).

For Gendlin, we dwell and speak directly in what he calls *the intricacy* of our situations. Old concepts, phrases, and social routines do always play a role, but the next thing we do, say, or think usually follows not just from the old forms, but from the larger situational intricacy. What language says and means is always more precise than what can follow logically from conceptual patterns. As both Wittgenstein and Heidegger showed, the nature of language far exceeds logic. Although Gendlin is concerned with logic, and develops new conceptual patterns that have logical power, he first shows that making sense (or following someone who makes sense) involves *implicit functions* that exceed logic and patterns. He shows a great deal about a whole range of such implicit functions.

But how can one discuss functions that always remain implicit? It is made possible by what I would call his "reflexively constituted practice": a practice by which *what* he asserts is also just then *happening* in how his words make sense. This allows the words to mean the process that is happening as we make sense of the sentence, so that the words say (something, never the whole of) the process by which they make their new meaning. Thereby a word can go beyond its old meaning. In this way the major words all change in Gendlin's philosophy. That makes the philosophy exciting, but also impossible to summarize in old phrases.

In a recent work of memory, Gendlin recalled that, when he began his studies in philosophy, he was fascinated by the fact that there were so many different systems of thought, and found himself challenged by the question of how one could make use of two or more different systems. In an unpublished manuscript describing the beginning of his intellectual project, Gendlin said:

> As an undergraduate, I developed a method for communicating with religious people *and* atheists, Marxists *and* McCarthyites, behaviorists *and* Freudians. My method was to accept each one's entire system—for the moment—so as to use *their* terms to express whatever point I wanted to make. I would explain that I did not agree with it all, and that I was only postponing all other arguments, so that I could make just one point. In this way, I found out that I could always formulate this *one* point in *any* system. I knew, of course, that "the" point was not the same in the different terms of the different systems of thought, since "it" also had all the different implications I was postponing. The differences were clear to me. But what was the sameness? In what respects was "it" still "that" point, moving across all the different formulations? For myself, when I "had a point," I would try to formulate "it" another way, and then another. "It" was *not* the

common denominator—which is nearly nothing. Rather, "it" has this odd "order" of responding to different formulations differently—but each time *very exactingly,* just so to each one. And not only to different systems. "The" point would also respond just so when put in relation to different purposes, different backgrounds, even loyalties to different groups. What seemed to me, if anything, *more* interesting than the meanings that my "point" formed in each of the different contexts in which I put it was the fact that no single consistent pattern could incorporate *all* that "the point" could be. In this way, I gradually learned that, when I had a point to make, I did not need to frame it in one of the systems already existing. I learned that I could create a quiet space within me and let my own words come. If interrupted at that stage, I might of course forget *what I was about to say.* But then I would simply burrow in some murky way to get "it" back again: "Oh . . . yes! . . . *that's* what I was about to say!" And that "that" was charged with implicit language, but was not a set of words. . . . I didn't want to think only with concepts. I wanted to *think with . . . that.*

What, in particular, claimed Gendlin's attention was the preseparated, directly sensed nature of *what we are about to say* in any situation. If we first "dwell" or "focus" so that it comes to be an "it" (a bodily sense), we can notice that it is very precise and yet it is not a formed entity. Its identity comes from our more intricate life in situations, and does not depend on our choice of logical forms. Different systems can then carry it forward differently, yet always in a very exacting way, only just so in each. If "it" were ordered only by forms and distinctions, the different versions would contradict and cancel each other; nothing would remain. But a "what we are about to say" has that radically different kind of "order" which can respond and develop in different conceptual systems. From the start it seemed to him that there was little philosophical understanding of how different conceptual systems cross and interact, that there was little attention to how words are actually used, and that our uses of words— and the philosophical accounts intended to interpret them—have been concealing their rootedness in the body of felt experience. By letting new conceptual structures form from his new use of words, he found ways in which our bodies of experience generate concepts.

For a first reading, some of Gendlin's work may appear to be very narrowly focused on the details of our experience in using words. This appearance is not the truth. First of all, this attention to experiential detail is, in fact, one of his work's greatest strengths. No other philosopher has given so much attention, step by step, to actual processes of meaning-formation.[8] This attention to the intricacies of meaning has turned out to be extraordinarily rewarding: it has enabled him to create a language for the examination of language. Secondly, as the papers in this collection show, this part of his work affects every other philosophical topic. Thirdly, as we think about what we are actually doing when we use words—for example, when we rearrange the old words in new phrases to make new sense of our situations—this process of concept-formation, this process of forming meanings, can also be a process of self-formation, a practice of caring for the self. Fourthly, moreover, as we find that what we want to say and do goes beyond old phrases and forms imposed on us from outside, we discover a freedom and empowerment, and a new conception of the individual, which can also lead to the progressive enlightenment of our social relations and perhaps also to an improvement in the social, public use of language and in the conditions that would enable people to speak with one another about what really concerns them. Thus, as a careful reading of Gendlin's writings, and of the critical papers in this collection, would show, Gendlin's theory and practice of language must ultimately be understood as a major philosophical contribution to the life of reason: a contribution that has radical implications for our interpretation and realization of the ideals affirmed throughout history. These are the ideals of mutual recognition and respect, equality, justice, freedom, and— insofar as possible—the fulfillment of their *promesse de bonheur*.

Early in this century, as we know, philosophers turned to our use of language in the hope that reflecting on this use would make it possible to work through old and intractable problems. Now, at a time when this attention to language has increasingly been brought to bear on the contemporary problematizations of rationality, Gendlin's work takes on a singular significance, for his analysis of the creation of meaning and the formation of new concepts is at the same time the exploration and demonstration of a radically different form (understanding, conception, practice) of rationality, more intricately reflexive than any other in our tradition. This rationality is a reflexivity in language that is connected, on the one hand, with the capacity for reflexivity distinctive of the "postmodern" individual, and, on the other, with the possibility of building more "democratic," more reflexively constituted communities. In Gendlin's theory and practice, the proliferation of social spaces where individuality would be able to flourish is connected to the reflexive formation of new meanings, new concepts, and consequently, also, to a real social and political respect for the unique body of cultural experience that each individual brings to the life of the community. In Gendlin's work, these dimensions of concept-formation, of language—ethical, moral, sociocultural, and political—are given the kind of theoretical and practical support that they require.[9] (In *The Archaeology of Knowledge*, Foucault turned to language in an attempt to challenge the way we think and communicate. Since he was familiar with the phenomenological movement, this turn could perhaps have suggested to him an examination of language as a meaning-forming practice: a practice, for example, of the self, or a practice of empowerment, that works for the emancipation of individuals belonging to oppressed groups by respecting the reality of their own experience as lived and liberating them from socially constructed interpretations of their experience imposed on them by the hegemonic culture. But his confinement of discourse to an archive of statements sentenced this contribution to the present appropriation of the project of Enlightenment to inevitable failure. Due to limitations of space, however, I cannot argue this point here.)

2

In his *Logic*, part 1 of the *Encyclopaedia of the Philosophical Sciences* (1830), Hegel observes that thought, as understanding, stops at concepts in their fixed determinateness and difference from one another (sec. 80, a), whereas in the dialectical movement of the "speculative" stage (sec. 82), thought free of the reifications of traditional logic works "affirmatively" with concepts "in their disintegration and transition," deconstructing them and, as Gendlin would say, carrying them forward. We come to regard the nature of language in a different way once Gendlin demonstrates very precisely how the body of feeling usually figures, and could figure differently, in our uses of language; how a new kind of concept can be formed; how the old meanings of a word function to enable *just that word* to acquire *just that precise new meaning*; and how the formation of meaning can be in closer contact with ongoing processes of bodily felt experiencing.

Gendlin's new terms arise from "stories" he tells about common situations, for example a poet working on an unfinished poem, a person walking into a meeting room and sitting down, or a snide remark. In his stories, the old words make new sense in new phrases that tell about perfectly recognizable aspects of the situation for which our language has as yet no familiar phrases. In his new phrases, the meaning of the major words changes—or as he puts it, their new use "retrieves" the words from their old schemes. The word would not be *that word*, if it did not actually *bring* its old uses and schemes *into* the new situation, so that old meaning and new situation "cross," and just this new meaning results.

For example, in a passage I quote later more extensively, the word "body" acquires a new and vastly greater meaning when he refers to the "philosophical discomfort" which he knows he has just generated in the reader: "This philosophical discomfort is bodily, a physical sensation, isn't it? Yes, our bodies are capable of *philosophical* discomfort! But the word 'bodily' changes in our saying this" ("TBP," 52).

In Gendlin's examples and stories, the word "bodily" makes sense about the body as sensed from inside. (Husserl, of course, must be recognized as the first philosopher to formulate a theory of meaning that is grounded in a methodology committed to respecting our experience just as it gives itself to us. Unfortunately, however, his commitment to the articulation of our experience as lived is betrayed by his commitment to a metaphysical dream: tracing the constitution of meaning back to its origin in the meaning-bestowing acts of a transcendental ego. Equally unfortunate is Husserl's reluctance to recognize the body's role in the formation and articulation of meaning. To his credit, Merleau-Ponty broke away from Husserl's metaphysical program and recognized the body's role in the forming of meaning, but he never understood how to work with the hermeneutic interactions between experience and language. In particular, he never recognized at the level of methodology that, and also how, his "descriptions," often in fact not at all true of our experience insofar as the experience is lived superficially, could nevertheless be true, and phenomenologically "faithful"—but only because they worked with, articulated, and carried forward the deeper, more hermeneutically implicit dimensions of experience.)[10] Gendlin shows in many stories that the body has intentionality, something like Heidegger's being-in-the-world, since we find that much of our situational knowledge is implicit in such a bodily sense, if we dwell on it and enter it. We *sense* all of a situation; in contrast, we can *think* only a little of it at a time. In his example, the philosophical discomfort implicitly contains a great many books we have read and chains of thought we have had. We cannot think all of those explicitly in any one moment. Similarly, in any ordinary situation we cannot separately think each aspect that is involved. We move and speak from our bodily sense of the situation. If we attend to this sense, we can find a few of the many factors that worked together to generate what we said or did. The factors we find are changed by being found, separated, and articulated, but before we did that, *they* functioned without being separate. But now the word "they" speaks of a preseparated kind of many, a "*preseparated multiplicity*" which we can find in any situation.

Gendlin does not only deny the old representational conception of language; he develops an alternative. Language does not represent; rather it *carries forward*. Speaking is not mainly "about": speaking is itself a further living in a situation. In this very precise sense, the functioning of language is always metaphorical—or rather, it is *always already* metaphorical, and yet, in another way, it is *not yet* metaphorical: not until this process of "carrying forward" is understood and put into practice reflexively. Symbols do not represent; rather, they relate to what we want to say in much the way that feeding relates to hunger. Feeding does not *represent* hunger; nor is there a *hidden* feeding underneath hunger.

Gendlin traces back and rejects the assumption that plants and animals are simply repetitive mechanisms. They are self-organizing life-interactions that easily develop something new. ("Put an ant on a fuzzy rug: Now it crawls quite oddly, a new more intricate crawl that was never part of its repertory.")[11] Culture and language elaborate but do not destroy this organic interactional capacity for novelty. Gendlin shows elaborately that our situational bodies can *imply* something new that has never as yet been done or said. We see this best when we are at a loss for words, not because what we want to say has no order, but because it is more precise than the available common phrases. Gendlin indicates this situational moment with a " . . . . ." The . . . . . *implies* more than we can phrase at that moment. The phrases to say what we want to say are not somehow hidden in the . . . . . ; they do not yet exist and we must await their *"coming."* If we do not compromise and accept something simpler, if we bear the discomfort, it may soon lead to new phrases to say what has never been said before. This *coming* is another implicit function of the body. If the phrases come, we seem to say what the . . . . . *was*, but Gendlin denies this. There is no equation, but nonetheless a very special relationship between such a . . . . . and what we later say "it was." While many other phrases leave the . . . . . behind unchanged, the special phrases *"carry it"* along with them, but not as it was, not in its insistent implying of something not here yet. Rather, the new phrases carry the . . . . . into speech or actions that are more than it was; they *"carry it forward."* This "carrying forward" exemplifies and clarifies what is at stake in Heidegger's distinction between "original" (*ursprünglich*) and "originary" (*originär*) uses of language: in the latter, poetizing (*dichterisch*) use, the "repetition" is not the transcription of an identical meaning-content, but rather an engagement in the process of meaning-formation which, by virtue of its poetizing, imaginative, and evocative qualities, responds to the challenge of the "original" meaning-forming moment and carries it forward, "redeeming" its implicit promise of meaningfulness.

The . . . . . to which Gendlin draws our attention comes many times a day in our ordinary situations. When we don't know what to do, we are not empty; it is rather that we sense *more* than the available routine can carry forward. We are stuck because we sense the situation more intricately than the usual routines can meet. Gendlin notes that we must improvise in our roles as mother, father, child, wife, husband, employee.

The old forms and roles fail us many times a day. We must and do develop new and more intricate actions to carry our situations forward. New ways can come spontaneously, but usually they require some minutes of dwelling with the . . . . . , entering it, drawing from it some new and more precise speech and action.

3

Pascal, challenging the rationalism of his time, the metaphysics that insisted on keeping reason and feeling split apart, proclaimed a different logic: "The heart has its reasons," he wrote, "which reason does not know."[12] Disturbed by the skepticism that was beginning to take hold in the seventeenth century, he wanted to argue for a logic of the heart, a discourse born of feeling, that could make sense out of connections that reason refused to recognize. Our own century is of course very different from Pascal's. And yet, we still seem to need the affirmation of a rationality that is embodied and in touch with embodied feeling.

Perhaps no one has given the grain of truth in Pascal's affirmation of a different rationality a more timely, more convincing demonstration than Gendlin. His work has put into practice a new critical understanding of how experience comes into language. This understanding is formulated in a practice of language that has brought to light some surprising ways in which language actually works. Drawing on these, Gendlin's use of language reveals how, in the very process of forming meanings, the words of our language can call upon, and articulate, certain roles that the body performs. In Gendlin's work, Pascal's affirmation of a reason of the heart has become a practice of language: no longer a mere declaration of faith, it has become the practice of a rationality actually grounded in the body of felt experience. This rationality is not at all hostile to the rationality of the objective sciences; but it denies their "objectivity," and it insists that even the most abstract thought—logic and mathematics, for example—and the most technologized processes of reasoning are rooted in, and continue to be dependent on, what might be called the *logos* of the experiencing body. The "rationality" that Gendlin practices is one that respects and works with what I would call the wisdom, or say the sense, implicit in our sensibility, to constitute new, truly emancipatory processes of thinking, learning, and communicating. When the . . . . . plays a role, what one wants to say and do arises in a much different way: one discovers a self-grounding process, rather than the social imposition of meaning.

Gendlin's work with language involves profound changes in our habits of thought, our traditional forms of experiencing and understanding ourselves, and even our ways of living. His work demonstrates a new sense of embodiment. His thinking works with a kind of experience that philosophical discourse has not yet properly and sufficiently recognized: the "bodily felt sense" of the situations in which we find ourselves. In effect, his theory of how language works—and the way he actually works with words—constitute a new "language," a new way of using the resources of our language.

Everyone today speaks of the need to think of reason as intersubjective and embodied; but no one surpasses Gendlin in attending to the question of what, very concretely and very precisely, this actually means and involves. With a deep and deliberate respect for our experience as we actually live it, Gendlin is almost alone in exploring the intricacies of this question.

The papers in this collection show just how Gendlin's philosophy of language is different from the philosophies we associate with rationalism, empiricism, and romanticism. Although it appropriates important elements from each of these schools of thought, it masters and goes beyond their problems by virtue of its attention to the process of conceptualizing felt meaningfulness. From rationalism, Gendlin takes over—and profoundly revises—the principle that meaningfulness depends on and requires conceptualization in language. From empiricism he takes over the principle that meaningfulness resides in a practical, embodied, experiential commerce with the world. But his more radical empiricism rejects classical empiricism because of its ontological commitment to atomism, mechanism, and objectivism, its doctrine of the primacy of perception, and its understanding of the body, the senses, experiencing, conceptualization, and the way language works. And finally, from romanticism he takes over, and alters, the principle that meaningfulness is not only cognitive or intellectual, but is deeply rooted in a changed understanding of the nature of feeling, of sense and sensibility.

Gendlin's relationship to the inherited discourse of rationalism is, I think, twofold. On the one hand, he is critical of its long-standing dualisms—dualisms that set the mind against the body, reason against feeling, and reason against the body; dualisms that isolate the self from the other, withdraw the individual from society, and sever the bonds of awareness that keep culture in harmony with nature. In other words, he frees what I call "rationality" from the epistemology and metaphysics of rationalism—and from the equally oppressive aspects of positivism, empiricism, and nominalism. Thus, he is strongly critical of a rationality that is conceived as disembodied, solitary, monadic, subjective, dispassionate, disinterested, disengaged, and incapable of feeling. On the other hand, Gendlin has carried forward an emancipatory potential promised by the philosophical tradition, introducing into the theory and practice of language a dimension of rationality that the traditional schools have always excluded: the reflexive intelligence, intersubjectivity, and sociability of the lived body ("PE," 69–87).

I believe that the true dimensions of Gendlin's work will only appear when it is contextualized within a larger historical framework: the historical horizons of Western culture. The radicality, magnitude, and originality of his work really become apparent only when read against this larger framework. I have already discussed him in relation to rationalism and the Enlightenment. It is also instructive to read him in relation to the discourse of romanticism. There are striking affinities, as well as some large differences, which come to the fore when his work is read in relation to the vitalism of Jacobi, Kant's contemporary;[13] the attempts at a reconciliation of reason and sensibility in the work of Herder and Schiller;[14] and the naturalism of Rousseau, who argued for the importance of not disengaging reason from our inner nature, and especially not from the inherent good sense of our feelings and sentiments. (However, Gendlin rejects the romantic longing for an immediacy and unity free of all forms and interpretations.) Indeed, there are even some fascinating resonances between Gendlin's conception of a "bodily felt sense" and the moral sense philosophies of Shaftesbury and Hume. Finally, moreover, it can be useful to think about Gendlin's work in relation to a tradition of reflexive inwardness, of practices of the self that can be traced back, in our Western history, to the Hellenic and Roman stoics of antiquity, the confessional self-examination of St. Augustine, the narrative self-explorations and self-constructions of Montaigne, the *Pensées* of Pascal, Descartes's methodical return to the authority of his own "inner" experience, and Emerson's reflexivity in his essays in personal experience. Although Gendlin himself has not made these connections, I suggest reading his work with this historical tradition in mind.

Returning to our contemporary situation, I would like, now, to indicate, very briefly, where Gendlin stands in relation to the debate over structuralism. Although he has drawn important lessons from both structuralism and poststructuralism, he has gone far beyond them to formulate a theory and practice of concept-formation that brings to light their numerous weaknesses and inadequacies—and shows us how to overcome them. The reason that he can negotiate between them is that he appreciates, and knows how to work with, the *process of explication*, whereas they, blind to the formative process, recognize only the conceptual structures that are produced—the one consenting to live entirely with these structures, the other choosing disorder as the only apparent option to life within ready-made and completely determinate structures. Against structuralism, which acknowledges only explicit, determinate structures, he has insisted that there are many different ways of ordering, many different ways of systematizing, many possibilities for the construction of meaning, and that experiencing—bodily felt experiencing-in-situations—is their source. Resisting the dogmatism, its assumptions of continuity, necessity, and totality, he has argued for a rationality that entails structural change and draws on implicit contexts to articulate a sense of new possibilities. But he argues just as strongly against poststructuralism, insisting that the alternative to the prevailing structure is not a space of limbo or disorder. Drawing our attention to the implicit dimension of our situations, he shows that it is not a texture of already given conceptual distinctions. The error of a certain structuralism has always been, of course, to suppose that it is. But when poststructuralism attempts to correct this error, it falls into the opposite error—with equally unfortunate consequences. For it misses the implicit contexts, which are a *greater* kind of *order* than structures: the order in which the meaning of a word can change, as the word "order" does here. The order of intricacy can be carried forward in many ways, but always very exactly and with more emergent detail than could follow from the concepts one used. To prove his claim about the multiplicity of orders and systems, and demonstrate that there are ways for us to inhabit our language that neither structuralism nor poststructuralism can see, Gendlin brings out how implicit contexts function in a kind of order radically different from that recognized by any other philosopher.

At any given time, new, more intricate possibilities are always already implicit in the space in which the dominant structure is articulated. By being able to speak from these implicit contexts, showing them in their functioning, Gendlin grounds his claim that the alternative to a structure is not disorder. Structures are always in fact implicit, but by demonstrating each time how new meaning exceeds them, he shows that the implicit dimension of meaning is not a texture of conceptual distinctions.

Neither the doctrine of structuralism, which implies the possibility of equating what is with *existing* conceptual structures, nor the doctrine of its contemporary antagonist, poststructuralism, which *denies* implicit order in the spacing between conceptual formations, can be used to represent Gendlin's much more intricate understanding of the ways we inhabit our language.

It is because he constantly shows the intricacies that he can resist Adorno's despair regarding the seemingly utopian possibilities in language that were affirmed by the philosophers of the Enlightenment. At the heart of Gendlin's project is his demonstration of rationality—

rationality in a new sense—in a practice that works with embodied meaning. (He calls its *psychological* use "focusing.") It is perhaps tempting to compare this practice with Foucault's "practices of the self," since Gendlin, like Foucault, seems concerned to "promote new forms of subjectivity through the refusal of the kind of individuality imposed on us for several centuries."[15] But Gendlin's practice is very different from Foucault's, for the only practices of the self that Foucault considers are practices of subjugation, processes of subjectification through which the body submits to an imposition of forms. By contrast, the "bodily felt sense" of a situation to which Gendlin calls our attention is more intricate, precise, and more enabling of creativity than are the meanings imposed on us by social training ("PE," 69–87). Moreover, he shows that our possible explications of what is intolerable about imposed meaning draw on our articulation of this bodily felt sense.

In a textual passage that demonstrates the reflexivity which needs to be encouraged in our use of language, Gendlin objects to the common belief that we should be able to substitute conceptual forms for what we say—especially in the discourse of philosophy. He believes—and his own use of language demonstrates—that the meaning achieved by a sentence is far greater than the categories we try to substitute for it. Thus:

> If someone asks, "What do you mean?," we feel a need to answer with clear categories and known meanings. We defend what we said by claiming that we "really" meant those clear categories. If we cannot say we meant *them*, if they don't *cover* what we said, then what we meant is *uncovered*—naked in what we said. But such "naked" saying makes us uncomfortable. This philosophical discomfort is bodily, a physical sensation, isn't it? Yes, our bodies are capable of *philosophical* discomfort! But the word "bodily" changes in our saying this. For example, what does the phrase "philosophical discomfort" mean? Nakedly, it means *this*, which my sentence says. But is it our old habit, or is it a fear of not being able to defend, or is it what we think philosophy should be, or what is it? ("TBP," 51–52)

"We can pursue the question," he tells us, "if we *think from* this discomfort—and if we let it continue to function, whatever we say about it."

Experience is neither the interpretations that we can make of it nor an already formed given. In response to any interpretation, the body of experience talks back with more intricacy than was contained in the interpretation. To notice this intricacy one needs to attend to one's sense of the implicit meaning and its response to what one attempts to say.

There are many different kinds of such response. The implicit sense one made before may "shrivel" and disappear, or remain simply the . . . . . , the implying of what is not yet said, showing that the attempted statement does not carry forward. Or, the implicit sense may move into many steps of carrying forward, showing new detail that was only implicitly (not as such) there before. The implicit dimension plays many roles, and gives rise to a whole new experiential "logic" in which uniqueness can give rise to universals, in which a small detail seemingly "under" a category can give rise to many further steps that are not subsumable under the category, in which a precise new aspect can always be created to relate any two things, and in which the more requirements one has at the start, the more new meaning can be created ("TBP"). Thus, for example, Gendlin's understanding of the implicit dimension of language, and his way of working with it, go far beyond Heidegger's efforts to "poetize" the "monotone" of philosophical reason and bring out the resonances of meaning which the "univocity" of standard usage conceals.[16] They also go far beyond Adorno's efforts to recognize "nonconceptual" meaning,[17] and Marcuse's efforts to break out of the one-dimensional functionality of our language, which he connected to an authoritarian, totalitarian politicization of our cultural life.[18]

Of course, our experience can be carried forward by new uses of words only to the extent that the words are *making sense*. The very nature of language is a new metaphorical sense-making which involves the body of felt experience in situations. Felt experience is never purely interior. Gendlin argues that even the plants live interactively, and intricately— even without perception and language. According to him we should not begin with perception and make it the model for experience. Perception and language only elaborate the already intricate bodily interaction. Human experiencing is always a bodily life-process, an interaction in situations with others. It always implicitly includes culture and language— but the bodily intricacy always also exceeds them. Therefore, when new sense-making emerges within existing society, it could transform social and cultural forms.

4

What is it that connects Gendlin's work in psychotherapy with his work in philosophy? I suggest that what connects the two disciplines is the problematic of the formation of meaning. Philosophy and psychotherapy in different ways both involve a process of reconceptualizing patterns of interpretation by moving beneath existing meanings in a way that lets new meanings emerge. For Gendlin this process cannot be captured by psychological or philosophical theories; it can at most be carried forward by them, and then only if the terms in which we speak of the process of meaning-formation emerge from it in that very moment.

These new practices and uses of language are crucial for a new development of the individual—what Foucault called "new historical forms of subjectivity." They are also the key to new forms of social relationship—forms in which individuals live from out of the intricacy of bodily sensed meaning-making and respect this way of living in each other ("PE," 69–87). There is, here, a learning process. In attending to, and speaking from, our bodily sense of a situation, we can discover the fact that what we want to do and say is more intricate than custom, habit, convention, socially imposed meanings. It is more than self-discovery or self-invention, when speech and action are more intricately shaped by carrying forward individual experience. Our capacity to break out of ready-made language and old constellations of meaning extends the horizon within which we have lived. We develop other forms of experience, other terms of life.[19]

In "Subject and Object," Adorno argued for his conviction that "The categorial captivity of individual consciousness repeats the real captivity of every individual."[20] Thought dialectically, this statement should be coupled with a statement in *Negative Dialectics*: "The utopia of knowledge would be to use concepts to open up the nonconceptual with concepts, without making it [the nonconceptual] equivalent to them."[21] Unfortunately, Adorno's failure to examine prevailing processes of concept-formation and work through a critique of these processes that would reveal, at the appropriate and necessary level of specificity, their obedience to the "logic of identity" makes it impossible for him to move beyond the futility and despair of two equally undesirable alternatives: either an abstract critique or an abstract utopianism. Working at the right level, Gendlin can overcome this dilemma, elaborating a critical theory of conceptual innovation that is also, at the same time, a critical and liberating practice. What Gendlin shows is a way to keep the forcefields (Adorno's word is *Kraftfelde*) of conceptual meaning always open to innovative formulations of sense.

The practice of meaning-formation that Gendlin shows us can enable us as individuals not only to resist the social imposition of meanings, but also to become skillful in carrying our own experience forward in new forms of meaning and action. Thus, when we go to the heart of Gendlin's philosophy of language, we encounter a deep and abiding concern for freedom, and that is because our freedom is dependent on our capacity to break out of ready-made language and carry forward the ready-made language we inherit and always find ourselves already using. New forms of subjectivity and new forms of community require that we learn how to think more creatively with words, that we learn how to form new concepts, new constellations of meaning ("PCN," 251–304).

Social forms can be altered and opened up to make a place for this greater experiential intricacy. With this in mind, Gendlin has devised and proposed a kind of social situation which includes in its very structure the expectation that each participant will restructure it further ("PCN"). He has also explored some new ways to build new kinds of community, communities in which social relations are founded—perhaps for the very first time—on principles of meaning-formation, rather than on already shared, ready-made meanings. Here one discovers that the interplay between language and embodied experience is more intricate than the usual social patterns. Potentially, this skillfulness could make us, as citizen individuals, more sensitive to the inadequacies of prevailing structures and institutions for communication and better able to speak with one another about things that presently cannot be discussed.

In a society that has made room for implicit meaning and its artic-ulation there would be a profound alteration of political processes and public spaces ("PCN"). (Indeed, schools and places of work were changed when they included the practice of new meaning-formation that Gendlin has taught.) In the new kind of community that Gendlin's work perhaps makes possible now, the communicative processes might be genuinely rooted, phenomenologically rooted, in the implicitly intricate interac-tions of our individual bodies of experience. Gendlin's methodologically grounded process—or say practice—of languaging lived experience con-stitutes a political experiment with potentially far-reaching and radical im-plications. For there is an essential relation of interdependence between processes of individuation and processes of socialization, and the very definition of the public and private spheres of life is mediated by processes of meaning-formation and communication. Therefore, the new type of individual toward which Gendlin's theory and practice of language points will never be able to flourish without a correspondingly transformed society, a society less repressive, less organized by and for relations of dom-ination. But how actually to achieve this transformation of society remains a problem. Concept-formation must play a crucial role in this regard, since individuality involves the capacity to develop distinctive forms from experience, and the social institutions toward which we are thinking and working require the creation of more opportunities for us to discover and discuss whatever is of concern to us in our lives. (Drawing out the implica-tions of his philosophy of language for a theory of democracy, Habermas would want to speak, here, of discursive opinion- and will-formation. But

Gendlin, while acknowledging the worthiness of Habermas's objectives, is not satisfied with his approach, because, as the very language that Habermas uses to formulate his theory of deliberative democracy tells us—and as Gendlin's very different way of using language enables us to realize—this approach is still too entangled in the aporia of modernity that the peculiar reflexivity of postmodern discourses has brought to our attention, and still too bound up, theoretically and methodologically, with institutions and practices that function in oppressive ways.) According to Gendlin, a society that has truly made room for implicit meaning and its ongoing articulation would generate new forms of social relationship— forms which would, in turn, help us as individuals to find the intricacy of our bodily sensing and bring this intricacy into the situations of our lives, recognizing and respecting it in each other.

Gendlin's attention to the carrying-forward of meaning-formations, the formation of *new* constellations of meaning, *new* conceptualizations, reveals a crucial theoretical and practical dimension that is insufficiently elaborated in the Habermasian theory of communicative action. Habermas understands the importance of rational communication in the life of a democracy; he understands how communication figures in the discursive formation of public opinion and the determination of a collective will. But his emphasis is on the achievement of mutual understanding— the communicative exchange of *already formed* meanings. And yet, a crucial dimension of this process is, and must be, the collaborative formation of *new* meanings, processes of communication that facilitate the shifting and altering of the ways we have been conceptualizing our situations, conceptualizing what our situations (implicitly) mean to us.

Thomas McCarthy recently argued that, "If deconstructionist concerns were to become an abiding feature of ethical-political thinking, the exercise of public reason might be carried on with greater sensitivity to what doesn't fit neatly into our schemes."[22] In this regard, it seems to me that Gendlin's theory and practice of meaning-formation could have some significant implications for the transformation of intractable relations of power and the current boundaries between the public sphere and the sphere of our private lives; that their application in our public discussions about what matters to us could significantly change what has been referred to in liberal theory as the public use of reason—the way that "citizens" listen to one another and communicate their needs, interests and concerns; examine, debate, and negotiate their differences; constitute their individual and collective identities; and deliberate on matters of common cause. (In the preceding sentence, I have put the word *citizen* inside quotation marks because, for Gendlin, the modern concept of "citizen," as used in that sentence, also needs to be rethought.)

The realization of a democracy in which these things would be possible depends, I think, on precisely the reflexive, deconstructive kind of rationality that figures in Gendlin's practice of meaning-formation. For, among other things, such democracy depends upon the respectful recognition of each individual's bodily felt sense of justice—and enables us as individuals to ground the deliberative conclusions achieved by the body politic, or at least to ground the process of reaching agreement on meanings, not only in abstract principles of justice, but also in our practical *sense* of justice and civility, that sense which articulates the moral sensibility always present, always carried, however primitively, in our individual bodies.[23] Gendlin has clearly shown that significant social and cultural change is possible only if, in our use of language, the body can give sense to words that exceed custom, habit, convention, socially imposed meanings—and speech and action are more intricately shaped by carrying forward individual and collective experience.

In *Dialectic of Enlightenment*, Horkheimer "rooted" morality in the moral feeling of compassion, which he described as "the sensuous awareness of the identity of general and particular, as naturalized mediation."[24] But he had nothing more to say about the formation of this "sensuous awareness." Nor could he shed any light on the process of its conceptual articulation and elaboration—how it engages a situation and can carry it forward through bodily felt interaction. In *Negative Dialectics*, Adorno broaches the very radical idea of a new categorical imperative carried by the body of feeling—but he makes the fatal mistake of denying this body any subjectivity, any capacity to articulate its felt experience discursively, and falls inevitably into the dialectic of despair. He says that this imperative is to summon people to their moral responsibility for others: "to arrange their thoughts and actions so that Auschwitz will not repeat itself, so that nothing similar will happen." But then he elaborates: "this imperative is just as *unruly* in regard to its own grounding as the givenness of Kant's once was. Dealing discursively with it would be an outrage [one that I suppose I am committing] for the new imperative enjoins the moment of the ethical supplement as a bodily feeling—bodily, because it is the practical abhorrence of the unbearable physical pain that the individual is exposed to, even as individuality is about to vanish as a form of mental reflection. It is only in the naked materialistic motive that morality survives."[25] For Adorno, then, mourning the loss of our ability to recognize and respond to the injurability of the other, there is little to hope for from the present and future of humanity, except—perhaps— a world in which the Holocaust will not be repeated. If Gendlin is not as despairing, not as hopeless, that is, in part, I think, not only because he works with an understanding of the body of felt experience that can release it from the reification that Adorno's way of thinking, in spite of good intentions, imposes on it, but also because, unlike Adorno, he can spell out a *discursive* practice, a subtle and intricate process of explication, through which—provided, of course, that the necessary favorable social and cultural conditions obtain—the body's experiential order, an order that Adorno seems to be calling a bodily felt moral "imperative," can be contacted and brought forth, rendered articulate and developed, or (in his own terminology) carried forward, as the "touchstone" for a more mature way of engaging the possibilities of ethical and moral life.

After Gendlin's work, we can understand much better—and know how to alter—the role of meaning-formation in two major spheres of life: how meaning-formation can function not only in processes of self-formation, but also in processes of democratic social interaction. Perhaps we can now envision the time when there will be a society of individuals better able to resist the social imposition of meanings and more skillful in giving independently meaningful form to their own experience. Perhaps we can even imagine a more radically democratic model of public space: the time of a space in which we, as citizens, could gather together for rational deliberation.

What if, when making sense with words takes place in the social domain, the domain of public discourse, what is at stake is ultimately a process that must also fit, or rather *make*, our bodily felt sense of justice? Gendlin shows how and why making new sense with words, if it *carries forward* our bodily sensing, and the affective and communicative capacities each one of us embodies, can contribute not only to the formation of the individual, but also to the formation of a social universal.

Everything hinges on the reflexivity-potential in language. This, I would say, is the key to the formation of the mature individual—the key both to its achievement of moral and political autonomy and to its self-fulfillment in authenticity. Correlatively, reflexivity is also, I believe, the key to the improvement of democratic institutions, because such institutions essentially require communicative infrastructures and processes that promote the ongoing conceptual reconfiguration of individual and collective experience, making it possible to carry this experience forward in significant new ways. To be sure, the importance of understanding and practicing reflexivity in language is being increasingly recognized—not only in critical social theory, for example, but also in philosophies concerned with new forms of subjectivity, the ethics of virtue, and the ideal of authenticity. And yet, it is painfully clear that individuals and institutions are still far from putting the ideal of reflexivity into practice. At the theoretical level, what is needed is a fine-grained, microscopic understanding that can bring out the intricacies and complexities of reflexive processes in the formation of meanings and concepts: a truly micro-level modeling of the logic of this reflexivity in the languaging of our experience. At a more practical level, what is needed is an understanding of how to incorporate reflexive languaging processes into our individual lives—and how to structure these processes into our social, political, and cultural institutions. Considered in this light, the historical significance of Gendlin's work lies in his contributions to our theoretical and practical understanding of the ways in which experiential processes and the formations of language can interact. There is no other theory and practice with a comparable power to show the creative possibilities inherent in reflexively constituted interactions between experience and language, nor is there any other practice and theory so capable of working creatively with these interactions in all their intricacy, complexity, subtlety, and richness.

In *Truth and Method*, Gadamer observes that, "Concept formation, born of Western philosophy, has held, throughout a long history, that mastery is the fundamental experience of reality." This reflection prompts him to ask: "Must we now be content to say that we are beginning to recognize this as such? Is our Western experience an insurmountable barrier?"[26] Like Gadamer's contributions to the hermeneutics of language, Gendlin's work has been normatively directed to the achievement of a practice and theory of communication based, not on domination, but on mutual recognition and respect for differences. Although I consider their projects to be similar, with significant affinities, I also want to call attention to a striking difference in their *levels* of analysis. In contrast to Gadamer's more general, more abstract account, Gendlin's analysis always directs our attention to the phenomenological and hermeneutical *intricacies* of meaning-forming and meaning-altering processes: it shows the hermeneutic logic of experience where it needs to be shown, namely at the micrological level. Let me briefly illustrate this point with some textual passages from Gadamer's *Truth and Method*, passages in which Gadamer explicitly takes up the same problems that concern Gendlin.

"In reality," Gadamer writes, "language is the single word whose virtuality opens up the infinity of discourse, of discourse with others. . . . Language is not its elaborate conventionalism, nor the burden of pre-schematization with which it loads us, but the generative and creative power unceasingly to make this whole ['of words and phrases, concepts, points of view and opinions'] fluid."[27] Gendlin would certainly concur. But he can carry this affirmation much farther—and in fact has done so. In Gendlin's work, one can always locate very precisely those moments where the "virtuality" of a word "opens up the infinity of discourse." Thus, moreover, one can see thereby exactly *how* this opening takes place. One can see very precisely that, and also how, there is, in the resources of our language, a "generative and creative power" that can *free* us from the "burden of pre-schematization"; but Gendlin also demonstrates how and why we are *dependent* on conceptual constructions for the very possibilities that could take us beyond them. In Gendlin's writings, Gadamer's genial affirmations are given microscopic demonstration.

Gadamer writes: "In a statement, the range of meaning of what has to be said is concealed. . . . [In other words,] as meaning thus reduced to what is said, it is always distorted meaning."[28] Earlier, I argued that Foucault's account of meaning in *The Archaeology of Knowledge* suffers from the very reductionism that Gadamer is here lamenting. Gadamer speaks of "distorted meaning." One might also speak of reification. (But this then calls for a theoretical analysis of power—something that Gadamer is not prepared to handle.) Gadamer continues: "To say what one means . . . means to hold what is said [in statements] together with an infinity of what is not said in the unity of one meaning." Elsewhere, Gadamer elaborates this point, arguing that "every word, in its momentariness, carries with it the unsaid, to which it is related by responding and indicating. The occasionality of human speech is not a casual imperfection of its expressive powers; it is, rather, the logical expression of the living virtuality of speech, that brings a totality of meaning into play, without being able to express it totally. All human speaking is finite in such a way that there is within it an infinity of meanings to be elaborated and interpreted."[29] Unfortunately, Gadamer does not actually *show* us just how words carry the unsaid with them. To this extent, then, the relationship between the said (the explicit) and the unsaid (the implicit), and the relationship between the said and the saying, remain obscure. By actually *showing* us how these relationships function, how they are formed and how, in the interplays of their intricacy, they work, Gendlin turns a theoretical and methodological doctrine into a truly *empowering* practice.

5

In closing, now, I would like to adopt a more critical perspective and point out that I have taken the time, in this chapter, to spell out in some detail what I believe to be the historical connections and contemporary implications of Gendlin's work because, to some extent, Gendlin himself has not done so. Nor has he yet sufficiently articulated how his reflexive practice of language would function in our ethical life and in the social, political, and cultural spheres. We still need, after reading him, to formulate and examine in detail just what difference his philosophy of language would actually make if it were put into practice in the communicative processes called for by a "deliberative democracy." And we need him to make explicit, and argue for, the functioning of *normative* assumptions behind the conception of human nature that is engaged by his philosophy of language as a practice and theory that brings the body of felt experience into the process of meaning–formation. That his reflexive use of language should enable people to carry forward their experience in a meaningful way, and that this *ought* to contribute to the public use of reason seems quite clear to me. But Gendlin himself has thus far left this matter untouched. His restriction, for the most part, to individual processes of meaning-formation—to the individual's languaging of experience—has been extremely fruitful, especially in the context of psychotherapy. But this restriction can unfortunately give the impression that his practice and theory of language, having been designed especially to fit the individual's expressive needs, cannot be carried forward into the diverse contexts of intersubjective life—the public sphere of political deliberation and cultural representation, for example—where new ways of saying and thinking are desperately needed. This impression would be a serious mistake. But it cannot be denied that Gendlin has not yet demonstrated the promise of his theory and practice with regard, for example, to the conflicts that arise in the social construction of shared meaning and the hermeneutics of cross-cultural dialogue. So far, he has not shown how our capacities for personal meaning-formation are (to be) connected with our capacities for participating in the practices of meaning-formation that are necessary in a deliberative democracy, for successful opinion- and will-formation. Nor has he shown how his practice of meaning-formation can work with collective conflicts (e.g. between employees and employers) to turn them into dialogical opportunities for all parties to achieve new meaning-formations and new self-understandings. But this is just to say that his work is not finished. I hope, however, that I have at least indicated some ways in which the extraordinary promise of his work would be realized.

If I end this chapter on a critical, provocative note, that is because I am convinced that his practice and theory could contribute more significantly than it has so far to the formation, not only of new forms of subjectivity, but also of new forms of intersubjectivity, and thus to the improvement of our existing democratic practices and institutions—and because I would like to see Gendlin think through and elaborate the historical connections and social-political implications which I have attempted to make explicit here in this chapter.

3

Filling in the Blanks

David Kolb

Eugene Gendlin claims that he wants "to think with more than conceptual structures, forms, distinctions, with more than cut and presented things" ("WCS," 29).[1] He wants situations in their concreteness to be something we can think with, not just analyze conceptually. He wants to show that "conceptual patterns are doubtful and always exceeded, but the excess seems unable to think itself. It seems to become patterns when we try to think it. This has been *the* problem of twentieth century philosophy" ("WCS," 29). As a result he has "long been concerned with what is not formed although always in some form" ("TAD," 1).

In this essay I would like to explore some of the issues surrounding the relation of the unformed and the formed. Gendlin says that "we get beyond the forms by thinking *precisely in* them" ("TAD," 1). The two emphasized words have to be considered separately as well as together. In many essays Gendlin's main concern is with the "precisely": Can something that is not fully formed and definite still direct us as we carry forward language and action? My discussion begins with that issue; I suggest ways that Gendlin's proposal connects with and differs from some current ideas in epistemology and the philosophy of language. Then my discussion moves to the "in": What sense can we make of the formed being unformed? Finally I suggest that Gendlin's program runs into some difficulties in this connection.

As always, Gendlin is concerned with the sources of change and growth in meaning. He offers the following example:

> Consider the silence of a poet with an unfinished poem: The already written lines want something more, but what? The poet may be only stuck

and confused, no mysterious call for thought at all. Just trying this line and that; many lines come. Some seem good. The poet listens carefully into each, rejects, and reads the written lines again—and again. The poet re-reads the written lines. The poem goes on there, where the lines end. Suddenly, or perhaps all along, the poet hears (senses, knows, reads . . . . .) what these already written lines need, want, demand, imply . . . . . Now the poet's hand rotates in the air. The gesture says *that*. Now the lines that come try to say, but do not say—*that*. The blank still hangs there, still implying something *more precise*. This blank seems to lack words, but no. The blank is very verbal: It knows the language well enough to understand—and reject—all the lines that come. The blank is not a bit pre-verbal; it knows what must be said, and that the lines which came don't say that. The blank is vague, but it is also more precise than what was ever said before—in the history of the world. But in another way, of course the blank is said—by the lines leading up to it. The poet can have (get, feel, keep . . . . .) this blank only by re-reading and listening to the written lines—over and over. They say what is further to be said.[2]

Eventually the poet finds the words; a line occurs and is accepted as saying what was to be said. Neither the previous lines nor felt blank meaning alone have directed the poet, but some situation in which the previous lines and the blank interact and inform each other.

How does the blank contribute to this process? Does the poet turn a mental eye to consult some fully definite felt meaning and then read off the new line (or perhaps the criteria for a new line)? No, Gendlin's story is not a tale of inner foundations. Whatever felt or bodily experience the poet is working with, it has no straightforward propositional content, or else producing the new line would be a simple matter of transcription.[3]

Inner experience has not had great philosophical success in this century. Bergson's appeal to lived time was put aside. Husserl's foundational inner science has been seriously challenged by Heidegger and Derrida. Empiricism's simple appeal to basic experienced data ran into difficulties. The logical positivists and their successors tried innumerable ways of connecting beliefs with immediate inner evidence. No way worked, and the enterprise has been crippled by attacks from Wittgenstein, Sellars, Quine, and Davidson, among others. The enterprise was doomed, it seems, because if the inner experience was to provide epistemological evidence for a belief the immediacy of the experience could not be maintained. Roughly speaking, if the inner experience had propositional content it was not immediate experience in the sense required, and if it did not have such content it could not be so directly related to the beliefs it was supposed to found.

Donald Davidson has argued that while it is obvious that experience is in some sense a source of belief, that does not mean that there is some special kind of inner nonpropositional evidence.[4] He claims that "evidence" is a logical relation by which one proposition supports another; the only thing that can provide evidence for a proposition is another proposition. Experience is not evidence in that sense. Its relation to our beliefs is causal (rather than intentional or logical or epistemological). Experience causes us to have propositional beliefs. Beliefs are connected in logical and evidential ways to one another, and the whole net of beliefs is connected causally to the world. The two kinds of relation are distinct.

The poet's new line, however, seems to stand in neither logical nor causal relation to the situational felt meaning that Gendlin describes. If anything, the relation is more causal than evidential, but neither of Davidson's relations quite fit the example. But then why should they? Gendlin's is not really an example of an experience relating to a belief. For one thing, the felt meaning involved is not a separate experience from the overall attempt to write the poem. The case is not parallel to watching the result of a laboratory experiment or looking into a room to check one's beliefs about its contents.

On the other hand, if we look back at Gendlin's first book (*ECM*) we do see him putting forward his theory of felt meaning as an alternative to the attempts by the logical positivists and others to explain the role of experience in the workings of language. So we cannot so easily dismiss as irrelevant to Gendlin's program the conclusions reached by thinkers like Sellars, Quine, and Davidson, who helped dismantle positivism.

The experience that Gendlin discusses is not so much evidence for beliefs as a guide for actions. Unlike the positivists Gendlin has never sought an epistemological foundation for beliefs. He has been concerned about the source of creativity and innovation that allows us to move forward in language, art, and behavior, and he has a special interest in controversies about method in psychology and psychotherapy. He is concerned with showing how there can be change that comes from other sources than the relation of concepts to one another. These are areas where Davidson's discussions of causal relations are relevant, especially as they have been picked up and extended by Richard Rorty.[5]

However, before we could deal with those larger issues, we need to get clearer on what Gendlin is proposing. The present essay makes some steps in that direction. First, I explore a bit further the implications of the idea that felt meaning does not have propositional content, then I look at some ways of conceiving the interpenetration of form and unformed that Gendlin speaks of, and I close by pointing out some difficulties.

The poet in Gendlin's example cannot be described as simply reading off meaning from an inner experience that can be consulted as something complete and meaningful on its own. This example and others, as well as Gendlin's extended descriptions of psychotherapeutic process, all show that his felt meaning is not something to be consulted as complete and definite on its own.

One way of putting this point would be to say that Gendlin rejects a lingering Cartesianism that still infects most anti-Cartesians. Even the enemies of Descartes still tend to envision inner experience as something that parades before a mental eye, with the items on parade each fully definite with its own content. When today's anti-Cartesians discuss intentional content they usually demand that we choose either some kind of self-luminous inner episodes of belief and desire, each with its inherent propositional content, or a third-person attribution of beliefs and desires to entities whose public behavior warrants such an interpretation. Unchallenged in that dichotomy is the demand that intentionality be located in a set of beliefs and desires with propositional intentional content.

Gendlin's examples challenge that presupposition. There is no clear intentional content to the poet's felt meaning, yet it functions meaningfully within an intentional process as some sort of criterion and source of content. Experience, Gendlin is suggesting, cannot be adequately described as a sequence of perceptual episodes, beliefs, and desires each fully formed with its own content. The situation exceeds these forms. This idea fits neither the standard appeal to inner experience nor Davidson's causal model.

Part of the problem is our tendency to analyze consciousness as the occurrence of felt qualities (colors, pains, sounds) plus intentional episodes (meanings, concepts, beliefs). The traditional division of body and soul thus persists, now as brute facts versus meaning facts (or causal relations versus logical relations).[6]

Gendlin's felt meaning is not in itself a separate experience. The poet does not really have an independent inner experience to consult. Gendlin has never said that the felt meaning he investigates could be separated from symbols and propositions: "experience, observation, and living are always already significant, always signifier-and-signified. There are no mere givens and no pure reports. Let us reject the assumption that there is somewhere, underneath or behind, a given to which signs 'approximate' or which they merely 'represent.' Language and thought carry forward what they signify, they can never be merely about" ("NLM," 389).

In his early work Gendlin's position on this was already complex and nuanced. He says there that without connection and specification by symbols felt meaning is "incomplete" and "not really a meaning"

(*ECM*, 28). Felt meanings can be the source for "countless possible meanings" (*ECM*, 208), depending on the symbols used to distinguish and schematize aspects of the experience. There are no "units" of felt meaning (*ECM*, 29, 41), and felt meaning can be variously individuated (*ECM*, 98); it is in itself "nonnumerical" (*ECM*, 151–53) and only after felt meaning has been differentiated by means of symbols can we make direct references to it (*ECM*, 109, 218).

Nonetheless, for Gendlin the felt meaning has a certain kind of independence. This is shown by the situation's ability to guide new formulations. "Any slot enables more moves than those consistent with the theory that helped to lead you there" ("TAD," 13). "The independence of the experienceable aspect [the felt meaning of a situation] is at any rate possible only after it has been lifted out by some formulation. . . . The aspect demonstrates its independence to this degree, from its initial formulation which gave birth to it: it can function in other formulations, and it can also give rise to sub-aspects which the initial formulation could not have led to. . . . It is in the power of the movement of steps from one experience-formulation pair to another, that the independence respect of an aspect lies" ("TPD," 328f.).

So the felt meaning is neither a given inner meaning-fact, nor a Davidsonian causal antecedent. Yet there is some intentional "shape" to the blank that the poet experiences. This raises the question just how Gendlin envisages the interpenetration of felt meaning of the situation with the symbolic, propositional meaning of the previous lines.

There are two stories at the extremes of what could be said about the example. According to the first of those stories the already written lines of the poem set up a structure that has only one inevitable continuation. When the poet perceives that structure, the next line is defined. Gendlin, however, insists that an examination of the experience of creating shows that the new line was not latent in that way. The new line is "an implicit which is not merely a hidden explicit. . . . Not . . . something hidden but fully formed." That the new line was in some sense "determined does not say [that it] can be derived. If the poem's next line were determined in that sense, the poet could figure it out logically. Finishing a poem would be easy" ("TAD," 9f.).

The second story speaks from the opposite extreme. According to this story the previous lines leave open an indeterminate space that imposes no restrictions at all on a new line. Gendlin denies this. "If the next line were indeterminate, most any line could fit in. That way, too, poems would be easy to finish" ("TAD," 10).

Both of the extreme stories take the previous lines of the poem as in a sense complete. If the lines left the field wide open, that would be because on their own they made something sufficiently whole in itself that it did not demand any particular further completion. Whatever comes would be to some degree an external addition (though it might create a new whole when it joined with the previous lines). On the other hand, if the previous lines demanded one and only one continuation, that would be because they had already set up some complete form that was present so that its demands could be followed. In both cases there would be a structure or order that was complete and present.

Gendlin denies that there is such a complete structure: "the implicit functions more intricately than patterns do" ("WCS," 32). Yet it functions: "when the words at last do come, they work in some way in and from that erstwhile blank" ("TAD," 11). We might read this as suggesting that the line between the formed and the unformed to come should be drawn between the old lines and the space for the new. I will argue, however, that Gendlin should be read as suggesting that the previous lines as well as the blank are not totally sharp and formed.

Just what kind of middle ground is Gendlin seeking between the two extreme views? We can approach this by looking at some other stories that try to occupy that middle ground. The first is a pragmatic story involving levels of generality. According to this story, the poem's previous lines get interpreted as setting up expectations and defining possibilities on a general level (the product will be a poem, an elegy, in modern diction, expressing sorrow rather than irony, etc.). Those generalizations shape the blank and suggest particular continuations. The poet chooses those that best fulfill the general plan. Thus, the formed and unformed aspects of the poem are sorted out by assigning them to different levels. The universal description is definite but the particular description (of both old and new lines) is still undetermined.

The pragmatic story has a complication. For it may be that the poet finds a line that upsets the generalization characterizing the previous lines. This may recast the poem (the diction begins to change, or irony enters in). These changes lead to new projections of the whole, new particularizations, still further generalizations, and so on. The process is complex but no more so than the familiar process of having one's expectations about a text altered by one's reading of the text, or having one's theory changed by the empirical investigations that were meant to confirm it. Of course the case of the poet is not completely parallel to that of the empirical observer, but the idea of guidance from heuristic generalizations seems to be transferable.

Straightforward as this pragmatic story may be, something is still lacking in terms of Gendlin's example. For one thing, it reduces the felt meaning Gendlin discusses to an artifact of the process of generalization. The formed and unformed aspects of the experience have been transformed into a relation of universal and particular. What is unformed is the possibility of different particularizations, but each generalization and each particularization is fully formed in its own right. There is nothing left with the curious double quality Gendlin describes. His thinking with the situation as a formed/unformed whole that can be carried forward has been turned into a process of theorizing about data.

We can see another problem if we consider the pragmatic story in the light of a more drastic Darwinian account. In the Darwinian story the earlier lines of the poem stand as they do, and new lines are generated by some random or in any case nonrational process (perhaps Davidson's causal relation?). When that happens, some innovations "catch" and some don't. There is no explanation for the new line's success except this: it recreates the whole that it makes with the older lines in ways that are useful for some purpose (for perception, for expression, for coping, or whatever the purpose of the poem is, and that purpose can change). Various generalizations and narrations about the new whole are then tried and discarded until one is accepted as justifying the lines that work. The generalizations come later; they don't guide either the generation or the acceptance of the successful line. This story is not too far from what Richard Rorty says about the function of creativity and metaphor.[7]

Again there can be a cycle: the previous lines, the generation of alternative continuations, the survival of one of the continuations, the new whole, the retrospective justification, then new innovations, and so on. This story is Darwinian because it separates the generation of alternative continuations from the test for survival. Unlike the pragmatist story, which still gave the generalizations a guiding role, the Darwinian story separates the contexts of discovery, acceptance, and justification.

This Darwinian story fails in two ways as an account of Gendlin's example. It makes the previous lines something complete, which Gendlin denies. And it makes the generation and the acceptance of the new line into two separate processes, neither of which have intentional guidance. But what Gendlin is trying to understand is the guidance exercised by the combination of the previous lines, the "blank" they create, and the felt meaning that is a part of both. The fourth story defines away the question that interests Gendlin.

In comparison with the Darwinian, the pragmatist story allows for guidance in the generation and acceptance of alternatives. But when we note how it differs from the Darwinian story, it becomes more obvious how it also differs from Gendlin's example. In the pragmatist story the previous lines become passive data for the activity of generalization and particularization. The question about how the previous lines interact with the blank becomes a question about the activities of the poet as creator. Activity and passivity are distributed in traditional ways.[8]

How can we talk about form and the unformed coexisting? We have tentatively rejected the idea that what is unformed is simply a further particularization of a generality, or of the activity of the creating subject. Perhaps we should say that the words and lines are formed, complete in themselves—there they are lying on the page—but what is unformed is the potential whole to be made out of these already formed parts. But this still avoids the odd status of the blank. What kind of possibility or potentiality could be present, coexisting with form and expressing itself across time but without being reduced to a simple temporal assemblage?

Others have explored this area before. In the ninth book of his *Metaphysics* Aristotle attacks the views of a group of philosophers from nearby Megara who deny that beings have potentialities. They accept Parmenides's arguments against any reference to nonbeing: whatever is, is totally what it is in the present. The Megarians conclude from this that all descriptions should be in terms of purely actual and sharply present entities, and therefore they demand that a being be described only in terms of what it actually is at this moment. Reference to past or potential future states is not allowed. If John is standing, we should say he is standing, but not that he has a power or potential to sit. The puppy at your feet is only what it is now.

Aristotle has little difficulty showing that ordinary language is shot through with references to past and future, and that without being able to talk about potential actions and states we could not say even the things the Megarians are willing to allow. But the dream that the Megarians represent has not died. Would it not be wonderful if knowledge and language could be anchored in some entities that were fully definite, just were what they presented themselves to be, and were available for this anchoring function?

We recognize here one version of what Heidegger identifies as the metaphysical drive to total presence, in this case emphasizing not the presence of the grounding entity but its nature as fully packed into its limits, with no inconvenient extensions. In modern philosophy mental objects such as sense data or meanings have been offered as such grounding entities.

One threat to this neat picture is the temporal reference that seems intrinsic across experience. The obvious defense against such a threat is to invoke the idea of a temporal assemblage. Time is understood to include a series of momentary experiences which remain self-contained but also enter into relations with other momentary experiences. These relations could be inferential or causal, or they could be part-whole relations whereby the individual slices, each complete in itself, make up a cross-time whole which is a new object. In any case the cross-time relations would not really affect the formed being of the individual slices. The individual experiences or temporal parts remain self-contained wholes on their own level.

Gendlin's poem example questions this account, as would Aristotle. For Aristotle, the individual temporal stages of a being are what they are, even on the "basic" instantaneous level—which is not basic—because of their insertion in the teleological process that leads to a goal, a final state or activity. The puppy is and acts as he does now because he is on the way to living a grown-up dog's life. Without that informing teleology the matter of which the puppy is made would not take on the form and activities it does. Similarly the lines of the unfinished poem are not self-contained; they would not be what they are if they were not produced within a teleological process that aims to make a poem.

But poems are not organisms. Unlike a puppy, a poem is not a self-developing instance of a natural kind. Natural substances, for Aristotle, develop to manifest a form of activity shared by members of the species. Poems do not have such a form.

Besides the kind of potentiality that defines the puppy, there is another kind of potentiality in Aristotle, a kind that would be possessed, for example, by a heap of lumber. The boards could be made into a house, or a table, or a bridge, or a toy, and so on. Matter has the potential to be shaped into many different substances.

A poem does not have this kind of relatively indefinite potentiality. As a sequence of words the poem can indeed be used for many things (wallpaper decoration, handwriting practice, a key to a cipher, and so on). But as a poem it is already within a type, though not a natural kind.

For Aristotle, the potentiality possessed by a poem is that of an artifact with a purpose. In his *Poetics* he describes the functions of artworks and how to build them to perform these functions. If one is building a boat there are constraints on how one can continue and still have the resulting artifact fulfill its intended purpose. If one is building a poem there are constraints as well. The functions the poem will fulfill exercise constraints on diction, subject matter, and other dimensions. These help constrain the kind of line that would be an appropriate completion to a poem, though there is still room for the individual talent of the poet, just as there is room for the individual style of the boat maker.

Unfortunately for this theory, poetic practice has widened immensely since Aristotle's time. While it is true that a poem belongs to a kind more particular than "marks on a page" or "words in sequence," our theories and practices of art have made the function and form of poems more and more open. Today the poem could be finished in a great many ways, with few or no constraints of the sort Aristotle would recognize. Suppose we added to the previous lines a line in a violently different diction. No surprise; this happens all the time. Suppose we added something we would not recognize as "a line of poetry," perhaps a quotation from the telephone directory, or half a paragraph from a VCR instruction manual. Or we might append a recorded speech by FDR, or a picture of a bathtub. Even in these cases the poem could still be a poem, given our practices of collage and irony, and our hermeneutical expectations about making and encountering art (and anti-art art) today. Perhaps in Aristotelian terms our notions of art have moved away from the category of artifacts towards that of actions.

This means that the possibilities "in" the previous lines are not those of an Aristotelian substance or functional artifact. The teleologies involved are not constant enough for that. Though it remains true that there are teleologies involved at all times, they are continually being revised and in a very fluid social context. There is no steady form, no repeatable *eidos*, so we have left the Greek scene.

Yet the fundamental point Aristotle made against the Megarians remains. If it is meaningful at all, the poem is not composed of entities that are complete in themselves at each stage. All the parts of the poem are both actual and potential (formed and unformed) at the same time. The previous lines and the blank are both formed and unformed. This unformed is more than the alternative usability of something already definite (like Aristotle's lumber), and it cannot be attributed to the activity of a supervising subject; it is part of what it means to be the lines and the blank.

So how do the formed and unformed interpenetrate in the experience of a meaningful situation? It seems to me that Gendlin is on the right track when he seeks to talk about a situational thickness that is more than the result of a complex form (though surely the forms involved are complex). He is right to point to an excess beyond conceptual patterns, to deny the adequacy of an analysis of the content of experience as a set of beliefs and desires, and to insist that our use of language is not simply governed by rules but pervaded by innovation and metaphorical creation that alters meaning as we carry it forward.

There are several ways a discussion might move to try to clarify this unformed quality. One traditional route would lead to the question of determinative and reflective judgment in Kant's third critique. The most important current route would lead to Heidegger, for whom time is not a series of complete self-contained nows and experience is neither the taking up of passive temporal data nor the linking of fully actual items into sequences.[9] An extreme route would generalize Gendlin's descriptions and come up with an ontology (perhaps related to Whitehead) which downplays the ultimacy of definite form.[10]

But we cannot now follow any of these routes, because we must examine some problems with Gendlin's formulations. I think that these problems arise because Gendlin has defined his own position in opposition to an inadequate theory of meaning, of which, oddly enough, there are too many traces in Gendlin's own theory.

Gendlin's 1962 book (*ECM*) was written against (among others) the logical empiricists, who tended to think of the structure of language in terms of formal systems of logical implications. These logical moves were given meaning through their being tied to sensory experiences by some sort of awareness of the content of experience that could be immediately put into propositional form. Gendlin certainly does not agree with this; his felt meaning has a complex two-way relation with propositions and symbols. Nevertheless, there are traces of the logical empiricist picture in his early book. He talks of felt meaning (such as the poet feels) as something we "have" (*ECM*, 13) as an "inward datum" (*ECM*, 15) that is then "represented" (*ECM*, 27) by concepts although it is had "in itself" in feeling (*ECM*, 27) and can be an object of "direct reference" (*ECM*, passim, esp. 91–92, 109, 218). The "intellect" can be in "direct contact" (*ECM*, 220) with these felt meanings. Later on Gendlin would stop talking about inward data and representation (compare the passage cited earlier: "there are no mere givens and no pure reports").

However, Gendlin continues to talk after the manner of the logical empiricists when he speaks of "concepts" and "logical relations" as systems of inference moves. For instance, attacking that idea, he says, "Rendering in clean conceptual constructs that make logical steps is not word-use" ("NLM," 392). This implies that "conceptual constructs" consist of "logical steps." The conceptual system is conceived as a series of rule-governed moves rather than also incorporating the net of structural contrasts studied by structuralists and attacked/embraced by the poststructuralists.[11]

Why should this be a problem? We can get a hint of the difficulty by recalling Gendlin's claim, cited earlier, that without connection and specification by symbols felt meaning is "incomplete" and "not really a meaning." Felt meanings can be the source for "countless possible meanings," but just which meaning becomes salient depends on the particular symbols used to isolate and schematize aspects of the experience. Now, for there to be a choice among symbols or propositions there have to be many of them, standing in contrasts to one another. So symbols have to have some prior definiteness and independence in order to be able to specify different aspects of felt meaning (and also in order for symbol

DAVID KOLB

use to be carried forward or changed). Were there the wrong kind of indeterminacy in the symbols, the felt meaning would be not be specified the way Gendlin wants it to be.

Gendlin has an argument in *Experiencing and the Creation of Meaning* that even symbol-to-symbol connections are mediated by felt meaning and not just logical relations. "The felt meaning functions . . . to select the further symbols that explicate [the meaning of a proposition or word]. Without bringing home to oneself the felt meaning of a term, such as democracy, one cannot define. The verbal sound alone could not lead directly to other verbal sounds that define 'democracy' " (*ECM*, 107). This claim is misleading. Of course the verbal sound qua sound would not lead to other sounds, but to speak of it as "verbal sound" is already to find it within a series of contrasts, and to speak of it as a "word" finds more, and to speak of it as the word "democracy" is to indicate its place in a series of contrasts and inferences observable in language and behavior. These contrasts and connections do link this sound to other sounds without reference to felt meanings. Symbols have contrasts and connections that establish their definiteness and their individuality independent of their relation to felt meaning. Otherwise they could not function as Gendlin wants them to do.

For Gendlin, a meaningful situation involves a complex interpenetration of some particular symbols and a felt meaning. But if the way signifiers get their individuality depends on contrasts with other absent signifiers, and if there is any underdetermination in those relations with the other absent signifiers, then an indeterminacy is introduced that is not the same as the unformed Gendlin has spoken about.

We could ask: What is the shape of the slot the poet experiences? Does it have a single shape if the propositional meaning of the previous lines is constituted by relation with absent others? If meaning comes by contrasts with absent possibilities, and there are many such sets of contrasts possible, then the previous lines can be different signifiers in different systems of relations. They can be individuated in various ways, projected to describe the context differently, and the context(s) can have different continuations. The tentative shapes the contrasts suggest will radiate in too many directions. Which context, which system, which slot is the actual one? This line of argument is familiar in different ways from the writings of Quine and Davidson, and of Derrida.

In ordinary cases we invoke settled practices that fix actual interpretations: we do stop at red lights and we know how to continue laundry lists. But there is no settled form of life to tell us how to go on with the poem.[12]

Part of Gendlin's answer to this objection might be to deny the kind of total indeterminacy that he attributes to Derrida. But he misreads Derrida,[13] and in any case a more contrastive theory of meaning does not require total indeterminacy in order to cause Gendlin problems. If any degree of contrast or (even regional) holism is involved in the individuation and meaning of propositions and symbols, then the tight interpenetration Gendlin wants between symbols and felt meaning is opened up toward other absent symbols and feelings in a way that confuses both sides in Gendlin's story.

There may be another problem. What if the felt meaning itself ("on its own," to whatever degree it is such) also depended on contrast, in this case with other possible but absent bodily meanings? If it does not so depend, then Gendlin may have to deal with the problems that plagued the logical empiricists and led eventually to Davidson's causal theory. If felt meaning does depend in some way on contrast and differences, then there is another dimension of indetermination different from the unformed richness Gendlin wants.

Gendlin does say that felt meaning is not purely personal. "The seemingly wordless 'sense' of which (and from which) Proust writes is not at all *pre*verbal. All of language is implicit in it, and the situations, living arrangements, the political and historical world in which language is used; that is why his words can come from it. But that is not easy" ("NLM," 396). But as far as I can tell Gendlin does not want these systems and forms of life to involve the felt meaning in constitutive relations of contrast with absent but possible other felt meanings.[14] But this seems to make the living arrangements and political and historical situations into something like causes that leave imprints on the bodily meaning.

I wonder then if it would not be helpful for Gendlin to distinguish the unformed he wants to talk about from the indeterminacy or underdetermination talked about by Davidson and Derrida. I think that for this purpose he needs to speak more about propositional or symbolic meaning, and about the possible constitution of meanings through contrast with absent feelings and signifiers.

One place where such discussion might find a base in Gendlin's text is his remark that "Meaning is experiencing qua instance of itself" (*ECM*, 202). This could lead to a discussion of "seeing as" or even "being as," and the ways that instances are and are not constituted by contrast with absent others.[15] This might lead us into the thickness of experience and let us carry forward Gendlin's own theories.

Reply to Kolb

Professor Kolb sensitively examines a major theme of my philosophy. He firmly defends the determinative role of experienced meaning (felt meaning, situatedness, intricacy . . . . .), and shows that others have not taken account of it. He says it needs to be pursued, but then he turns to an objection. I will first answer his objection and then some of the lovely array of questions he poses for me at the end.

His objection assumes that I hold what I actually consider to be a great error: I do indeed say that different symbols (signifiers, concepts, rules, distinctions . . . . .) can bring different results from a felt sense, but I deny that the results depend on the signifiers. This is also the error that leads people to think of science as mere construction: they see that different hypotheses lead to different findings, so they conclude that the hypotheses determine the findings. I seek to correct this! There is a *"responsive order"* which can indeed be carried forward in different ways, but always only in very exacting ways, because *experienced meaning* (*intricacy* . . . . .) *plays a determinative role.* If this is missed, my "reversal" of the usual philosophical priority is lost again.

We see the loss, as Kolb develops the objection: if meanings depend entirely on signifiers, he argues that they must "have some *prior* definiteness and independence." I agree that they have some definiteness but it is not prior. Experiential meaning plays a crucial role in determining and each time redetermining the signifiers. Now that he has dropped the determinative role of . . . . . which he pursued through most of his commentary, it seems to him that signifiers can get their meanings only from each other.

Kolb first asked about "form and the unformed *coexisting.*" He saw that they cannot be separated. Now he speaks of "the *un*formed" alone. But its inseparability has been central to my whole enterprise. I have insisted that there is no *un*formed or *un*symbolized experiencing. Experiencing is always symbolized at least by events. There is not always a wordless . . . . . but when there is, it is symbolized by our attention to it. *The experiential* side . . . . . is *never just unsymbolized, never just one side.* We cannot ask about it *alone*, because it is never alone.

The signifiers are never without some experiencing either. Kolb mentions my saying this in *Experiencing and the Creation of Meaning*, and agrees. But he is committed to the assumption that only the signifiers determine anything. So, when *he* then says that the signifiers never become definite either (citing Quine, Davidson, and Derrida), he thinks we are back to the problems of those authors. We would be, if moves from the *un*formed were totally up to the signifiers, since they are indefinite too.

But this is just the crux of the argument: in the tradition it was assumed (and it is still assumed!) that the indefiniteness of the signifiers belongs just to the signifiers, that it is nothing but *their* breakdown, so that there is nothing else. Kolb assumes that experienced meaning is indefinite since what we say from it depends partly on the signifiers, but that they are indefinite on their own hook. It does not occur to him that the indefiniteness of the signifiers *is* the *determinative* role of experienced meaning! That is the answer to the puzzle we could formulate from his comments: Why does "a combination" or "coexistence" of the two "guide us"(as he says), whereas each is indefinite when considered alone?

It is artificial to consider either experienced meaning or symbols alone since each has already involved the other and they don't happen alone. So we do not need to say how experienced meaning is formed or unformed alone. We do not avoid the question, but we need not answer it in terms of signifiers *alone*. We can deliberately enter and go a few steps into the . . . . . , so that our answers will be more precise and go further. *Such an entry and the further thinking it enables (just where some see only stoppage) is a major import of this work.*

If we enter our . . . . . (our sense of the discussion at this point), we find not only his question, but the whole context, the role of the question in the argument, and why it would have been asked. This is a very common transition made many times in most arguments. Of course it is not a logical deduction; it is rather a function of the . . . . . We realize that Kolb's question concerns how the experienced side can possibly contribute anything, how it can have its guiding role, if it were just *un*formed, and dependent on signifiers, themselves indefinite.

We reject formed or unformed, but we don't have to stop there. Kolb's "unformed" (I don't call it that) involves the traditional assumption that form is the only order: by *unformed* he means that it can contribute nothing. We answer that there is an intricate responsive order (not just neither form, nor unformed). We want to show its contribution.

While we cannot separate experienced meaning from the forms *in any one spot*, we can show its contribution *in transitions* from one experienced symbolization to another. In a move we notice when more than form was involved. The experienced side performs functions that are not due just to the forms. We can speak with and from those functions (roles, effects . . . . .), and I have specified many of them.

Transitions happen from one saying to the next, from one step of thought to the next, for example from a question to the sensed relevance (. . . . .) of the question, and from that to a new answer. Or, when someone misses our point, we move to the . . . . . and from that to another version which the hearer might grasp more easily. Such transitions happen also when there is no . . . . . for example when we move *from* being engaged in events *to* speaking, without a . . . . . happening in between. We can distinguish what follows logically *from the previous form*, and what does not, but makes sense because it follows from the experiential "side" of what we had before. We can notice and speak from its role, even though it was never alone, but formed both before and after the transition.

Kolb wants all determination to be by "contrasts and inferences." Yes, we can render them all as differences, but after McKeon, Heidegger (and Derrida), can Kolb really want to settle for just one traditional account of signifiers? Can he want to grant a founding role to just one of the well-known variety of signifiers (differences, commonalities, conceptual patterns, logical forms, rules, symbols, sets, gatherings, categories . . . . .)? Each can explain the others, and has often done so in the history of philosophy. They did not succeed each other in a linear way, as is sometimes alleged. (Dialectic came after Kant and Descartes, but before Aristotle and the atomists.) Actually they have been contemporary since the pre-Socratics. Each can come into any sentence-slot where one of the others works. It helps to let them all work implicitly, whichever one we utter.[1]

We do not deny the ancient truth that a word's meaning includes *not* meaning everything else, and that it involves a vast system of implicit relations to other words. Knowing this approach protects us from many errors (for example, from taking positives as just alone). But other strands of the tradition protect us too. Kant showed that what unifies the sentence unifies the concrete objects too. Wittgenstein showed that words are related not just to each other; their relations are embedded in relations of situations. These conflict, taken just as signifiers. But when they are at work in the intricacy they do not conflict. No aporia there. They function so that our further thinking is not stupid about what each has shown. From the . . . . . that comes after the string of them, our next step will be *new and more precise.*

Our next step here can say: when a word is used in a new way, we *immediately* understand ("Oh . . . . .") the odd way in which the word has just changed the situation. The language-situation system (its contrasts, differences, similarities, syntheses, uses, ideas, references, denotations . . . . .) *develops further implicitly, as we interact and speak.* I could not have said this without the tradition, but it goes further (and it is about going further).[2]

Just because all forms and distinctions break down is no reason not to see what each can bring (show, lift out, synthesize, differentiate, entitize . . . . .) *there,* in the intricacy (situation, experiencing, context . . . . .). We want to see just where each breaks down. We also keep the problems an approach *makes visible,* as well as those it *hides,* which only other approaches reveal in it. We cannot keep it all, but the more we have recognized, the more is implicitly at work when we think our next step.

The . . . . . does not let us say whatever we like; it is not looser or less precise than logical precision. The more different forms (including the traditional ones) we recognize, the more further possibilities *implicitly govern* (see chap. 1, "A New Kind of Concept") our next step. Mutually exclusive forms can do this only because we let them work in the . . . . . (which is alive in us, is our living in situations, our interactions with others, and is much more [. . . . .] than the signifiers to begin with).

The great variety of concepts, theories, and approaches seems to be an embarrassment of riches; there are too many. But when we are working on something (a practical situation with other people, or a theoretical problem) we often try all available approaches and find that none carry the problem forward. Then we wish we had more approaches to try. Now there are *too few*!

Of course we are not always meeting difficult situations, or working on something. I have distinguished several cases (in *ECM* I call them "functional relationships"), and various ways of making distinctions among them. When we only play, we can listen into many possibilities. Even so, each step must still make sense. But felt meaning functions in another way when we already have a demanding situation (interaction, problem, felt sense . . . . .). That is when it may reject all attempts to carry it forward. Then too there might be more than one way, but even one is hard to devise. If one does come, then it can be further reformulated in countless ways in different further steps.

When we are working on a problem, we do not denigrate the fact that conceptual patterns cut (or unify, itemize, organize . . . . .). We wish ours were sharper, so that they would lift out (reveal, find, make, differentiate, synthesize . . . . .) more. The fact that different signifiers give different results does not worry us, because the difficulty (problem, situation . . . . .) remains hanging and thereby gives us the "guidance" that Kolb was tracing.

While Kolb was still tracing my argument, he understood how we recognize when a . . . . . is not being carried forward: "Then the blank still hangs there, still implying something more precise." Also in cases where there is no . . . . . , Kolb recognized that experienced meaning performs a determinative role that is not accounted for by the signifiers. Yet he was able to lose track of it so quickly! Let us specify it much further.

Let us enter the intricacy here: a felt meaning may be carried forward in different ways, but we see its determining role because:

1. *Each way* is precise, just so, or it fails to carry forward; we cannot change the signifiers at will. Something else (the situation . . . . .) requires and provides this precision. There may be another way but it too will be

DAVID KOLB

precise and not variable at will. Most proposals do not carry forward at all. That is why life and thought are hard.

2. What we study responds *to each way* with more than could be consistent with (more than could follow from) our signifiers (our hypothesis, conceptual form, distinction, theory, or symbols . . . . .).

3. What certain signifiers bring out (find, make, synthesize, differentiate . . . . .) can force us to revise *the very signifiers which* brought it out. We see that the result is not entirely the creature of the signifiers; if it were, they could not lead to results that are inconsistent with them.

4. Different results of carrying forward do not contradict each other, even if they involve contradictory signifiers. For example, in a difficult situation with complicated other people, one theory makes certain facets of the situation leap out at us. Those do not disappear if we now allow a second theory to make other facets leap out. We are grateful to have seen both sets of facets, and we are wise to keep both in sight. Theories can contradict each other; facets of a situation (of a . . . . .) do not.

In these and other ways we can recognize the determinative role of experiencing, even though signifiers are inseparable from it, and different ones can carry it forward differently.

But isn't what we find in the intricacy determined by the position or statement from which we enter it? No, it isn't! (see 3 above). That is just the point! But can we not find other specifics as well? Yes, but they will not contradict those we found (see 4).

Kolb attributes my concern with logical forms to my opposing (and therefore being influenced by) logical empiricism, which he calls "an insufficient theory of meaning." But there is no sufficient *theory* of meaning. I am concerned with logical form (or whatever that is which generates logical implications . . . . .). To ignore logic and mathematical science seems simplistic, as well as helpless in the face of their power. We can move with logical (as well as experiential) implications at any point. Logic seems "too tight" to Kolb. But logic is just as lost by a little looseness, as by a lot. The tightness is what has the power.

Kolb says he finds a happy medium between tight and loose in "the net of structural contrasts studied by structuralists and *attacked/embraced* by poststructuralists." But look at "attacked/embraced"—the two are played against each other; aporia is no happy medium. One loses what logical forms can bring out, without gaining a way to think with more than logic.

When I examine that "net," I find mutually exclusive determinants *working implicitly together,* not as "structural contrasts," nor like logic with a little looseness. When they work implicitly *in* the intricacy, they can *cross* and open so that a single, more precise step is *focally* implied.

The *net* of life in situations (. . . . .) does not consist just of contrasts, not even attacked/embraced ones. If we *enter* where poststructuralists attack/embrace, we find an intricacy with which we can think, and which can protect our next step better than contradictory positions in aporia.

How is it that a situation (experience, felt sense . . . . .) has such a demanding precision? How is a . . . . . individuated? How is it that a troubling situation is so stubbornly precise, even when only half known?[3]

I answer that we speak as we live—*immediately* in our situations, as living organisms, as plants live. What is individuated and determinative? I say it is, for example: what someone is working on, interested in, or trying to avoid. It is a point someone makes, or a situation that needs to be met. If you try to explain what is meant by "a person working on something," "meeting a situation," or "making a point," you find that these phrases are not signifiers that define what happens. Rather, *the reverse*: the phrases are familiar from many situations; those define the phrases. Or, better: words and situations determine and constantly *recreate* each other. But let "recreate" mean what just happened to that word: else it will not make sense.

The reversed priority (*ECM*) can make my philosophy seem hard to understand, but the reversal *can* be grasped all at once. We can see the meanings of words being remade in use. They do not need to lie ready, "definite" in advance, as Kolb wants. Kolb did recognize this so well, when he wrote:

> Gendlin is on the right track when he seeks to talk about a situational thickness that is more than the result of a complex form . . . and to insist that our use of language is not simply governed by rules but pervaded by . . . metaphorical creation that alters meaning as we carry it forward.

> For Gendlin the felt meaning has a certain kind of independence. This is shown by the situation's ability to guide new formulations.

> Neither the previous lines nor the felt blank alone have directed the poet, but *some situation in which* the previous lines and the blank interact and inform each other.

> What Gendlin is trying to understand is *the guidance exercised* by the combination of the previous lines, the "blank" they create, and the felt meaning that is a part of both.

> What is not fully formed (although in the forms) can still direct us.

4

Tacit Knowledge and Implicit Intricacy

William James Earle

> The complexity of the word is simply the complexity of the topic, and the linguist cannot pretend to tidy it up.
>
> —*William Empson*[1]

> There would be no surprises in anything he would say—because he knew exactly what to say.
>
> —*Gordon Lish*[2]

Let me begin by remembering for you—there is, of course, a me remembering and writing and, I hope, a real you somewhere reading and, again I hope, appreciating, despite the contrary conventions of academic discourse—a puzzlement of mine from the shallow past which illustrates and is illuminated by Eugene Gendlin's understanding of language. This is the puzzle. Although a standard scientific article of the sort published every week in *Science*, the official journal of the American Association for the Advancement of Science, will typically cite ten or fifteen other scientific articles, there is never any discussion of what the cited authors mean—nothing, in other words, resembling the interminable hermeneutics of the humanities.

Is this because scientific writers are clearer and more unambiguous? Is it because scientists are better readers? Not likely. It is just that the sentences they write have as their more-or-less immediate context the actual laboratory work which supports them. It is, furthermore, *normative* that a scientific article should be at least an implicit recipe for reproducing its experimental basis. The sentences in scientific articles are as general as other sentences and at least as abstract, but nevertheless refer, for those who can really use them, to recoverable practice. This familiar fact is, I think, most commonly adduced to make a *narrowly* epistemological point about corroboration or crosspersonal verification. The emphasis, here, is different.

Scientific activity, the total practice of which the writing of scientific articles forms a significant part, requires that the distance between words and world be always, at least in principle, a transversible distance. In a story or novel I can write—especially if I am not a very evocative writer, not a very good writer—"The sky was blue," and readers, with all the good will in the world, will not be able to get back to the blue I had in mind if I did have a particular blue in mind and, in any case, will not be able to get back to any real, particular, and interesting blue. Suppose the writer of the short story or novel had to provide a sample (perhaps a color chip) of every mentioned color. This would then be something like a scientific article. Scientific writing doesn't, itself and as such, have to be evocative because it includes, by specification, the relevant samples, the color chips, the laboratory equipment, the experiments, the technical performances. A good deal of the recent "ethnography" of science—for example, the work of Latour and Woolgar[3] and Lynch[4]—as well as the related "neglect of experiment" literature[5] reminds us, or redeems from mere abstract, negligent, or distracted assent, Wittgenstein's insight that to understand a language is to understand a form of life.[6]

Eugene Gendlin's work can be read as a development of this Wittgensteinian insight. (My guess would be that Gendlin's thinking, growing out of his own therapeutic practice, was formed in substantial independence of Wittgenstein so that he fulfilled the requirement laid down by Wittgenstein in the Preface to the *Tractatus*: "Perhaps this book will be understood only by someone who has himself already had the thoughts that are expressed in it—or at least similar thoughts."[7]) More importantly, Gendlin's work helps us to understand Wittgenstein and, thereby, to make some real philosophical progress.

Let me begin with one of Gendlin's explicit comments on Wittgenstein:

> Wittgenstein showed that the meaning of a word lies in how it is *used* and that it is used in a *variety* of situations. He would show that the same word could be used in many situations and would mean something different in each. He would offer, not three or four, but perhaps thirty-four examples of such situations, each quite different. None of them would fit the pattern that initially seemed to define the word.[8]

Other commentators on Wittgenstein have made the same point in similar words, *but*. Let me see if I can be explicit about this felt *but*. Here are five (complementary) approximations: (1) *But* Gendlin makes the point ungrudgingly. He does not share the typical, almost definitional, philosophical distaste for numbers larger than three. (2) *But* Gendlin is not trying to change Wittgenstein's insight into an ignorable "of-course-we-all-know-that" familiarity. (3) *But* Gendlin really has overcome the philosophical resistance to an "examination of details [*Einzelheiten*]."[9] Gendlin likes details. (4) *But* Gendlin does not notice (or notice Wittgenstein noticing) situational context merely to disambiguate the otherwise ambiguous. Situational context, according to Gendlin, continues to work in the words we use giving them a positively valued (and a really, though not always obviously, benign) complexity.[10] (5) *But* Gendlin believes what he is saying. This question of belief is rather tricky. Let me address it in the next paragraph.

Rodney Needham makes the point that, while an ethnographer may worry a lot about *which* beliefs to ascribe to the natives he studies, "He does not find it necessary, however, to specify what he means by belief or how it is known that men in New Guinea believe what they say. The tacit assumption, rather, is that this common psychological category in the English language denotes a common human capacity which can be immediately ascribed to all men."[11] Paul Veyne faces the same problem of the "*pluralité des modalités de croyance*" as he tries to answer the titular question of his book *Did the Greeks Believe in Their Myths?*[12] This is also the problem faced again and again in the therapeutic context. This is nicely illustrated by Serge Leclaire, a French psychoanalyst, who reports that all his sophisticated Parisian patients believe, on arrival, that they have oedipal complexes—they have, after all, read Freud—but not in a way that does them any good relative to the problems that led them to seek psychoanalytic help.[13]

This applies to Gendlin in two ways. *First*, what he believes in philosophy he believes fruitfully. *Second*, in his therapeutic practice, he attempts to show his patients the way to fruitful belief. "Real belief" and "fruitful belief" are, of course, just phrases gesturing toward those modalities of belief—there is likely to be more than one—that make a difference, in therapy, in our intellectual lives, in our lives. Peirce wrote: "Let us not pretend to doubt in philosophy what we do not doubt in our hearts."[14] Let us not pretend to believe in philosophy what we do not believe in our hearts. Peirce's advice has two—complementary—aspects both of which are, I think, taken seriously by Gendlin. To speak in inexact and provisional disciplinary terms, one aspect is sociological, the other is psychological.

The Sociological Aspect. The phrase, "in philosophy," though its practitioners—professional philosophers—tend to deny it, indicates a set of addresses in social space; and someone, a particular philosopher, will find certain beliefs, doubts, and arguments irresistible in direct proportion to their utility in moving him to better addresses within the space in which he lives and moves and has his being. Philosophers are far too naive—even, mainly, too nice—to calculate their social advantages and, in any case, they can do better "living" a policy of sincere intellectual adhesion. You cannot exit social space but, like Gendlin, you can complicate your position within it, playing many roles—academic psychologist, philosopher, radical therapist—simultaneously and incompletely, exploiting slack and leeway as well as your own insoucience,[15] and using, craftily, the not inconsiderable advantages of marginality and maverickhood.

These remarks may sound deflationary and discouraging, but actually provide a basis for limited optimism along the lines of Bourdieu's remark that "if we have any chance of having personal opinions, this is perhaps on condition that we know our opinions are not such spontaneously."[16] Social determinism in most spots (though not, for example, pertaining to caste in perfectly intact caste societies) is soft and can be struggled against. This, to put it in terms of an objective correlative of its phenomenology, is like swimming against the current in a very viscous fluid and not like cutting through a steel door with an acetylene torch. These images are meant to suggest something that can be done with difficulty but without special tools, gifts, or exemptions, something that is marginally, but really, possible because it involves beating the statistical odds—like taking a good photograph, writing a provocative sentence, or remaining interesting as well as courteous to one's spouse after thirty years of marriage. The struggle here envisioned, instanced by the artist's or the intellectual's struggle to stay creative, is a struggle against limited and limiting (or conventional and conventionalizing) success. What psychology supports this possibility of constrained, but genuine, social transcendence?

The Psychological Aspect. What is needed here, and what I take Gendlin to be working toward, is a non-Cartesian, or psychosomatic, theory of belief and knowledge. Many philosophers are officially (as well as attitudinally and optatively) non-Cartesian and regard themselves as having given up mind-body dualism. Gendlin is, for philosophers, a good case study of someone who has really abandoned dualism. I want to make a case for the claim that Gendlin's abandonment of Cartesian dualism is effectual and fruitful. I shall say nothing about the metaphysics of these matters because all questions about what there is, in any fundamental sense, belong to the natural sciences and, in any case, how such questions are answered has very little—perhaps surprisingly little—connection with properly philosophical or properly psychological questions. We see, in Gendlin, what happens when belief in self-transparent minds with clear-and-distinct ideas subject to tidy discursive encapsulation is *really* given up. I shall in what follows look at some central features of this process. In the course of this examination, I shall also try to make evident the connections between Gendlin's psychological views and the possibility of (limited) social transcendence.

I said at the outset that Gendlin's views help us to understand why ordinary scientific articles fail to generate hermeneutic wrangles. The competent readers of such articles are always able to get back to the relevant world of scientific practice. They understand language—the articles—because they understand, as fully enculturated participants or initiates, the form of life—a scientific discipline—to which the language belongs. Wittgenstein's *Sprache-Lebensform* link is, I believe, given a distinctly un-Wittgensteinian inflection by Gendlin. For Wittgenstein, what we go back to—when we return from conceptual holidays, from cognitive downtime—is public practice, a shared, teachable, learnable, essentially rule-governed world in which experience, also known as "subjective experience," is insignificant or at best epiphenomenal. For Gendlin, what we go back to—when we return to ourselves from the conventional world of stereotyped emotions and expected sentiments—is our own messy and murky, but richly significant, bodily experience. Despite this difference, Gendlin is applying what Wittgenstein described, at the end of the *Tractatus*,[17] as the only "strictly correct [*streng richtige*]" method in philosophy: "whenever someone wanted to say something metaphysical, to demonstrate to him that he had failed to give a meaning to certain signs in his propositions." This is, I would argue, if not the only strictly correct, certainly—and *still*—a centrally important method in philosophy which Wittgenstein never abandoned and which Gendlin consistently employs in therapeutic practice. "Metaphysical" is what sounds good, sounds important and deep, but is deadened, disconnected, and finally useless. The reader can supply his own philosophical examples. The equivalent of the "metaphysical" in Gendlin are the quick and glib remarks we make about our lives (à la the Gordon Lish epigraph) which lead nowhere, which constitute a kind of pseudo-understanding, and which Gendlin, as he describes the process in *Focusing* and *Let Your Body Interpret Your Dreams*,[18] is constantly urging people to get beyond. Language isn't something bad or inimical (Gendlin is no Bergsonian ineffabilist), but still it is (sometimes) necessary to say: "don't answer in words."[19] Why? Because for most people most of the time the available words are "ready-made"[20] for purposes of serviceable communication and not for purposes of inner exploration or self-knowledge.

"Language," Gendlin writes, "includes situations as well as words. It is not 'just verbal.' It brings with it the bodily feel of living in the situations. Words change situations. Human situations are lived and changed largely by talking."[21] Of course, talking can be, mostly is, just verbal recycling of *doxa*,[22] the familiar and agreed upon mixture of platitudes and false-hoods, non–eyebrow-raising to *les bien-pensants*. But Gendlin is *stipulating* a use of language that "includes situations." Gendlin's situationalism, or contextualism, is not the linguistic commonplace that demonstratives, or indexicals generally, mean (in some broad sense of "mean") by indexing items in their environments. For one thing, indexicality can be, even perhaps, as Quine once put it, "must be supplanted."[23] For any sentence containing indexicals, we can devise what Quine calls an *eternal sentence*: "a sentence whose truth value stays fixed through time and from speaker to speaker."[24]

For Gendlin, in contrast, context cannot be eternalized away. Sentence and situation interanimate. Indeed, sentences, as artifacts with polymorphous causal powers, are not really separate from the situations in which they are said. And because of their causal powers, sentences also resonate, complexly, in the organisms which produce them. It is indeed the causal powers of sentences, not their representativity,[25] that make poetry possible and that explain the general irreplaceability of sentences. So two sentences that mean *exactly* the same thing, if they have different effects, may have a quite different therapeutic efficacy.[26]

There are many illustrations, in Gendlin's work, of the causal powers of sentences and even of words and phrases. Gendlin does not himself use the phrase "causal powers" but I think this is a reasonable—though doubtless not the only helpful—gloss on his practice. He says throughout *Focusing* that as you try to understand your own life, you may produce "accurate" descriptions or "cogent" analyses of your problems, but nothing happens. The descriptions or analyses are *causally inert*. "This book [*Focusing*] will let you experience and recognize when actual change is happening in you, and when it's not. There is a distinct physical sensation of change, which you recognize once you have experienced it. We call it a body shift."[27]

It would, of course, be possible to argue that the shifts and changes that occur during, that perhaps constitute, the therapeutic process are devoid of cognitive significance and that sentences involved in the process, even if they happen to have—as they might well not have—truth-value relevant meaning, are no more than catalysts of patient improvement, fine if they work, useless if they do not. I should begin to sketch the counterargument as follows. This is really nothing new. When you give up the Cartesian model of mind, you should also give up the idea of representations, or sentences-as-representations, irresidually—and, as it were, instantaneously—legible to minds which in a quick two-step procedure distinguish their cognitively relevant from their cognitively irrelevant features and then evaluate them for truth. Cartesian minds know what they know and, because they have no depth, regard "tacit knowledge"[28] as a category mistake. Non-Cartesian minds recognize degrees of cognitive availability and find themselves always transacting, and indeed negotiating, at the unstable interface, not of the cognitive and the noncognitive, but of the cognitive and the potentially cognitive. Intimate, wide-bandwidth causal contact with the implicit intricacy[29] of our own bodies and their circumambient worlds slows down non-Cartesian minds and explains the gradualist, patience-requiring[30] character of significant cognitive process—everything from personal enlightenment to scientific advance.

Something like this also explains the entrenched character of false philosophical pictures which survive in our intellectual practice after their official abandonment. The Cartesian picture of mind is a case in point. Few of us believe in soul-like minds, but we may still act as if our own minds were enough insulated from their causal (or bodily) circumstances to produce representations of the world that are either true or false simpliciter, judged from some—imaginary—extraterrestrial point of view. This is nicely brought out in a recent discussion, by Rorty, of Putnam. According to Rorty, Rorty accepts, whereas Putnam does not, "a story about humans as animals with special organs and abilities: about how certain features of the human throat, hand, and brain enabled humans to start developing increasingly complex social practices, by batting increasingly complex noises back and forth. According to this story, these organs and abilities, and the practices they made possible, have a lot to do with who we are and what we want, but they no more put us in a *representational* relation to an intrinsic nature of things than do the anteater's snout or the bower-bird's skill at weaving."[31] In crude summary, we have two main stories: in one, humans, detached from causal influence, represent the world accurately or inaccurately; in the other, humans, because of their own environmentally relevant causal powers and design, cope with the world—anyway, some of them, some of the time—a bit more cleverly than their animal competitors.[32] It seems to me that Gendlin is *already* working out in concrete detail the consequences of accepting—here again, I should underline *really* accepting—the second, or causal/coping, view.

"In action," Gendlin writes, "we must think situations to cope with them."[33] This is more radical than it sounds because, on the more common view, we don't think, and indeed can't think, about a situation in its individual particularity, in its category-evasive implicit intricacy, but think, and can only think, about its general description or representation, which can be detached from the situation itself and communicated to others, even others devoid of firsthand experience. According to Gendlin, "We do not have to think only the general concepts about 'what went on the other day.' When we think a situation, its whole past history functions in how we think it. We think 'Michael does things like that.'"[34] The phrases "what went on the other day" and "Michael does things like that" have no general communicative utility and probably strike most educated speakers as phrases of laziness. But I am not being lazy— merely economical or finite—when I say "how things are in Ptashne's lab"[35] or "the intellectual climate at the Institute for Advanced Studies"[36] or "what they're really into at CERN."[37] I am, of course, evoking for insiders or participants or initiates what may or may not be communicable remainderlessly to outsiders.

"You had to be there" and "you can't know what it's like because you're not an X" are among the most annoying remarks in the language, blending socially exclusionary gestures with a philosophical confusion of knowledge and experience. But it is important not, in our annoyance, to commit an *overcorrection*.[38] The annoying remarks reflect the view that all cognitive significance is based ("based," here, being no more than a placeholder for an analysis not attempted) on the experience of the persons to whom the significance is available. The overcorrection is that no cognitive significance is based on experience. The *via media*, or Gendlin's view, is that some cognitive significance is based on the experience of persons who have special relations to it in virtue of their experience. Mistake: language is always essentially evocative. Overcorrection: language is never essentially evocative. *Via media*: language is sometimes essentially evocative. "What went on the other day," for whom it works, works by evocation.

Can every evocation be replaced by a detachable (or perfectly general) representation? Probably some can. In any case, our stock of resources, linguistic and other, for framing representations is by no means fixed. But it is likely, at whatever level of representative ability we currently operate, that we can notice more and feel[39] more than we have words to describe. For example, most of the very definite, or precisely shaped, suggestivities of paintings evade our general descriptive resources.[40] So we end up talking about paintings by evoking them through the use of their proper names—a procedure which, whether we like it or not, excludes the unacquainted.

All of this implies a kind of realism. The paintings are there and affect us in ways we cannot anticipate. The paintings may affect us in ways that subvert current art-historical understanding. We don't notice only what we have been taught to notice. Causal traffic, patterns of irradiation, sensory impingements, are much richer than the standard perceptual codes. We are not prisoners of our culture. This is a perfectly general point: "Instances," as Gendlin puts it, "are more than their categories." "A situation [Gendlin again] has no fixed number of details."[41] I find this same realism, exactly this kind of realism, in Michel Foucault. Besides the "fundamental codes of a culture" and its high-level "scientific theories" and "philosophical interpretations," there is something else:

> It is here that a culture, imperceptibly deviating from the empirical orders prescribed for it by its primary codes, instituting an initial separation from them, causes them to lose their original transparency, relinquishes its immediate and invisible powers, frees itself sufficiently to discover that these orders are perhaps not the only possible ones or the best ones; this culture then finds itself faced with the stark fact that there exists, below the level of its spontaneous orders, things that are in themselves capable of being ordered, that belong to a certain unspoken order; the fact, in short that order *exists.*[42]

Gendlin has developed a methodologically individualized version of these thoughts.[43] The officially imperceptible deviations are nonetheless felt by patients and others. Our culture provides us with quick and, in some ways, efficient categories in whose terms we habitually perceive, judge, and value. If we are properly enculturated ("properly" as in "properly brought up"), the categories, codes, and concepts we use will have immense psychological plausibility, will strike us as altogether "natural," and will, as Foucault realized, operate almost everywhere "spontaneously." Nevertheless, something seeps in around the edges of the official grid or wells up from below it. Here is one of Gendlin's descriptions: "You make contact with a feeling and you say, 'Yes that's it!' Then you feel something below it or behind it or alongside it and you say, 'Well, no, that isn't it after all.' "[44] What is felt in this way is likely to be felt vaguely, precisely because the precise categories were made for something else. As Gendlin puts it, "The felt sense is the holistic, unclear sense of the whole thing. It is something most people would pass by because it is murky, fuzzy, vague."[45]

Murkiness, fuzziness, and vagueness, as I understand them, are neither final features of the world nor byproducts of the insuperable limits of our representative capacities. They manifest the "unspoken order" of the world whose raw[46] causal power is unconstrained by our conceptual arrangements. Not everything is social. Even pharaonic regimes crumble. No one is in a position to control all the causality. Representations are imposed, but are also subverted by stray signals. There is hope because there is complexity. There is cognitive advance because signals get through from outside the cognitive systems we have inherited or designed. We can feel what we are not supposed to notice. The complexity of the world, in any case disruptive, Gendlin teaches us to transmute into usable intricacy.

Reply to Earle

With few exceptions I declare myself happy with Professor Earle's rendition. I enjoyed his vivid writing. How shall I reply, since I agree? But do I really agree? I have long argued that one cannot say what is new in my philosophy unless the words change their meanings in the process of saying it. Does Earle let his words do that? Yes, but so unobtrusively that readers might not notice. I will specify how his words change in their new setting, here.

For example, Earle's word "causal" would be wrong if taken in the usual way. The previous commentator showed this.[1] I might wish that Earle had *deliberately* marked how the very causation of which the word speaks here *causes* the word's meaning to change so as to say it when used in this context. But the crucial question is: Has Earle kept my "reversal" of the order? In his sentences, does the old meaning of "causal" define the situational felt meaning, or does it *redefine* "causal"?

Causality is usually said to be a connection between two separate things, a Humean-Kantian relation imposed by an observer. The word might seem to place *situational meaning* within the scientifically constructed universe, with all the familiar assumptions and problems this would entail. But we cannot conclude that this *must* have happened just because Earle used the word. Then we could never say anything new, since all words bring old schemes. The question is rather: Does he move only from the old schemes, or often also from the felt sense of the present context?

How can we make and recognize moves from the felt sense? By entering into the intricacy I can offer two sets of what I call "specifics." I use (1), (2), (3), and (4) to show that each is a specific:

1. *The new sense is created by new phrases.* He writes: "*category-evasive* implicit intricacy" and "sentence and situation interanimate."

2. *A new pairing can make new sense.* The pair in "the *causal/coping* view" shows that "causal" does not exclude a person working on something, making a point, trying to change a situation, rather than the usual causality between merely observed things over there. Notice three words together, when he denies that "our minds are insulated from our *causal*

(*or bodily*) *circumstances.*" Now causal means bodily! And circumstances are bodily!

3. *Letting just the felt sense be there for a while.* In trying to think how my reading of Wittgenstein differs from the usual, Earle first has only a felt sense and the word "*But* . . . . .": "Other commentators on Wittgenstein have made the same point in similar words, *but*. Let me see if I can be explicit about this felt *but*." Earle's felt sense turns out to imply many complex strands of philosophical discussion.

4. *Conveying just the felt sense.* This is the reverse of (3). Sometimes Earle has already worked out a long philosophical argument, and can convey it metaphorically without philosophical words. For example, social determinism "can be struggled against . . . [It is] like swimming against the current . . . not like cutting through a steel door."

5. *The steps move from the felt sense.* We follow Earle's steps of thought, but they would be non sequitur if we tried to derive them from the old scheme of causation.

Now I turn to a second set. Let us see how new phrasings come, how words change in meaning. How can they move beyond their old schemes? At first they don't. I specify seven stages (6–12):

6. *At first there are no words we can use.* If taken as usual, Earle's words would say something else:

"Causal" would fail as we saw, but so would any other word:

"Bodily" would mean a physiological brain process.

"Situational" would mean cultural patterns.

"Immediate" would mean a magical intuition such as Aristotle is said to have asserted.

"Precise" would mean fine distinctions.

"World" would mean the external science-observed or culturally created world.

"Immediate engagement" would mean unexamined practical action. "Evocative" would be merely psychological.

I teach students to bear up under this first stage, when *none* of the words carry the felt sense forward. I say: drop all the words quickly, so that they don't destroy the . . . . . !

7. *We can let the felt sense redefine the word.* Reversing the usual priority, we can insist that a word (for example, *causal*) shall be redefined by the felt sense. This is a strong move simply refusing to lose hold of the felt sense. But it is only a stand-off. We *say* "causal" but *think* the felt sense . . . . . Or, we say "immediate," and think that same felt sense.

8. *The word may speak from the felt sense.* Now, if we look closely, the felt-sense–defined word actually makes sense.

9. *Each word says something specific from the felt sense.* We can try

one word after another in the spot. Now each says something different, specific, and from the felt sense.

10. *Now the various words do not contradict each other.* Their differences are now not between their usual meanings, not the old schematic issues that were between them! For example: the unity of immediacy *versus* the two events of cause and effect. *This* "immediate" does not contradict *this* "causal." They say different but not contradictory aspects of the felt sense. So do Earle's other words ("body," "situational," "precise," "world," "engaged," and "evocative"). At first *no* words worked; now they *all* do.

11. *Other words retrieved from the old tradition.* To put into other words what these words newly say is not at all easy, but if we do, then the change happens also in them. For example, we explain: Here "immediate" means we don't perceive through an interpretive screen but can immediately do (say, be . . . . .) something *new*. Now "new" means not abruptly new, but how a new use (of "new" or any other word) *changes*—now not a "change" to something else; the word keeps its old uses and acquires one more.

12. New uses change the concepts implicit in old uses. From those changes we can build new conceptual models, especially where the old ones imply that novelty is impossible. For example, we can formulate concepts about how the body enacts and redefines language, rather than being "destroyed by history" as is currently assumed. I have developed such a theory (*PM*).

Of course we need not spell all this out for every word. Earle's spirited commentary would be impossible if all this had to be overt. But these specifics must become known and deliberately used. Mine are only one version, but even one can enter this new arena (this old but avoided arena). Two or three would enable us to find our way in it.

Earle calls my philosophy "methodologically *individualized.*" This is exactly right, but might be misunderstood as individual *rather than* social or historical. The historical process *is* individual when we think further. History moves through individuals because only individuals think and speak. I spell out how I think further, of course from the tradition and from Wittgenstein, McKeon and Heidegger, from Husserl, Dilthey, and Derrida, and in the world in which they thought, and you now think.

Yes, thank you Mr. Earle, for saying: "Gendlin is *already* working out in concrete detail the consequences of . . . *really* accepting the . . . causal/coping view."

I would carp at a few of his words near the end, which seem to fall back into an old philosophical picture: Earle says that experiential intricacy is due to the fact that "*sensory impingements* are much richer than the standard *perceptual* codes," and that "stray *signals get through* from outside the cognitive systems we have inherited or designed." These words fall back in two ways: they make what exceeds the codes and systems seem unusual, an occasional extra, a stray aberration. This would deny what Earle has said so well, that language and meaning *inherently and always* speak and act in the intricacy.

Secondly, "sensory" and "signals" invites the old assumption that all knowledge is based on perception or sensation, as if the five senses were our only access to the world. The world would be over there, outside us, without us, known only through mediation by perceptual signals. Percepts come *between* us and the world. If perception were our primary way of being in the world, we would lose what Earle so effectively emphasized: the immediacy of acting and speaking in the world of situations.

Actions (and speech) are neither just the person nor just the environment, but both without first splitting them. We are *immediately* both when we breathe, eat, become hungry or upset, and act or speak so as to change a situation.

In the tradition all knowledge is often said to begin with perception. We see that animals perceive, without language. But this is no reason to begin with perception; plants live without perception. I say ours are (elaborated) plant bodies. But rather than deriving ourselves from theories about animals and plants, we find the immediacy directly in our action and speech in situations.

The bodily tissue-process we feel (are, speak from . . . . .) is an *immediate* environmental interaction even without perceptions. It is only elaborated by perception and language. We live *immediately* in our situations; we physically feel the point of what we do, and of what happens. We speak as we breathe, digest, get angry, or cry. Our words come *immediately* from (and are part of) living in the situation. So we don't want to fall back into the old assumption that the world we live in is only *presented before us*, only perceived and observed, only signaled from the outside.

Like Wittgenstein we can reject the assumption of an only externally perceived world. Wittgenstein spoke from what Earle calls "our immediate situational engagement."

Earle sees that I am not an "ineffabilist," nor is Wittgenstein, although many commentators call him one. They assume that what is not defined by concepts, rules, or propositions must be ineffable. But if this were so, we would be in great trouble. In practice we must think and discuss our situations directly. We think "what went on the other day." We might have a category for what went on, but we would not do well if we derived what we say and do from categories. The situational intricacy is what we *say* (and change by speaking), so of course it is not ineffable.

5

The Situatedness of Thinking, Knowing, and Speaking: Wittgenstein and Gendlin

Hans Julius Schneider

Ever since the first edition of Hubert Dreyfus's book[1] about the limits of "artificial reason" appeared, one of its theses has struck its readers as particularly surprising: the claim that the main disadvantage of computers as compared to humans is their lack of a body. From the point of view of an intellectual tradition that cherishes the phantasy of a nonembodied, effortless and perfect understanding among angels,[2] the clumsiness and vulnerability of the human body is more likely to be seen as a hindrance for thinking as well as for communicating with others. So it sounds like a paradox that the computer's lack of a body, a feature that it seems to share with the angels, should be a disadvantage for its intelligence.

In this paper I shall explore the situatedness of human thinking, knowing, and speaking as it is treated in the philosophy of the later Ludwig Wittgenstein: the roots of language (and consequently of thinking and knowing in a narrower, i.e., language-dependent sense) in human activities, i.e., in "forms of life" and in "the common behavior of mankind."[3] This "activist" picture of thinking and knowing that Wittgenstein draws can then be complemented and enriched by considering occurrances that are more like events *happening to* the thinking person. These have been of special interest to Eugene Gendlin.[4] By treating the characteristic relatedness of thinking, knowing, and speaking to the embodied human subject, I shall focus on that side of the mental, the lack of which seems to result in a disadvantage on the side of the computers.

97

HANS JULIUS SCHNEIDER

1. General Perspectives

Two images are likely to come to mind when we talk about the situatedness of speech in activity. The more common one is that of different places or sites in a landscape. As the Latin word *situs* suggests, the situations can be conceived of as different places or regions on a *surface*. One can imagine that in these different regions different "forms of life" (to use Wittgenstein's term) are at home. According to this picture, the situatedness, the embeddedness of speech in an activity, is its relatedness to a *particular* region. If such a picture is used in an epistemological context, speaking of the situatedness of (articulated) knowledge can be expected to raise problems concerning the restricted, "local" validity of (some or even all) knowledge claims. "Relativism" and "points of view" are associations that come to mind.

The other, less common image does not have a horizontal, but a vertical orientation. Instead of speaking of the "situatedness" of speech, one could as well talk about its being "rooted" in activities. According to this image, not the different regions with their characteristic plants and trees are of primary concern, but rather the normally hidden, the "underground" parts of single exemplary plants, as they appear on close investigation. According to this picture, speaking and knowing appear to be (rather small) visible parts of a bigger whole. And pointing to their situatedness means to call attention to the fact that a proper understanding of these visible parts has to include a clear grasp of the roles of the less visible or less prominent ones. In our case these are the nonlinguistic (but language-related) activities and experiences in which the body plays an indispensable role.

In using this image, the problems in focus will be the following: the relationship between knowing-how and knowing-that, between meaning and saying something, between a purported "implicit" knowledge and its articulated, "explicit" counterpart, between rule and rule-formulation, etc. In particular, here we face the question in what sense and to what degree it is possible for the "theoretical" part of these opposites (i.e., articulated knowledge; rule-formulation) to get hold of the respective "practical" part (know-how; regular activity). Can the practical part be completely described? Can it be supplied with theoretical foundations? Can it be modeled by a theory?

In this paper the situatedness expressed by the second picture will be my main concern. I shall explicate and argue for a reversal of the traditional view of the relationship between thinking (meaning, knowing) and acting. This reversal can be found in Wittgenstein's writings and can be characterized by the following claims.

1. Our know-how always exceeds our know-that. Although all practical knowledge can in many ways be related to language, our theoretical knowledge about our practical abilities will never catch up. A complete grasp of our practical by our theoretical knowledge is impossible; it is not even clear what "completeness" could possibly mean in this context.

2. The "ability-to-say" is a special case of the (normally nonlinguistic) "ability-to-do"; the first always remains embedded in the second and has to be understood as so embedded, if pseudoproblems are to be avoided (e.g., the problem of how an action can be meaningful and not "mindless," without the acting person having entertained a thought while performing it).

3. The realm of *meaningful* "intelligent" activities is larger than that of rule-governed activities, and it has priority over it. In most cases rule-formulations are secondary even to those activities that can *ex post* be profitably described as regular. Rule-formulations typically are means to particular ends (e.g., language-teaching). In this sense they are of local interest only. Their articulation normally is not a case of "making explicit" something that has "implicitly" been there all along. To conceive of them in this manner would be to falsify the relationship between language and action.

4. A practical engagement and rapport between at least two acting persons (paradigmatically: mother and child) is the basis for speaking and consequently for thinking and knowing. It is not the case that genuine actions (as opposed to "mere behavior") can only be found in cases where a knowing-that or an "inner" activity of "meaning something" precedes or accompanies the activity. This is also true for speech acts, and consequently it is a mistake to regard (constative) speech acts as an externalization or "transfer" of knowledge. In the primary case, practical engagement and rapport is not the *result* of an exchange of knowledge, but a *condition* for it.

5. The practical involvement is closely interwoven with the "common behavior of mankind," including the human body. This also means a common possession of the ability to have certain "passive" experiences, experiences of events happening to us, like the experience of feeling pain or having a significant dream. The existence of such events is not denied by Wittgenstein, even if some of his remarks sound as if it were. Although it is an important feature of such events that they can be experienced as meaningful, the corresponding *linguistic* activity most of the time is secondary: the "report" of a dream, e.g., is more than a mere mirroring of a ready and fixed "inner" occurrence. Such a passive occurrence can itself have linguistic "components" or aspects; but this does not mean that the linguistic activity connecting to it is nothing but an explicit

formulation of an implicitly given, language-like "inner event" that is just "read off."

To avoid misunderstandings I shall add two caveats right away. The first will make the claims more pointed by rejecting two versions of rendering them inoffensive: claiming the situatedness of thinking, knowing, and speaking means more than claiming that *res cogitans*, our angel-like mind, *in the beginning* needs a body. There is more at stake than the proposition that our legs surely have to supply the power for the takeoff when this admission is combined with the conviction that the kite of pure thought, once it has been raised, can fly all by itself. Additionally, I want to claim more than the inoffensive thesis that this "pure thought" remains tied to the body in the way that all computer software remains tied to some piece or other of hardware. The hardware is necessary, but it is irrelevant, in the sense that its specific realization (mechanical, pneumatical, electronic, . . .) does not matter on the level on which the software is described. So the point will neither be to demonstrate a base or humble *beginning* of language and thinking, nor to show the unavoidability of a "material substratum" or "bodily correlate" for it. Instead, the claim is that a neglect of the situatedness of thinking, knowing, and speaking will also lead to mistakes in the higher spheres, the thinner air of highly developed language. How it is possible that some quite special linguistic activities can indeed develop a certain autonomy is a matter deserving some extra attention after the basic traits of the situatedness of language are understood.

The second caveat is meant to help avoid an interpretation that generalizes the claims, and is (in relation to this interpretation) a softening: the claims I have formulated are not meant to deny (1) that there are cases in which a *particular* know-that is ahead of a *particular* know-how (e.g., the person who knows "in theory" at what point to keep her center of gravity does not necessarily know how to act as a tightrope walker); (2) that to some linguistic activities there is no corresponding specific realm of nonlinguistic activities (as, e.g., in the case of uninterpreted calculi); (3) that some activities (for persons who are in command of a language already) can be constituted with the help of rule-formulations (as in the case of newly invented board-games); (4) that in some cases agreement in a certain know-that (e.g., knowledge of a theory in physics) can be the basis for a rapport concerning a certain know-how (e.g., to set up an experiment); (5) that a practice like telling someone a dream, i.e., the social practice of producing a linguistic rendering of an "inner event," plays a role for determining the identity of this event. From the point of view of the problems discussed here, none of these cases are counterexamples, because they concern specific relations inside a highly differentiated realm of possible activities. They give no evidence against the claim that our most basic forms of speaking are situated or "rooted" in nonlinguistic forms of acting.

So the point of the claims can also be formulated in this way (and here their relation to Wittgenstein is more readily seen): it is not a purely mental act of "meaning something," in the sense of an inner speaking or thinking, or an "unconscious knowledge" of rules, that transforms an occurrence of "only physical behavior" into one of meaningful or intelligent activity (or into a meaningful experience). The body is not a "stupid block" (*PI*, 430; literally "dead block") if it is not inspired by mental or "inner" speaking. In cases in which communication is problematic, so that the partners have to reassure each other about the meaning of certain of their actions, this reasurance does not consist of propositions about the characteristics of mental events, or about the existence or nonexistence of such purported events. Nor does it necessarily consist in "making explicit" internally given "implicit rules." Accordingly, the imperfect explicitness of such rules cannot be blamed for the communication problem to have occurred. Wittgenstein shows that such "logocentristic" efforts, according to which purely physical activities can be secured as being what they seemed to be (and indeed are) only by postulating additional mental activities, are erecting a make-believe scaffolding. (The parrot does not really speak, because it is unable to perform these mental activities.) The grammar of our language may make such mental scaffolding appear natural, but if we look closely, we can see that it does not support anything. What does give support to our bodily movements, what marks them as being more than *mere* physical events, is their embeddedness in the context of the "common behavior of mankind," with all its activities and experiences.

2. To Say Something and to Mean It

The idea that the body should be a hindrance for communication fits well into a common picture of language. This is the picture of language that figures in the quotation from St. Augustine that Wittgenstein has chosen as the starting point for his *Philosophical Investigations*, and his thoughts develop as an attempt to show again and again how it misleads us. According to this picture, acquiring a primary language is similar to learning a second language, insofar as also in the primary case the new material that has to be memorized is taken to consist of unfamiliar *sounds*.[5] They have to be correctly paired with already familiar "meanings," i.e., with contents that are taken to have been "meant" before the sounds are learnt, independently, in advance. (In the case of learning a second language, these "contents" are indeed "given": they can be formulated with the help of sentences from the primary language.) According to this picture, the young child can think already (i.e., it can engage in the inner activity of "meaning something" in the medium of a not-learned, "private" language); only to speak, i.e., to articulate the socially accepted sounds, is what it has yet to learn.

Communication, according to this image, is a kind of transfer or translation, conveying something "inner," something in the mind of the speaker, to the mind (the inner understanding) of the hearer. So it seems natural to expect that something that the speaker had "meant" correctly (inwardly spoken to herself appropriately) sometimes gets a wrong or incomplete "expression." Suffering a deterioration on its way from the inside to the outside, it arrives in the mind of the hearer in a shape that will mislead her. This danger of "damage in transit" seems to have at least three sources. One is of an external kind, when, e.g., noise disturbs the correct "reception" of a message. A second is internal, when, e.g., the "sender" does not focus carefully enough on the correct inner meaning, a situation comparable to the case of a mistaken reading in a telegraph office. And a third source seems to result from limited capacities: when we perform the acts of "meaning something" we seem to be much faster and to act with less effort than in the acts of speaking. In order to avoid unbearably long utterances, what we actually say will mostly be elliptical compared to what we meant, and it will for that reason be less than perfect. The parallel inner activity of meaning something, according to this picture, is what gives meaning to the bare sounds which, taken by themselves, could as well have been produced by a parrot. And from here it is a small step to the wishful dream already mentioned: if we were able directly to watch each other's activity of meaning something, without the intervention of language (without a body, as one *res cogitans* watching the activities of a second), we would be spared the characteristically human transfer operations that always tend to lead to imperfect results.

Let us first observe what aspects Wittgenstein does *not* take offense at when he expresses his doubts about the usefulness of this picture in certain (mainly philosophical) contexts. He is of course aware that there are many forms of expression in natural language that make use of this picture or a similar one, and it is a basic trait of his philosophy that he is not interested in advocating a change in forms of expression where they are "performing their office" (*PI*, 402). When we say, e.g., "his name is on the tip of my tongue" or "I did not mean it in this but in another sense," not these expressions themselves pose a problem, but only some of the ways that they might be taken up. Concerning the first example, the request "show me your tongue so I can tell you the name" would certainly be a case in point; concerning the second example, the question "did your meaning start simultanously with your speaking, or a bit earlier?" appears to be at least dubious, but we must admit (with the history of philosophy in mind) that its oddity is not universally felt.[6]

Furthermore, against recurrent misunderstandings, it is worth stressing the fact that Wittgenstein does not deny that sometimes we dream, have sudden ideas or flashes of wit (among them linguistic ones), that something we remember we can "see quite lively in front of us," even with our eyes closed, or that we can silently rehearse a sentence before starting an important negotiation. If he were to deny these things he could hardly be seen as sharing important points with Gendlin. But he reminds us that in *some* cases we are confronted with figures of speech containing nouns to which no corresponding entity can be found. Rather, they function like the word "lurch" as (currently) used in the phrase "he left her in the lurch." But neither does Wittgenstein in general deny the existence of "inner events"; nor does he (like some forms of behaviorism) take them to be inaccessible. On the contrary, he invites his readers to check the validity of certain claims about the role of such inner events by considering their own cases, and this would not make sense if he in general denied their existence.

What he does indeed take offense at is the idea that in the case of meaningful speech there must always and necessarily be two parallel actions or processes: the "external" act of uttering something and a parallel "inner" act of meaning something. The inner act is thought (according to this mistaken picture) to have either the same structure as the external act, or an even more perfect one, namely a "logical" structure, which shows the forms of thought directly, without the imperfections of grammar. It is a part of this picture that the inner act gives meaning to the external, purely physical act, so that the existence or nonexistence of the inner part decides over the meaningfulness of the overt "external" act. It is an important aspect of this wrong picture that it tempts us to see the inner act as being more perfect than the external: a speaker often "means" correctly what she expresses incorrectly; and most of the time we mean much more than what we explicitly say. This seems to be confirmed by the boundless possibilities in answering inquiries about what we have said.

We cannot delve into the many subtle points of Wittgenstein's discussion, where he tries to convince his readers of the misguiding character of this picture. Nevertheless, it is necessary for our purposes to summarize some of his main critical claims.

1. By way of introspection we cannot confirm that repeated utterances of the same word are always accompanied by the same inner acts or events that could be convincing candidates for an act of "meaning something" or for the thing meant (the meaning of the word). Whatever inner events (pictures, bodily sensations, etc.) may in fact occur, their occurance is not regularly tied to the acts of "saying something and meaning it." These events are neither what makes the utterance-act meaningful, nor are they what the hearer has to infer for her to grasp the meaning of the utterance.

2. To inform a hearer about the particular characteristics of such an event (in case there has been one) is not necessarily the same as explaining the meaning of the utterance to her. An explanation of what a particular expression of some language means (as type or as token) does not describe inner acts or events belonging to a speaker, but rather the use of the expression as part of a language (type) or in a specific utterance-context (token).

3. Questions such as whether a particular expression was meant as a word or as a sentence, to what grammatical category a word belongs, and whether an expression was elliptical are questions to be answered by recourse to the public system of the grammar of a language, and not by turning to the inner actions or events that may accompany the utterances. Before a specific language is constituted, these questions are meaningless. There is no "language of pure meanings" with its own grammatical categories and forms of inflection, in addition to which only conventional sounds would have to be learned in the primary language acquisition.[7]

As a step to an alternative picture that does not so easily invite the kinds of errors Wittgenstein tries to exclude, imagine a situation of the following kind: someone says something and, interrupting herself in the middle of her sentence, goes on with the words "no, I meant . . ."; then she continues, and no additional correction is necessary. According to the *old* picture, two *simultaneous* actions have been performed, one of which (the act of meaning something) is an *inner* action; it is taken to have been correct from the start. The other (the utterance-act) is an external action. As a copy of the inner one it was wrong the first time, but was then followed by a correct version. Now, in order to get a new, alternative picture of the same situation, we could describe it by saying that what we are confronted with are not *simultaneous* actions, one internal, one external, but rather a *succession* of two equally "external" (i.e., public, linguistic) actions, occuring one after the other, the first of which has miscarried and (for that reason) was not completed, whereas only the second one succeeded. In the realm of nonlinguistic actions this kind of case is not uncommon. When in an athletic contest of long jumping a participant makes a mistake on her first attempt (e.g., by running too far and missing the line), she will try once more and probably do it correctly. When we take such a case as an orientation for the linguistic one, we can see that in *both* cases there is normally no reason to say that *internally*, in an invisible realm, the action had been successful and complete ("meant") on the first attempt and only failed to get "externalized" properly. It is enough to say that there were two attempts and only the second succeeded. In this way we would avoid a duplication of meaningful actions, resulting for every action in an internal and an external version. What appears to be a retrospective claim that the second, successful attempt would show what "internally," from the perspective of how it was "meant," had also been present in the first attempt, would then be interpreted as a possible but not necessary metaphorical expression for the judgment that now we are content: on the second attempt the action succeeded.[8]

It is an important aspect of this view that it does not falsify the commonsense experience that linguistic utterances normally are meaningful actions; it does not, for the sake of exact, scientific describability, reduce the meaningful actions to acts of sound-production, as e.g., the founder of "descriptive linguistics," Leonard Bloomfield felt obliged to do.[9] When in this way we do not reduce speaking to a purely physical act or event at the outset (by admitting only limited means of description), we avoid the problem of explaining how such a purely physical event can have "meaning" attached to it.

Accordingly, the possibility of commenting on some prior utterance, which is available in all developed languages, would be seen as the normal and familiar possibility of performing follow-up actions, a point stressed by Gendlin. In such a commentary a speaker would not be seen as referring back to some internal event or action that had been present all along and that would now, on the second attempt, be more accurately *translated* into the "external" language that is audible for others. It is correct to say of the first utterance that it was "directed"; it had its place in a meaningful development of events and can in this sense be called "intentional." And events "happening" *to* the person (like sudden ideas, mental images, or bodily experiences like Gendlin's "felt sense") could be parts of this meaningful development. But still the commentary given later would not be an act of reference to "the intention," if this expression is understood as standing for a fixed and ready "mental entity" that has been present at the time of the utterance, and that could be described as a structured array of data—something that would in this sense be taken as a "linguistic" entity.[10] Formulating a slogan we could say: the second, commenting utterance is a *continuation* (since it takes up and carries further a movement); it is not a *translation*. With Dreyfus's reading of Heidegger in mind, we could say that the way of "being-in-the-world" that computers lack does not have the form of "to have something in mind," and that therefore what is lacking cannot be supplied by giving more information to them. Rather, it has the form of "to have it in the bones": what is lacking is the living body.

On the basis of this account a simple explanation (without additional and not so easily justified hypotheses) can be found for the fact that our ability to give commentaries on what we "had meant" is so boundless. Since what we give are commentaries, not descriptions, they are directed to the future, not to the past of a fixed and ready "event" that would only have to be "described." They are follow-up activities, and for this reason they can be continued indefinitely in a succession of additional steps, as long as the circumstances permit. If, on the other hand, we really were confronted with a subsequent description of a fixed and ready "inner state," we would have to expect either that such a description can be completed (which is implausible), or that the act of meaning something is performed extremely fast, so that what is covered by it is de facto limited, but is so unsurveyably large that it *seems* to be infinite. This also is implausible, but it would explain why it seems to be impossible to give a complete description.

According to the alternative picture I am proposing, acts of lying and of "thoughtless" babbling (like a promise that is not "meant" as serious) are actions that do not fit their contexts. Instead of the picture of a more or less powerful (or, in the case of lying, altogether missing) simultanous "inner" act of meaning something, the quality and strength of which determines the value of the external act, again we would see a succession of actions in time. The follow-up actions, the later conduct, will show of what value, e.g., a promise is.

3. To Know-How and to Know-That

After having investigated Wittgenstein's criticism of the idea that "behind" or "beneath" the perceivable acts of speaking there are parallel or foundational "inner" acts of meaning, acts that are themselves language-like and the presence of which gives meaning to the "external" acts, we now turn to the picture he draws of the relationship between an explicitly formulated know-that (i.e., a special case of knowing how to say certain things) and a practical know-how, i.e., the ability to perform nonlinguistic actions.

The famous scene of the building-site at the beginning of the *Philosophical Investigations* is introduced by Wittgenstein as an attempt to invent a language that comes as close as possible to the Augustinian picture that he had quoted in his first paragraph. And this means, from his own point of view, that the language of the builders is quite different from our real natural language. But soon Wittgenstein imagines and describes in detail what steps could be taken to extend this language in such a way that it becomes more similar to our own language, in spite of the strange character it showed in the first moments and in spite of the remaining differences. But the more steps one takes to extend the builders' language, the less appropriate are the claims St. Augustine makes about language. The Augustinian picture, which at first appeared to be unconvincing because a language that functioned as he had claimed *all* languages would function was so obviously different from *our* language, now appears to be unconvincing because we can see what special un-Augustinian extensions are required to make the language he pictures come closer to *our* language. Since these extensions do not fit his picture but are necessary to bridge the gap between the original builders' language and our own, they speak against the adequacy of the picture. And realizing this means at the same time to see the kind of error that is invited by propositions that are true of our language but only *seem* to confirm St. Augustine's picture. One of these is the proposition, "every word of a language means something" (*PI*, 10).

In a sense this sentence is true. It is part of the concept " . . . is a word of a language" that the objects to which it applies have meaning. But what this "having a meaning" consists in (and the fact that there can be substantial differences between kinds of "having meaning") can only be seen when we consider the contexts of possible utterances of it. Only in relation to such contexts can we classify something as a word, as a piece of language, in the first place. In the beginning of language-acquisition, with regard to the most simple language-games, this mainly means: the *nonlinguistic* context of shared activities has to be taken into account. Using one of Wittgenstein's pictorial ways of expression: Something "is" a brake only in conjunction with "the whole of the rest of the mechanism" (*PI*, 6). So our claim here is that something "is" a piece of language only in conjunction with "the whole rest of activities," a lot of which necessarily are nonlinguistic. This can be obscured by propositions like "every word of a language has a meaning" or "someone who talks does not merely make a noise but means something (has something on her mind)."

As is well known, in the beginning of his *Philosophical Investigations* Wittgenstein adopts a "genetic," developmental perspective by drawing a sketch of how a very rudimentary "language," a system of signals that serve to coordinate a few rather specific forms of acting together, can gradually be enriched by adding new forms. This sketch is meant to show (among other things) how fundamentally different the functions of words can be and that to someone who does not participate in these language-games (to a speaker of a quite different language) information about these different functions cannot be supplied by schematically using propositions of the form "the word x means . . ." Instead, using the hearer's language, one would have to describe the (different kinds of) uses of the words, i.e., describe the possible speech acts as they are embedded in nonlinguistic activities. So utterances are like the tips of icebergs, the invisible parts of which are bodily, nonlinguistic acts. To grasp their meaning in a way that appreciates their differences means to see their situatedness, the many different ways in which they have roots in nonlinguistic activities.

What then are the chances for lifting the hidden, nonlinguistic part of the iceberg out of the water by more and more extending the language? Certainly *at the beginning* a practical, nonlinguistic realm of actions is unavoidable to get the speech acts going; but can we not at a later, more developed stage *describe* the nonlinguistic parts and thus incorporate them in the realm of language? Can their descriptions replace the practical, nonlinguistic actions; will we be able to retrieve the nonlinguistic by using language and thus make the whole of the iceberg hover over the water?

With respect to an activity like erecting a building one might indeed be tempted to argue as follows: since the participants do not act blindly and at random, but are goal-oriented (reasonable, intentional), they must have "something in mind" when they act. We say about them, e.g., that they must *know* where the slabs are kept and accordingly which way they have to go to find them, they must know how to grab them in order to be able to lift and carry them, etc. And the more their language develops (so one might like to say), the more they will be able to make this tacit or "implicit" knowledge "explicit," until finally their know-how will in the end be completely transformed into a know-that. A part of this know-how will linguistically be rendered with the help of rule-formulations: "If you are bringing a slab and you see that someone else is just beginning to descend the ladder, then you should . . ."

The plausibility of this view depends on whether it is a necessary condition for a genuine case of action that the piece of "overt behavior" concerned be accompanied by (audible or "inner") *speech*. For, if speech were a necessary condition for action, and if, because of the effective way in which the builders are pursuing their aim, the character of their activity as a case of genuine action is indisputable, it would be this connection between speech and action that would oblige us to say that they must be "speaking internally" quite a lot—since they do act intentionally, but "externally" hardly any speech, except one-word sentences, can be perceived. If this were correct, the program to "make explicit all the implicit knowledge" would have a clear meaning: what it wants to make public is precisely that inner activity which has to be postulated in order for the overt behavior to qualify as a series of "actions." What from the outside seems to be the nonlinguistic side of these actions (what the acting people "have in mind") would in the end be transformed (in accordance with its hidden linguistic nature) into an overtly linguistic form. The iceberg would be hovering over the water.

A well-known articulation of this program is John R. Searle's version of speech act theory: language is not random, but rule-governed; the rules are not formulated, but "implicit"; the scientific goal is to make explicit these implicitly fixed and ready rules, to supply the *rule-formulations* to the *rules* that are necessarily given with (any particular) language.[11]

But we have seen already that the presupposition that there is a speechlike inner parallel-action which endows an external bodily behavior with meaning is implausible and is not supported by the experience we all have with our own linguistic activities. So the program to just make public something that implicitly exists and already has the form of speech has no foundation. A part of the reason why this is seldom noticed probably is the fact that indeed we have different kinds of linguistic follow-up activities that can shed light on the utterances and nonlinguistic activities that precede them. To take a closer look at these activities can help us to think of them no longer as cases of just "making explicit" something that is implicitly given. As has been hinted at above, the following forms can be distinguished.

1. Certainly it is possible to *safeguard* or support an existing practice with the help of linguistic differentiations. And where an (at first rudimentary) linguistic competence is growing by incorporating finer and finer distinctions, a progressively finer tuning of the activity is possible, as any individual history of language acquisition testifies. But it is clear that all these differentiations can never *go behind* all of the practical activities; they will never be able to replace them completely, to function as their substitute. The new differentiations constitute a competence *parallel* to the older, more primitive competence. The distance between the differentiating lines becomes smaller, but the *practical* competence to draw such lines and to act accordingly is not explained by these differentiations and cannot be substituted by them. This means that "what a speaker had in mind" is made *explicit* in this way only as far as the choice between two lines of distinctions is concerned. The point of drawing lines (and the

point of other linguistic activities that only *seem* to be similar, like e.g., counting) is linguistically not "expressed" in this way. The competence to draw finer distinctions is a further practical competence; it is not a *foundation* of practical competences in general.[12]

2. Furthermore, it is possible to *describe* activities and single actions as they are situated in their characteristic contexts and to describe them in a progressively more complex and rich way. Since our language contains words for actions, we can talk about them, and we can, e.g., explain how a complex action or succession of actions is constituted by single, constitutive actions. But it has to be kept in mind that to engage in such a description again means to perform certain actions. The description is not a kind of mirroring; it is not an unmediated representation that has an action as its object, without being one itself. In some contexts a description of an action can be used as a substitute for its performance. For example, reading a certain recipe can fill the place of cooking and tasting a dish, in case the reader knows that she would not like anything prepared with garlic. But still, descriptions cannot *in general*, independently of contexts, substitute for activities and play a foundational role.

For this reason the phrase "*complete* description of an action" is always in need of a clear specification of the chosen perspective. A recipe, an instruction for a bodily exercise or for a scientific experiment can be called "complete" if this means: for the practitioners of the relevant field these descriptions are intelligible (i.e., they are able to follow them) in the sense that the relevant social group (e.g., the scientific community whose members share a certain paradigm) normally would come to a unanimous opinion about the correctness or incorrectness of a particular attempt to perform the action. This specification shows that the possibility of *describing* an action is not sufficient for the possibility of defining a corresponding concept of a *complete* description for the relevant action. With respect to descriptions of human actions under a psychotherapeutic aspect, this can be expected to be the normal case. There can be progressive steps of getting clearer about one's own motives, about interconnections between episodes in one's life, etc. But it is impossible to formulate in advance a matrix so that the degree of completeness with which items have been filled into its slots would be a measure for the *completeness* of the relevant actions' description. The very expression "complete description" is meaningless in cases like these, because it is impossible to specify at what point completeness would be accomplished.[13] And in some contexts it even seems advisable to give up the word "description" altogether. Especially in the psychotherapeutic process as it has been convincingly described by Gendlin, the utterances of the participants will often be more aptly seen as follow-up actions, continuations, unfoldings, than as acts that communicate something that is fixed and ready, but invisible.

4. Activity and Passivity

So far, our discussion of the situatedness of language has examined what can be characterized as the relatedness of utterances to contexts of quite specific social activities. "Building a house" is a paradigm case. It can be clearly separated from other activities; the related competence will probably be acquired by way of explicit demonstrations, and to acquire it is optional. So when Wittgenstein (using the comparison already cited) says that a single utterance has meaning only in conjunction with "the whole of the rest of the mechanism," the standard case of such a "mechanism" is a surveyable social activity.

It is an important addition (or at least a helpful shift of focus) when Gendlin includes the personal histories of individual speakers as a dimension of situatedness. As a consequence of this step, the "mechanisms" that have to be considered are not only clear-cut, more or less optional activities with socially well-established relations to their linguistic "parts," but also preverbal experiences in early childhood. By participating in countless little dramas, the infant acquires a preverbal understanding of what it means to be alive as a human being who is growing up in a specific cultural tradition.

Experiences of this kind, many of them perhaps more "passive" than "active," are related to language in a way different from the social activities like building a house. Firstly, they happen before language is acquired, so that the fitting words have to be found at a later stage. Nevertheless, of course, they are experienced as meaningful. Secondly, in the beginning the child is more or less drawn into the scenes of the drama; the roles she is going to play are not "taught" or demonstrated. There is no explicit instruction, but surely a lot of learning. This "personal," partly preverbal, and mostly passive kind of situatedness will then more and more overlap with the situatedness of social activities and will thus be increasingly connected to the realm of language. More and more aspects of these little dramas can be articulated via language, and what has been learnt by direct participation can now be criticized, developed, explicitly shared.

As Gendlin has pointed out, the trails or "memories" of these dramas are located in the living, goal-directed body; they can be experienced as a "felt sense." To be open for them and for the process of their "finding words" has a certain "passive" aspect: one has to attend to what is "coming." When enough connections with language are established, "active" steps like trying out interpretations of the past and taking new steps into the future are possible. It is very clear in Gendlin's writings that the subtle balance of "passivity" and "activity" that he reminds us of cannot be captured with the help of the traditional image of an inner, personlike "subject" who is confronted with "ideas" in the sense of empiricists like John Locke. The "inner realm" we experience here does not consist of entities like "word-meanings"; it is no reduplication of the "outer" realm of speech. Our experience of "listening" to what "comes by itself" (passivity) and finding ourselves able to carry on with words and sentences (activity) certainly is *related* to language. Our ability to move freely in this realm is indeed indispensable for even the most ordinary uses of language, like "getting the point," "finding a better formulation," etc. But this does not mean that in the "passive" moments there are "objects" of experience which themselves are linguistic or conceptual in character.

In this respect Gendlin helps to clarify what to many readers of Wittgenstein seem to be counterintuitive claims: Do we not have "something in mind" before we talk? Do not thoughts come to us that we then proceed to express (or that we sometimes would like to get rid of)? The detailed "experiential" way in which Gendlin makes us aware of the functioning of such experiences, of their role in understanding and indeed in every but the most mechanized instances of language use, accomplishes two things. Firstly, it justifies our intuitions that "something" indeed can "come to us." It may be disturbing when we sit for meditation, or it may be welcome when we try to remember a forgotten name. And secondly, we see how different the instances of such experiences are from "internal" reduplications of "external" words. They cannot be "made explicit" by conceptual patterns, by rule-formulations. The formulation of a rule can be a *result* of such an experience; it is one possible way of carrying on. But the rule does not "make explicit" what we did/experienced in the "space" between any two or more given rules. So although Gendlin discusses "mental entities" (or processes and activities) of some kind, he carefully avoids falling back on a pre-Wittgensteinian theory of meaning.

As has been mentioned above, Gendlin introduces the expression "felt sense" to signify the bodily experience that supplies the inspiration and the guidance for our "working with language" (and for other, nonlinguistic ways of "carrying on" an activity). It is important to see that what Gendlin calls a "felt sense" is not the same as an emotion. Instead, the term invites associations with sentences such as "I sense something" and "This is how something feels." Furthermore, the ambiguity in the word "sense" is deliberate: it means "related to the senses" and at the same time "making sense, being meaningful" (an aspect shown by the fact that originally he used the term "felt meaning").

Of the many examples that Gendlin, on the one hand, reminds his readers of, and that, on the other hand, he makes his readers experience as an integral part of reading and understanding his texts, I would like to mention just one: walking in a street, I am greeted by a person. I answer to the greeting because I am aware that I know the person, but I do not know at the moment who she is, where to place her. Gendlin gives a lively and convincing description of how I can have a bodily sense, e.g., of the problematic relation I have to this person. I am sensing my attitude toward her; in my face and in my uncontrolled gestures I may unintentionally show or express my attitude, and this can occur before I fully realize whom I have met, i.e., before I can identify her by placing her into a wider context. So we can say for the discussed example that to have a "felt sense" is to be aware of the kind of relation I have to this person, the particular way of my situatedness in respect to her. This felt awareness is not a "knowing that"; it is not that I know some clearly separable and readily classifiable bits or pieces of "information" or some "propositional content." Rather, it is the ability to go on, to take a next meaningful step, be it a bodily move or a move in a language-game.

One can stay with a felt sense (one can learn to open up toward it); and then a next step will "come" from it in a way comparable to the "coming" of tears. I might approach the person with a particular bodily posture or mimicking expression, or suddenly her name might simply "come to me." I may begin to explain to someone the problems I have with the person. In spite of the linguistic character of these particular follow-up activities and in spite of the fact that they may contain statements of fact, the felt sense by itself is no "knowing-that," it is no "implicit knowledge" about a particular "content" about which it would be meaningful to say that at any particular moment it had been made completely explicit. Certainly it is possible to tell a story and thereby to give a hint about how I perceive my situation. But still the nonconceptual, "bodily" side of my felt sense remains richer than any description of it can tell, or, more correctly: richer than any linguistic instance of carrying on can tell. The felt sense is the basis of all such stories, the place from where endless new versions, different interpretations, enrichments, etc., can spring. And they all should be seen as ways of carrying on, not as "improvements" or "corrections" of older versions, with the help of which the speaker tries to finally arrive at "the" one complete and truthful representation of a past incident. Thus, the nonconceptual can never be captured by a complete description, can never be completely transformed into something conceptual.

It is especially important for Gendlin that this realm of the nonconceptual is by no means chaotic. It is not a "limbo" in which conceptual systems can or have to be randomly "chosen," so that only after such a random choice something orderly begins. Instead, we normally find an order in this realm that again and again turns out to be farther-reaching than the order in the realm of conceptual knowledge (e.g., in the realm of a person's self-knowledge). From this orderly realm of the nonconceptual, new creative steps are possible that transcend the conceptual order available at that particular moment. These steps can be deeply meaningful, and thus be the very opposites of random choices.

One background component of this view is Gendlin's experience with psychotherapeutic work. One has to keep in mind that "healing" processes on the psychological level often if not always occur as a result of the therapist's listening to and mentally accompanying a client, not as a result of actively intervening or "manipulating" her. A second background component is the (later) philosophy of Wittgenstein. Wittgenstein investigated the kind of competence that is necessary to find one's way in "the grammar of our language," in his special, not rule-oriented sense. And one of his results is that this competence can be talked about in terms of citing paradigms, that one can be conscious of it and can rehearse it, but that it is impossible to model it as a form of calculation, because every new (more refined, more "dense") system of concepts and rules again has to rest on a practical understanding of its situatedness. There can be no "rule behind all rules." So the ability here in view, and its relatedness to the body, should not be confused with the totally different ability to operate with rules; only for this second ability is it possible to develop mechanical, computational models.

And there is another kinship in the thinking of Gendlin and Wittgenstein: Gendlin wants to show how it is possible to *work* with language by moving back and forth between its conceptual and its nonconceptual sides. The result is a kind of versatility, an ability to make moves, not a fixed, complete conceptual system. This has a parallel in Wittgenstein's view that philosophy is an activity. Its goal for Wittgenstein is not an ideal conceptual system, a reformed language, but clarity. This practical orientation toward an activity and the explicit recognition that the conceptual and the nonconceptual sides of language cannot be separated enables both Wittgenstein and Gendlin to avoid a mystification of language—in particular a mystification of its nonconceptual side. Not an enraptured listening is what is called for, but careful work, sensitive to the intricacies of language-use and our felt sense of these intricacies. Admittedly, this work again and again requires us to pause and become aware of our situatedness in a particular moment. But the felt sense leads to a next communicative, practical step. The pause is necessary to avoid getting into mechanical routine, restricted to the domain of traditional concepts and well-trodden paths. But it is only half of the work to be done. Its worth will show in the next step—in how we "carry on."

5. Unembodied Intelligence?

I would like to finish with a brief look at a problem that will not be discussed here in any detail. What are the implications of our discussion for the endeavors to make models for intelligent activities and to simulate them on machines like computers and robots? As a first step it is useful to recall that there are certain clearly delimitated areas of action that have been made "independent" of the contextual bodily abilities of acting subjects. This can be done by seeing to it that such abilities are relied on in only one and the same unaltered way. A relatively surveyable domain, e.g., is that of mathematical or logical calculi. Here the necessary activities are not only restricted (as in some areas, perhaps, of poetry) to *language-internal* activities (so that all questions of use reaching beyond the linguistic marks can be skipped), but furthermore language itself is considered only under the aspect of the formal properties of its signs.

By considering simple devices like the abacus, one can easily see that in the field of such activities mechanical means not only can be applied meaningfully, but complicated sequences of actions, like the addition of numbers, can be substituted by the (production and) handling of these devices. And this invites a way of expression quite common in ordinary language, namely to say about the mechanism that *it* (not its user) would calculate or compute. Here we have the limited autonomy of some linguistic activities (the independence of the body that some ways of "thinking" achieve) that has been mentioned above, in the first caveat: once the activity of calculation has been started via the living body (by drawing strokes, arranging little stones, or in whatever way), it is no longer dependent on the body in every single step. This is what distinguishes this case of language-use from the uses of most other words and phrases, which again and again ask for body-related mental flexibility and competence of judgment.

When we consider this special case of a mental activity, one that can indeed to a certain degree be separated from the body, we see how different it is from standard cases of intelligent actions: from painting or contemplating a picture, playing music, ordinary or poetic speaking. Steps toward a separation of these activities from the body would have to be accomplished through their rendering in language. Some of my considerations were meant to show why such a rendering is possible in quite special cases only, and even there only to a certain degree.

The connexionistic, nonrepresentational approaches to artificial intelligence might be seen as attempts to supply bodies for the machines used, to give them their own ways of "being-in-the-world," with their own bodily situated intelligences. With machines of this kind we would not share the "common behavior of mankind"; if they would talk, we probably would not understand them.[14] Their strangeness for us would be a strangeness concerning mind *and* body. Facing them we would not be confronted with "minds" that are like ours, except that they are contained in metal or plastic "bodies." Instead, they would be beings with their own peculiar characteristics, more like fish from the deep seas in their strangeness than like the computers in our offices. So it seems that it is not so much the body, after all, that sharply distinguishes us from the angels. Getting rid of it (or never having inhabited one in the first place) seems to be of no advantage, neither for the computers, nor for us. The situatedness of our thinking, knowing, and speaking in our bodily activities should therefore not be seen as a regrettable boundary. The search for a way to transcend boundaries will not be successful as an overcoming of the body, but rather as a mind-bodily experience of the order Gendlin has been concerned with, an order that is more comprehensive than the (often necessary but not sufficient) order of the rule-governed part of our thinking that can be rendered with the help of mathematical or logical calculi. Gendlin has shown us a way to work with this kind of experience, and he carefully avoids mystifications. Neither an unknown realm of "the inner," nor "language" itself, is conceived by him as a power beyond the realm of our daily experience. We will find creativity and freedom when we pause to realize and appreciate the obvious: the situatedness of our thinking, knowing, and speaking.

Reply to Schneider

I need to argue with Professor Schneider's use of "active" and "passive." We need to make specific new distinctions from how a felt sense comes and works. This gives me an opportunity to illustrate how we can enter this arena.

Like all distinctions, "active/passive" brings a welter of uses, as well as the felt sense of one present use. Let us enter this one here: Why does Schneider call Wittgenstein's approach "activist"? It is because meaning is understood in the context of practical action. Of course this does not mean that we are always the *active* ones; it includes how others act on us.

Conversely, we are not always passive in a felt sense. Schneider says that we move and act from it. He calls the felt sense "passive" only because it must *come* to us; we cannot create it. But even in its coming we are not only passive. Usually we must *actively* seek it by disposing our attention so as to *let* it come. "Active letting" is not a contradiction or an aporia of the two concepts. It is much more intricate. We can further specify several strands: we actively review what we already know, step by step, until the steps lead to a . . . . . Then we *actively* hold our attention there where we sense what we call a "lead" (a little half-step, idea, image, thought, phrase, impulse to act . . . . .). Now we *actively* hold our attention there, and (here at last is a passive aspect) we *wait* for the lead to come into focus. When it does, we *hold* on to it tenaciously (again active), while waiting (passively) for words to phrase themselves in relation to it. So this is far more intricate than "active," "passive," or just both.

These new distinctions are not ultimate; we can always open them and enter further from a . . . . . But even these few terms take us several steps into this arena which has been avoided so long.

Similarly, Schneider is right that the "history of individual speakers" is implicit in it, but a felt sense is not something past. The past is only one dimension of (the felt sense of) *present* situations. This is more intricate than either present or past. If the past were not implicit *in the present*, we would not know what we are doing. But it is *implicit*: we attend to the present without reviewing memories. The past is an *implicit function*.

I am happy that Schneider keeps me company in understanding Wittgenstein. He shows Wittgenstein's refusal to read *later-formulated rules* in behind practices that occur without them, as if the later rules determined the performance. Schneider alludes to my "reversal of the usual philosophic procedure" when he calls this "the reversal" in Wittgenstein.

Schneider shows that Wittgenstein does not deny experiences such as dreams, feelings, and pains, only that they are internal duplicates of meaning. Like words, feelings have meaning as part of the situational event, "in conjunction with the whole rest of activities." They "concern specific relations inside a highly differentiated realm of possible activities."

What Schneider says shows that Wittgenstein speaks from our immediate engagement in situations, rejecting the distinction between inner and outer, subject and object. He shows that Wittgenstein did not (as is so often thought) base his sayings on an "external" world that is only observed. The "embodied human subject" is involved in activities that are not just outwardly observed. Schneider quotes Wittgenstein: the body is not a "stupid block," not like a wooden copy of our outward appearance. It lives and moves in the immediacy of situations. Schneider says: "What marks . . . our bodily movements . . . as being more than *mere* physical events, is their embeddedness in the context of the common behavior of mankind with its activities and experiences."

The internal/external distinction cannot be assumed, if we want to understand Wittgenstein. For example, he asks: "Why cannot my left hand give my right hand money?" (*PI*, 268). In terms of outward observation, of course one hand *can* visibly put money into the other hand. But this would not be "giving money." It would not bring the change in the situation, which we mean by "giving money." We need to grasp *where Wittgenstein is speaking from*. This is what has been so widely misunderstood.

It is not that Wittgenstein *adds* something unobservable to the perceived world. To so read him would assume the kind of "external world" he criticized and rejected. With that assumption, if "giving money" is not an outwardly observed behavior, it must be *un*observable. But Wittgenstein's point is that what we call "giving money" changes a situation. The point is not that we cannot observe the change. We can observe some of it, and some of the consequences. But the change happens in the situation, not in a merely observed world, nor in an interior one. The distinction misses situations altogether: they cannot be found in external or internal realms.[1]

When Wittgenstein says that the meaning of words is not *conceptually* definable, many readers conclude that it is ineffable. But then it could not be said, whereas the meaning of our words *is* what we say. Conceptual definitions and rules can be useful but they are a *further* saying; they do not duplicate what we said.

Since the later-formulated rule is not somewhere in or under the performance, what then is its status? Schneider is right that Wittgenstein left us with the question of "the relationship" of "an explicitly formulated know-that [for example, a rule] . . . to the practical know-how, i.e., the ability to perform nonlinguistic actions" without a rule. Schneider agrees with Wittgenstein (and me) that rule-formulating is "a *continuation* (it takes up and *carries further* . . .)." Rules are "not the finding of preexisting facts" but "follow-up actions, continuations, unfoldings."

Such statements (including mine) are not exclusive. Although a rule may fit a performance, other systems could let us formulate other rules that fit. (But it is not easy! Most attempts fail.)

Schneider says: "Since what we give are commentaries, not descriptions, . . . they can be continued indefinitely in a succession of additional steps." The behavior fits the rule both before and after it is formulated, but the formulating or making/finding of rules (distinctions, patterns, concepts . . . . .) is always a "carrying forward." This point has been hard to state, and my concept of "carrying forward" carries it forward.

We *can* philosophize from the place from which Wittgenstein speaks, since we cannot help but be and speak from there. We need not pretend to leave that ordinary place, and speak "from nowhere" as Nagel calls it. My way goes on from Wittgenstein's showing, but he did not move on in this way. He did not say what he was doing, nor where he stood when he did it. One could not use language to tell about its working. Wittgenstein might have loved to straighten out the persistent misunderstandings of him, but he was convinced that one cannot. Why not? Why have most twentieth-century philosophers been unable to say what they were doing? It was certainly not from feeling no need. It was because they knew—*quite rightly*—that any talking-about, any supposed ninety-degree turn purporting to tell about the work of language *from the side,* is always again just more speech in situations, and not from the side.

Rather than being stopped by this seeming limitation, or trying to overcome it, I find it an advantage that has not been deliberately employed. Why deplore it? Why not employ it, intend it, count on it? If we are not mesmerized by the search for conceptual formulations *to replace* speech, then it is a happy fact that speech about speech is always again an instance of speech. The implicit functions of speech are at work in our speaking of them; therefore we can also speak from them.

6

The Implicit Intricacy of Mind and Situation

Meredith Williams

The long-standing philosophical problem with which Eugene Gendlin opens his "Thinking beyond Patterns"[1] is that of disentangling nature from convention. How much of our ways of understanding and ordering things is natural and how much is conventional projection? This problem applies as much to our own lives as it does to rest of nature, both animate and inanimate. The classical solutions to this problem have been realism, with its commitment to a determinate structure of nature that is mirrored in veridical thought, and constructionism, with its opposing commitment to a chaotic nature whose only structure is derived from the arbitrary imposition of form by human beings. In "Thinking beyond Patterns," Gendlin seeks to undermine these solutions as overly simplistic and to put in their place an alternative which focuses on the relation between what he calls "the intricacy" of particular existence and the applicability of forms or patterns. In brief, his view runs as follows: there is a contrast between the elaborately rich detail, or intricacy, of any particular existence and the forms that might be used to describe, categorize, or in any other way distinguish this intricacy. Intricacy is always more than any form that might be applied and in this way is beyond patterns. This apparent concession to a constructionist strategy is matched by a realism of sorts. The forms that successfully apply are not arbitrary or willfully imposed upon a pliable intricacy. On the contrary, the intricacy of the particular is itself ordered and orderly, and thus constrains the range of forms and patterns that we might apply. This order of intricacy, however, is not captured by any of the sciences, which deal with reality solely in terms of forms, so Gendlin's realism is not scientific realism. This account of intricacy as always more than form and yet constraining form I shall call Gendlin's "intricacy thesis": "Forms never work alone, always within a wider and more intricate order" ("TBP," 21).

The primary concern of this paper is to gain a clear view of the intricacy thesis as it applies to thinking and situated action, and to evaluate it from a Wittgensteinian perspective. Wittgenstein also sought an alternative to realism and constructivism, but his alternative consists in descriptions of practices, or language-games, that do not themselves admit of Gendlin's distinction between intricacy and form. Wittgensteinian criticism becomes interesting precisely because it shares Gendlin's philosophical ambitions and assessments of the traditional options, but takes us in a direction, I shall argue, quite distinct from Gendlin's. Gendlin seeks a phenomenological solution in which bodily experience is a criterial marker for that intricacy which always eludes complete description and yet orders our experience. Wittgenstein looks to the outward circumstances of a thought or action and subsequent action. He is suspicious of privileging the phenomenology of our experiences, arguing that such an account provides at best a description of "more or less characteristic *accompaniments*" of understanding or thought.[2] To take these accompaniments as essential or as indicative of something hidden and yet important, according to Wittgenstein, is a deeply rooted philosophical mistake. Gendlin would deny that he is making this Cartesian mistake. Rather, he would claim to develop a phenomenological approach that adequately captures the experiential role of feeling in thought and action without subscribing to a Cartesian conception of an interior life of essentially private experiences. The question here is: Has he succeeded in this?[3]

To pursue this evaluation of the intricacy thesis, I shall restrict the discussion, as does Gendlin, to cognitive innovation (the intricacy of thought) and behavioral responses (the intricacy of situations) and the role that bodily sensation plays. His point is that if we fail to take into account the intricacy of thought and action in behavior, we will miss one of the most important sources of orderliness in our behavior. We will instead attempt to reduce all behavior to either rule-obeying action (i.e., consciously and explicitly following an order or rule) or law-instantiating behavior (i.e., behavior subsumable under causal laws). Such accounts must fail on Gendlin's view, because (though he does not put it this way) neither account recognizes the role played by the intricacy of thought and action, which carries with it an orderliness that is metaphysically more basic than either rules or causal laws. In section 1, I shall take up the intricacy of thought and the nature of conceptual innovation. In section 2, I argue that the intricacy of action (or situation) is importantly different, though Gendlin does not note this, from the intricacy of thought. Finally, in section 3, I focus on the claim that the order of intricacy is metaphysically basic. What I shall argue is that Gendlin cannot get the metaphysical mileage he seeks out of the notion of intricacy, and that Wittgenstein, with his notion of practices in which the natural and conventional cannot be disentangled, opens the way to a more plausible alternative to classical realism and constructivism.

1. The Intricacy of Thought

The intricacy thesis states that intricacy is always more than form. "Form" is the generic expression Gendlin uses to designate any abstraction from concrete particular existence. Concepts, patterns, distinctions, rules, categories and the like are all forms. The difficulty, of course, is in saying what the relation is between forms and the intricacy within which they operate, since any attempt to describe the intricacy will thereby involve the use of forms which *ex hypothesi* cannot capture intricacy. Intricacy cannot be described or categorized in any way without thereby distorting what it is and the role it plays in organizing thought and action. So the first hurdle Gendlin must cross is to find an acceptable way of characterizing the relation between intricacy and form that does not involve direct description. This is further complicated by the claim that much of the intricacy within which forms operate is implicit. So, any explication of intricacy must also clarify the way in which it is implicit.

One might well expect that the only strategy available would be that of Wittgenstein's *Tractatus*,[4] namely, to find a way of showing what cannot be said. But drawing an analogy between Wittgenstein's doctrine of showing and Gendlin's account of intricacy cannot be a straightforward matter. In the *Tractatus*, the very intricacies of nature that Gendlin maintains cannot be fully described or said are the only things that can be said. Elementary propositions do this by picturing in the same degree of detail the intricacy of the state of affairs that is being pictured. Propositions can do this, on Wittgenstein's view, because names (which stand proxy for simple objects) in concatenation with each other, not general terms, are the fundamental semantic units. Names are not patterns or forms, though how they name and concatenate with other names is formal. These formal features, including most importantly the naming relation itself, cannot be described or named. They can only be shown. Wittgenstein's general point is that all semantic, logical, or evaluative "properties" and relations can only be shown through the use of meaningful propositions, i.e., propositions about matters of fact, because logical form is shared between the proposition and its corresponding state of affairs. But logical form is one of the most formal and abstract of forms, and so is disqualified from being part of the intricacy Gendlin seeks to understand. For these reasons, Gendlin cannot make use of some variant of the Wittgensteinian notion of showing what cannot be said. Intricacy is not shown through what we say; it is felt as a determinant of what we do or say.

Gendlin's point seems to be that this intricacy within which forms operate can neither be said nor shown in the *Tractatus* sense, but it is nonetheless the ordering ground of action which can be *felt* in a physiological or bodily way. Bodily experience, under certain conditions, enables us to become aware of this ordering intricacy. Gendlin's strategy for pursuing his project is to draw on two cases—writing poetry and psychotherapy—that he takes to be exemplary in revealing the role played by intricacy in constraining concept-formation and use. These are cases, Gendlin thinks, in which intricacy is made "visible" as it were. There are, however, grounds for being skeptical about assigning this exemplary role to these two cases. The very features that make writing poetry difficult and therapy valuable are what make these two modes of discourse different from ordinary speech situations. The normal features of a speech situation are eliminated, intensifying the focus on the actual words produced. Typically, speech is embedded in an activity or practice that does not make the actual words themselves the salient feature of the activity. Yet, Gendlin is treating these two atypical cases as revealing what goes on ordinarily, for his thesis about intricacy and forms that he draws from these cases is stated in a fully general way. This methodological role assigned to poetry and therapy will come under fuller scrutiny later.[5] For the time being, let us grant that these are paradigmatic and illuminating cases of the development of thought and speech.

Gendlin introduces a technical device in his discussion of these cases. It is what I shall call "the significant silence" sign, the " . . . . . ," used to mark the point at which the subject can become aware of the intricacy of thought at work, thereby establishing its reality as something more than patterns and yet as constraining the choice of words made by the poet or client. It is no accident, I think, that Gendlin uses a device that is very close to the conventionally accepted sign for the phrase "and so on" to indicate continuation in the same way. Two important differences between the conventional " . . ." (continuation sign) and Gendlin's " . . . . . " (significant silence sign) are that the " . . . . . " has temporal duration and it marks an apparent discontinuity in the speech of the poet or client. This temporal duration of the silence itself suggests or supports the idea that something more is actually going on but in a hidden way, something that will bridge the apparent discontinuity in speech. The bridging work of the silence indicates its affinity with the conventional ". . . ," suggesting that the silence marks the work of a normative principle of continuation that determines (timelessly) its correct future applications. This Gendlin expresses by saying that "the . . . . . is an implying" ("TBP," 48). Thus, Gendlin can draw on both a temporal and an atemporal characterization of the way in which the intricacy marked by this sign is implicit.[6] One might think that the intricacy is implicit because it is implied without actually having been drawn. The implicit intricacy . . . . . might be assimilated to the continuation expressed by a rule like "Continue the sequence '2, 4, 6, . . . ,' " where the ". . ." indicates how the sequence is to be continued, namely, in the same way as the preceding three numerals. Here "implication" is used in the atemporal sense associated with logical implication or entailment. On the other hand, the temporal dimension invites the thought that the intricacy is implicit because it is hidden from view, that unconsciously perhaps the sequence has actually been carried out. Subsequent speech then is a report on what has already occurred or, more likely, the effect or outcome of that unconscious occurrence. Gendlin would be unhappy with either of these characterizations of the implicit character of intricacy. Implicit intricacy is presumably neither logical entailment nor unconscious cognitive processing. Yet, we are not given a clear understanding in what sense intricacy of thought is implicit. I shall return to this shortly.

We need to ask again, what explanatory role does the . . . . . play? For the time being, whatever way one takes the notion that intricacy is implicit, we can say that the occurrence of a . . . . . indicates the work of an implicit intricacy which in some way mediates and links the language before and after the silence. The silence is a way of becoming aware of that intricacy and also letting it do its work without insisting on untimely categorization. That allows for the development of new meaning or sense (new patterns), as opposed to the repetition of canned or familiar phrases. Presumably, if we can understand what makes for meaningful progression in the development of a poem or an advance in therapy, we can shed light on what makes even familiar speech meaningful.

In writing a poem, the poet finds herself searching for the next line, which does not come immediately to her. This search is expressed by a significant silence. It is this silence "the . . . . . that *determines* the next line, it says (in other words:) that most lines will not do" ("TBP," 57). In other words, it is not the poet who determines the next line, nor is it the previous lines of the poem, but the blank or silence itself. Now what can Gendlin mean by this? He might mean that finding the appropriate words for the next line is not a matter of the poet *deciding* that certain words will do. As Gendlin interestingly points out, decisions are made when time runs out and action must be taken whether or not it is really appropriate. The poet's choice of words, on the other hand, is severely constrained. What constrains the poet in her acceptance of words for the next line is, according to Gendlin, the implicit intricacy of the thought marked or signaled by the significant silence. It is intricate thought that is doing the real work here.

Now why does Gendlin want to separate the work of intricate thought from what the poet herself does? For the same reasons, it seems to me, that Descartes thought that mathematical objects must exist and that Popper introduces a third world of abstract objects. Descartes emphasizes the fact that "my mind is necessitated by the mathematical object and not the other way around and so the object must exist independently of my mind."[7] For Popper, there is a logic or structure to problems, arguments, mathematics, poems, and other abstract entities that is independent of any individual's choices or beliefs, and it is this logic that determines the development of the problem.[8] Both are saying that the object of thought constrains thought, and so the individual does not decide what is to be said next or what follows. The concept of the mathematical object or the problem itself determines what follows. The important difference between Gendlin and either the Cartesian or Popperian views is that intricacy, unlike Cartesian mathematical objects or Popper's third world, is not an abstract evidential, logical, mathematical, or conceptual structure, or indeed any kind of pattern—the intricacy of a thought or action or situation is *not* the *logic* of that thought or action or situation, but something more. It is this something more that is alleged to constrain the logic of the situation or action or thought and to create the space for creativity and new meaning by determining which words are appropriate. What Gendlin does hold in common with these two philosophers is the guiding idea that intricacy *determines*—in some sense—what is to follow. It is precisely this locution and the picture associated with it that Wittgenstein examines and challenges in his *Philosophical Investigations*.[9]

Let me approach this challenge by pointing out three tensions or problems in Gendlin's account. Is the intricacy that "determines the next line of the poem" a thought? It is natural to construe the silence as marking the occurrence of unconscious thought. Yet the ordinary idea of unconscious thought points to the occurrence of patterned conceptualizing processes out of the conscious reach of the subject. This is ruled out by Gendlin in his elaboration of the sense in which this intricacy is implicit. He tells us that " 'implicit' *used to mean* that something fully formed is hidden, folded in" ("TBP," 56; my italics). In other words, the idea of unconscious but patterned thought is the old notion that Gendlin is seeking to displace with his changed understanding of "implicit": "My word 'implicit' changed implicitly in the . . . . . which changes how a word will work before it comes" ("TBP," 56). So is Gendlin's hypothesis that there is another kind of thought that is unconscious and nonconceptual (i.e., unpatterned), but the source of words and new meaning? So, in explicating the explanatory role of the . . . . . , ordinary patterned thought is replaced by some kind of special unpatterned thought about which nothing can be said without transforming it into ordinary patterned thought. Here is the first tension: it is expressed in the contrast between the ordinary conception of thought as itself inherently conceptual and so patterned and Gendlin's unpatterned special kind of thought that is nonconceptual and yet somehow "implies" ordinary thought. Ordinary unconscious thought makes it intelligible how the right words are found for the next line of the poem in the space indicated by the . . . . . Yet, ordinary thought is patterned and so undermines Gendlin's thesis that intricacy is more than patterns and only as "more" determines the right words. Unpatterned implicit intricacy is alleged to spawn the right words, yet we have no idea how it is supposed to do this or even what this intricacy consists in. The silence is a blank.

We are left with the following picture of the poet struggling to find the right words. The silence marks an unconceptualized form of thinking which itself implies (in a nonlogical and nonevidential way) that a certain sentence string is acceptable. The role of this peculiar form of mental activity seems both productive (it takes time and it produces a linguistic string) and normative (it provides the criterion of acceptability, a criterion, however, that cannot be expressed in a patterned way, i.e., in language or in ordinary thought). But this does not fit well with another aspect of Gendlin's development of this notion of a significant silence. He also treats the . . . . . as a *variable* for which a concrete value can be substituted as a function of the preceding words: "The . . . . . is held by all the words around it. And it . . . . . s the schemes that work in it implicitly. This way of a slot says something of how schemes work implicitly" ("TBP," 58); "Forms and patterns do not work alone, even in pure logic. In application they work-in more (the slot, the situation . . . . .). But forms are always at work, at least implicitly"; "In our instance the poet's . . . . . comes at the end of the already written lines. So the forms of these *are* at work in it" ("TBP," 63). On this account, *the preexisting lines imply* the next sentence, or how the blank is to be filled in. This is quite different from the claim that the blank implies the next line. Yet Gendlin says both: "The . . . . . is held by all the words around it" ("TBP," 58); "The . . . . . is an implying" ("TBP," 48); "At first you may be just confused and stuck, but then a . . . . . can come. 'To imply' is what the . . . . . does" ("TBP," 52).

This is the second tension: Gendlin conflates two distinct pictures of how we are to understand this . . . . . , and then uses elements from each picture that are most appropriate to the topic at hand. What are the two pictures? One has been sketched: it is a picture of an unconscious or preconscious mental activity out of which words come. We can only describe it as something rich, detailed, and mysterious. We identify it by way of certain typical physiological symptoms—a feeling of blankness, a tightness perhaps in the throat, head, or middle of the body. This picture reifies the object or process marked by the occurrence of a . . . . . It creates the sense of great depth and complexity that always eludes our attempts at description but in the end is the most important thing. This is the mistaken picture that Wittgenstein argues we are driven to by our inability to explain how the next line is determined by what has gone before: "In our failure to understand the use of a word we take it as the expression of a queer *process*. (As we think of time as a queer medium, of the mind as a queer kind of being.)."[10]

The second picture is quite different. The occurrence of a . . . . . does not signal or denote some hidden reality, but is a placeholder or variable for which the poet seeks to substitute a sentence string given the context of the poem, that is, given the preexisting lines as well as the various conventions demarcating poetry from other forms of writing, the intentions of the poet, the problem being addressed in the poem, and so on. In other words, the criteria for assessing the appropriateness of proffered lines are statable although multiple. On this view, the blank itself implies nothing, does nothing; it is a variable or placeholder only. This is an instrumentalist or functionalist view of the . . . . . , not a realist view. This makes writing the next line of the poem more closely akin to solving the arithematical problem "$57 + 65 = n$."

Gendlin needs the first picture, the realist picture, to generate the air of mysteriousness, depth, and paradox: intricacy is both vague and precise ("TBP," 49); it determines what is to come and yet it does not ("TBP," 53); it can be indicated and felt but not said. His justification for this picture is that if the functionalist construal were correct, then the next line would follow in the way that "4" follows from "$2 + 2 = n$." All implyings would be like logical entailment or mathematical derivability. And clearly the lines of poem cannot be derived in that manner from the previous lines. That is true, but it does not support the temptation to realism about the silence. A blank does not imply or determine anything. The blank is not itself an intricacy. What is intricate or complex is the array of factors that contribute to finding the appropriate line. It is precisely because the poet knows how to weigh the previous lines of the poem, the conventions surrounding the writing of poetry, her intentions, her exploitation of new possibilities. The feeling of blankness the poet might feel in the search for the next line is not the critically important matter. A very poor poet might feel the same blankness and yet be unable to generate an appropriate new line. Even a good poet might well experience a significant silence and write down a continuing line with the accompaniment of relief, and yet realize that the line is no good.[11] What matters is the context in which the poet writes and what the poet goes on to do, not the silence. The functionalist reading of the . . . . . is far more persuasive than the realist reading.

This functionalist account is deflationary, and precisely for this reason is congenial to the Wittgensteinian perspective. Implicit implication is no different from, and so no more mysterious than, our ordinary notion of implication. The "more" of intricacy that can never be captured in a single pattern reflects the multiple factors involved in finding the next line of the poem. This interpretation of the . . . . . is completely consonant with the view that there is only ordinary thought, thus eliminating any theoretical need to hypothesize a special kind of thought. Gendlin himself seems to support such a view when he insists that implicit thought is not to be viewed as "thought already there." So what supports Gendlin in his more realist remarks about implicit intricacy?

The temptation to a misplaced realism can be traced in part to Gendlin's use of cases from psychotherapy. The therapeutic situation is a highly artificial one in which the client is trained into what is taken to be as an appropriate awareness of her body. The client must learn to abstract her physical feeling from any normal course of activity and reconceptualize it as providing the key to her problems. The clear logical discontinuities in the client's discourse invite reading into the silences the connective logical or conceptual tissue binding together trains of discourse into an intelligible whole. In this way, silences can be seen as producing new meaning or new sense. Moreover, therapeutic discourse is taken to have a direction, or better a progression, with its implication of movement toward what is better for the client. That progression is marked primarily by a movement from tension to relief of tension. The reason, then, that the . . . . . can be seen to imply subsequent speech is that often there is no logical relation among the sentences uttered by the client in the therapy session, and indeed no obvious principle of connection to link the sentences and the feelings with which they are associated in a coherent or meaningful fashion. The silences themselves become the perfect medium for filling in whatever content is necessary to turn the disjointed discourse into a progressive articulation of the client's problem(s). The flexibility built into the notion of intricacy is further expanded by the fact that the meaning of the actual sentences uttered is assigned retroactively through constructive interpretation. This is yet another construal of "implicit intricacy." On this view, the intricacy marked by the silence does not exist until some later time when an interpretation is constructed. Here, all that is required for connectedness or the silence's "determining" what is said is logical compatibility, not evidential or logical derivability. The only independent evidence for the acceptability of an interpretation and so the significance of the silence is that, though inarticulate, the client "knows" what it contains by way of bodily feeling. It is "the unclear sensation of the problem in the middle of one's body" ("TBP," 68). But this physiological marker of implicit intricacy fits the realist picture associated with the writing of poetry, not the constructivist picture associated with therapy.

Finally, there is a third tension: the intricacy felt in a bodily way is a problem, that is, a pattern. It is very difficult to maintain the distinction between intricacy and pattern, for what is sensed physically is a problem, i.e., a pattern of a rather high order. The steps that are taken are now seen as steps in the articulation of that pattern, and so can be said to be implied by it. Once more, the contrast between intricacy and pattern is obscured. All that sustains the contrast is Gendlin's insistence that the intricacy is always "more" than any pattern, which is to say that it always eludes full or complete description. But unless the notion can be tied down more firmly, it looks as though it will face the same fate as the philosophical notion of substance, which became "a something, I know not what" that plays no explanatory role at all either normatively (in setting the standards for evaluating what follows) or productively (in explaining the genesis of the new words). The very flexibility of the term "intricacy" becomes its own undoing as a theoretically significant term. To mark progress, intricacy must be describable or interpretable. Otherwise, any notion of progress or implying is utterly empty. Yet, always to be more than any description or group of descriptions, it must be ineffable and so beyond descriptions. Gendlin seems to face the following dilemma: either intricacy is ineffable, in which case it plays no explanatory role in accounts of thought and action; or it is describable, in which case the striking contrast between intricacy and patterns is lost, and Gendlin's central thesis that we think beyond patterns is undermined.

These three tensions—ordinary thought versus a special kind of thought, the realist account of the . . . . . versus the functionalist account versus the constructivist account, and intricacy as describable versus intricacy as ineffable—raise questions about Gendlin's methodological approach. Why should two atypical human situations—writing poetry and engaging in psychotherapy—be taken as the exemplars of the relation between language and reality? What justifies Gendlin's extending what happens in these situations to all uses of language or patterns? Both are sophisticated activities that presuppose the person to be an assimilated language-user. The poet searching for the *mot juste* and the client seeking to articulate her problems are to be taken as the most revelatory about the relation between language and the world. What is the evidence or grounds for this extension? None are offered. Until that is forthcoming, there is simply no reason for accepting this methodological assumption.

More limited claims are warranted from an investigation of these two cases. A functionalist account of the . . . . . is quite plausible in its own right and is a useful antidote to the temptation to hypothesize mysterious but unknowable mental episodes that provide the logical or quasilogical links between sentences uttered. Gendlin's account of writing poetry makes us aware of the multiple factors that go into determining how the poet is to continue. The discussion of psychotherapy cases emphasizes the importance of retrospective interpretation placed upon disjoint utterances. Accepting these points, however, is much more modest and deflationary than the larger theoretical claims Gendlin makes on behalf of implicit intricacy.

2. The Intricacy of Situation

The account of implicit intricacy at work in the specialized and sophisticated domains of therapy and writing poetry is not restricted, Gendlin maintains, to these narrow domains. The intricacy thesis holds for situations in general, where a situation concerns the relations of a living organism to its environment and its array of available behaviors given its nature and circumstances. As Gendlin expresses it, a situation is a "preseparated multiplicity" ("TBP," 92) which he further explicates as an array of "implicit action-possibilities" ("TBP," 94). A situation then is not just the describable features of an event at a particular time; it also implies an array of further events. Gendlin holds that situations are ontologically and epistemologically more fundamental than the objects that are elements of situations. His central thesis is that the living organism "knows" its environment in a behavioral and visceral way; that is, its behaviors implicate an environment of a certain sort and vice versa. Gendlin thinks that the explanatory concepts he has introduced in connection with the way in which the . . . . . works can be used to describe the intricacy of situations. Yet, the implicit intricacy of a situation, I shall argue, is significantly different from that of thought as characterized by Gendlin, and does not stand in any important theoretical way upon Gendlin's account of the intricacy of thought.

There are two salient disanalogies between a significant silence and a situation. The first and most important is that the implications that a behavior or action has for an environment and vice versa are all *internal* to the situation in that they are logical or rational or adaptive relations on the surface of things, as Wittgenstein might put it. The implyings allegedly provided by a significant silence in therapy, on the other hand, occur at those points where there are logical or rational gaps between sentence and sentence. The logical and rational gaps that occur in therapy create the space for hypothesizing the occurrence of a *significant* silence as opposed to simply a silence. No such gap opens up in the living organism's relation to its environment. The second, and perhaps derivative, disanalogy is that the array of action-possibilities created by (and constituting) a situation seem much more limited than the array of action-possibilities (lines of thought) implied by the significant silence. The former are limited because they are governed by principles of rationality and adaptiveness; the latter, however, given the role of retrospective interpretative construction, require only logical compatibility. Logical compatibility is much weaker than evidential inference.[12]

Both disanalogies need elaboration. Let us consider Gendlin's simple example of a bird flying away from a perceived cat ("TBP," 114). A bird flees a cat. The very flight of the bird indicates that the situation is a dangerous one; the cat-inhabited situation implies flight for the bird. There is no temptation here to treat the perching of the bird before flight as a . . . . . , for that would suggest that the flight was implied by the . . . . . rather than by the situation itself. The entry of the cat and the perched bird have the internal relation of predator and object of predation. The creeping of the cat shows (or implies) this as plainly as the sudden flight of the bird. The situation for the bird is one of danger, open space, and avoidable obstacles. The bird's action-possibilities once it has taken flight include continued flight, alighting on a branch of a different tree, alighting on a telephone wire, and so on. There are no logical gaps among the elements of the situation (provided the elements are behaviors and actions, not, say, bodily movements). Even if the bird flew into the cat's mouth, that would only show the way terror can blind. In other words, actions within the situations of living organisms are not arbitrary or random but are rationally or adaptively connected on the surface of things. Gendlin views this as evidence of the self-ordering nature of organisms.[13] Chains of sentences in poetry or therapy, on the other hand, may display no overt logical or rational connections among the sentences, and these logical gaps can be matched by silences in their construction. Gendlin's hypothesis is that these chains are not arbitrarily or randomly constructed but are ordered by the intricacy of thought rather than the patterns of logic or rationality. If the intricacy of thought marked by the . . . . . is construed functionally, this is acceptable; if construed realistically, it is not acceptable. But with situations there is no need to hypothesize a . . . . . to explain the connection between features of the situation. We are not tempted to construe the bird as considering its alternatives in a hidden or preconscious way.

The second major disanalogy concerns the nature of the implication that the situation and the . . . . . have for action-possibilities. There are two ways to express this point. Put simply, we can say either that the range of action-possibilities for situations is more limited than the range for significant silences, or that situations involve rational or adaptive implication whereas silences involve logical compatibility. The array of action-possibilities for the bird in a dangerous situation doesn't seem that large. Basically, it can flee or fight or freeze. The range of actions for animals is, for the most part, limited to the canned response. In the same way, it seems clear that the range of situations a bird can be in is fairly limited. This is why it seems natural to say that the bird responds to the cat as a whole rather than to some part of the cat, such as its eyes, or to some abstracted pattern, for example, the characteristic shape of the ears and crown of a cat ("TBP," 115). As Gendlin expresses it, the intricacy of situations implicates the whole organism. The grounds for holding that the bird, in its action, responds to the cat as a whole support my contention that the range of situations that a non–language-using animal can be in is limited. Consider the wide range of particular objects that can cause the bird to fly in fear: a stalking cat, a barking dog, a playing child, flapping laundry, and an indefinitely large number of other objects and events. It seems quite plausible to say that the bird responds to danger rather than to a cat or a dog or a child or laundry, and that the bird is highly risk averse, which is measured by the large number of what ethologists call "false positives," like the flapping laundry, which stimulate the flight response. Is it more plausible to hold that the bird during each of these flights is responding now to a cat, now to a dog, now to some wind-blown laundry? Or are each of these the same situation for the bird, namely, one of danger for which there are really only three behavioral possibilities—flight, fight, or freeze? The point of introducing this problem of individuating the object to which the bird responds, and so the range of situations that a bird can inhabit, is to show that that range is determined by an abstract pattern (what is dangerous), which is delimited by the behavioral response of the bird. On this reading, the number of situations that a bird can be in is highly limited and is determined by an abstract pattern, namely, the pattern of the bird's reaction to events in its vicinity.

By contrast, the logical space of discourse within which the poet or client works creates ample room for alternatives to adaptive behavioral responses. This is a function of our compositionally and symbolically rich language and not the hypothesized intricacy of the . . . . . The range of what is logically compatible is much greater than the range of what is adaptively suitable. The range of actions for animals is, for the most part, limited to the canned response. But the range of possible descriptions or interpretations available to the reflective person is indefinitely large, especially if the primary constraint on acceptability is logical compatibility with earlier utterances. Consider two examples taken from the therapeutic situation. One client moves by way of a . . . . . from the utterance "I keep feeling a sense of no meaning to my life" to "I just want to leave everything" ("TBP," 70); another moves from "It's too sore to touch" to "I've waited all my life" ("TBP," 68). Certainly an interpretive narrative can be constructed to connect these sentences (with reference of course to the larger context of the utterances), but displaying this kind of logical compatibility is not implication, either logically or evidentially. One can readily imagine quite different sentences being uttered that would be equally compatible with the earlier utterances. This is not the case with the relation between perceived danger and flight or fight. To individuate the situation and its implicit range of action-possibilities, it is necessary to see less of the intricacy.

It is possible to miss this point by confusing situational implication with richness of detail. The very language of Gendlin threatens to conflate these two. He identifies a situation with a "preseparated multiplicity," which he further explains as an implicit array of action-possibilities. The problem being raised here is how to individuate action-possibilities. Gendlin's very argument that the bird responds to the cat as a whole underscores the internal relation between this instance of wing-flapping and the presence of this animal. That relation is one of danger, so the relevant action-possibilities are fleeing (by taking flight) or fighting. This is distinct from the details of any given flight. But the preseparated multiplicity seems to concern the indefinitely large number of describable details of any situation. Now the exact trajectory of any given flight or the exact number of feathers ruffled in any given fight or the exact angle of the cocked head frozen in fear will vary and cannot be captured in any single description. But, does the bird's situation imply all possible tilts of the bird's head or the total number of ruffled feathers? If Gendlin says no, then, *in what relevant sense*, is intricacy more than patterns? If Gendlin says yes, then he must forfeit his claim that the bird responds to the cat as a whole, which he took to be a crucial part of his account of situations and which distinguished his theory from any form of stimulus-response theory.

What we are facing is the difficulty in specifying what intricacy consists in and what makes it always more than any pattern, description, conceptualization or distinction that we can make. It seems to me that Gendlin introduces at least four ways in which the intricacy of thought and situation is always more than what is captured by any category or pattern or distinction.

1. The first sense is completely uncontroversial with no interesting metaphysical consequences. It is the *thesis of the generality of categories* or patterns. Descriptive terms or categories are general, and so of necessity do not capture the uniqueness or the full details of any object, event, or situation. So if intricacy refers to the richness of detail of any concrete particular, then that richness of the individual situation will always exceed any particular description. From this, however, it does not follow that intricacy is indescribable, only that it hasn't all been described. Though Gendlin would endorse the thesis of generality, he certainly intends something more substantive and even surprising than this truism.

2. Two of the forms that intricacy takes concern the way in which intricacy is implicit. These are developed in connection with his discussion of action and situations. What I shall call a "*criterion of wide identity*" must be used, according to Gendlin, to individuate any situation or significant silence. A silence or a situation has implications for further speech or action which are part of the identity conditions for either form of intricacy. This is why they involve an *implicit* intricacy. The implicit intricacy of thought, marked by a significant silence, implies precisely and determinately the appropriate continuations of speech or writing. I have already argued in section 1 that Gendlin's account of the intricacy of thought conflates two distinct pictures of the . . . . . , the realist picture and the functionalist picture. The realist picture I argued is unacceptable and the functionalist picture carries no greater metaphysical baggage than does the thesis of the generality of categories. The implicit intricacy of a situation implies a range of possible actions. Showing that we need a criterion of wide identity for situations and actions brings out the theoretically important difference between a physical system of minute changes and an ethological system of internally related circumstances and actions. For animals, situations are adaptationally coherent. For human beings, situations are further mediated by cultural institutions and of course language. But however these matters are worked out, it is surely a sound point that the identity conditions for situations include what Gendlin calls "implyings" for subsequent events.

3. The intricacy thesis can be construed even more strongly to state that the identity conditions for the original situation undergo change in the very occurrence of any of the implied subsequent actions. This is a *thesis of the indeterminacy of identity* of situations. In describing it as an indeterminacy of identity (as opposed to wide identity), I want to underscore that, on Gendlin's view, there is no way, not even in principle, for individuating a situation or a thought once and for all. This thesis is closely tied to his concept of retroactive revision ("TBP," 84), according to which, in the context of therapy, the previous step implies the next one because "we *retroactively revise* the previous step—looking backward from the next" ("TBP," 84). This clearly supports the functionalist interpretation of the . . . . . and suggests that the relation between what precedes the . . . . . and what follows is not one of implication but one of logical compatibility; that is, ongoing interpretations are constructed to make whatever is said part of a single problem or narrative.

I want to contrast this with the way in which situations are indeterminate. Here Gendlin says that "a situation has a complex pattern: It implies not only how it now implies, but also a change in its implying" ("TBP," 94). This is obscure as stated. It seems to me that what Gendlin is getting at is that in acting in a particular way in a situation, one thereby changes the situation itself by altering the range of subsequent action-possibilities. Since part of the identity of a situation is its range of implied actions, to alter that range is thereby to alter the identity conditions of the situation. A consequence of this is that no action or situation is ever complete. What a situation is will depend on all subsequent changes to the range of possible actions, but since this kind of implying never ends (even if the physical world were to do so), there is literally no fact of the matter concerning the identity of any situation or action. The cat approaches the tree in which the bird is perched, thus creating a dangerous situation. That situation is individuated by the current relation of cat to bird and by all that is implied by the actions and relations of the cat and the bird. The range of possible actions implied by the proximity of the cat to the bird includes the cat's creeping with eyes fixed on the bird, the cat's sitting in a fixed position, the cat's lashing its tail, the cat's lying down for a nap, as well as the bird's continued perching, flight, or dive-bombing of the cat. The actual behavior of the cat and bird, taken from the range of possible actions, retroactively changes the identity of the situation by altering the range of further possible actions. If the cat lies down for a nap, that behavior shows that the cat is full or has not seen the bird, thus altering the identity of the original situation. What was initially and correctly taken as a dangerous situation is in fact a peaceful one.[14]

When we compare the indeterminacy of the identity within the therapy session and the indeterminacy of the identity of a situation, we can see that they differ. To say that the . . . . . implies the next utterances of the client is in fact to say that the next utterances can be made logically compatible with the previous ones by interpretation. This can only be done retroactively; it carries with it no possibility of prediction. What a situation implies, on the other hand, is changed by the *actual* occurrence of one of its array of implied, i.e., rationally or adaptationally warranted, possible actions. Actual (but implied) consequences of an action override possible consequences in fixing the identity of the situation. These are two ways in which identity can be indeterminate, but one (the . . . . .) is open because it can only be constructed after the fact. The other (a situation) is open because the future is open, and there is no principled way of drawing a limit to the temporal reach of a situation.

4. The fourth way in which intricacy is construed is not so much stated as insinuated by the air of paradox, inexhaustible detail, and indeterminacy of identity that accompanies the writing of poetry or engaging in psychotherapy. This is an almost mystical sense of the unutterable complexity or *ineffability of reality*. Intricacy is something that can neither be said nor shown (in the Wittgensteinian sense), but only felt in a bodily way. The intricacy of thought is literally felt as some kind of physiological discomfort and in some mysterious way orders our speech. The intricacy of the situation is bodily enacted, it is the self-ordering yet mysterious and unknowable principle of organic activity. None of the other three versions of the intricacy thesis support the ineffability of reality. Support for the crucial causal role of an ineffable reality in thought and action can at best be provided indirectly. But precisely because it is ineffable, even apparent indirect support (the client's feeling of tension while quiet or the bird's sudden flight) provides no real support for this alleged underlying reality, this multiplicity that cannot be spoken or shown. If it really is ineffable, then it would not be possible to ascertain whether the intricacy of thought remains constant, elaborating as it were a single problem, or shifts, changing problems, or has nothing to do with the client's problems at all but is only mistakenly interpreted that way by the therapist. Given the ineffability of what is "hidden" behind the . . . . . , there is no way to distinguish these. What matters is what the client actually says and whether there is an actual reduction in tension or confusion, and presumably what she goes on to do after therapy. Moments of silence may well be indicative that the client is not going to use canned or repetitive responses. The only reason that it is so indicative is that the client usually goes on to say something more interesting or at least helpful than unbroken speech typically allows. The danger here is parallel, it seems to

me, to what Wittgenstein saw as the danger in philosophical puzzlement and its distinctive phenomenology: "[philosophers] see in the essence, not something that already lies open to view and that becomes surveyable by a rearrangement, but something that lies *beneath* the surface."[15] The crucial difference between the philosophers Wittgenstein discusses and the illusions created by their philosophical demands and Gendlin is that philosophers seek a simple order lying behind the multiplicity of ordinary life or discourse, whereas Gendlin seeks an ineffable multiplicity behind the patterns and forms we use to simplify that multiplicity. These seem to be two sides of the same metaphysical coin. My point is that insofar as intricacy is ineffable it too is an illusion created by the phenomenological features of the therapeutic session. It is the metaphysical urge to find meaning or order beyond the scope of ordinary action and life.[16]

In sum, the generality thesis and the ineffability thesis are the two least interesting construals of Gendlin's intricacy thesis, the first because it is a truism without serious metaphysical import, and the second because it is an empty hypothesis. But the criterion of wide identity and the indeterminacy of identity provide insight into the structure of situations. Both help elucidate the way in which intricacy is implicit in action without, however, supporting Gendlin's thesis that intricacy is metaphysically richer or ontologically more basic than patterns.

3. Intricacy and Patterns

What argument does Gendlin give for the claim that intricacy is ontologically more basic than form? The primary argument is philosophical:

> Currently, everything is studied in terms of formed forms, patterned patterns. But, patterns are passive; they are observed but not observing, seen but not seeing. . . . For example, the growth of a plant is explained in terms of patterns we sense and construct. We are not tempted to assume that the plant lives by thinking or sensing these patterns. But, since the plant can't do that, we have no concept at all about how the plant could organize and continue itself rather than being organized by the continuity of the "ideal observer." How could the plant imply its own further life-process? . . .
>
> We need concepts of a self-ordering . . . self-ordering cannot consist of formed patterns, because patterns are always ordered, passive, already requiring an external observer. ("TBP," 111–12)

MEREDITH   WILLIAMS

The structure of Gendlin's argument seems to be the following: the changes and developments that occur in the life-process of any living organism are orderly. There are two traditional ways of accounting for this orderliness: (1) The orderly behavior and change is the result of the organism's recognizing a pattern or rule and following it. This explicit rule-obeying behavior clearly does not apply to plants or animals or even all human behavior. Rule-obeying actions require sophisticated cognitive resources, for the agent must be able to recognize and understand normative principles and apply them. (2) Orderly change is the instantiation of causal laws. Law-instantiating behavior is the object of the patterned explanations of science. But causal explanation cannot provide an account of orderly change because "patterns are passive; they are observed but not observing, seen but not seeing" ("TBP," 111).[17] Causal patterns are the projections of the observer onto the observed system. Here Gendlin endorses a very strong version of constructivism, the view that "the mechanical order is projected" ("TBP," 120), and that "as scientists we impose the empty space of time and space patterns, and thereby make-and-discover the mechanical causes" ("TBP," 121). These remarks, taken together, suppose that change can only be the result of an active agency, and so a pattern or law which is not such an agency can't produce change. Any causal connections we hypothesize are in fact sustained only by the active observings of the ideal observer. Their reality is in the mind of the observer not in nature. Neither rule-obeying explanations nor law-instantiating explanations can account for the orderliness of behavior. The former is cognitively too sophisticated for most behavior and the latter is a scientific projection requiring an observer and so cannot be the source of order within nature. Both of these forms of order, according to Gendlin, depend on an observer or agent who is independent of the rules or laws. Rules are followed by agents and laws are projected upon nature by observers. Given this character of patterns, patterns cannot be the source of order. Gendlin therefore rejects the assumption that there are only these two forms of orderly behavior. He further draws the inference that there must be some form of order which is self-ordering.[18] He claims that this self-ordering order is what he intends to capture with his notion of bodily intricacy. Such intricacy is a "bodily implying,"[19] and so explains change in virtue of this special kind of implication.

There are two important features to this argument. The first is that entities or events hypothesized by traditional modes of explanation are ontologically dependent, presupposing another form of existence. The second feature reveals Gendlin's assumptions about what would count as an adequate theory of orderly change or agency. He resurrects the old conception of causation or agency as involving necessary connection. This is the force, it seems to me, of using the phrase "bodily *implying*." "Implication" is necessary connection, but since it is the implication of intricacy rather than patterns, it cannot be described or made to fit a logical pattern. Before evaluating this argument, let us consider Gendlin's second argument for bodily intricacy, this one being an empirical argument.

Gendlin cites certain scientific studies that he holds corroborate his intricacy thesis ("TBP," chap. B-5). These are ethological studies, which have uncovered a wide range of inborn behavior sequences in various animals, including the web building capability of spiders, nest building by birds, mating rituals, and the like. These behavior sequences cannot readily be assimilated to either of the traditional explanations of regular behavior. These orderly and repeatable behaviors are not mechanistically instantiated but display a subtle and continuous adaptation to the existing conditions of the environment and the organism's own body. Nor can we imagine that the bird or spider literally follows rules in the construction of its nest or web. So, this type of sequenced behavior is neither mechanistically realized nor self-conscious rule-following. It belongs to a another category, and as such requires a different kind of explanation, one that appeals neither to laws nor rules. For Gendlin, the explanation once again lies with the self-ordering intricacy of the organism's body. The actual behaviors that constitute any given orderly sequence are implied, in all their precision and richness as well as in their regularity, by the organism's body, an intricacy which no patterned explanation can capture. It is concluded that the intricacy of the body is ontologically basic and attempts to describe this intricacy are explanatorily basic.[20] This conclusion is drawn, although Gendlin does not put it this way, on the basis of its being the best explanation of the empirical data gathered in ethological studies.

To a considerable extent, I agree with Gendlin's primary argument that rejects the long-standing idea that orderly behaviors are to be understood either in terms of normative rules or causal laws, although I do not accept the conclusion he draws or all the arguments he uses to support that conclusion. Gendlin cites the complex behaviors of lower animals that resist simple causal explanation in terms of stimulus-response chains and yet clearly cannot be rule-governed. These behaviors include nest building, mating rituals, web spinning, and the communicative dances of bees. It is the activity of the implicit intricacy of the body of the bird, spider, or bee that ontologically grounds these complex patterns of behavior and explains them. By locating the source in bodily intricacy, Gendlin hopes to explain the apparent innateness of these patterns of behavior, the internal orderliness of these sequenced behaviors that is so striking, and the precise adaptation the animal makes to its concrete situation as it carries out its project. Gendlin's notion of bodily intricacy cannot carry this explanatory burden. There is an alternative way of conceptualizing the sequenced behaviors of the ethological studies that both recognizes a form of regular or orderly behavior that is neither rule-following nor law-instantiating, and prepares the way for a naturalistic explanation of such sequenced behaviors without appeal to the notion of bodily intricacy.

This important class of behaviors that does not fit categorization either as rule-following or law-instantiating I shall call, following Wilfrid Sellars, "pattern-governed actions."[21] Pattern-governed behavior is such that it would not have occurred except as part of a complex abstract pattern. The wing-stretching behavior of the albatross performed during its mating ritual would not have occurred except as part of that ritual; the wiggles of a bee when it returns to the hive after locating a clover field occur because they are part of a complex dance. These individual behaviors are performed because they are part of a ritual or a dance, though they do not follow from a conception of the ritual or dance. The explanation for, and individuation of, the particular movement is given by its relation to the complex patterned ritual or dance as a whole.

What is it to say that a behavior or action is performed because it is part of a complex pattern without, however, being performed through a recognition of that pattern? To clarify this, let me distinguish between a behavior that is done because it is part of a pattern and a physically similar behavior that is done for other causes. A bee wiggles because a drop of acid touches its body. Though physically like the wiggle that, in the context of a dance, indicates the direction in which the flowers are to be found, this wiggle does not indicate that. It is only a physical reaction to the irritation of its body's surface; it is not done because it is a *part* of a dance. The causal explanation for this part-of-the-dance wiggle will reside in a causal, perhaps evolutionary, explanation of the survival value of such patterned dances. We cannot understand the individual wiggle independently of its part in the complex dance. It seems to me that much that Gendlin is trying to capture in his notion of the body's implying is better characterized as pattern-governed behavior. This view does not entail that intricacy (presumably the individual dances of individual bees) is more basic than the patterns that are instantiated. But it clearly does not reduce pattern to mere stimulus-response regularity or elevate it to the cognitive recognition of a choreographed recipe for the dance. This is because the individual behaviors are what they are only in virtue of their part in the pattern. In evolutionary terms, the *pattern* of behaviors is selected for, not the individual behaviors. This means that patterns are as metaphysically basic as intricate individual behaviors. The implication for Gendlin's argument is that the ethological studies do not corroborate his intricacy thesis alone.

Not only are patterns as "real" as intricacy for the reason just given, Gendlin's grounds for denying this involve a fallacy. Gendlin confuses an ontological order with an epistemological order. From the fact that to identify patterns as patterns they must be abstracted from the concrete case (what he calls "doubled perception"), Gendlin infers the claim that patterns cannot be ontologically basic. An analogous line of reasoning would be to hold that since the chemical composition of water was only discovered after 1750, water was not H_2O before 1750. This degree of social constructivism is simply not plausible, not even to Gendlin.

Finally, recognizing this third kind of behavior—pattern-governed behaviors—provides an alternative ground for rejecting the second premise of Gendlin's reductio ad absurdum. There are not just two forms of orderly behavior, and in introducing this third kind, I am not introducing a self-ordering order if that means an order without explanation. The complex dance of the bee, the web spinning of the spider, and all the rest can themselves be explained, typically in evolutionary ways. But the individual wiggle or thread production is explained by showing its function within the complex pattern as a whole. So Gendlin and I agree on the force of the argument and where to locate the unacceptable premise, but we offer very different alternatives to that premise. On my Wittgensteinian alternative, patterns are as basic as intricacy, and certain aspects in any case of what Gendlin wants to explain in terms of implicit intricacy are explicable as patterns.

What this indicates for Gendlin's argument is his deep philosophical commitment to the idea of a fundamental self-ordering order which is beyond description or explanation. This is what the living body is to provide with its implicit implications for future action-possibilities in concrete situations. This can be construed in two ways at this point in the argument. Pattern-governed behaviors cannot be assimilated to any form of patterned explanation, Gendlin maintains, because patterns only exist abstracted from organic intricate "order." We have already seen that this way of arguing for the basicness of bodily intricacy is fallacious. The second construal of Gendlin's claim is that only bodily implicit intricacy can account for the myriad of precise adaptations the organism must make to its actual environment in any particular instance of nest building or engaging in a mating ritual or indeed any kind of behavior at all.

This, of course, is one of the problems over which behaviorist theory foundered. Nor can evolutionary theory shed light on this problem. Does, then, Gendlin's notion of implicit intricacy constitute an explanatory advance in our understanding of this aspect of all activity?

In what way does bodily intricacy explain the minute and precise adjustments and coordinations of physical action to the environment that are a constant part of all behavior? I think that the sense of explanatory gain is, in the end, illusory. It derives from two sources. The first is implicit intricacy is a kind of implying, not identical to logical implication but clearly related. What this comes to is a revival of the classic notion of causation as a *necessary* connection, a rationalist conception of the order of the universe in terms of which the cause must be such as to rationally necessitate or determine its effect. Not only has this view of causation had a long philosophical history, but there has also been a long history of attack on this notion, from David Hume's critique of necessary connection on. An important part of Wittgenstein's later philosophy is a critique and rejection of his own earlier commitment to such a notion. That early commitment, stated forcefully in the *Tractatus*, identified that metaphysical basis of all necessity and possibility with the idea of the logical form of reality. Though Gendlin's notion of bodily intricacy is clearly not that of logical form, intricacy is to do the same work as Wittgenstein's logical form. It is the self-ordering metaphysical basis for everything else. The skeptical attacks on this idea, from Hume to the later Wittgenstein, lead to the second source of the illusion of explanatory gain. That is that intricacy is an ineffable something that can be obscurely sensed in certain unusual circumstances and that displays and determines an order that is distinct from causal or rational or logical order. But what is ineffable cannot explain anything, but can only give rise to the illusion of having explained something.

4. Conclusion

Gendlin has challenged the adequacy of the terms in which two long-standing metaphysical debates have been conducted. He is looking for a form of realism that is not a simple scientific realism and a mode of behavior or action that is neither rule-obeying or law-instantiating. This is an important undertaking. I do not, however, think that the phenomenological approach he espouses can solve the important problems he raises. A Wittgensteinian approach with its emphasis on practices as pattern-governed activities is much more promising.

Reply to Williams

Professor Williams presents an array of interpretations of my term "intricacy," and shows why each is impossible. She implies that there are no others, but I am grateful for the careful discussion of these. They show how my approach differs and cannot be grasped in old terms. She also finds a series of "tensions" in my work. These will help me to make myself clear.

Williams reads Wittgenstein in the usual way, as if he "looks to the *outward circumstances*." I agree about "circumstances," but he did not look to—he strongly mistrusted—outward observation. He did not assume the world of science, of external perceptions connected by an observer, the world of things over there, the picture-world that is merely presented before us. He rejected the external/internal distinction and spoke instead of doing. Doing is neither outward nor inward. It is not what fills a picture. It is not an observation before us.

Of course, Wittgenstein did not deny that there are things outside us. Just as surely he did not deny what are called "internal" experiences such as pains. For example: "If someone has a pain in his hand . . . one does not comfort the hand, but the sufferer: One looks into his face" (*PI*, 286). Wittgenstein could speak of (what is currently again called) "the human subject," without falling into the subject/object split. He speaks of pain and person as he speaks of words, as part of interactive doing.

I wish Williams shared some of Wittgenstein's skepticism about science. Mine is far less than his. I find a *responsive* order unlike a single conceptual system, but orderly in giving precise results to each procedure, although different results to different procedures. We can see this order both in situations and in science. If the responsive order is omitted, what I mean by "intricacy" does indeed become puzzling.

We need a term for what Williams (and Putnam) rightly need to be able to say: there is *some relation* between "H_2O" and what *was* there before 1750 (and after). But what stays the same is not the pattern. Science changes its patterns every few years; the valences and bonds that are said to connect the H_2 with O are not now those of 1750. On a given date science is arranged with logical consistency from premises, but there is no such consistency across the changes from year to year. This does not mean that the findings of science are just constructions. There Williams and I agree. Science is hard work because obviously there is some feedback that refuses most attempts to characterize and predict it, yet it does yield to some. It is not arbitrary; neither is it just what science says in 1995, 1750, or 2050.

We need what my concept of "intricacy" provides: a way to think about *an orderliness that responds always exactly*, yet always with more than could follow just from the hypotheses. It responds with exactness to different conceptual systems, and is therefore obviously not one of them (nor all, since they contradict each other). It is *more* orderly and *more* demanding than conceptual systems, but open for carrying forward.

For Aristotle, steam and water were different elements. The distinction still holds for cooking, house-heating, and power companies. Polynesians had many kinds of water, and Eskimos of snow. Fish distinguish different kinds of water, and so do we city people. H_2O is only one of many kinds of kinds.

We need terms like "intricacy," "unseparated multiplicity," "responsive order," and "carrying forward." Yes, water *was* H_2O before 1750, but we must examine how the word "was" works here. It asserts a relation, but a more intricate one than was-so or was-not-so. I call it "carrying forward." We *now* assert that how we *now* construe something is not found behind us in memory or record, but does have an important continuity (not an identity) with what we do find recorded there.

The relation is not "was" or "was not," nor is it an aporia of both, was/was-not. Carrying forward is more intricate, and differs in different contexts. It can be entered and spelled out in each context. For example, some say that science begins anew arbitrarily every few years; others insist that all past findings are carefully taken account of. These are two general positions. Entering the intricacy of carrying forward in the case of science, we find, for example, that the later assertion need not achieve everything the earlier ones did, because the questions change. In other respects the earlier findings cannot be wiped out. If later explanations fail to cover them, they remain at least as "anomalies." Modern science need not account for all that Aristotle could (for example, how animals move from themselves), but it must account for the change from ice to steam, if both are now water. These examples show that the specific facets go beyond the two competing generalities.

I share Williams's commitment to account for science. I go further in her direction than Wittgenstein, since I do devise concepts (of a special kind), although no single set, and never as read back. Williams is right that intricacy is "an order without explanation." This is my reversal: Which defines which? Do our activities in the intricacy define our concepts, or must we read one set of those back, to "explain" the intricacy?

Without the concept and the intricacy of "carrying forward" we would lose the reversal, and fall back into the traditional assumption that everything comes to us already conceptualized, patterned, differentiated, cut into "factors" we enumerate. If nothing like intricacy is recognized to govern the factors, they are arbitrary; naive realism shifts easily into constructionism.

I agree with Williams that "it all depends on the *context*," but a context does not come to us in conveniently separated factors that a poet need only "weigh."

To Williams I seem concerned with novelty just for its own sake, but I use novelty to show that certain approaches must be wrong, since novelty would be impossible if they were right.

I agree with Williams that Wittgenstein left the account of science problematic. But did he find the intricacy? Yes, indeed. He showed it in many examples of using a word in new situations, in which it makes new sense in a whole gamut of ways.

Intricacy and the responsive order enable us to establish a new empiricism, and not a naive one. Instead of realism or constructivism, we can study how intricacy *functions* in scientific research, neither arbitrarily nor by antecedently existing patterns, but a responsive order for carrying forward.

No, I do not propose the impossible task of "disentangling nature from convention." Since the Greeks it has been understood that nature (at least human nature) allows itself to be elaborated in many different ways without a line between nature and nurture. But recently this is being forgotten; now it seems there is no (human) nature at all, only conventional construction. I argue that nature has an *order* that is open to being *carried forward*, but always only quite precisely. Like Williams, I deny the notion of merely imposed "conventions."

I am not an ineffablist, nor is Wittgenstein, although he is often read as one. "Ineffable" means what cannot be said. Against this reading Williams rightly points out that the situational meaning is what Wittgenstein *does say* (and says that *we say*). The implicit meaning *is* what is said; it is how the situation is changed by the saying.

Although Williams recognizes that I seek to undermine both simplistic solutions, realism and constructionism, she decomposes my new way into "tensions" between the two old approaches. She insists that I *must* mean either a given "determinate structure" or an "arbitrary imposition of form." So she reads some parts of my work as saying the one, and some the other. Naturally I lose, but her careful points can help me clarify the new alternative.

Her first tension is between forms and something just *un*formed (omitting my more-than-formed, which responds nonarbitrarily to many forms). She has me making a "distinction between intricacy and form," whereas I emphasize that it is always only in and with some existing forms that we can think more than forms. There is no sheer unformed, nor pure form. Everything is formed and distinguished already, but *from* it certain moves let us find more than follows from the form.

Her second tension renders the . . . . . either as a mysterious "mental activity," or as a "placeholder signifying nothing." But the . . . . . is (our being in) the context, the situation, including the words around the blank. She can seem to do without it because she thinks of "the context" as already-defined factors and given possibilities.

"Since Gendlin . . . insists that implicit thought [her term] is not to be viewed as 'thought already there,' what supports Gendlin in his more realistic remarks [her division] about implicit intricacy?" I think her question is: Since what she calls the "thought" is not yet there, how can our sense of the situation be realistic or pertinent to the situation? I answer that what supports me is the role that implicit intricacy plays. It is not the thought that supports the realism. Rather, what determines the thought (when it does come) is that it emerges from (and carries forward) how we live and speak organically in our situations.

The third tension is "either ineffable or describable." Williams sees me chasing what "always eludes description," but my agenda is not to describe. Nor to *explain.* I am concerned with functions performed by a situation, sometimes by a . . . . .

She is right that poetry and therapy are special cases. My main instances include science, everyday speech, difficult practical situations, snide remarks, and philosophical thinking on the edge. I use poetry because many philosophers respect poetry more than philosophy.

I agree that the . . . . . is "a *continuation* sign," but Williams does not recognize its kinship with Wittgenstein because she renders his *knowing how to go on* as "logical entailment." She divides between "atemporal" (logical) and "temporal" (causal) ways of interpreting the role of the . . . . . Kolb also tried these and showed why neither applies.

For me new meanings come in life and situations, not from some *other thing* called "thought." Williams takes meanings as thought, and says that "ordinary thought is patterned." Patterns are indeed always at work, but I don't agree that "ordinary thought *is* patterned." If it were, one could not move to new meanings from it. The term "thought" needs to be newly *thought* in a context in which new meanings are possible.

It is unfortunate that Williams adds the word "whole" to my cat. When the cat's two-ear pattern is painted on a windowpane, I argued that the bird flees *not from a pattern* but from *a cat.*

Now let me take up each of Professor Williams's carefully examined alternatives of what "intricacy" might mean:

1. Intricacy is trivial as "*unique*" detail in Williams's sense, but to dismiss the "not subsumable" one must assume a category system, and

that we care only for what fits it. Even then, implicit intricacy is involved in applying categories, including (among much else) the implicit rules for ignoring intricacy. This is sometimes what we want, but usually we ignore what is called "uniqueness" at our peril; what does not fit our categories can radically affect us. The more unique something seems, the more universal significance it will have, when carried forward and explicated (*ECM*).

So-called details often overthrow our categories. They can force us to new distinctions. But intricacy is neither old nor new distinctions, nor is it unique. New distinctions are ever possible. There are no fixed levels of specificity. The most specific further distinction can overthrow the most overarching one (*ECM*).

2. She grants implications for further speech and action, (3) and that action can change the alternatives a situation seemed to pose, but she thinks of this as merely making a new step retroactively "logically compatible" with what went before. This concerns the "retroactive" revision I talk about (in "TBP"). Retroactively we can fill the gaps, to make an experiential step seem logical. It would be up to me to show that the step was more than that. My point was that in advance we cannot deduce the step logically. Logical compatibility is not what functions when new steps come. It isn't the same thing as the retroactive view. So I deny that "To say that the . . . . . implies the next utterances [or actions] . . . *is in fact to say* that the next utterances can be made logically compatible with the previous ones by interpretation."

4. I don't share the current love of remaining in paradox. When I speak paradoxically I soon move from the seeming paradox to state ordinary but philosophically odd *functions*.

7

Embodied Meaning and Cognitive Science

Mark Johnson

Eugene Gendlin's most profound philosophical achievement has been to show us a way to recover, and to think by means of, the vast realm of embodied meaning that exceeds all our concepts, distinctions, and symbolic forms. In a number of works over the course of his career, Professor Gendlin has brought to our attention the amazing intricacy of our experience, understanding, and thought that has been overlooked and marginalized by mainstream philosophy since the Enlightenment, including, most recently, all first-generation cognitive science. By "first-generation" cognitive science I mean the functionalist view that the mind and reason can be studied in terms of their functions alone and that these functional relations can be represented by formal symbol systems, especially formal logics. On this view, which underlies generative linguistics, information processing psychology, and classical artificial intelligence, the fact of human embodiment plays no essential role in the functions of mind and reason. This conception of disembodied reason is rooted deeply in our Enlightenment view of the person that underlies not just our dominant philosophical theories but also makes up much of our common cultural understanding.

In contrast, "second-generation" cognitive science treats the mind, concepts, meaning, and rationality as embodied, and therefore as not reducible merely to functional relations or programs. Recent empirical studies from such fields as linguistics,[1] psychology,[2] anthropology,[3] philosophy,[4] and neurophysiology[5] have revealed the role of our bodily experience in the grounding and structure of our conceptual systems, in the nature of our reasoning, and in the ways we communicate.

Gendlin approaches the embodiment of meaning from a unique perspective that comes out his intellectual training and clinical work. First, he was educated as a philosopher with a strong background in phenomenology, which accounts for his deep insight into lived experience and the realm of human meaning and order underlying our formal and conceptual distinctions. Second, as a practicing psychotherapist, he is adept at helping us become aware of hitherto hidden dimensions of our experience and understanding. Just as psychotherapeutic methods seek to uncover experiences and structures that have been submerged in the unconscious, similarly, Gendlin's philosophical method highlights dimensions of meaning of which we are hardly ever aware, and that lie beyond formal relations and articulate symbols. His works, therefore, are more than theoretical investigations. They are also practical exercises in self-understanding intended to change our lives. They do this by dipping down, over and over again, into the reservoir of meaning and thought that makes up our embodied experience and that goes beyond our formal distinctions and patterns of thought. Gendlin thus employs a unique blend of phenomenological and psychotherapeutic methods that lets us think and feel our way back into the complex intricacy of our experience from which the structured, formal aspects of meaning and conceptualization arise.

Gendlin's work raises a deep philosophical question concerning the possibility of gaining access to a meaningful order that exceeds formal patterns. What I want to ask is whether Gendlin's way of recovering this submerged continent of embodied understanding can give us any sort of empirically responsible theory of meaning and of inference structure. Second-generation cognitive science certainly shares Gendlin's concern with the embodied and imaginative nature of human understanding and reasoning, and it wants to do justice to the workings of this part of our experience that has been ignored in most theories of meaning, concepts, language, and knowledge. However, Gendlin thinks that it is a serious mistake to assume that our situated understanding consists solely of forms, patterns, and relations that can be symbolically articulated. He argues that, as soon as we specify these forms and patterns, we necessarily overlook or suppress the intricacy of experience that gives rise to these forms. Consequently, Gendlin thinks that even second-generation cognitive science must be guilty of the same mistakes of blindness and exclusion that he thinks plague any structural modes of explanation. My central concern in this paper is to examine whether this charge is legitimate and

MARK JOHNSON

to ask what a satisfactory theory of meaning, understanding, and reason should involve.

The question, in other words, is whether our methods of structural analysis and explanation limit us to no more than naming what we experience as form/structure/pattern and thereby cause us to miss *the way* our experience does what it does—the way it implies, points, opens up, and transforms itself. Do our methods of analysis necessarily cause us to overlook the working of these dimensions of meaning, because we can only articulate them via symbolic forms? Is it possible to give an empirically responsible theoretical account of the embodied dimensions of meaning and understanding that underlie our symbolic forms?

1. Gendlin's Project: Thinking beyond Patterns

Gendlin's main project is to recover the situations out of which forms and patterns emerge. This is the core of his entire philosophical program, and he argues that we suffer from a massive cultural forgetting of all of the intricacy that goes into the making up of our world. As he says, "My project is to think—about, and with—that which exceeds patterns (forms, concepts, definitions, categories, distinctions, rules . . . . .)."[6] Notice the precision and economy of this summary thesis. Gendlin wants not only to *theorize about* these nonformal dimensions of meaning, figuring out what they are and how they work. In addition, and more importantly, he also wants to think *in* and *with* them in this very inquiry, for only in that way can we grasp that which exceeds forms.

But now we might ask why it should be necessary to try to think in these ways. Gendlin's answer is that the failure to do so condemns us to never being able to understand who we are, how language works, or how we reason. A mode of thinking that employs only forms, distinctions, patterns, and rules will necessarily miss the very embodied situational experiences that make these forms meaningful in the first place. The fateful error, which Gendlin attributes not just to Western philosophy, but to our general cultural understanding, is to miss a large part of what goes into making something meaningful to us. We then are tempted to mistake the forms for that which they inform, and we fool ourselves into thinking that it is the forms alone that make something what it is—that make it real and knowable.

Such a strategy of exclusion leaves out the body and our situated, embodied practices, along with all their intricate, complex meaning. Lakoff and I have documented the denial of the body in contemporary theories of meaning and mind, and we have traced this prejudice at least as far back as Enlightenment philosophy.[7] In order to get a sense of what this suppressed bodily dimension of meaning and experience consists in, let us consider one of Gendlin's favorite examples, that of a poet searching for the right words in an unfinished line:

> The poet reads the written lines over and over, listens, and senses what these lines need (want, demand, imply, ...). Now the poet's hand rotates in the air. The gesture says *that.* Many good lines offer themselves; they try to say, but do not say—*that.* The blank is *more precise.* Although some are good lines, the poet rejects them.
>
> That . . . . . seems to lack words, but no. It knows the language, since it understands—and rejects—these lines that came. So it is not pre-verbal; Rather, it knows what must be said, and knows that these lines don't precisely say that. It knows like a gnawing knows what was forgotten, but it is new in the poet, and perhaps new in the history of the world.
>
> Now, although I don't know most of you, I do know one of your secrets. I know you have written poetry. So I can ask you: Isn't that how it is? This . . . . . must be directly referred to (felt, experienced, sensed, had, ...). Therefore, whatever terms we use for such a blank, that terms also needs our direct reference.
>
> The blank brings something new. That function is not performed by the linguistic forms alone. Rather, it functions *between* two sets of linguistic forms. The blank is not just the already written lines, but rather the *felt sense* from re-reading them, and *that* performs a function needed to lead to the next lines.[8]

Whether in poetry or in the activities of our day to day lives, we all know the kind of experience Gendlin is describing—that experience of, first, coming up with new candidate words for completing the line; second, of testing them out to see whether they are "right," or at least "better"; and, third, of finding the words that seem appropriate and that carry us forward in our thinking. Several important points need to be emphasized regarding such experiences and the ways they reveal important aspects of meaning and reasoning.

1. There is a nonlinguistic dimension—the nonformal side of the relation between our intricate experience and our words, symbols, or other patterns—that gets its fulfilment in and through the words we try out as candidates to complete the line. This other part, this . . . . . , is not itself linguistic, in that it is not the word(s) we are seeking for.

2. Yet, neither is it utterly distinct nor separable from the words or forms or distinctions. That is why Gendlin says that it is not preverbal,

since it "knows" when we come up with the best (or at least a better) linguistic or symbolic expression to fulfill it. Gendlin cautions us against the mistake of thinking that there are two distinct and autonomous sides of any experience—the felt sense and the formal expression—that could exist without each other. These are not two independent entities that are only externally related. Instead, they are two dimensions of a single, ongoing activity, each one intrinsically related to the other.

Thus, Gendlin argues that we must never think of the formal, patterned, "objective" side as somehow copying the subjective side, for that would entail that the words could stand in for, or represent, the subjective side, and thereby replace it. As he says, "Between the subjective and objective sides there is not a relation of representation or likeness. The words don't copy the blank. . . . The explication releases *that* tension, which was the . . . . . But what the blank was is not just lost or altered; rather, *that* tension is *carried forward* by the words."[9] So, we do not have two independent entities externally related, but one continuously developing situation that we identify, via reflection, as having these two intimately interwoven or blended dimensions. It is for this reason that the words or formal distinctions are not adequate in themselves. If they copied the "subjective" side, then that side would be eliminable, replaceable by the forms and patterns. Conversely, the subjective side, the . . . . . , is what it is only in relation to the forms that give expression to it.

3. Notice especially that this nonformal side is not vague, mushy, empty, or chaotic. It is, as Gendlin says, extremely *precise*. It knows which words or forms are appropriate to carry forward the meaning that is developing. It is so precise that it rejects many candidates as inadequate. It is vague, but only in a rich positive sense, namely, it is full of possibilities that are not yet realized, and so it only *seems* to lack precision. I would say that it is full of embodied *structure*, if that term had not been lumped together by Gendlin along with "form" and "pattern."

4. The blank, the . . . . . that the poet seeks to realize or fulfill, "carries forward" the meaning that has been developing in the poem, or in some ongoing experience we are having, and it points toward what is to come next. Gendlin says that the situation "implies" (in a very broad and enriched sense) what is to come next as the situation develops. It implies various possibilities for experience, not in the sense that they are logically deducible from the situation as it is presently formed, but rather insofar as the situation can be carried forward by our pursuing one or more of these possibilities.

So, we are living in and through a growing, changing situation that opens up toward new possibilities and that changes as it develops. That is the way human meaning works, and none of this happens without our bodies, or without our embodied interactions within environments that we inhabit and that change along with us. A "situation," as Gendlin uses the term, thus has as two of its abstract aspects an organism and its environment. But it would be a mistake, as Lewontin and Levins observe, to think of the organism and its environment(s) as autonomous, independent entities that are only externally related. Rather, organisms and environments are co-evolving aspects of the experiential processes that make up situations.[10]

This explains why we should not think that our embodied meaning, understanding, and reasoning could ever be adequately thought or grasped by our concepts, symbols, rules, or patterns. Our situations, with all of their summing up, implying, and carrying forward, are *embodied situations*. Meaning, therefore, is embodied. And neither the "subjective side" (the nonformal, the nonconceptual, the . . . . .) nor the "objective side" (the forms, patterns, words, concepts) is the meaning in itself. Meaning resides in their situational relation as that relationship develops and changes.

Gendlin is both careful and elegant in spelling out the complexity, the intricacy, and the richness of situations as they work in our lives.[11] But the most urgent question that his subtle analyses raise for me is whether it is possible to incorporate these profound insights into a more adequate cognitive science. Over the last fifteen years George Lakoff and I, along with many others working in second-generation cognitive science, have believed that our studies of the embodied and imaginative nature of concepts, meaning, and reasoning are steps toward a cognitive science that does justice to the embodiment of all human understanding. Recently, however, Gendlin has argued that our methods do not really allow us to get at the kinds of nonformal thinking that he is investigating. Let us look at his argument as to why no account of metaphor, or even embodied metaphorical meaning, can capture that part of thought that exceeds all patterns.

2. Embodied Metaphorical Meaning

Besides the phenomenological tradition, the only major orientation to take seriously the embodiment of meaning is cognitive linguistics, or, a little more broadly, second-generation cognitive science. Cognitive linguistics argues that model theory, objectivist semantics, and all formalist approaches that rely on formal logic are necessarily inadequate, because they cannot account for either the embodied or the imaginative dimensions of meaning and conceptual structure. The fundamental assumption of cognitive linguistics is that meaning and value are grounded in the nature of our bodies and brains, as they develop through ongoing interactions with various environments that have physical, social, and cultural dimensions. The nature of our embodied experience motivates and constrains how things are meaningful to us. But besides being embodied, meaning is also imaginative, in that it involves image schemas, metaphors, cognitive prototypes, metonymies, and other types of imaginative structure out of which our world is worked.

Classical objectivist semantics treats meaning as an objective relation between inherently meaningless symbolic forms and mind-independent states of affairs existing in the world. Languages are regarded as formal systems to be modeled using formal logics. The vast majority of semantic theory and theory of knowledge in the twentieth century is some version of this basic idea, from generative linguistics, to model theory, to artificial intelligence, to theories of epistemic justification. Such views give rise to the view that all meaning is propositional, and this, in turn, supports "truth-functional" theories of meaning, in which the meaning of a proposition is taken to be the conditions under which it would be true or false, that is, the conditions under which it would have a truth-value. Theories of knowledge from this perspective are theories of representation concerning how a proposition can stand in a correspondence relation to some state of affairs in the world.

What all orientations of this kind miss is the embodied and imaginative nature of concepts and the reasoning we do with them. None of them has any place for the role our bodies play in how we experience and make sense of things, since they mistakenly assume that words and concepts can get their meanings solely by picking out objectively existing states of affairs. Moreover, there is no place in these accounts for the central role played by various kinds of imaginative structure in our concepts and reasoning. The reason for this is that concepts are supposed to be "literal" and either to fit or not fit the world. These are supposed to be objective matters, having nothing to do with how people make sense of things, and especially having nothing to do with imaginative devices such as metaphor, which is thought to lack any determinate literal meaning (and, hence, any determinate truth-conditions).

In radical contrast with this traditional objectivist view, recent cognitive science has revealed that the human conceptual system, human languages, and human reasoning are all irreducibly and pervasively metaphoric and imaginative in nature. Furthermore, we have discovered that these metaphors that make up our situations are grounded in our embodied interactions. The metaphors and other imaginative structures that make up our embodied understanding are not merely in the *words* we use—they are not merely linguistic. Rather, they make up the very structure of our embodied understanding, and they are thereby structures of our conceptual system, of our inferences based on those concepts, and of the language that emerges from those concepts. That is why we call the metaphors "experiential" and not just linguistic, because we are claiming that our very understanding—our mode of being in and having a world—is metaphoric and imaginative.

Obviously, it is impossible here to survey all the types of embodied, imaginative structures of understanding that we have been studying, but they would include at least the following: prototype effects in categories, radial categories, image schemas, semantic frames, experiential metaphors, and basic-level categorization. To give some idea of the kinds of structures involved, let us consider briefly the nature of semantic frames, image schemas, and experiential metaphors.

Semantic Frames and Idealized Cognitive Models

Human beings understand their world by means of idealized cognitive models[12] for the kinds of entities, events, and situations we encounter in our everyday experience. Recent empirical studies in lexical semantics have shown that words do not map directly onto states of affairs in the world, but rather are defined by their roles in idealized models of situations, which are holistic structures called "frames."[13] Words get their meanings by the roles they play in frames. A semantic field of words is a group of words defined with respect to different roles in a single frame (e.g., "buy," "sell," "goods," "price" are defined relative to a commercial event in general, for which we have a "commercial exchange" frame). A single situation in the world can be framed in different, and often mutually inconsistent, ways. When frames have structure that extends over time, they are called "scenarios" or "scripts." And when they characterize our common understanding of how something works in the world, they are called "folk theories." Frames are *imaginative*, not only because they are idealized models that do not exist objectively "in the world," but also because they are defined partly by image schemas and experiential metaphors.

Image Schemas

Systems of spatial relations have been found to differ considerably among the languages of the world. However, they all appear to use a single set of "primitive" image schemas, that is, schematic mental images. Examples

MARK JOHNSON

of such image schemas include containers, paths, links, compulsive force, attraction, contact, balance, center-periphery, orientations (e.g., above-below, front-back, up-down). All of these are recurring structures of our bodily interactions in the world, and they exist across *all* our perceptual modalities (visual, tactile, olfactory, aural, etc.). They are not fixed structures or images, but rather dynamic patterns of our interactions within various evolving environments. At present, they are being modeled in terms of known types of neural structures in the brain, such as topographic maps, center-surround architecture, orientation tuning cells, etc. Such modeling indicates that image schemas can be characterized neurally, and that their peculiar properties arise from the neural structures peculiar to our brains, given the nature of our ongoing interactions with the kinds of environments we inhabit.

Image schemas define spatial inference patterns. For instance, if object A is inside container B, which is inside container C, then object A is inside container C. Such spatial inference patterns can be the basis for abstract inference patterns. Conceptual metaphorical mappings appear to preserve image-schematic structure (e.g., patterns of containment), and, in so doing, they map spatial inference patterns onto abstract inference patterns.[14] Thus, for instance, we reason abstractly that if concept A is "contained within" concept B, which is "contained within" concept C, then A is contained in C—that is, if A is in B, and B is in C, then A is in C. There is considerable evidence of this sort to suggest that abstract reason arises from the interplay of metaphors and image schemas, and that it is grounded in our bodily experience.[15]

Since image schemas are not in the "objective world," but arise from properties of our bodies and brains acting within environments, they do not have a purely objective character. But since they are determined in part by our biology and by the world as we experience it, they are not purely subjective either.

One of the most philosophically important consequences of what has been discovered about image schemas is that they both characterize basic inference patterns and are themselves characterized by the nature of our bodies and brains, relative to our purposes and situational interactions. The idea that inference patterns can have a bodily basis is utterly inconsistent, both with objectivist views of pure, transcendent reason, as well as with deconstructivist views of reason as the arbitrary play of an unfettered imagination.

Experiential Metaphor

Research in cognitive linguistics has revealed a vast system of thousands of mappings across conceptual domains that permit us to understand more abstract concepts in terms of more concepts tied to our embodied interactions.[16] These mappings preserve image schemas, and thereby allow us to use the "logic" of physical space and our spatial experience as the basis for abstract inference. They permit abstract inference by mapping knowledge about concrete domains onto abstract domains. The "container logic" of classical Aristotelian syllogistic logic is a good example of this bodily based reasoning and of the way meaning is embodied. Over the last two decades numerous studies have appeared that show how our most basic concepts in virtually every area of human life (such as, morality, politics, economics, social relations, science, art, and religion) are understood by us via experiential metaphorical mappings.

For a number of years Lakoff and I called these "conceptual" metaphors, in order to emphasize two basic points: (1) that metaphors are not mere matters of words, but actually structure our concepts and our reasoning; and (2) that they are not merely formal structures, but rather are embodied imaginative structures. Since many people have misinterpreted the term "conceptual metaphor" as referring only to abstract, formal, propositional structure, when, in fact, these metaphors depend on our nonpropositional embodied experience, it is perhaps more accurate to call these "experiential" metaphors. This captures the fact that they are not just intellectual forms, but rather are the very stuff of our world as we experience, conceptualize, and reason about it.

As an example of embodied, experiential metaphor, I gave an extended account in *The Body in the Mind* of some of the ways in which metaphors of balance are tied into our bodily experience of balance. Beginning with the *balance* image schema that is present in our bodily sense of being balanced and losing our balance, I then argued that our other, less obviously bodily, senses of balance were metaphorical mappings that carry forward a basic *balance* image schema. These metaphorical senses included the notions of psychological balance, emotional balance, perceptual balance (as in our sense that a painting is balanced and well ordered with respect to its color values, negative and positive space, and visual "forces"), moral and political balance (as in equality, justice, fairness), and mathematical balance (as in arithmetical equality, or balancing of equations).

The point of this analysis was to help us to stop thinking of meaning as disembodied and formal, by showing how it grows out of our embodied experience in the world, which it calls up and draws upon even in our most abstract conceptual understanding. It is in this sense that meaning is embodied and imaginative. It is in this sense that we speak of metaphor as experiential and conceptual. On this view, even our understanding of "balancing" a mathematical equation is tied up with our mundane sense of bodily balancing. The balancing we do with, and feel within, our bodies is submerged and not attended to in our mathematical reasoning, but it is nonetheless there, by virtue in part of the *balance* schema that works in our metaphorical understanding of mathematical equality and balance.

3. Gendlin's Critique of Cognitive Linguistics

Gendlin applauds the emphasis that cognitive linguistics places on embodied meaning:

> Both Lakoff (1987) and Johnson (1987) in their new books talk of something that is not just a pattern or a logical form. Johnson speaks of "concrete and dynamic, embodied imaginative schemata," which are surely not just logical patterns or images or diagrams. Lakoff talks of something "non-propositional." They have taken up an excellent strategic position, right on the interface, where they can assert both this embodied character, and also work on the logical side to collect and formulate what I have been calling "patterns that can be the same."[17]

Although Gendlin approves of our focus on the bodily basis of meaning, he worries that cognitive linguistics works exclusively "on the logical side," and thus risks missing the full richness of the situation itself. The source of the problem, according to him, is that the cross-domain mappings that define experiential metaphors (i.e., the mappings of entities and structures in one domain onto another domain of a different kind) are seen as being too *structural*. Gendlin proposes that "the embodied non-propositionals should not be thought of as if they were commonalities, classes, structures, or image schemata, although, we do also want to formulate those. I will try to show that the embodied non-propositionals function differently, not like commonalities or image schemata."[18] Gendlin's strategy is to show that we are not limited merely to thinking "*with* forms," which is what he thinks cognitive semantics is restricted to. In addition, we can learn to think "how they (the forms) are exceeded in use."[19]

I will argue that Gendlin's criticisms bear only on the classical theory of metaphor and not on a cognitive semantic theory. In fact, cognitive semantics lends empirical support to Gendlin's point of view. Still, it must be acknowledged that no current theories, either those of cognitive semantics or any other perspectives, have so far given an adequate account of the nonpropositional dimensions of metaphor, or of meaning generally. I shall end up suggesting that, indeed, this inability to capture that which exceeds structure is a fundamental problem for all theories of meaning. About this, Gendlin is right, but his own account has certain limitations, too. In particular, it is not clear how his view can lead to empirical generalizations of the sort needed for a semantic theory and a theory of reasoning.

Gendlin's criticisms are directed against the traditional view of metaphor as a pairing of preexisting commonalities between two conceptual domains that exist independently, each with its own fixed structure. Gendlin correctly challenges this view on four counts. I want to support each of Gendlin's four critiques with evidence from cognitive semantics, and thereby to show that cognitive semantics has considerable resources for a theory of meaning and of metaphor of the sort Gendlin is proposing.

1. According to the classical view, a metaphor operates by highlighting preexisting similarities between two conceptual domains: "Classically, metaphor was said to be a crossing between two single situations."[20] The metaphor supposedly pairs up fixed structure in one domain (the source) with that in another domain (the target) so as to emphasize features that are similar across the two domains. The metaphor "Love is a journey," for example, would be understood under the classical view as matching preexisting features of journeys with those of love that are the same or similar.

Gendlin correctly observes that this cannot be all that metaphor does, for then there would really be no point in using metaphor. Beyond its possible rhetorical effects, such a metaphor could be replaced by a list of literal similarities between the two domains. Thus, Gendlin's first modification of the classical view is to insist that what is crossed in a metaphor are not two preexistent situations, but rather a whole "use-family" of the source domain term with the present situation in which the term operates as a metaphor.[21] By a "use-family" Gendlin means the entire family of situations in which a term has been, is, or can be, used.

Gendlin's notion of a "use-family" is captured in cognitive semantics by the notion of *semantic frames*.[22] Frame semantics shows that any given term will get its meanings relative to one or more semantic frames in which it is situated. As we saw earlier, within a given frame a term is defined in relation to a cluster of other terms that fall within that frame. For instance, one semantic frame for the term *drive* would include a complex cluster of terms related to all of the things we do with automobiles, including such terms as "vehicle," "start," "accelerate," "steer," "brake," "car," "stop," and many, many more. This would be merely *one* of many possible frames, all of which would form a very complex category structure for the concept *drive*, including frames that involve boats, golfballs, baseballs, hammers and nails, progress toward a goal, and many other frames.

Gendlin is correct, then, to insist that the whole use-family comes into play in metaphor, and that no traditional similarity theory of metaphor can be adequate to this dimension of metaphor. Metaphors are almost never simply matters of matching preexisting cross-domain similarities. The problem is not just metaphor, but rather the entire objectivist and literalist theory of concepts that underlies the similarity view. By employing a frame semantic analysis of concepts, cognitive semantics thereby avoids this kind of reductionism and literalism, and it is compatible with Gendlin's notion of the use-family.

2. Gendlin's second criticism is that "the commonalities do not determine the metaphor. Rather, from the metaphor, and only after it makes sense, is a new set of commonalities derived."[23] Again, Gendlin is right to claim that in many cases the meaning of a metaphor is not determined by some underlying set of features that are common between the source and target domains. In *Metaphors We Live By* Lakoff and I argued this same point at length by showing that in many cases we perceive similarities only as a result of the metaphorical mapping that induces them.[24] We described five kinds of situations in which metaphors "create" similarities. The crux of our argument is that many metaphors are based on *experiential correlations* that then make possible our subsequent perception of commonalities between the two domains. For example, while there is no intrinsic commonality or similarity between "more" and "up," we have the basic conceptual metaphor *more is up* in our culture (and apparently in all cultures) that is *based on* experiential correlations of the following sort: when we add more entities to a pile, the profile of the pile rises (goes *up*) in our perceptual field. The same experience occurs when we add more liquid to a container—the level rises. This experiential correlation is one possible basis for the *more is up* metaphor (as in, "The number of murders committed *keeps going up* each year," "The divorce rate is *rising*," "The gross national product *reached a peak* last quarter, and now its starting *down*"). Because of the *more is up* metaphorical mapping, it then seems natural to us that there are commonalities perceived between "more" and "up" that we do not perceive between "less" and "up."

In *The Body in the Mind* I also gave an extended example of the experiential correlations that ground the *purposes and destinations* metaphor and that create our sense of commonalities between the domains of physical motion and the achievement of some intention or purpose. The experiential basis for the metaphor is the frequent correlation that we experience between the achievement of a purpose or the satisfaction of an intention, on the one hand, and movement through space to some destination, on the other. An example of this would be the case of a baby satisfying her purpose of getting the rattle by crawling to the place where it is and grabbing it. The experiential pairing of moving to a destination with achieving a purpose gives rise to the following *purposes are destinations* mapping:

Physical Motion Domain		*Intentional Domain*
Starting location A	⟶	Initial state
Goal (final location B)	⟶	Final (desired) state
Motion along path (from A to B)	⟶	Intermediate actions

Our sense that there are commonalities between the domains of physical movement and achieving purposes is thus based on this metaphorical conceptual mapping, which is, in turn, based on the experiential correlation between structures in the two domains, as noted earlier.

It is a mistake to think of a metaphor as a set of similarity statements in the first place. A set of cross-domain mappings *is not* a set of similarity statements. In order to see this crucial point, consider the mapping for one of our culture's basic conventional metaphors for love. Someone who experiences their love relationship to have "hit a dead-end" and to be "going nowhere" is conceptualizing love as a journey, according to the following conceptual mapping:

The *Love is a Journey* Metaphor

Journey Domain	*Love Domain*
Travelers	Lovers
Vehicle	Love relationship
Impediments to travel	Difficulties
Destination	Common goals

This mapping, which underlies the *love is a journey* metaphor, is the basis for all kinds of inferences we make about our love relationship. Based on these ontological correspondences given above, we use our knowledge of the source domain (journeying) to understand and reason about the target domain (love). Consequently, the way we conceptualize, reason about, and talk about our love relationship will be determined by the epistemic entailments that are based on the ontological correspondences given above. Which parts of our knowledge are brought into play, and how they are developed, will depend on the context. If, for example, one of the lovers should complain that, "This just isn't going anywhere," we can use the epistemic correspondences (based on our knowledge of the source domain of journeying) to understand what they mean and to reason about what might be done. If the love-vehicle isn't moving ("going anywhere"), then there must be a reason. Perhaps there is a breakdown in the relationship (i.e., the "vehicle" has ceased to function properly). Then we must decide what is malfunctioning, whether it can be repaired, and whether it is worth the effort that would be required to fix it (i.e., "to get it going again"). Or, perhaps the relationship isn't going anywhere because it (the relationship-vehicle) has run out of fuel. Maybe there's a way to energize the relationship to get it going again. Or, we might find that we're not going anywhere because our progress is blocked (as in, "We've hit a road-block in our marriage"). Then we have to figure out whether we can go around, or through, whatever is blocking our path (where, for instance, the metaphorical blockage might be a financial, sexual, or communication problem).

Notice that the reasoning we do in this case is *not* based just on commonalities or similarities between the two domains. There is a shared image-schematic structure between these two domains, namely, the *source-path-goal* schema. On the basis of this shared structure, we go further to take the logic of the source domain and project it onto the target domain to give rise to *new* structure in the target domain. This projection is actually cognitively constitutive—it is a partial structuring of our concept of love. It is not the case that the two conceptual domains, journeying and love, each had the entity "vehicle" in them, and that the metaphor merely highlights these preexisting common features or similarities. Instead, "vehicle" is an entity in the source domain that gets mapped onto the love relationship in the target domain. Only on the basis of this mapping can we then draw the appropriate epistemic entailments about how we might possibly get a *stalled* relationship going, or *get beyond* or *through the roadblock*, or *overcome* some *obstacle* in our path. We understand why the "course of true love never did run smooth" in terms of inferences like these that are based on our knowledge of the source domain. In itself, a love relationship has no vehicles, no roadblocks, no dead-ends, no breakdowns. It acquires all of these, and the epistemic entailments that go along with them, from the metaphorical mapping.

Notice that the metaphor doesn't work by specifying some fixed similarity statements concerning the two domains (journeying and love). Rather, based on the correspondences, we make inferences, given our knowledge of the source domain. Consequently, the structure of a concept is not an all-or-nothing matter. It is not the case that conceptual structure either preexists in a fixed and completed realm of its own, or else that it is all radically constructed. As with our concept *love*, most of our basic concepts are defined by multiple conceptual metaphors that are sometimes mutually inconsistent (though not incoherent). There will always be preexisting conceptual structure in both the source and target domains (as the invariance hypothesis demands), but conceptual metaphor will also be partially constitutive of our grasp of the target domain, by virtue of *additional* structure carried over from the "logic" of the source domain.

Work in cognitive semantics, therefore, has given a body of evidence that supports Gendlin's claim that metaphors are often the basis for *derived* commonalities between two domains of experience. Moreover, it goes beyond Gendlin's account to provide a theory of how these apparent commonalities can emerge for us in the first place.

3. Gendlin's third modification of the classical theory rests on his rejection of the view that a metaphor is defined by a single pattern of commonalities between the two domains. Instead, he argues, "a metaphor generates an endless chain of commonalities, not a single pattern."[25] His argument is that any present situation does not just contain structures or patterns that define the "here and now"; rather, a situation implicitly contains all the possibilities for what will happen in the future and how things will change over time.

Certainly, any metaphor has a measure of open-endedness about it, since it can be extended in many directions, subject to certain limits on the nature of the mapping.[26] In this sense, a metaphor used in a present situation has the potential to be elaborated in many possible ways, developing in a limited set of directions opened up by the mapping. But to say that there is a "limitless" chain of commonalities that can be generated seems to be an overstatement, at best. If Gendlin means only that there are a large number of future situations in which the metaphor could generate new meaning, then he is correct. However, the commonalities generated are indeed "limited" by the nature of the mapping and by the kinds of situations human beings can experience. Otherwise, a given metaphor could conceivably mean *anything*, which is clearly not true of metaphors in use within actual human contexts.

4. Gendlin's fourth and last criticism is the most profound, for it claims that the meaning of a metaphor is never reducible to a set of commonalities, patterns, or forms. Since Lakoff and I define metaphors as cross-domain conceptual mappings, it does seem that Gendlin is criticizing our kind of theory as being too structure oriented, and thereby missing an order that exceeds forms.

But just what is Gendlin's argument for this key claim? First, he defines a pattern as a fixed, logically consistent, unified conceptual structure. For Gendlin, a pattern must remain the same wherever it is asserted or affirmed, and it must be capable of being either true or false.[27]

Based on this narrow conception of a pattern as specified within formal logic, Gendlin's argument runs as follows: a metaphor may be used in two succeeding situations, such that a pattern that we would deny in the first situation would then be affirmed in the very next situation. But, if these patterns really are inconsistent, then the meaning of the metaphor cannot be derived from the original pattern alone. There must be something beyond the patterns that gives rise to them. He gives the example of a poetic line in which a girl standing in a field is called a rose. In our initial understanding of the metaphor we are unlikely to think that the pattern "rooted to the ground" would be part of the meaning. But what if, in the very next line, the poet says that she "stood stock still, timeless, rooted to the ground"? Obviously, "rooted to the ground" *can* mean something and be appropriate in that context. It could say a great deal about the kind of person she is. Gendlin argues that the metaphor of the girl as a rose cannot, therefore, be defined by patterns that represent commonalities that remain unchanged across all situations.

While Gendlin is correct in observing that we must account for the open-endness of metaphor, I want to suggest that there is something misleading about the way he frames the issue. From the perspective of cognitive semantics, this is not a case of, first, denying that the proposition "she is rooted to the ground" applies, and then, second, affirming that it does apply. Rather, this is a case of how our knowledge of the source domain comes into play as a situation develops. It *is* part of our knowledge about roses that they are rooted to the ground. In the first instance, however, *that* particular knowledge is not brought forth by the situation. In Gendlin's terms we would say that the crossing of the use-family of "rose" and the situation does not highlight *rootedness*. But as the situation develops in the poem, that very knowledge about roses becomes quite important, and it becomes part of the inferences we might draw about the girl.

So it is somewhat misleading to describe this example, as Gendlin does, as a case of first denying the proposition "she is rooted to the ground" and then turning around and affirming it. It is far more accurate to say that, *as the present situation develops*, we make use of different parts of the mapping, along with the corresponding knowledge we have about that particular part of the source domain. What was potentially present in the logic of the source domain becomes actualized within a particular context. George Lakoff and Mark Turner have recently employed this cognitive semantic theory to show how poetic metaphors can be creative by drawing on typically unused parts of conventional metaphorical mappings.[28]

4. Meaning That Exceeds Structure

We have seen that the traditional similarity theory of metaphor can treat only the fixed, preexisting conceptual structures. Consequently, it necessarily misses the nonpropositional and embodied experiential basis out of which the formal structure emerges, and relative to which it means and infers what it does. I have argued that cognitive semantics, with its emphasis on the embodied and imaginative character of meaning and reason, can explain many of the semantic phenomena that Gendlin rightly sees traditional metaphor theory as being incapable of explaining. Nonetheless, Gendlin correctly asserts that there is an inherent limitation to any theory of metaphor (or meaning generally) that gives only a structural analysis. *What will always be missed by such a view is the affective dimension, the mood, and the felt sense that lies at the heart of our experience of meaning.*

Cognitive semantics must face this limitation of its methods and recognize that it can never tell the whole story about meaning. But this is a limitation that will pertain to *any* empirically responsible theory. The reason for this inherent limitation is the following: an adequate semantic theory must make empirical generalizations concerning the phenomena it studies. These generalizations are not necessarily limited to propositional rules or principles. As we have seen, in cognitive semantics the generalizations can include such structures as cross-domain conceptual mappings of the sort that define conceptual metaphors. The reason cognitive semantics can go beyond the traditional theories of meaning is because it recognizes these other, nonpropositional, forms of explanatory generalization. In addition to conceptual metaphor mappings, there are metonymic correspondences and also counterpart relations between entities within different "mental spaces."[29]

However, cognitive semantics is limited to identifying and making generalizations about *structures* of various sorts (whether those structures are propositional, nonpropositional, image-schematic, or logical), in order to explain semantic phenomena and inferential structure. While I acknowledge this methodological limitation of cognitive semantics, I want to ask whether Gendlin's way of revealing the "order that exceeds forms" can actually lead to generalizations about meaning and inference, or whether it can only serve as a corrective to other semantic theories. In other words, my final question is whether Gendlin's view can contribute constructively to a semantics of natural language, or whether it can only point out the shortcomings of all semantic theories.

As an example of both the power and limitations of cognitive semantics, I want to consider a particular experiential metaphor, in order to examine its embodied dimensions, and also to determine what in the metaphor cannot be captured by our analysis. Steven Fesmire has given an extended analysis of the experiential metaphor *mental disquietude is inhibited breathing*,[30] in which we understand various aspects of mental unrest and distress in terms of the phenomena associated with inhibited breathing. This experiential metaphor is typical of a general conceptual pattern people use to understand the mental realm in terms of the more concrete and highly articulated operations of the body. Eve Sweetser has named this universal generic mapping the *mind as body* metaphor, and she has documented its pervasiveness across many cultures.[31]

The *mental disquietude is inhibited breathing* metaphor is the basis for a large number of related expressions that we use to describe anxiety and mental dysfunction, such as:

"She was *choking with anxiety*."
"Harry *choked* on the exam."
"Until she arrived, I was *breathless with anticipation*."
"Don't get *all choked up* over a little test."
"Let's *take a breather* from this debate."
"The interrogation was *suffocating me*."
"Your solution to the problem is certainly a *breath of fresh air!*"

Our understanding of mental disquietude in terms of the physical experience of inhibited breathing is but a part of a larger metaphor system in which we conceptualize mental functioning as breathing. The *mental functioning is breathing* metaphor consists of the following mapping:

Breathing		*Mental Functioning*
Flow of air	⟶	Flow of ideas
Constricted air flow	⟶	Disrupted flow of ideas
Inhibited breathing	⟶	Mental disquietude
Restored air flow	⟶	Revived free-flow of ideas

Fesmire identifies other related metaphors that interweave with *mental functioning is breathing*, especially those involving the relation of breath ("spirit") to consciousness, and the notion of the *flow* of ideas in thought. But, for our purposes, it is his analysis of the bodily grounding of the *mental disquietude is inhibited breathing* metaphor that is most relevant. He observes that the metaphor is based on a strong experiential correlation between mental tension and restricted breathing. Restricted breathing can generate tremendous anxiety and mental distress within us. Also, heightened anxiety is often accompanied by inhibited breathing.

Noting these experiential correlations, Frederick Perls even went so far as to claim that "suppression of excitement produces the breathing difficulty which is anxiety."[32]

We can see how this correlation of anxiety with inhibited breathing gives rise to the *inhibited breathing* metaphor by examining three kinds of mental disquietude.

1. Consider the case of actual restricted breathing due to a blocked air passage. If something is not done to relieve the blockage, you could die. That is why inhibited breathing generates tremendous anxiety. Once breathing is restored, you can, quite literally, *breathe again*, and this is accompanied by a felt lessening of anxiety.

2. Consider, secondly, a situation of high anxiety, such as when you are in a life-threatening situation or are subject to some other highly stressful condition. Your mental tension will typically be accompanied by, as its physical counterpart, inhibited breathing. As the anxiety lessens and the tension releases, you can *breathe once again*. This experiential pairing of mental tension and inhibited breathing can give rise to an experiential metaphor. The emerging metaphor can be seen in the ambiguous case where someone in extreme mental distress complains that she is "suffocating." She might, indeed, be actually finding it hard to breathe. But she might also mean, via metaphor, that she is suffering great anxiety.

3. This emerging experiential metaphor can then be extended to cover clear cases of metaphor in which there is no actual restricted breathing involved. To find a relationship, or a high-pressure meeting, or a heated discussion, *suffocating* may not involve any kind of apparent physiological distress. However, even in these explicit cases of metaphorical understanding, the physiological symptoms are often just below the surface of consciousness, and they are operating even though we are not presently aware of them. It is often quite difficult to distinguish the suffocation you experience in a relationship from an actual sense of physical tension and constricted breathing.

The key point I want to make with this example is that the meaning this metaphor has, and the way it operates in our conceptualization and reasoning, is thoroughly dependent on its bodily, experiential basis. In other words, how the metaphor works in our thinking depends on experiential pairings, feelings, and the felt sense that accompanies certain types of situations. Cognitive semantics can describe this experiential basis of meaning, in the same way I have given a very partial account of the *mental disquietude is inhibited breathing* metaphor. What cognitive semantics cannot capture in its generalizations, however, is the affective dimension of this experiential grounding of meaning. We can *point* to it,

MARK JOHNSON

but we cannot include in our mappings and generalizations the *felt sense* that is part of what the metaphor means to us, nor can we include the way it works in our experience.

As far as I know, there is no theory of meaning or metaphor that can capture this deeply embodied dimension *via empirical generalizations.* I am attracted to the cognitive semantics orientation chiefly because it can at least talk about and explore embodied meaning, whereas most semantic theories are objectivist in nature, and they pay no attention to the embodied and imaginative nature of human concepts and reasoning.

What I find that Professor Gendlin does better than anyone else is to lead us back down into that vast submerged continent of meaning that exceeds our logical forms and patterns. As I said earlier, he does this by an almost incantational technique that helps us dip down further and further into the situation in which meaning is *happening* here and now. Gendlin's remarkable blending of phenomenological and psychothera-peutic methods can open up hitherto hidden dimensions of the process of meaning and experience.

But what Gendlin's method cannot do is to give us semantic and inferential generalizations that purport to explain the phenomena of meaning and reasoning. Nor does he pretend to do this. Instead, he wants to assist us to think about, and with, an order that exceeds our logical forms and patterns.

What we need, then, if we want a more empirically adequate theory of human meaning, understanding, and reasoning is an ongoing dia-logue between cognitive semantics and Gendlin's method for recovering the meaning and thought that lies beneath logical forms. We need to explore back and forth across the shifting boundaries that distinguish structures and forms from the embodied realm of experience out of which those forms emerge and in relation to which those forms have meaning. We need to seek semantic and inferential generalizations, but always keeping in mind what those generalizations miss. As Professor Gendlin says, we need to learn to think, not only *about* that order which exceeds and grounds forms, but also to think *in and by means of* it. Otherwise, we lose touch with the embodied situations that are the locus of our experience, our thinking, and our acting.

Reply to Johnson

Ours is a friendly discussion. Johnson says his findings corroborate my theory of metaphor. On my side I have argued only that if he were to give a role in his theory not to "affects" or unspeakable realms as he seems to think I want, but to our sense of acting and speaking in situations, we would arrive at more and better formulations; we could cooperate in a "third-generation" cognitive science.

Empirical findings cannot adjudicate philosophical issues because philosophy can reinterpret findings and generate new variables. My philosophy should be able to meet Johnson's challenge. From the arena of intricacy which it opens we can specify many new parameters which can be operationalized. This has already led to what is now the most replicated finding in psychotherapy research.[1] As I go along here, I will set out specific predictions that my theory of metaphor generates.

We have three main disagreements:

1. I am far from rejecting or lacking theory: I offer a new type with both logical precision and experiential connections (see *PM*). Johnson summarizes and likes my theory of metaphor, but he takes me as opposing purely conceptual theory. I do not oppose this at all; I am only against reading concepts back as if they were "the basis of" the process that gives rise to them. That falsifies and hides the process. Without doing that, we can still gain all the advantages of conceptual models and logical inferences. Concepts expand experience, practice, and thought. They *carry* experiencing *forward*. "Carrying forward" is itself a concept which does that. We can use its logical structure, but we can also dip into its experiential way of working, and think further from that as well.

Johnson's concept of metaphorical "frames" lays open the metaphoric nature of speech. This success neither requires nor proves that metaphors are "based on" the frames and correspondences.

I take Johnson's empirical findings as seriously as he does: I let his findings stand on their own, and I think further from *them*; he reads his theoretical framework in behind them, and thinks further from his *framework*, rather than from what he has found.

2. I think that *all* word-use involves metaphorical crossing. I know that Johnson also rejects the notion of "literal" speech along with the whole "objectivist" approach, but he sometimes sounds as if he were speaking literally about the physical motion domain as if it were original or "basic."[2]

3. Thirdly, we differ in our conception of the body. Johnson has included a role of the body in speech, but he speaks of the body in terms of spatial movements, up, down, or "motion along a path." For me, the body's living-in its *environmental situation* is prior (already in plants), and continues with us also as more "basic" than the spatial grid. We move as part of living in situations, and only derivatively in a spatial grid. Johnson

MARK JOHNSON

does not include the role of the bodily sense of speaking, or of wanting to say or do something to change a situation. He thinks of the body in *space*; I think of it *in situations*.

Now I will reply to Johnson's critique of the four planks of my theory of metaphor.

1. Contrary to a long history, I have argued that a metaphor does not consist of two situations, a "source domain" and a "target domain." There is only one situation, the one in which the word is now used. What the word brings from elsewhere is not a situation; rather *it brings a use-family*, a great many situations. Which of the many uses now obtains is known only if one grasps what the word says now, in the present situation. To understand an ordinary word, its use-family must *cross* with the present situation. This crossing has been noticed only in odd uses which are called "metaphors."

Since metaphor is the crossing of a use-family and a present situation, we realize that *all word-use requires this metaphorical crossing*. Johnson agrees that what he calls the "source domain" is really a use-family, not a category system, but he also writes of a "very complex category structure, for example, for the concept *drive*," including "vehicle," "accelerate," "car," "brake," "golf balls," or "nails." I think he means that it is not a single order of subcategories. I agree with Wittgenstein that a use-family does not operate by categories or a concept at all; it is "only a family resemblance." How a use-family functions is not determined by a concept. Wittgenstein brought up one situation after another in which, as soon as we use it, the same word immediately has a new meaning, often unrelated to any category system or concept.[3]

I would urge going *more deeply* into the question how we can sense, for example right here, that in the phrase "going deeply" *more is down*. Johnson has studied what he calls "inconsistent frames," but I ask: How do we sense which one now obtains? We know it only from grasping what the word says.

Johnson backs away from concepts that include more than their schemes. But concepts like "family resemblance," "unseparated multiplicity," and "crossing" enable us to think how the metaphorical meaning can be new. If Johnson included the role played by his bodily sense of the ongoing metaphorical *mapping*, he would find not only concepts, but also two unseparated multiplicities. Because he does not speak in this way, he sounds as if he assumed that a metaphor is "based on" already discrete correspondences.

2. I have argued that commonalities do not determine a metaphor (or word-use). Rather, *from* the metaphor, only *after* it has made sense, can a set of commonalities be derived.

Johnson first agrees, but then says that I have no theory to explain how the commonalities arise. I do have a theory and I do explain it, but my new kind of concepts do not import their schemes behind something. I will also *explain* this kind of "explain."

Johnson praises me for recognizing that the commonalities don't precede, but rather *come from* the metaphor. He says that he too has made "the same point." As he puts it *"in many cases* we *perceive* similarities only as a result of the metaphorical mapping that induces them" (my italics). He limits his agreement with "in many cases" and also by saying that some similarities were there in advance; only our *perceiving them* comes from the metaphor. He says: "The crux of our argument is that [in Johnson's view] many metaphors are *based on* experiential *correlations* that then make possible our *subsequent* perception of *commonalities* between the two domains" (his italics). He wants to distinguish between *basic* "correlations" and *resulting* "commonalities." For example, he thinks he knows that *more is up* is "based on" the "correlation" with the experience of adding more to a pile, so that "the profile of the pile *rises.*" But I think prices *"rise"* because the numbers get larger, and we count *up* from 1. I know that he has analyzed these and many other cases. He imports a cognitive scheme in which *he* formulates the "correlations," and then selects the fewest that could account for the variety of instances. But what he calls a "basic" or "experiential" correlation seems no different in character from all the rest, which he calls "resulting" or "subsequent."

An empirical question is generated here: I predict that, if asked for basic correlations, different subjects will come up with different ones, and that Johnson's "profile of the pile rising" will correlate no more highly with those, than some of them with each other.

I don't think the similarities he calls "correlations" are formulated before Johnson formulates them. They don't exist before the metaphor happens. Even afterwards we don't formulate such correlations, unless someone fails to understand the metaphor. Then we take time and thought in order to come up with similarities to explain the metaphor, and differences to say what is *not* meant. "The girl is a rose"—how? She is similar in being soft, fresh, vulnerable, but different in that (for example) she is not rooted to the ground. We say what is similar and what is different. We explain: by "the pile rises" Johnson means that *the top* of the pile rises, not that the whole pile rises.

We both want to speak of the *activity of* mapp*ing* rather than antecedent or imposed traits. If allowed, words speak from mapping as it happens. This word "mapping" would acquire a more precise meaning right in this sentence, if we would let it speak from how it changes in the process it tells about here. *This* mapping changes (carries forward) *both*

172

MARK JOHNSON

what is "mapped," and what is mapped upon, just as the word "mapping" does when used in this context, here.

We could show empirically that people grasp a word's precise situational meaning immediately, without first separately perceiving discrete correspondences. I predict that people could immediately answer intricate questions about the meaning of an oddly used word, but would have to think a while before they could derive correspondences. I also predict that their answers about the meaning will correlate significantly more than their proposals for correspondences.

3. The third plank in my theory is that one can generate *an endless chain* of similarities and differences from *one* metaphor or word-use. For example, girls and roses are both living, beautiful, soft, fresh, natural, vulnerable, both grow for a long time and then come into bloom for a short time, on and on. We can also derive endlessly numerous differences from one metaphor.

Johnson reads my "endlessly numerous" as if I had said that one can assert just anything. Yet they all arise from the single, determinate way the word made sense. "Oh!" we say, "Yes, I get it." Then we can say in endlessly numerous ways what the metaphor meant, and did not mean. Its sense is *carried forward* by each such statement. Then people say (inaccurately) that each similarity and difference "was" implicit in the metaphor. So many are possible because a metaphor is an *unseparated multiplicity*; it can be carried forward by isolating (finding, making, differentiating, synthesizing . . . . .) an endless number of factors. A use-family is an unseparated multiplicity, and so is a situation.[4] A metaphor is their crossing, a new unseparated multiplicity.

A *crossing* is not the lowest common denominator, as it would be if the two domains had only fixed characteristics.[5] *Crossing lets each play a role in shaping the result, but crossing also opens the constraints of how each is already schematized, and reveals that each is also an intricacy.* That is why the meaning cannot be determined from the antecedents, only from the effect of the word in the situation.

I predict that if individuals are asked to make an inference from a metaphorically used word, they will justify and explicate the inference in terms of the *new* precise meaning, not in terms of the general definitions they listed before knowing the situation.

The new meaning of a word is precise. Yet it need not *follow deductively* from how one would have defined the use-family and situation before the metaphor or word-use. Of course, what the word means does *follow* from (the crossing of) the use-family and the situation, but we can know *this* (nonlogical) meaning of "follow" only if we let it say how we follow someone in ordinary speech.

Johnson wants to emphasize that the new meanings are not deducible from the old ones, but he lacks the terms for a nondeductive "following." I urge him to adopt my terms to say this. Then he could still formulate the neatest array of similarities that could organize the most instances, without having to read back as the cause of the process the same sort of things that result from it. Johnson makes it clear that he does not intend it so.

The process by which we speak every day is more precise and intricate than a scheme; we have to let it happen also in how we explain. Concepts such as "crossing" work like word-use.

Johnson speaks of correlations and resulting *similarities*. For Derrida it is *differences*. But both similarities and differences are implicitly generated by the use of a word. If they are read back behind the process of speech after it has happened, it seems as if speech derives from them. Then the process is covered, made to seem its own products. I also like products as well as process. I am not one of those who say that only the *journey* matters, not the destination. I value the existing network of metaphors Johnson shows. I value destinations and products, only I don't reduce the process to those. Let us think from and with how it exceeds its products. I reverse the order: samenesses and differences are generated from making sense in speaking and living.

Now I want to meet Johnson's challenge, and send a challenge back: I want to show that my theory of immediate new meaning (how saying these words changes *this* situation) can explain something that Johnson says but cannot explain: he emphasizes that we can make *valid* inferences about the "target domain" from a metaphor, but he accounts for this as applying "knowledge from the source domain to target." But if we know something *only* about the source, and apply that to the target, we are likely to be misled. Such a transfer of what we know about one thing to another of which we do not know it, is the sort of case that gave metaphor its bad reputation. *If the word did not acquire a new meaning governed by the present situation, inferences from source to target would mislead us.* We would surely be in jeopardy, if we imputed something to our love relationship, only because it is true of journeys!

Johnson says that *love* "acquires . . . vehicles, roadblocks, dead-ends . . . *and the epistemic entailments that go along with them. . . . Based on the correspondences* we make inferences, *given our knowledge of the source domain.*" He means that we know something about roadblocks. What do we know? For example, we know that a roadblock does not damage the road. If a roadblock is removed, the road is as passable as before. Johnson says that this knowledge enables us to infer that if what troubles our love relationship is removed, the relationship will be as before. *But we cannot infer this at all*! What two people *call* "the roadblock" may well have damaged the road. Assume that one person did something disturbing, and has now stopped doing it. That person now says: everything is all right, isn't it? I'm not doing that anymore. But the other may say: "But I remember it every time we try to make love. When I turn on to you, I hit this *roadblock*. I can't keep on doing it." In *this* use the word "roadblock" generates a different correspondence. It's not like a roadblock that leaves an undamaged road. The "correlation" is rather with something that is harmless when one is standing still, but disastrous when one hits it after getting up speed.

Metaphors do involve *valid* correlations, but they are generated by the metaphor when the word makes new sense in the situation. The new correspondences are generated there. *The inferences are valid because they are generated from the precise new meaning in the target situation.* I think this is what Johnson means, and he could adopt my kind of concepts to account for it.

But if we are right, then why is metaphor so famous for fooling people? *Metaphors can fool those who do not know the target situation well enough to let it give the words a new meaning.* Then they are led to make inferences just from the source domain!

It is important to free "metaphor" from naming only misleading cases. We are quite dependent on new uses of words, so they had better not be *necessarily* misleading! We have always only the same words of the language to use, after all! Metaphor is more precise and more likely to be true to a situation, than predefined terms.

4. Johnson reads my fourth plank as if I wanted to encompass all eventualities, all future uses. But that is not why I speak of new uses. They show us something about *all* uses of words. Johnson has done a great deal by studying the network of metaphors. Yes, we often take well-traveled roads. I do not denigrate his beautiful work in showing the vast textures of metaphors.

The fourth argument of my theory says that even when we do formulate statements of samenesses and differences from a metaphor, these do not function only as patterns would. Samenesses and differences function in *two other* ways, which enable us to explain two kinds of truth: when it is said that the girl is a rose, we explain that it does not mean that she has roots. Then, if one does say that "she is deeply rooted," this must make sense: for example, "she is deeply rooted in her native soil." The requirement that a new use must make sense is *one kind of truth.* But we don't thereby give up our denial that she has roots; that is *another kind of truth.* (Doesn't the word "truth" make sense here, both times?)

We don't give up our earlier denial, although now we no longer deny *the word* "rooted" when *taken* in its new context. (The capacity to *take* in various ways is an implicit function [see chap. 1, "Functions of the Implicit"]). But we do continue to deny what we denied before. No flux here; this difference between flowers and girls is a lasting truth. Neither of these truths is a pattern (conceptual structure, rule, form, distinction, category . . . . .). For example, it might seem that "roots" is the spatial pattern of long strings dangling down. It seems safe to deny this pattern of the girl, but someone might say, for example, that vines clung to her, long tendrils dangling down from her, as her lover carried her. Neither the lasting truth nor new sense-making are governed by patterns, but in these two ways metaphor (word-use) is truthful and precise.

Johnson and I agree that new metaphorical meanings are not derived from preexisting similarities, and that metaphors can be true. I propose a kind of concepts that enable us to think with and about how that happens.

8

Experience and Meaning

J. N. Mohanty

I take it that one of Eugene Gendlin's central thoughts is that *meanings* arise from *experience*. Stated in this way, the claim is not startlingly new. One may immediately think, as a precursor, of David Hume who, as is notoriously well known, held that ideas are but copies of impressions. But clearly this is not what Gendlin means. In this essay, I will focus on this thesis of Gendlin, try to understand what he means, and make some critical remarks on it and suggest some changes.

1. "Experience" and "Experiencing"

The word "experience," even as used in the classical philosophies, is ambiguous enough. Kant, for example, used "*Erfahrung*" sometimes to mean sensations, and sometimes, and more typically, to mean perceptions ordered by "the analogies of experience." In the latter sense, it is empirical knowledge. Gendlin does not want to restrict "experience" to this. For him, what is most important is that there is a "*felt* dimension" to every experience. It is this that he has in mind when he speaks of "experience as actually lived and felt" or of "living experience" or of "felt experience."[1] The German language has at its disposal two different words for "experience": *Erlebnis* and *Erfahrung*. Part of what Gendlin wants to focus upon is *Erlebnis*. *Erlebnis* and *Erfahrung* are not numerically distinct occurrences. Rather, an *Erfahrung* is also *erlebt* by the subject whose *Erfahrung* it is. As *erlebt*, it is an *Erlebnis*—a lived, felt experience. (In this sense, Whitehead held that every experience is basically a feeling.

Dilthey also held that the psychic life of a person is an *Erlebniszusammenhang*.) Gendlin also calls it "experienc*ing*" (note that the emphasis is on *ing*, the act-character and not on the content). Every moment we have this "stream of feeling" or stream of *Erlebnisse*. Perceptions, thoughts—even abstract logical thoughts—desires, volitions, are all, in this sense, experiencings, feelings, *Erlebnisse*. So are Husserl's intentional acts. Thus, when I perceive an external object, the perception is an *Erfahrung*—the empiricists are generally concerned with it or its kind. But the act of perceiv*ing* is also lived through (*erlebt*) by me; this *Erlebnis* is a direct feeling of my experience. The same is true of my experience of thinking about a mathematical problem.

The difference between "experiencing" and "experience," however, for Gendlin, is more than that between *Erlebnis* and *Erfahrung* as I have stated it. He goes on to draw the following distinctions (*ECM*, 242f.).

In the first place, experienc*ing* is directly observable by its subject. It is immediately felt, if not known. *Experience*, on the other hand, is a construct. Secondly, experiencing is characterized by a *preconceptual* meaning (*ECM*, 8). As a *felt* datum, it includes one's "manner of experiencing" (*ECM*, 243, fn. 9), contains richness of details, but none of these has yet been conceptualized. Experience, on the other hand, consists of conceptual contents. As Gendlin appears to understand it, one may not be aware of one's experience. When the *contents* are contents of awareness, Gendlin will speak of "experience in awareness" (*ECM*, 242). In fine, experience is a conceptual construction.

A brief note on this last point. Husserl famously held the view, in the *Ideas* I, that the noetic act consists of hyletic data and the interpretive act, but there are also the so-called *Fülle*, the details as Gendlin puts it. Out of this lived-through fullness of details and data, there are constructed the so-called *noemata*, the contents of the acts. On Husserl's theory, we are not immediately aware of the noema, but we can be aware of them through a change of attitude brought about by a "reduction." But Husserl, unlike Gendlin, does not want to call experience with its contents "conceptual construction." He cannot say that, for on his view concepts are rooted in the noemata of appropriate acts.

It should be noted that Gendlin's characterization of "experience" as a construct in terms of concepts would seem to most philosophers as being rather odd. In its standard use in philosophy, "experience" stands for the immediately lived-through preconceptual sensing and/or feeling. But Gendlin's use must be familiar to psychologists who posit "experience" as a construct mediating between sensory stimulus and observable behavior. As regards his idea of experiencing, Gendlin finds suggestions for it in Husserl, Sartre, and Merleau-Ponty, but I must say the idea, as he formulates it, is his own. It may be closer to the concept of *Erlebnis* in Dilthey and G. Misch.

Gendlin gives various examples of experienc*ing* which, he holds, can be *directly referred* to by language. This would seem, again, to be an unusual position, for it is one of the common assumptions of modern semantics that language refers to things through the medium of senses or meanings. But that standard semantics is not sacrosanct, and we can agree that language may directly refer. What we need to do, according to him, is to attend inwardly to feelings in their precise nuances—like the "feel of my body," "feeling tense," or "feeling at ease," to what he also calls the "felt meaning." Such meanings are always there, he tells us, as identifiable features of our experiencing at any moment. Gendlin uses "felt meaning" in such a broad sense that even the (allegedly theoretical) meaning I grasp when I hear a sentence (in a language I know) is also *felt*, and so comes under "felt meaning." Experiencing *is* feeling (*ECM*, 15).

Now this thesis about the possibility of "direct reference" is very important for Gendlin, for only when such direct reference is possible will it be possible to make psychology directly experiential (and, I should add, phenomenological). The reason many philosophers have questioned this possibility is that every experiencing is incurably temporal, so that attending to it can only occur after the experiencing has taken place. In that case, attending would be a kind of trying to reach back to what is already gone, a sort of *nachschwimmen*, to use Husserl's striking phrase. I am not, however, completely happy with this argument. There is also what Husserl calls "primary retention," which is not remembering, but which retains the original experiencing in its grip. It is only an extremely atomistic conception of temporality which renders the above argument compelling, but that conception of temporality itself is not acceptable. So I will let Gendlin's point about the possibility of directly attending to one's experiencing stand. But what is Gendlin saying? He need not maintain that the experiencing with all its rich details, its *Fülle*, its *hyle*, is, or can be, attended to. He needs only to say, and this is what he in fact says, that it is the felt *meaning* that can be directly referred by being attended to. Phenomenological psychology needs to be able to describe such meanings, not the *Fülle*.

Gendlin seems to me to hold two different theses in this regard: first, he holds that every experiencing, being a feeling, *is there* with a (felt) meaning. He also holds that every experiencing can be symbolized and interpreted variously so that we can ascribe to it various meanings. These two are not the same thesis. However, in Gendlin's view, these two are parts of one thesis, for he also holds that felt meanings are always symbolized in some way, though not necessarily always linguistically. Meanings on his theory are always interactions of feelings and something else which serves as a symbol: this latter may be an event, a word, or a concept. Thus, saying that experiencing has always a (felt) meaning and saying that experiencing is always symbolized are saying the same thing. The mistake we should avoid is that for an experiencing to have meaning we must symbolize it by words. While thus felt meanings are always symbolized, they become reified, "entitized," by direct attention. In this sense, a felt meaning of my present (or better, just past) experiencing is the referent of my inward attending (*ECM*, 12).

2. Levels of Meaning

Provisionally, then, there are three levels of meanings on Gendlin's theory:

1. The most basic level is the felt and preconceptual meaning of an experiencing, which can be inwardly attended to.
2. Then there are the mean*ings* that arise out of the interaction of experiencing and language. These are, let me suggest, *experiential concepts* still referring directly to the primary level, but which require linguistic, symbolic interpretation.
3. Finally, there are the *logical concepts*.

Note that Gendlin aims at avoiding two extremes that philosophers tend to favor. At one extreme is the view that experiencing is a chaotic mass and has no meaning, all meanings are logical. At the other extreme is the view that true meaning is experiential, and logic distorts it. Gendlin wants to have both experiential meaning and logical concepts. To have both, especially logical concepts not as distorting media but rather as positive contents, he needs a third, a mediating *Zwischenglied*. We see why the three levels of meanings are necessary. This *Zwischenglied*, however, Gendlin tells me in a letter (to which I will refer several times below), is what he insists is "direct reference" which makes it possible to move from the felt meaning to the logical concept or from the latter to the former.

In the subsequent parts of this essay I will modify this three-level thesis, partly in conformity with Gendlin's own thinking and partly under the guidance of what I take to be better phenomenology.

The first thing to be noted is that according to Gendlin the same word can stand for a logical concept as well as for an experiential meaning of the second level. Such a word as "hostility" or "jitteryness" may do both the jobs. But here, Gendlin is not merely describing how concepts work. He is also *suggesting* a new sort of conceptualization which can do justice to both the second and the third levels, to both concrete, experiential and abstract, logical thinking. He suggests that if our prelogical (and corresponding logical) concepts are to retain, and refer to, their preconceptual, experiential basis, we should replace "content" concepts (also called "Newtonian" concepts, should I call them "thing" concepts?) by "process concepts." Content or Newtonian concepts are always "static," while the actual contents of our experience—according to Gendlin—are always changing. This aspect of our experiencing will be better captured by process concepts. I take it that he is not suggesting that the third-level, i.e., logical concepts be "process" concepts. That would make them cease to be logical concepts. So the most reasonable construal would be that he wants the second-level, prelogical, experiential concepts to be "process" concepts. Now I feel a certain uneasiness with the sort of self-evident character many thinkers ascribe to "process." Philosophers find the concept of identity, of sameness unacceptable, and appeal to the *alleged* fact that everything—in the case of experience, certainly experience itself—is in a ceaseless flux. And yet these philosophers do not care to advance one single argument why they think so. It is taken to be obvious that things, and experience, are in a flux such that nothing is ever the same. This may well be so, but that is not what my experience tells me. Some reason needs to be given for the thesis. Some reason needs to be give why our everyday common experience that we see, experience, encounter the same thing, person, or situation is only an illusion fostered by our inability to discern minute differences or by our use of logical concepts. Even our experiencings, it may be claimed, exhibit patterns of sameness, contents recur and return, all is not unmitigated process. One truth misleads, namely, that all is in time. To be temporal is not to be a process. Duration is also a modality of time. What I am for the present claiming is that the process thesis is a *metaphysical* thesis, as much as the substance thesis is. If we get rid of both, we shall be in a better position to describe our experiencing. Contents of experiencing may recur and not vary from moment to moment. Yes, content$_1$ may soon be replaced by content$_2$, but content$_1$ need not be irretrievably lost in the abyss of nothingness but may very well reappear at a later time. This is why Husserl characterized contents as "idealities"—neither substantial things nor perishing instants. To be fair to Gendlin, I must recognize that he too does not expect a process logic to be fully adequate to experiencing (*ECM*, 33). He would even be willing to reject the claim that there is a basic opposition between process concepts and logical concepts, for process concepts can just be as logical.

The second point to which I want to draw attention is this: Gendlin holds that the felt meaning is "incomplete" (*ECM*, 28), an experience contains an inexhaustible fund of implicit meanings. But the experiencing does *contain* those implicit and incomplete meanings (the first-level meanings). This "containing," we are rightly told, should not be taken "in the sense of marbles in a bag" (*ECM*, 28). And yet these implicit, incomplete meanings—those of the first level—can be directly referred to and inwardly attended to. I find here both truth and, in my view, muddle. The truth, in my view, is that any actual experiencing *has* different meanings (though *not* inexhaustible meanings, there is only a finite set of possible meanings), but the muddle arises out of the ambiguity of this "*has*." Even if we are careful enough not to think in terms of marbles in a bag, there nevertheless are other misleading pictures one may be operating with. One question that may be asked is: If the meanings are implicit, does it matter if they are also incomplete (in their implicit state) or complete, and is it possible to say that they can be directly referred to or inwardly attended to? I think Gendlin will reply that there is an awareness by a subject of a felt meaning implicit in his experiencing. While I would admit such an awareness (which would leave me, if I were the subject, somewhat uneasy, puzzled, etc.)—I can be vaguely aware within me of an implicit hostility, although I would not name it hostility—I would still hesitate to concede that I can be aware of the infinite number of implicit meanings or even of all the finite possibilities inherent in my experiencing. It is of course the case that what meaning (still felt meaning) we find in an experiencing depends upon, as Gendlin rightly sees, the "point of view we take," the "question we ask," "the scheme we apply" (*ECM*, 28–29). But then saying that by the question we ask, the point of view we take or the scheme we apply, we pick out, make "explicit" (and also "complete") one of the many implicit meanings, and to say that we actually "confer" a meaning on experiencing are two ways of describing the same situation. In that case, I would get rid of level 1, in the three-level scheme given above, and say that experiences are meaningful insofar as we take a point of view on them, describe them with a scheme, look at them from a point of view. Recall further that symbolization through interaction need not be linguistic (according to Gendlin), and we can replace the three-level scheme by the following: (A) the experiential meanings arising from the interaction of experiencing and some symbol (not necessarily linguistic), these being the original felt meanings of experience; (B) the felt meanings as they are linguistically symbolized (and are still experiential concepts) and can be directly attended to; and (C) the logical concepts. The simple experiencing of level 1 in the previous scheme then, is useless—except as assuring that the meaning that discourse lays bare *was* already there implicitly. Scientifically, for psychology, what is relevant is A. The experiential meanings alluded to in A are the concrete phenomena which, as Gendlin rightly sees, can sustain many logical conceptualizations (*ECM*, 33). The best that one can claim for the level 1 is that A itself points to, suggests, perhaps implies *its difference from that which went before it,* to its own inadequacy to comprehend its genesis.

Trying to understand the genesis of meanings through symboliza-tion, one seems to be faced with the following dilemma: if felt meanings were already independently and completely there (in an experiencing), then symbolizing could only copy them, capture them; as in Plato's picture, one catches birds from an aviary. If, on the other hand, they are entirely dependent on how we choose to symbolize, then they would have no important role to play, for everything would be up to the interpre-tations one makes and the result would be a sort of nihilism. Obviously, Gendlin wants to avoid this simplistic either/or. As he puts it in a letter to me, "Felt meaning never lets us say nor do just whatever we please with it. It talks back. If it didn't, life and thought would be easy." The felt meaning of "hostility" or of "suspicion" cannot just be ruled out of existence by subjecting the experiencing under consideration to a different interpretive framework. I think the problem here is that, while through new symbolization an entirely already existing felt meaning is "comprehended" anew, the question still remains: At what point does it amount to "comprehending" the old felt meaning, and at what point does such "comprehension" yield something new, a new meaning? The line of demarcation must be difficult to draw, but since the experiencer, on Gendlin's theory, can directly attend to his felt meaning, he must be able to say when one is not any longer the same as the other.

3. Gendlin and Phenomenology

Gendlin's thinking is grounded in phenomenology. As a true phenome-nologist, he recognizes that the questions of truth or validity have to be bracketed and the question of meaning brought to the thematic center (*ECM*, 57f.). He also excludes the question of causation, of the origin of meaningfulness of experience (*ECM*, 60). To recall his beau-tiful metaphor, if consciousness is an "island" (as Dewey calls it), then Gendlin wants us to keep in mind that this island "stops on one side at the waters of its origin and on the other side of the waters at its validity or objectivity" (*ECM*, 60). This is a nice formulation of the limits within which phenomenology must begin, to say the least. There is of course an extension of phenomenology into what Husserl called "genetic phenomenology," which brings into the domain of phenomenology the question of noncausal genesis. Let us recall that it is by following—possibly by misconstruing—this idea of genesis that Derrida proceeds to "deconstruct" transcendental phenomenology.

I find the following important connections between Gendlin's theory and Husserl's.

First, consider Gendlin's "IOFI" principle: that any meaning is an instance of the experiencing involved in having that meaning (in other words, that a meaning is an instance of itself) (*ECM*, 185). An experience has meaning insofar as the experience is an instance of that meaning. This was precisely the theory of meaning Husserl had in the first edition of the *Logical Investigations*, where meaning was regarded as a species of which the act intending that meaning is an instance. In the second edition of that work, Husserl abandoned it just because he thought he had overlooked the distinction between meanings and species (by which he meant universal classes), but I think the theory of noema by which he replaced the earlier theory is still compatible with a *modified* version of the earlier theory.

Second: in the *Ideas* I (sec. 124), Husserl makes a distinction between preexpressive *Sinn* and the linguistic *Bedeutung*. He writes: "Whatever is 'meant as such,' every meaning in the noetic sense (and indeed as noematic nucleus) of any act whatsoever *can be expressed conceptually* [*durch Bedeutungen*]." Then he tells us that expression raises every meaning to the realm of the "Logos," of the conceptual. Also: "expression is not of the nature of an overlaid varnish or covering garment; it is a mental formation, which exercises new intentional influence on the intentional substratum and experiences from the latter correlative intentional influences."[2]

Third, Gendlin is willing to admit—despite his preference for what I call the process *dogma*—that meanings are universals (in Husserl's language idealities), i.e., "respects in which occurrences can be said to be repeatable, or to be instances" (*ECM*, 192).

While so far agreeing with Husserl, Gendlin offers one major comment on Husserl which is worth looking into: he regards Husserl's conception of "act" and "intentionality" as not data of awareness but rather as principles presupposed by such data. Meanings and experiencings, however, are such data. This reading of Husserl's concept of "act" and "intention" we find already in a famous psychologist (whose lectures Husserl attended in Leipzig), Wilhelm Wundt. Wundt regards Husserl's "act" to be completely formal and empty. This empty concept of act needs a concrete "intention," so that on Wundt's reading, the intention relates the act to an object through a *Vorstellung*. All these concepts, according to Wundt, are produced by scholastic "word-definitions" and are not truly descriptive.[3] However, both Wundt and Gendlin are wrong on this point. For Husserl, "act" *means* "intentional experience," and "intentional experience" means an experience that has a meaning. The latter is an *Erlebnis*, an act is also an *Erlebnis*. What is a *principle* is "intentionality in general."

Gendlin is right, in my view, in holding that "Husserl does not explicitly state that the datum given in awareness when meaning is had is a *felt* experiencing" (*ECM*, 276). After rejecting Brentano's theory that every intentional state (or, in Brentano's language "mental phenomena") is also an "inner perception" of itself (because one act cannot have two act-qualities on his view), Husserl makes use of "reflective glance" at an act, but, faced with the question of temporality of experiencing, had to say that in such reflection we are only trying to "swim after" what is gone. He did not assert unambiguously the thesis of reflexivity that Gendlin does. So he is faced with the question: How are we aware of our meanings? For this he had to fall back on his methodologies, such as "reduction." He could have said that what the methodologies do is to raise the prelinguistic, felt meanings to the level of clarified conceptual meanings, without at the same time wanting to identify the two levels.

4. Back to the Levels Again

Thus, we are back with the question of levels. Gendlin's final scheme would look somewhat like this: (I) Experiencing with implicit, incomplete felt meanings; (II) Explicit, felt but prelinguistic (though still symbolized) meanings, inwardly attended to; (III) Experiential concepts (arising out of the interaction of felt meanings with language); and (IV) Logical concepts. Of these, in accordance with my remarks in this essay, I would regard the level I at best as a presupposition, and not as a datum for psychology. Psychology can begin only with II.

Reply to Mohanty

I appreciate Professor Mohanty's sensitive examination of a central issue: Can experiencing be meaningful without form or symbolization, or is that impossible? His paper is a kind of conversation with himself; later in it he corrects earlier misapprehensions. So he first objects to privileging process schemes over thing schemes, then finds that I also insist (in *ECM*) that one should not fall exclusively into either, although their differences must sometimes be pursued. He realizes later that I share his abhorrence at the "flux" notion that everything always simply changes. I am concerned with relationships that are more precise than either sameness or change.

Mohanty asks why I say that "experience" has been *a construct* in philosophy. *Experiencing and the Creation of Meaning* is a critique of "experience" rendered as a construct, an organiz*ed* system, the result of known or knowable "conditions" or "relations." Usually it consisted of finished objects, often already classified, or to be gathered in groups. In these ways it was usually a construct.

Mohanty speaks of the "experience" of the empiricists as "perceptual sensing." But this was a construct too. One was supposed to believe that our experience of the ordinary world could have been constructed out of bits of color, sound, and smells, although no attempt was ever made to construct even the simplest ordinary situation out of these bits. This "empiricist" account was as much a construct as the idealist one. It is only one turn from Hume's "natural and philosophical relations" to Kant's a priori categories. We need not fall into these traditional forms. Rather than a concept about experiencing, we can think with (from, into . . . . .) experiencing. Doing so is not *replaced by* concepts about it. On the other hand, experiencing always *involves* concepts (symbols, forms, differentiations . . . . .); it is symbolized at least by events and interactions in situations with other people. Direct attention in the coming of a felt meaning (. . . . .) is also a kind of symbolizing, like the word "that."

Mohanty sets up tables of "levels," looking for a level of unsymbolized experience, which he then rightly rejects. I would add that there is also no given order of levels. One can find (make, lift out . . . . .) levels in many ways. Each way is a further symbolization. So even if there were an unsymbolized experiencing, one could not assign it level 1 (or any level).

If not *un*formed, is it *incompletely* formed, not fully symbolized? But what is completely formed is also implicitly intricate and capable of *further* symbolizations that do not follow from its seemingly complete form. Not one but many "complete" forms (whole philosophies and social patterns) are implicit in any human experiencing, yet meaning is never derived just from them. Even the most fixed routine, however stable and repetitious, can be carried forward in many ways if one lets a felt meaning come, and moves on from the felt meaning. (This is why, with Heidegger, we can reopen traditional forms if we "dwell" in them—not just *in them* as forms, but in the situations they involve and formulate.)

The incompleteness of experiencing (meanings . . . . .) cannot be a level 1, since experiencing is always *with and after* language, concepts, and social forms, but it exceeds them, for example when we are at a loss for words or a course of action.

Mohanty understood that experiencing can be symbolized by events as distinguished from symbolization by words, or by direct attention to a . . . . . Using Roman numerals this time, he places as "level I" what he calls our "prereflective engagement in events," even if there is as yet no way to speak from it. Then, if we let it come as a felt meaning to which we refer, that is his "level II." So Mohanty calls speaking "level III." But I would argue that ordinary speech (level III) arises directly from our prereflective engagement in situations, and was implicit in it, so that levels I and III usually happen together, without a felt sense.

If we let a felt sense come, we encounter much more of what we then say "was" prereflective, and we can think and do much more, but the coming of a felt sense is unusual.

If we could not speak without first having a felt sense, then speaking would always be what occurs at level III, and our prereflective engagement would be only inferred behind the felt sense. We would not know the ordinary case, when we speak *directly from* our prereflective engagement. But since this is the usual case, the prereflective engagement is real and experienced. Mohanty is not right that his final level I is "only a presupposition." Together with his level III, the prereflective engagement is where we normally speak. He thinks of it as merely theoretical because he wanted it to be utterly *un*symbolized. If we consider it as it happens, implicitly full of language, social forms, history and our own past, opening into what we say or do next, then it is not merely theoretical. Although not *without* III, we easily find it as more than III.

My philosophy often differs from others in this way. Where they consider something a theoretical "presupposition," I find it experientially and directly. This gives us a way to reread the philosophies to let what they set out function for us directly. What Merleau-Ponty said about the body *before language* actually functions now, *with and after language*. Otherwise he could not have known of it. So it need not be read as merely a theoretical precondition (see "PB").

We can also let a felt sense (. . . . .) come, and enter there. Once it has come, many kinds of further steps become possible. But its coming is itself a *further* symbolizing; even without a felt sense, there is no unformed experiencing.

As I say in *Experiencing and the Creation of Meaning* and already explained in my reply to Kolb, there cannot be a line between experiencing and forms or symbols. We can make many other more precise distinctions but not that one. Mohanty well understood why not:

> If felt meanings were already independently and completely there . . .
> then symbolizing could only copy them. . . . If, on the other hand, they are
> entirely dependent on how we choose to symbolize, then they would have
> no important role to play, for everything would be up to the interpretation
> one makes and the result would be a sort of nihilism.

He also understood that we can recognize the contribution of felt meaning, because it talks back. We cannot carry it forward into anything we like. If we could, life would be easy. He knows that experiencing in situations is neither fixed nor open to just anything. And yet, when there is a further symbolization, Mohanty wants a "line of demarcation" between what experiencing *already* "*has*," and what is *new* in the further step. It would be sad if such a line were possible. It would pose just the alternatives he so well rejected above. The new step would only copy the portion that the felt sense already included, while the new part would have no relation to the felt sense, so that it could have played no role.

We can supply what Mohanty needs: when a step does follow, but not from the previous *form*, we see the contribution of the felt sense. But let us not assume that we ought to be able to split *this* kind of following into two portions, a same and a new part. Mohanty is right that something is needed here. It is of course the experiential concept of "*carrying forward.*"

Why does Mohanty suddenly assume that there must be a divide between the old and the new? I think it is because of the traditional assumption of a logical-mathematical reality. When we calculate, we must be able to trace all the units through at each step. But practice is more intricate than units. For example, in a revised paper we can certainly trace which words have remained, and which have changed from the previous version, but what is now said clearly cannot always be divided into a new part, and another part that was already there.

Carrying forward is "ambiguous" only if everything must be the same or different. Then most of life seems only paradox, aporia, same *and* different. Mohanty asks: What part is new, and what is the part that the felt sense already *has*? But what he calls "*the ambiguity of this 'has'*" actually *has* (can be carried forward by) a more complex conceptual pattern than same/different, and it is also exceeded by the carrying forward from which it speaks. To use this concept, we need the experience of an erstwhile . . . . . now no longer hanging there, not because it is lost, but because what "*was*" implied is no longer implied because it is being said or done. But this more intricate pattern *has* two pasts. Only in the retroactive past can we *now* say that our explication is what the felt sense implicitly *had.* The remembered or recorded past was only . . . . . Now we say that the words "imply" and "implicit" already *had* the carrying-forward pattern in them, but we carried it forward with this pattern. Carrying forward can be formulated in other ways, but always with more precision than just "same or different."

Mathematical units are simple and powerful. Experience responds to them with "necessary" results. But the slightest bit of explication can alter the units and undo the whole calculation. This shows that nature and experience do not come in units with lines of demarcation between them. It is a carrying forward to make units, to entitize a "this" and a "that." Whatever we entitize is actually an intricacy that is always open to being carried further and entitized differently. Anything in experience and nature is also an *unseparated multiplicity.*

If we grasp how logic works together with experienced meaning, we can keep the advantages of logical inference without losing the human world and falling back into the assumption of units (schemes, cuts, syntheses, entities . . . . .). That assumption makes everything that is not in units seem indeterminate or "ambiguous."

Philosophy has always undercut some of the assumptions, and sometimes it also developed alternatives. In recent times Husserl, Wittgenstein, McKeon, Heidegger and Merleau-Ponty have explicated (carried forward) some of the current assumptions. I have gone on to show some of them too (*ECM*, "TBP," A1–2). But the task is never finished; actually it grows as humanity continues to develop.

But if we *only* criticize assumptions, we do it on the basis of other assumptions, so that there seems to be a closed circle. We need to recognize that we think with more, and that we can deliberately let it play its roles. Only so can our thinking exceed the inevitable assumptions.

Two misunderstandings are invited by denying any *un*symbolized level. The denial could be misunderstood as if there were no nature, nothing but symbols, forms, social conventions, history. This is not so, as we see when we think at a new edge; we find that the . . . . . talks back and leads to new steps. The denial of an unsymbolized level must not deny that experiencing can talk back to symbols, forms, and history. But the talking back of the . . . . . invites an opposite misunderstanding: the . . . . . can seem to be merely individual, singular, personal, private, outside of history and society. This is not so. The tradition is implicit in a person's thought, and not only in old thoughts, also in the new ones that change the implicit tradition. Thought is inherently social. Even if you do not share your new thoughts, they carry the human world forward, and could open possibilities for me.

Various schemes of *time* can carry experiencing forward (*ECM*, 155–58). I do not share Husserl's and Heidegger's assumption that time is privileged and must be entitized and schematized before anything else. What they show is valuable, but the assumption that this *must* be the basic order is not. An order of more and less fundamental is a scheme and a carrying forward. There are always competing ways of doing that.

Mohanty does me the honor of reading Husserl through my work. He reads "act" as my kind of experiential concept. Can we read it that way? Certainly! It is what Husserl said he was trying to do, and almost did. But can we use the word "act," considering the old scheme that the word brings? Why not, since any other word will have to acquire this new use here, from which "act" speaks. No statement needs to capture; it can only carry forward. But then, does it matter what we call something? Yes, because if it makes sense at all, a different word will immediately create a different (although not contradictory) meaning from this felt sense here, the one Mohanty speaks from as an "act."

Now I can explain why I am not concerned with a "reflection" which seeks to mirror experience while only "swimming after" it. Mohanty sees that I don't share Husserl's assumption that a single act cannot be both meaningful and reflexive. Reflexive need not mean reflection. Reflection, like "swim after," is indeed a separate act. It means looking *back* at what just happened. We do indeed sometimes reflect, and this is a separate act as Husserl said. A felt sense *of* what happened also comes as a separate act, although it is a large change, not a reflection. But we usually *know what we are doing*, quite without any separate act, as I said above. Aristotle had no problem pointing out that perceiving and thinking are always inherently what he called "auto." That kind of *reflexivity* is not reflection. Mohanty allows me to "assert unambiguously the thesis of reflexivity," but we saw that this is an intricate relation, not the impossible identity between different times. An identity would turn the implicit into an explicit we want and fail to capture. The . . . . . is itself a carrying forward, and it is also not to be equated with how it is further carried forward.

Mohanty is not quite right to say that I "admit" that meanings are universals. It is my central principle in *Experiencing and the Creation of Meaning* ("IOFI," instance of itself), but "universal" and "instance" change to say that an experience is an instance in an unseparated multiplicity of ways. From a bit of experience (however formed) one can move to endlessly many old and new stated universals which it instances. Mohanty does not say why he assumes that there must be a fixed number.

9

After Dilthey and Heidegger: Gendlin's Experiential Hermeneutics

Robert C. Scharff

1. Introduction

To catch the spirit of Gendlin's writings—and to identify in a preliminary way what makes him easy for other philosophers to misunderstand—consider a few characteristic passages: "People who have no experience of psychotherapy sometimes think that the patient's therapy process derives from the therapist's theory. That would be like deriving the world from a few generalities. Theory certainly has an influence; but experiencing is not derivative from simpler, ordering principles."[1] The example is from therapy, but Gendlin's objection is to a widely shared philosophical assumption: "experiencing" is commonly construed as "derived from"—i.e., having intelligible order imposed upon it by—"principles" (theories, forms, rules, patterns, distinctions, categories, definitions). Broadly speaking, this assumption tends to follow either a rationalist or an empiricist line: in the former case, experiencing is taken to be a kind of unstructured mush awaiting "our" principles of understanding (reason, mind, language); in the latter, it is regarded as a sort of unprocessed sensuality from which nature's order has to be "abstracted" or "induced." Either way, experiencing is interpreted in terms of rational (logical, theoretical, conceptual) operations which render it intelligible; and either way, it thus comes to seem philosophically incidental. For if experiencing is beholden for its meaningfulness to whatever principles order it, then what deserves philosophy's main attention is not experiencing—not the mere element of "disorder" in or "raw material" for knowledge—but the ordering principles.

Gendlin argues, however, that this construal of experiencing cannot be right. If reason alone really was responsible for our ordering principles, then no genuine "interplay" between reason and experiencing would ever be possible; there would be only imposed or abstracted forms and beyond that "no order at all."[2] Yet life is full of occasions when principles (forms, concepts . . .) clearly occur *with* instead of imposing themselves *on* experiencing. In such instances, as Gendlin puts it, experiencing makes itself felt as a "more than forms"—a "wider order" of "greater intricacy" that "*functions in*" and "talks back to" conceptualization so as to "give the forms and rules their meaning and their work."

A poet, e.g., stuck with an unfinished line, "feels very exactly" what is needed (". . . . .") by the other lines. This very exacting . . . . . continues to "work with" the various words and phrases she tries until the right ones come; and finally, "when the next line does come, it nearly always forces some revision of the lines already written" ("TBP," 21, 47–49; cf., *ECM*, 91–111). Moreover, this experiential functioning is no rare or mysterious occurrence known only to talented people like poets. All of us go about "finding words" for what we mean in this way. Often it happens so readily that we fail to notice; but if the words do not come, the process is easy to spot. Confronted with just *this* question, e.g., about a person (place, job, book . . .) I know well, all the usual words may "feel wrong." Yet this is certainly no mere feeling. It has the power to guide me past some words that come which "almost do" but are still "not quite right"; and as my search continues (perhaps via mulling over my sense of this "not quite"), it takes me toward a way of saying "precisely" what, in a quite specifically experienced way, I "felt all along" I wanted to say. And yet if I then find I am not understood, I know perfectly well that "what I mean" is always "more" than the words I have already found; so, no matter how satisfied I may have been with these words, I can always start again with this "more"—this greater intricacy, Gendlin calls it—and other words will come.

It is this greater intricacy (wider order, more than forms . . .), then, that Gendlin calls "experiencing"; and against the usual philosophical view that imposed forms *make* experience meaningful, he argues that experiencing

> has an order of its own because it always *responds* with an unavoidable exactitude that vastly exceeds what could possibly follow from [any given] distinctions. So to say . . . the distinctions *made* (found, lifted out,

> synthesized . . .) what comes . . . [is to wrongly] attribute intricacy to *them.*
> While it is true that what comes is always orderly and exact, yet much more
> comes than could have followed from the order and exactness alone. . . .
> [W]hat comes is always ten thousand not-yet-separated-strands, never
> simply just what we said or thought.[3]

Conceptual formulations thus "only *seem* to work alone"; in fact, they
work within this always only partially said-and-separated experiencing.
Gendlin's writings are thick with examples of how it functions in every
sort of conceptualizing—even the philosophical sort. For when a

> philosophy re-positions the old words to make new sense[, t]hat is possible
> only because more than forms is at work in thinking. The process of
> making new sense involves more than new distinctions displacing the old
> ones. It involves functions of implicit intricacy. Most earlier philosophies
> did not overtly avow these functions, but no philosophy would have been
> exciting or even possible without them. ("TBP," 38; also, 41–42)

In philosophy, as everywhere, if our conceptualizing did not involve this
experiential functioning, we would be unable to understand the (old,
now being revised, new, still difficult, now bothersome again . . .) *point*
of "re-positioning" all those words. If, e.g., "we don't understand a book,
we can only quote it. To understand it is to dwell-think *in* [be attentive to
the experiential processing of] its forms, and that is *more precise* than the
forms" taken by themselves—more precise in being, among other things,
an "order-for-further-moves."[4] So, e.g., when we begin to understand
the book, we can explain "how it would have to handle" circumstances
or questions it never actually considers; and it is not just the already
"positioned" words that make such further moves possible.

Clearly, then, Gendlin's view of and approach to "experiencing" is
no variation on traditional themes, and it is set forth in explicit opposition
to philosophy's usual treatment of "experience." The point needs stressing at the outset; for anyone who fails to take it seriously is apt to hear
what Gendlin says with a tin ear. Two mishearings are especially likely.

On the one hand, when Gendlin speaks of experiencing's "wider"
order and "greater" intricacy, this not a sign that he so values it that
he seeks to study experiencing *instead of* rational forms. In fact, he flatly
denies there could even be such a "separate," i.e., non- or extraconceptual
way to treat experiencing and argues that the very idea is contradictory—
as if we could "study experiencing as it is when it is not studied . . . [or]
state it as it is when it is not stated" ("EP," 291). On the other hand, when
he depicts experiencing as "talking back" to forms, this does not mean

he thinks the traditional view should be *inverted* to make experiencing determine forms. All he says is that conceptualization never functions without experiencing; one must not conclude that concepts can only mimic it. For this conclusion would not just be unwarranted. It would also be, Gendlin argues, fundamentally antiphilosophical. Experiencing may be much more than the mere disorder or raw material it is traditionally assumed to be; but as a little reflection reveals and philosophers have always insisted, it is also rich with naiveté, confusion, and conflict—i.e., in need of conceptualizations that embarrass, clarify, or otherwise speak back to experiencing in the process of expressing it. Indeed, for Gendlin, even the traditional idea of "one-way" conceptual imposition, wrong as it is, arose out of a perfectly justifiable urge "to correct an earlier . . . mistaken view that science copies or pictures nature" ("TBP," 24). Hence, the way to deal with this idea is to remain a philosopher and see it as an "over-correction," not to become a mere empiric or anti-intellectual and embrace experiencing instead.

To understand Gendlin's treatment of "experiencing," then, we must see, first, that he does not conceive "experience" in either the rationalist or empiricist way and, second, that he considers it neither apart from nor instead of conceptual forms. In my project, he says, I ask "how experiencing *functions in* conceptualization."[5] A stuck poet, e.g., has *both* her felt sense of . . . . . *and* the lines that have already come, in the language she already speaks; and as she struggles to fill the line, the two "work together." The . . . . . cannot, of course, be satisfied by deduction from existing lines; but it does come after exactly these lines in just this language; hence, as she searches for the words, the already formed lines and language *work-in* her felt sense of . . . . . , and it *responds-to* these lines and language. It is this process of working-in and responding-to that Gendlin studies. He wants to "think with" this process, i.e., to see how experiential responding to given conceptual forms allows them to "work implicitly in" rather than "put themselves on," say, a poet's . . . . . —and so to witness the "creation" of new meanings.

The study of experiential *functioning in* conceptualization is Gendlin's alternative to the traditional overcorrection. Such a "one-way imposition" view secured reason's prerogatives by demoting experiencing to "experience," so that it appears, wrongly, as if existing conceptual forms "either only force consistency, or break and leave us in [unformed] limbo." Of course, existing forms *can* be analyzed abstractly, as if they "worked alone"; but Gendlin points out that usually when this has been done, "a *concept* was thought to be only the conceptual *pattern* . . . [and] all further steps could come only from the pattern's logical implications." So, while he fully agrees that "we still want those further steps of logic, and what they open on any topic," he argues that we must stop purchasing these conceptual gains at the profoundly impoverishing price of suppressing our direct or "naked understanding" of the variety of ways that any logical order actually functions experientially.

> Many people treat concepts as if they were a separate world. . . . They drop all of their naked understandings the moment they turn to theory. They try to operate just with formed conceptual patterns. But without their own naked understandings they can think nothing new. They can only rearrange concepts that are available in the library. And even these can be understood only very thinly in this way. But if we take the implicit intricacy along . . . then even the purely logical steps are powerful because they work *in it.* ("TBP," 60–61)

Consider, e.g., how "thin" our perception of Descartes's *Meditations* is if we only analyze its theories and arguments—as if the "power" of the Cartesian order of reasons, for its author, for modernity, or for us uncomfortable inheritors of modernity could reside entirely in these notorious, explicit "patterns." The point is, Gendlin argues, we must stop thinking of concepts as if they really operated in a "separate world" and only according to the logic of their settled meanings. In fact, forms can and for the most part do "work implicitly in" experiencing; and as they do, they too are "changed" in the process—not in contradictory or irrational ways, but in ways that do not merely follow from their given sense. When, e.g., the poet's words come and force a revision in previous lines, "the[se] already formed lines were at work in the implying of—a change in themselves." Put generally, "when forms [thus] work implicitly they do not work alone, and that is why they can work so as to change in the process of working. Surely we want to think about *that* way forms can work, that pattern here—which involves more than the pattern ("TBP," 63–64). Thinking-with this greater "pattern" is Gendlin's project. He studies "the function *of* directly referred-to experiencing *in* the creation" of new meanings.[6] In this, his study follows a reflective path that, in fact, is always open to us—viz., to turn toward and differentiate *this* currently felt sense of things (as the poet does in being aware of her . . . . .), and to consider how that experiencing works in the *coming of the words to say* just this . . . . . in some exactingly (albeit not exhaustingly) satisfactory way.

So far, I have sampled Gendlin's writings in order to identify likely misreadings of his "study" of "experiencing." For some this will, perhaps, be orientation enough. Yet it is, I think, a fair guess that most readers—especially those with primary roots in the empiricist-positivist

strain of modern philosophy—will remain skeptical. Isn't *the* philosophical problem of our time the conflicting multiplicity of concepts and
principles? Isn't Gendlin's appeal back to "experiencing" thus hopelessly
naive and beside the point? In studying the functioning of experiencing
"in" conceptualization, doesn't Gendlin simply forsake the prime philosophical duty of asking about the *legitimation* of some conceptualizations
over others?

As I see it, Gendlin's project has in fact nothing to fear from this
objection; but defending him against it will take some time. To put it in
a sentence, Gendlin collides here with what are perhaps the two cardinal
precepts of modern philosophical practice—viz., that experience (however defined) has no rights *against* reason (however defined), and that
the main task of philosophy is to enforce this priority by establishing the
criteria of *rational warrant*. In spite of all the recent displays of postmodern
revolt, great power remains in these precepts; and they can make it appear
self-evident that Gendlin's talk of the "implicit functioning" of felt (!)
experiencing in *all* conceptualization reaps nothing but chaos.

In section 2, I consider a bit more these two cardinal precepts and
the objection they might tend to spawn here. I want to show how they
presuppose, respectively, notions of both *experience* and *epistemic inquiry*
that Gendlin quite rightly rejects. Yet his own alternatives are, of course,
not without precedents. Gendlin, as he often says, "comes from" and tries
to "carry forward" especially Dilthey (on experience) and Heidegger (on
philosophical inquiry).[7] In sections 3 and 4, then, I consider how he
appropriates, respectively, their notions of *Erlebnis* and of *hermeneutics*. In
a fifth and final section, I turn briefly from defender to critic in order to
suggest a sense in which Gendlin seems to me guilty of some "naiveté"—
not about his project, which I believe he correctly judges to be a genuine
and powerful "carrying forward" of sources already transformative in
their own right—but about the extent to which the intellectual sea-change
needed to understand his project has already occurred. This problem, I
will suggest, is connected with Gendlin's somewhat ungenerous reception
of Heidegger's idea that hermeneutics has a "historical" dimension to
its task.

2. Experience and Imposed Order

To return to the initial problem: in modern philosophy, there is a dominant understanding both of "experience" and of what to do with it, and
both are very different from Gendlin's. At least since Descartes and Locke

and then surely not without precedents, experience is seen primarily as an un–self-conscious, receptive, sensuous (especially visual) relatedness to whatever is external to us. Sometimes emphasis falls on the location in us and effect on us of what is encountered, i.e., we *have* experiences, or *experience* something. Sometimes it falls on the independent things with which we presume contact, i.e., we encounter *something*, the *experience*(d object). Yet, with either emphasis comes the same strong denial: notwithstanding that such encounters figure centrally, happily, often even self-correctingly in everyday life, philosophically speaking they are from the outset completely unworthy.[8] It is not that, sometimes, experience gives us knowledge enough while at other times (sc., in science), it does not. Quite to the contrary, for the modern philosopher experience is as Descartes depicts it in the *Meditations*—i.e., merely the source of the totality of unsound opinion he acquired while still methodless and unable to help himself. And three and a half centuries, two rival traditions, and countless competing epistemologies later, the basic message remains: at best, experience is philosophy's inescapable point of departure; it is, however, so thoroughly untrustworthy and yet so powerfully attractive that the first philosophical task must be to *step reflectively back out of* any reliance upon it in order to ask what rational principles might protect us against its pull.

So successful has been modern philosophy's push for (let me call it) criterialogical separatism that now, even in those moments when our thoughts are simply taken up with comfortably pedestrian affairs, "experience" cannot shake its ruined reputation. A glance, e.g., at the *Encyclopedia of Philosophy* encourages in us the forced option: either experiential innocence/ignorance or its rational antidote. So it is that whether in the person of artisan, healer, or student of nature, "the mere empiric cuts a poor figure" among philosophers—precisely because empirics are content to rely upon the

> homely and substantial experience of a world of public objects, which forms for all sane and *unreflective* persons the basis of ordinary life. It has been regularly insisted, however, since the earliest times that experience in this sense is nothing ultimate: the paradoxes of motion and change and the more familiar facts of perceptual error and illusion are enough (it is thought) to show that it cannot be straightforwardly identified with the real. Hence, in addition to the rejection of habit-learning as a road to knowledge, there arises that further prejudice against the deliverances of the senses and in favor of necessary reasoning from first principles[9]

The prejudice in favor of "necessary reasoning" is, of course, as strong in empiricists and skeptics as in rationalists and idealists. The shared point is the separatist *rejection* of "homely" experience; for it would never do to split the difference, say, between an ordinary "habit-learning" that is often serviceable enough, and a more rigorous scientific "knowledge," which holds an additional kind of promise. Philosophically speaking, the former must disappear *in favor of* the latter. The only real issue is how much may reason "legitimately" make out of what can (cannot) be "given" sensually.

Writing in 1967, Heath concludes that the cumulative effect of so many failures to "reconstitute ordinary experience out of a mixture of sense data and formal logic" seems now to discredit the whole effort. Yet, as prescient as his conclusion clearly was, it seems equally clear that the old tendency to express distrust of experience by trying to gain reflective separation from it continues to dominate mainstream debate. To see this, we need only ask who—even among the most proudly postmodern revisionists—is ready to simply "return" to ordinary experience and, say, explore positively the ways of the empiric or, more pointedly in the present context, study with Gendlin the "function of experienced meaning in cognition"? The truth is, for all the new talk of respect for non-scientific discourse, conceptual relativity, or purely pragmatic edification, it is never long before assurances are given all around that (of course) experience/practice "itself" remains *one* (*prephilosophical*) thing, and how justified (true, useful or otherwise consequential) are the claims (beliefs, actions) "expressive" of that experience/practice remains the *other* (*philosophical*) thing. Criteria of rationality (truth, utility, conversational appeal) are everywhere being pluralized (historicized, recontextualized); but it is still widely assumed that at least *these* criteria must be *the* criteria, established in a properly detached, reflectively "separate" analysis—or else our whole philosophical practice seems threatened with corruption by precisely that illusion-prone, error-ridden, semantically uncrystallized, homely experience which was seen to need criteria in the first place.

Consider the lingering influence of this assumption even in the revisionisms of, e.g., Putnam and Taylor. According to Putnam, modern philosophy's radical distrustfulness of ordinary experiences and practices has culminated unsatisfactorily in both "ontological speculation that seeks to describe the Furniture of the Universe and to tell us what is Really There and what is Only a Human Projection . . . and epistemological speculation that seeks to tell us the One Method by which all our beliefs can be appraised."[10] Putnam tells us he has lately come to oppose such speculation—along with its "weird notions of 'objectivity' and 'subjectivity'"—precisely because it makes philosophers imagine themselves thinking from a "God's-Eye View" and so "unfit to dwell in the common." Appealing to James, Dewey, and Wittgenstein to help dispel this old attitude of rational reconstruction, he directs us toward "the

Lebenswelt, the world as we actually experience it," urges us to "regain our sense of [its] mystery," and reminds us that it is after all in daily life and not as epistemologists that we are first moved to call some of our ideas "unreasonable." Yet as forcefully as Putnam pushes for displacement of this old separatist idea of "what philosophical reflection can and cannot be," he continues to construe "unreasonableness," not as perhaps the new issue of what this might be in "life-worldly" terms, but in the old way—i.e., by approaching daily experience via the "claims" which emanate from it. I remain a "verificationist," he says, only now in the looser "pragmatist sense" of pluralistically "refus[ing] to limit in advance what means of verification may become available to human beings."[11]

A similar doublethink—in which fostering an enriched understanding of daily experience is continually interrupted by the old insistence that its "expressions" must meet "independently rational" criteria—appears in Taylor. On the one hand, he too wants philosophy to recover the lived circumstances of our practices and articulations from (capital "E") Epistemology. He calls his sort of revisionism "philosophical anthropology," and he begins with the "experienced motivational or emotional lives" of human beings considered as "self-interpreting animals" whose expressions are "always open to further articulation just because they already involve articulation." From the old reconstructivist standpoint, he admits, it may seem paradoxical that

> although [1] only an articulated emotional life is properly human, [2] all our articulations are open to challenge from our inarticulate sense of what is important. . . . [For] if one focuses only on the first point, one can believe that human beings are formed arbitrarily by the language they have accepted. If one focuses only on the second, one can think that we ought to be able to isolate the scientifically pure, uninterpreted basis of human emotion that all these languages are about. But neither of these is true.[12]

Like Putnam, Taylor interprets both mistakes as attempts to conceive human beings "as objects among other objects." In both cases, the motivation is to ground the merely "subjective" in something "really real"; so in both cases, Epistemological distrust of ordinary lived experience remains: whether exemplified by the employment of old classics like secondary properties or new favorites like folk-psychological explanations, there is the assumption that phenomena such as "emotional life," "our pre-articulate sense of our feelings," or the "inarticulate" have just *got* to be accounted for "in terms of factors which are not experience-dependent."[13]

On the other hand, unlike Gendlin—who at this point wants us to think the *functioning together* of our pre-articulate sense (= experiencing) and our articulations—when Taylor tries to evaluate today's post-Epistemological disputes, even his philosophical anthropology cannot neutralize the old separatist distrust. There are, says Taylor, two major factions among those who, like himself, no longer seek "total reflexive clarity about the bases of our beliefs," viz., the "neo-Nietzscheans" and the Habermasian "defenders of critical reason." Neo-Nietzscheans have concluded from what Taylor depicts as an endless interplay of the articulate and inarticulate that a meaningful life is "expressive," like a work of art, so that *any* use of external criteria to judge the worth of its expressions is inappropriate. Habermasians, however, refuse to "go all the way" in this Nietzschean direction. Out of "fear for the fate of a truly universal and critical ethic," they cling "to a formal [if also no longer monological] understanding of reason." Thus, for Taylor, the post-Epistemological movement splits into radical and revisionist camps, which raises the question of how to "adjudicate" the dispute between them; and facing this issue, his new sense of lived experience simply fails him. For he insists that "the dispute has to be fought on the terrain" of the Habermasians—because, he asks, assuming the question is rhetorical, "Where is the *argument* that will show the more radical Nietzschean ['aesthetic'] claim to be true and the [ethically universalizing] thesis of critical reason untenable?"[14]

Having joined in the post-Epistemological debate and knowing that even its revisionists want to reject the old idea of a Standpoint Above the Fray, Taylor now demands an "argument" to decide *between* the factions. One need not be a disciple of Foucault and Derrida to wonder where Taylor could be standing when he "articulates" this sense of argument. So does his new post-Epistemological possibility—the one, as I am suggesting, that Gendlin takes up—again threaten to get Epistemologically occluded. "Adjudication and argument" are precisely what Taylor at first deemed utterly foreign to life's endless interplay "between the articulate and the inarticulate"—in which interpersonal and social encounters are occasions for dialogue and further conceptualizing, and expressivity has not congealed into flat "claims" or asserted "conclusions." But now, apparently because neo-Nietzscheans say things about life after Epistemology that strike him as "incoherent," he demands a "justification" for their "aestheticism"; and here Philosophy returns, criterialogically taking on life's Expressions all over again.

My general point, then, is that in the climate created by our modern inheritance, philosophers cannot just "decide" to treat ordinary experience differently or more generously, since this alone will not make them any less Epistemological about it. In the old Cartesian model, reflection on experience is expressed as a radically separatist distrust that calls for truly *philosophical* reflection to attain a wholly neutral (ahistorical, God's-Eyelike, or otherwise *extra-experiential*) standpoint from which to properly evaluate experience. In my view, despite the many recent moves to soften, pluralize, and historicize the monological vision of rational "method" which accompanied this original model, the continuing power of its basic idea that philosophical reflection must be extra-experiential and that it must establish at least some criteria to impose *on* experience is greatly underestimated. And it is, I believe, the continuing power of this idea, much more than the unusual character of Gendlin's notion of experiencing, that makes him so easy to misread. For as the case of post-Cartesians like Putnam and Taylor can show us, it is possible to embrace the most richly untraditional notions of experience and—in an effort to make us philosophically "fit" to take them seriously—even to openly renounce traditional epistemology, yet continue to undermine precisely this new philosophical opening by covertly pushing some new version of the old commitment to extra-experiential standards.

As Gendlin rightly insists, his orientation really is quite genuinely *not* Epistemological. He does not—and given what he sees of how experiencing actually does function in all conceptualizing, he cannot—want an extra-experiential set of adjudicating criteria. To him, Epistemologists are among those who treat the conceptual as if it were in an "entirely separate world." This attitude is nicely captured in the following comparison. Consider the fact, notes Gendlin, that when we speak of poetry (or anything else, for that matter) we understand,

> we know what we are saying although we cannot substitute patterns for it. But, in philosophy . . . we think we must be prepared to do so. If someone asks, "What do you mean?" we feel a need to answer with clear categories and known meanings. We defend what we said by claiming that we "really" meant those clear categories. If we cannot say we meant *them*, if they don't *cover* what we said, then we are *uncovered—naked* in what we said. ("TBP," 51)

Such nakedness is intolerable to Epistemologists. For them, philosophy must consider only concepts (principles, rules, language) and their (equally conceptual) legitimation, or else there will bleed into the reflective field a flood of subjective, psychological, emotional (in a word, nakedly nonconceptual) material that threatens the very idea of legitimation itself. In this, the earliest Cartesian and the latest positivist agree: except on noncognitive topics, philosophy must always ask why we are *justified* in, not merely *predisposed* toward, affirming some conceptualizations but not others. And against just this sort of attitude, Gendlin urges us to learn to appreciate how to be philosophically "uncovered": for it is a fact—and one which will not go away—*both* that existing conceptual forms change in their interaction with experiencing *and* that using these forms to explicate experiencing changes it. Moreover, these two facts are also true at the reflective level, so that there will never be either "the" test for legitimate conceptualizing—or even "the" conceptualization of experiential functioning itself.

Gendlin knows, of course, that to Epistemological ears this emphasis on conceptual processing and pluralism, especially when linked with an express interest in the "experiencing" from which conceptualizations arise, sounds alarmingly relativistic; and it is important to understand his account of why this fear is groundless. Part of the problem is simply, one may say, Epistemologically fabricated. It is true that *differing* conceptual schemes, considered purely as conceptual schemes—i.e., abstractly and "in themselves"—transform easily into *incompatible* ones; and if we dwell on this purely conceptual incompatibility, it encourages us to convert every actual presence of differing accounts of something into an occasion for either (with the current majority) lamenting or (with a smaller neo-Nietzschean minority) glorying in the failure of traditional epistemic testing. Yet, for Gendlin, such "purely" conceptual exercises entirely ignore a crucial point about differing schemes, viz., that any experiencing is open to multiple explications, both at any moment and over time, because in every conceptualization there always remains an unexplicated felt sense of "more." Judged in terms of an experiential process, then, and not as pure forms, differing conceptualizations of something are understood to be not incompatible but differently explicative. So it is that we can even be of two minds, in which case we can produce explications that articulate "quite precisely" this condition; and if we treat these explications as the conceptualizations of an experiential process—and not just as finished "claims"—they are readily understandable as expressive of what it is to *be* of two minds, and not as two separate assertions possessing "contradictory" contents.

Gendlin therefore argues that a radically new, much more promising, and not at all relativistic approach to conceptual multiplicity is implied by his study. "So long as we only exclaim: 'But everything changes!' we view as merely troublesome the human functioning in which meaning and order are formed." There is, however, no need to assume this troublesomeness—and thus no need to dream of curing it with an ultimate (or even some less-than-ultimate) conceptual test. Rather, what is needed is "another Copernican Revolution" in philosophy, says Gendlin, in order for us to recognize felt experiencing as a center of consideration in its own right . . . [to] inquire into the ways in which logical order can relate to concretely felt experience . . . [and to analyze] the formation of meaning in the interaction of experiencing and symbols. . . . Such a philosophy could aspire to being not merely another scheme, but a *philosophy of the relation between any schemes and experiencing*. . . . [E]thical, political, and generally theoretical issues are entirely different when approached through this frame of reference. (*ECM*, 7–9)

Friends of Heidegger's Daseinsanalysis will spot easily here Gendlin's turn away from the production of "another [essentialist] scheme" that tries to fix "what" we are or ought to believe, in favor of a (hermeneutic) inquiry into "how" schemes and experiencing function together (in various modes of ek-sistence). Thus, ethics, e.g., Gendlin thinks is "best cared for as distinctions between kinds of [experiential] processes," not in terms of battles over rules or principles. Suppose, e.g., a friend plans to marry; you like the intended spouse; and marrying this person seems in general a good thing: "Is that enough for you to call the decision right? Would you not need to know more about *how* your friend decided? What if the decision was made on a drunken afternoon to get married that very day? Suppose your friend badly wants money and the intended spouse has some? . . . What if your friend talks mostly of not wanting to live alone?"[15] The problem here "is not exactly in the reasons themselves"; it lies in the "something more" that is indicated by these reasons, viz., "the lack of a kind of decision-making process we respect." Just as with finishing a poem, in which only a certain ending will "do," so it is possible to study also how it is to "live from" various moral decision processes. For it is the "experiential *process, not the value-conclusions alone*, [which] tells us what a value really is in an individual. The same verbal value-conclusions can mean very different concrete process conditions and very different resulting behaviors . . . [so we] value the experiential process (a certain manner of it), not the value-conclusions alone."[16]

In short, for Gendlin the fact of conceptual pluralism and controversy, in ethics or elsewhere, need no longer appear to either threaten the practice nor make us long for final criterialogical cures—*if* we start considering the various concepts, values, and principles *in terms of the steps they might bring in an experiential process*, and not as "merely float[ing] on an independent conceptual level." The secret is to stop treating the presence of multiple conceptual schemes initially as a terrible *problem*, so that even if it has now become optional whether philosophy should construe the problem as a soluble, devastating, or perversely pleasant problem, one always imagines the next task must be to discover (or to explain with relish why it is impossible to discover) which scheme is really "constitutive" or "representative" of experience. If conceptual schemes really did possess the sovereign power to make sense of experience, either by imposing order on it or copying something in it, then every time we were faced with more than one such scheme we would indeed be obliged to discover some criteria—possessing some sort of logical, rational, consensual, or otherwise extra-experiential prerogative—for choosing some scheme(s) over others, or else nihilism would always be near at hand. To Gendlin, however, this old story is quite wrong. Experience is not and cannot finally be "nicely sorted into essence-piles"; hence, we need "to study the formulating process itself, and the roles of experience in it, [in order to] find how experience can ground different formulations differently, so that we might then be glad (and also specific, and knowing) about different formulations."[17] Yet being glad, specific, and knowing—instead of perpetually nervous or joyfully relativistic—about different conceptualizations becomes possible only after the old idea of a Sanctioned Scheme for Needy Experience is abandoned. Only then can we learn to "think with" any experiential process, and so both to discern the possible influence of conceptualization "back" upon the experiencing it explicates and to understand that experiencing always involves a wider, deeper, and more intricate order than any conceptualizations of it. As Gendlin often remarks, the only thing strange in all this is that so many philosophers have to be told about it; for in their daily lives, as ordinary persons, they take it for granted like the rest of our species.

Today, however, these facts about experiencing are still routinely ignored even by postpositivists—covered over, e.g., in their images of pluralized verificationism or Habermasian rationality testing. As postmodern as they can be in opposing the scientistic, monological, male-gendered commitments of an earlier day, these thinkers fail to see their own revisionisms for what they are—viz., new "expressions" of the same old thoroughly determinate, anything but neutral, modern, Western, European, *experientially felt sense* that it is philosophy's job to treat all conceptualizations as making "claims" requiring extra-experiential "adjudication."

With this problem in mind, then, I want to explain further how Gendlin is able to get past all this epistemological backsliding by considering two more topics. First, there is (in the next section) his appropriation—and very definitely productive "carrying forward"—of Dilthey's enriched and nontraditional sense of *Erlebnis*. Second, if the idea of taking up Gendlin's project is not going to "feel" philosophically uncomfortable, one must learn how to accomplish his sort of "reflective take" on the process of conceptualizing. This latter issue will bring us (in section 4) to

Heidegger's claim in *Sein und Zeit* that a Daseinsanalysis—like Gendlin's "thinking-with" the functioning of experiencing in conceptualization—must be "hermeneutical."

3. Dilthey and *Erlebnis*

Dilthey has long been famous, of course, as the pioneering "philosopher of the human sciences." Today, however, we know it is misleading to give this phrase a primarily epistemic construal—i.e., to assume that Dilthey, like other early second-science advocates such as Rickert and Windelband, is most fundamentally concerned to defend the method of *Verstehen* against that of natural-scientific *Erklären*. He does indeed think that there is a second, "human" kind of science, and that its *Verstehen* is different from explanation; but whatever its procedural distinctiveness, Dilthey argues that *Verstehen* operates the way it does not because it follows a second type of logic or expresses a second sort of rational "interest," but because of the demands of its subject matter. What in the last analysis makes natural-scientific explanation unsatisfactory in such disciplines as history, philology, political economy, or aesthetics is that with its externalizing outlook, quantifying concepts, and concern for causes, explanation is barred in principle from dealing with "Life," in the sense of human affairs as they are directly lived through (*erlebt*).[18] It is not that these features of explanation are somehow mistaken. In fact, to the contrary, they make predictive/technologically controlling sciences possible. It is just that there is also another possibility, viz., the study of other aspects of our circumstances besides those which can be handled abstractly, mathematically, and from the outside. For the sake of this other possibility, we must ask what alternative sort of procedure is suitable when we wish to study not externally encountered nature but, in Dilthey's phrasing, the "total nexus of psychic/historical reality" as that is "possessed" in lived experiences (*Erlebnisse*).

As philosopher, then, Dilthey is consciously antipositivist. Instead of starting with the success of a (natural-)scientific activity already underway, embracing the topical and epistemic principles of its "observational" orientation, and turning to the usual task of defending and formalizing its procedures, he challenges the hegemony of this very scientific orientation. We "have" reality in another, more direct way than via external confrontation and abstract explanation, he argues; and in order that it may be studied, we must clarify the character of this other sort of possession and the other sort of experience which makes it possible:

Lived experience is a distinctive and characteristic mode in which reality is there-for-me. . . . [It] does not confront me as perceived or represented; it is not given to me, but . . . is there-for-me because I have a reflexive awareness of it, because I possess it *unmediated* and as belonging to me in some sense. . . . Everything I experience or could experience constitutes a nexus or system. Life is a process interconnected throughout by a structural system which begins and ends in time. To a spectator [Life] presents itself as a closed identity because of the sameness of the apparent body in which this process takes place. At the same time, it must be contrasted to the emergence, growth, decline and death of an organic body by noting the peculiar fact that every part of it is bound up with the other parts in one consciousness by means of some kind of lived experience of continuity, connectedness, and self-sameness.[19]

From passages such as this, we can begin to appreciate the enormity of the task that lies before anyone who, like Gendlin, wants to "carry Dilthey forward." In an intellectual atmosphere in which the ideas of experience and reality have long been formulated in ontological deference to natural science—i.e., where the paradigm of subjects sensually confronting objects and the companion concern about the warrant for conceptualization of such confrontations have ruled together for centuries—Dilthey's nonstandard descriptions of both experience and method are bound to seem subjectivistic and philosophically regressive. Dilthey himself, moreover, is no total innocent here. Part of the reason he needs to be carried forward is that he never found a completely satisfactory way of distinguishing *Erlebnis* from *Erfahrung*.

The late (1907–8) passage just cited captures two basic and unwavering features of Dilthey's idea of *Erlebnis*, viz., (A) its "inwardness," i.e., the fact that it always involves "having" my human and nonhuman surroundings, "here," for me; and (B) its "exteriorization," i.e., the fact that what this direct possession "means" continually manifests itself in expressions of life (*Lebensäusserungen*). Already in 1883, Dilthey explains in a now famous passage that to do justice to both A and B, he must completely reconceive the "whole context of the facts of consciousness," because

no real blood flows in the veins of the knowing subject *constructed* by Locke, Hume, and Kant, but rather the diluted extract of reason as a mere activity of thought. A *historical as well as psychological approach* to whole human beings led me to explain even knowledge and its concepts (such as "external world") in terms of the manifold powers of a being the wills, feels, and thinks.[20]

As the first italicized phrase indicates, Dilthey did not think the human sciences operate in the sort of intellectual atmosphere "constructed" by traditional epistemology, in which rational minds are depicted as confronting an external reality; rather he proposed a return to the "context of lived experience" within which such constructs are developed in the first place. I will return shortly to the basic challenge this return ultimately poses for traditional epistemology; but for now, I emphasize only the fact that on the approach to *Erlebnis* itself, the second italicized phrase identifies a lifelong problem for Dilthey. For neither his earlier "psychological" works like the *Ideas concerning a Descriptive and Analytic Psychology* (1894) nor the late "anthropological reflections" in the notes for his unfinished *Critique of Historical Reason* (1910–11) succeed in doing justice to both A and B at once.[21] In works like the *Ideas*, "descriptive and analytical" treatments of *Erlebnis* do typically focus on A rather than B, thus making them easy to misread as proof that Dilthey starts with a subjectivistic inclination to privilege "merely inner" states—and then in the *Critique*, overcorrects objectivistically in deference to B. Earlier he glosses A in terms of "psychic life's [inner] structure," pointedly excluding consideration of that "consciousness of an objective world . . . correlated and opposed [to me]" which he admits is always part of life as well.[22] But later, he says instead that if a mind tries to "hold fast and apprehend its own inner states and turns its attention upon itself, *the narrow limits of such an introspective method . . .* make themselves felt. Only from their actions, fixed utterances, effects upon others, can human beings learn about themselves."[23] In other words, where Dilthey could once appear to espouse psychological subjectivism, he seems later to sell out to positivist objectivism.[24]

Dilthey, however, rightly rejects both interpretations, and the 1907–8 passage suggests why. Accusations of subjectivism and objectivism both proceed from the "spectator's" perspective. For a spectator, who sees only human bodies confronting objects "outside" of them, Dilthey's interest in how we experientially "have" reality can only signify curiosity about what is "inside" these bodies—i.e., be evidence of his idealistically straying toward Mind instead of remaining realistically respectful of World. And it follows that if Dilthey later seems to turn away from this insideness in favor of understanding life's "expressions," this can only be a sign of his becoming properly (some might now say, too hastily) realist again.

Yet if Dilthey explicitly refuses to epistemologically privilege the spectator's viewpoint, he also fails to develop a philosophically adequate account of the "standpoint of life" he wants to assume instead. Analysis of Gendlin's way of carrying Dilthey's work forward, however, can show us both why this is so and what we can do about it. For Gendlin's own notion of "experiencing" is, in point of fact, a direct appropriation of Dilthey's *Erlebnis*; and in translating *Erlebnis* with a gerund, he is deliberately following Dilthey in stressing both the "process" character and the "concrete, ongoing functioning" of experience in all human life.[25] Still more telling than his appropriation of *Erlebnis* itself, however, is Gendlin's philosophically transformed idea of how to handle it. At first glance, his descriptions of experiencing can often *seem* as if they might just as easily have been Dilthey's:

> A phonograph record [or today: a computer] may "obey" all the rules of logic, syntax, and of objects about which it speaks, yet it has no experience of the meanings it speaks. When we humans speak, think, or read, we *experience* meaning. . . . Therefore, there are at least two dimensions of meaning: (1) the relations of symbols to each other and to objects, and (2) our experience of the meaning.
>
> We are most aware of this second, experienced dimension of meaning in those cases where the symbols do *not* adequately symbolize the meaning we experience. In those cases we go on talking around what we mean—we may wave our hands, point our fingers, tell long stories of events, give examples, invent metaphors, pause to grope for words. In such cases we are intensely aware that we are *experiencing* a meaning . . . we *feel* the meaning. We notice that . . . meaning is not only a matter of things and symbols and their relationships. (*ECM*, 45)

As we have already seen, it is clear that Gendlin shares Dilthey's primary concern for dimension 2. On close reading, however, one sees that his approach to it is fundamentally different from Dilthey's in two important ways.

First, as noted above, Dilthey tends either to speak of experience "itself," i.e., to stress its *inwardness* and psychic structure (as in the psychological works), or else to begin with "expressions" of life, i.e., to stress *outward* manifestations of experience (as in the late notes for the *Critique*). Gendlin, however, explicitly fashions his approach so that it avoids both tendencies. Whether in the human sciences, our social concerns, or philosophy, he says, for us to enter "upon the dimension of experiencing will require *both* experiencing and logical symbolization. Meaning is *formed* in the interaction of experiencing and something that functions symbolically. Feeling without symbolization is blind; symbolization without feeling is empty" (*ECM*, 5).[26] If pressed, Gendlin might have second thoughts about his Kantian metaphor, for he denies that there ever are any blind feelings or empty symbolizations. Yet carefully read, the orientation for all his inquiries is clearly displayed here. We need, he says, to "make a field of study out of what was an embarrassment"—to start "neither in statement, nor in an experience we can say nothing about," but to "study both experience and statement as they occur in the process of affecting each other."[27] First, then, Gendlin's approach to "dimension 2" differs from Dilthey's in being under an explicit requirement not to divide this dimension into inner psychic (and for traditional ears, mysterious-sounding) and outer (and all too famously "observable") halves. The second difference lies in what Gendlin does to meet this requirement, viz., favor consideration of experiences of being stuck, uncomfortable, or otherwise (as he says) *in transition* from extant conceptualizations to more satisfying ones. The reason for this focus is simple. These are the sort of cases most likely to reveal how experiencing actually *functions* in symbolization; whereas in cases in which statements, gestures, and actions come easily (or, typically in Dilthey, have already occurred), this functioning is more likely to go unmonitored and to be less noticeable (see, e.g., *ECM*, 230–31).

Much should be made, I think, of this matter of selecting either (let me call them) finished or uneasy cases. Dilthey's preference for the former and Gendlin's choice of the latter can illuminate for us why Gendlin's actual studies of experiential functioning are more successful than Dilthey's. Given Dilthey's primary interest in the needs of the human sciences, it is surely no surprise that he thinks mostly of finished cases, i.e., cases in which there are "manifestations" of experience already lived. Yet from this angle, it can seem most natural to think of experience not so much in its own right but rather as a topic one *returns to*–something of *epistemic* value whose clarification furthers the task of imaginatively *re*living and creatively *re*constructing (as Dilthey often calls *Verstehen*) its "expressive" *results*. The problem is, these continual reversions to the imagery of (inner) experience and (outer) manifestation violate the spirit of Dilthey's own caveats about the inappropriateness of a spectator epistemology for the human sciences. So here we must see that Dilthey, to vary Heidegger's phrase, actually knows more about how to treat experiencing than he finally tells us. Though he *understands* how experiencing always functions in expression, what he *says* prevents him from considering more thoroughly just how deeply this ontological (and not just epistemological) insight cuts.

Recall that already in 1883 Dilthey insists that his grounding of the human sciences will have to proceed from a standpoint—what he later calls the "standpoint of life"—that reconceives the "whole context of the facts of consciousness" in such a way that the very notions of "knowing subject" and "external world" are shown to be *theoretical constructs*. Yet this announcement has both an obvious epistemological and a far-reaching ontological implication; and it appears that Dilthey is clear from the start about the former, but only gradually and imperfectly works toward clarifying the latter.

The epistemological implication is that given the topic of the human sciences—i.e., given their concern to "understand [experienced] life in its own terms"—they can never find a home under the methodological conditions laid down for natural science. The deeper implication, however, is that Dilthey's "standpoint of life" is potentially much more than just the needed epistemic alternative for the human studies. Dilthey begins, of course, by rejecting the standard positivist demand that the human sciences, as "sciences," must conform to the same epistemic conditions already extant in natural science. This demand, he argues, simply universalizes the spectatorism of the natural sciences, so that *Verstehen* is illegitimately judged according to the model of "knowing subject-external world/explanatory theory-observational data." Yet merely in presuming this extension, positivism presents Dilthey with the task of not only *identifying* the epistemic conditions of the human sciences, but also of *differentiating* them from those of the already successful sciences. To the question of how this differentiating is to be done, Dilthey's earlier works give no clear answer. From the writings of his last decade, however, comes the explicit suggestion that the positivist universalization of the natural-scientific standpoint *has matters exactly backwards*. It is not spectatorism but rather the standpoint of life that should be granted such an extension. For prior to this standpoint being considered as the source of epistemic principles for the human sciences, "understanding and expressing lived experience" is what all of us already do. Speaking, then, in the most general philosophical terms (as Dilthey in fact sometimes does in his late notes for the unfinished *Critique*), the standpoint of life is not really a "standpoint" at all. It is simply the reflectively recognized version of how we always already exist; and it thus provides an angle of vision from which *both* "understanding life" *and* "explaining nature"—and indeed, any other "ways" of articulating experientially possessed "reality"—may be seen as expressive of "lived through" possibilities.

How is one to treat this deeper implication of Dilthey's "reconception of the whole context of the facts of consciousness"? How much of it can we assume he recognized himself? It is true both that he does not *say* "Philosophy must take its bearings from the standpoint of life" but also that his work shows how this can be *done*. In my view, dwelling on the former unfairly minimizes what he actually accomplishes—and also encourages giving some later thinkers (e.g., Gadamer) more credit than they deserve. Dilthey's late work is in fact full of references to a planned "broadened" version of anthropological (or sometimes, "hermeneutical," but in any case pointedly *not* "psychological") reflection, in terms of which philosophy would be able to relate human science experientially both to natural science and to other human activities.[28]

I therefore recommend that we follow Heidegger's suggestion. Writing without access to the crucial seventh volume of the *Gesammelte Schriften*, he nevertheless takes up what he (I think rightly) calls Dilthey's "ownmost philosophical tendency"—which means, in the first place, that he refuses to follow the usual practice of reading Dilthey's entire corpus in terms of its initially stated interest in a developing a "logic of the human sciences" and defense of non-naturalistic psychology. Instead, Heidegger argues, we must come to understand Dilthey's "elemental restiveness":

> Epistemological, historico-scientific, and hermeneutic-psychological investigations are forever overlapping and interpenetrating. Wherever one aim predominates, the others are already the motive and the means. What seems like disunity and an unsure, haphazard "trying things out," is really an elemental restiveness [*Unruhe*] in the direction of the one goal: To understand "life" philosophically and secure for this understanding a hermeneutical grounding in life itself.[29]

In Heidegger's phrase, Dilthey is thus to be seen as "above all on the way toward the question of life"—a question whose "essential point" is not the narrower and human scientifically driven one of upgrading the old ideas of "persons" and their "psychical structuration," but the really "substantial" one of "disclosing a new horizon for the question, . . . in the broadest sense, of the being of man."[30] Some discussion of what Heidegger means by this claim can, I think, provide a context both for addressing the problem of Epistemological misreadings of Gendlin's carrying forward of Dilthey's *Erlebnis*, and for appreciating his entirely transformed conception of how to treat it.

4. Heidegger and Hermeneutic Inquiry

For Heidegger, to "appropriate Dilthey's labors" we must actually start with the ontological objective toward which all his work is "restively" on the way.[31] As we know, Heidegger associates this task with a twofold problem. The obvious component is how to interpret *human* being. The ultimately more important but initially obscured component is how to secure a basis for doing this in our era's general ontological atmosphere, where *everything including humans* tends automatically to be interpreted "metaphysically," i.e., as being either a present object or a present subject that knows such objects. Here, according to Heidegger, we can see that Dilthey left us with something to appropriate on the question of understanding human life "in terms of itself." It is not simply that he did not try hard enough to characterize human being in a phenomenologically adequate way; rather, he failed to recognize this second component of the problem.

What Dilthey did not realize is that his reflections on life and lived experience could never cure his elemental restlessness, because his explicit conception of those reflections continued to bear the stamp of his original epistemic/human scientific concerns. To use our earlier imagery: it is as if, while writing poetry, he continued unawares to assume that poems can only have certain kinds of structure, no matter what this particular . . . . . in its particular context seems to call for. In retrospect, we can see that Dilthey was an insightful enough student of life (good enough "poet") that his actual accounts of experiencing and its understanding continually outrun the dictates of his "philosophy of the human sciences." But like other recent thinkers such as Putnam and Taylor, who also want to say Epistemologically unsanctioned things about daily experience, Dilthey is continually subverting his own findings— e.g., by making his characterizations of experiential "possession" of life fit the traditional Cartesian rubric of inner and outer. The problem is not with the third-person point of view as such. Spectators, just as spectators, are harmless enough; they are simply resolved, legitimately and fruitfully, to "have" reality only in cognitively represented external confrontations. But to reflectively privilege the spectator viewpoint in philosophy is, in Heidegger's language, to "be" ontologically forgetful. Philosophically spectatorlike minds only know "reality" as that which is comfortably thinkable along the lines of external nature, and "human beings" as either part of nature or as bearers of criteria for adjudicating claims made about it. For spectator minds, "living through" representable confrontations with purely external things no longer "appears" as a life option—i.e., is no longer available "in terms of itself" as an experienced phenomenon. Rather, spectatorism rules silently as the philosophically respectable attitude, invisible even to itself, insofar as all efforts to reflectively attend to it as an *Erlebnis* find only a suspiciously unobservable and thus rightly suppressed (inner, merely subjective) part of (outer, objectively warrantable) *Erfahrungen*. Spectator minds, in Heidegger's phrase, treat a "founded mode" of being-in-the-world as if it were identical to being-in-the-world as such; and as long as philosophers continue—either enthusiastically, like happy moderns, or restively, like Dilthey, Putnam, and Taylor—to do this, they will never succeed in explicating that idea of a genuine plurality of experiential modes implied by Dilthey's own lovely suggestion—scarcely deserving to be confined by human-scientific designs!—that *Erlebnis* expresses itself in every thought, practice, and production and is the way we originally possess "reality" in any of its possible senses.

Gendlin is interested precisely in carrying this lovely suggestion forward. Indeed we can say he is attracted *as such* to the study of Dilthey's idea of understanding lived experience as an inexhaustible source of meaning—i.e., an "experiential intricacy that is always more than forms" ("TBP," 29; and *ECM*, 2–10; "EP," 300–306). He too wants to bring this point into service everywhere and has himself done so for psychotherapy, for some of the sciences, and for various other endeavors.[32] But unlike Dilthey, Gendlin is not responding *primarily* to these needs. Here his philosophical outlook is in agreement with (though he did not get it from) Heidegger, viz., that to carry Dilthey's work forward one has to follow the lead of the "direct analyses" of *Erlebnis* and not be put off by the epistemic- and research-mindedness of his general ("Kantian") viewpoint.[33] Gendlin thus sees himself contributing to a time when, as I would put it, an ontological atmosphere such as our present one no longer tends to herd the virtually limitless "kinds of experiential processing" into a few epistemically respectable pens.

At the same time, Gendlin's appropriation of Dilthey is not the same as Heidegger's. More especially, it is for him no means to a larger end, as in *Sein und Zeit*. To put their difference in one sentence, Gendlin wants to practice everywhere the hermeneutics of facticity that Heidegger treats only as an entrée to raising the Being-question again. One obvious consequence of this difference is that Gendlin rejects—and knows that he is rejecting—the idea that the general philosophical reception of his kind of study of experiential functioning depends in any important sense upon either the undertaking of a fundamental ontology or on a radical reevaluation of Western metaphysics. When he plays this point off against *Sein und Zeit*, he expresses it in two parts: First, he skips all the introductory material on the relation between the Daseinsanalysis and the Being-question and proposes straightaway to "understand Heidegger experientially." *Sein und Zeit* already shows us, Gendlin argues, how to "understand the inherent relation between living, feeling, understanding, and cognitions of any kind"; and for justification, he points to Heidegger's own claim that his *Existenziale* function "hermeneutically." When this phrase is explained, says Gendlin, it is quite clear that the *Existenziale* are always meant to function as more-than-concepts—"phenomenologically lifting out," as Heidegger puts it, what "concretely shows itself from itself" about human living, and never offering merely "free-floating theses," valued in themselves for the content they pass on from one "vacant understanding" to another ("B," 55, 64). Second, however, Gendlin criticizes Heidegger for tending to lose sight of his own intended hermeneutic openness, precisely in the moment that he thinks his existential analyses have done enough (i.e., in Gendlin's phrase, made the "one step" needed) to further his overall ontological project. Taking the two points together, Gendlin concludes that although Heidegger did bring

> forward a line of development from Schleiermacher and Nietzsche through Dilthey and Husserl, the founding of our assertions directly on our living, as we experience . . . he always goes only one step, *from* the living experiencing *to* his formulation of the structure implicit in it. The reader thereby has lifted out some aspect that "was" already being lived, but was not seen as such. But other authors lift out other aspects, or one could say, they formulate "the same" aspects differently. *My interest is . . . the question: How might we think about that much finer and different organization of living, such that "lifting out" is possible?* . . . As capable of giving explicit birth to all these liftings out, the character of th[is] organization of living is much more fundamental than even the structure of *Being and Time.* And it can be studied! ("B," 69, my emphasis; cf. "TBP," 30–31)

It is not, says Gendlin, that Heidegger utterly fails to find this "finer . . . organization of living [= experiential intricacy]"; yet he draws on it only once—to lift out its "existential structure" and, informed by the result, move on with his Being-question. Accordingly, Gendlin often identifies his own project by explicitly contrasting it with Heidegger's at this point. Instead of diverting attention to a renewal of ontology, Gendlin proposes to stay with that "finer organization" with which *Sein und Zeit* so promisingly starts, in order to study the "lifting out"—i.e., the hermeneutical—process itself. In the rest of the paper, I shall consider a bit further how this move ensures both a fundamental similarity and profound difference between Gendlin's approach to experiential intricacy and Heidegger's.

As to the similarity, in my view Gendlin's writings show decisively both by example—i.e., in the sheer number and variety of cases in which he "thinks with . . . more than forms"—and via methodological reflection—i.e., in addressing the question of "what language do we use to speak [after all, in forms] of what is more than language"—what the "hermeneutic" philosophizing first pioneered in *Sein und Zeit* can really become. In the nature of things, I cannot fully defend this claim here; for its true defense would entail the annotated review of Gendlin's many successful thinking-with's. At least, however, I can explain how I see Gendlin carrying forward the hermeneutics of *Sein und Zeit.*

To begin with, Gendlin did not originally formulate his project as such a carrying forward; but he does now think of himself as engaged in one—with Heidegger, among others. He is thus sometimes willing to characterize his own approach in the language of *Sein und Zeit*'s "hermeneutic of Dasein." Like Heidegger in that work, he explains, my "beginning is always how we sense ourselves, find ourselves already with . . . whatever we study, in an implicitly 'understood' way, in our living [so that] whatever conceptions are developed, in any science [or elsewhere], they need to be related back to the implicit lived understanding we already have of the topic, and need to be viewed as articulations of that" ("B," 48; "EP," 290ff.). Like Heidegger, Gendlin here depicts his inquiry as attuned to the sensed "way in which human beings are always open to anything"—and thus places all the "ontic" experiential explications he studies in a space initially cleared by *Sein und Zeit*'s ontological characterization of the human condition.[34] Here, as in *Sein und Zeit*, "understanding" signifies our "situated" being-in-the-world; and Dilthey's pioneering conception of interpretation is carried forward in the portrayal of explication (creative expression, conceptualization, symbolization, etc.) as the way "speech" is always "interpretive" of this situated (one recent paper tries "moody")[35] understanding. For Gendlin himself, then, "explication" may have "come from" Dilthey; but it also later became his translation of Heidegger's "*Auslegung.*"

Given this orientation, it is clear why Gendlin is attracted to what I called above "uneasy cases." For in such cases, available concepts either already do or seem as if they would function metaphysically, i.e., as hegemonically forgetful of their experiential roots. If, however, we begin like Gendlin—which, as I see it, is also like Heidegger, hermeneutically—the virtue of uneasy cases is that by studying the obvious tension in them between established concepts resisting change and a felt sense of their being or their having grown expressively inadequate, we may come to recognize more readily how the implicitly understood (felt meaningfulness, more than forms, greater experiential intricacy, finer organization . . .) functions in *any* conceptualization.

As to Gendlin's differences with Heidegger, I believe the most important one is this. He sees Heidegger's pursuit of the destruction of Western ontology in the middle works as a selling out of the hermeneutical promise of *Sein und Zeit*. Although Gendlin praises the destruction for what it has revealed, he rejects what he sees as Heidegger's eventual "metaphilosophical" privileging of this critique, on the grounds that it implies, wrongly, that the hermeneutical opening discovered in *Sein und Zeit* cannot be carried forward under current conditions. On the contrary, it seems clear to Gendlin that millions of persons—including many who begin quite without any help from Heideggerian critique—are today being moved simply by their own uneasy and poorly conceptualized situations to recognize "experiencing" as the source, both of their expressions of growing dissatisfaction with inherited ideas about how to think or behave, and of the felt rightness of at least some of their creative transformations of these ideas. Of course, Gendlin is not romanticizing the wisdom of nonphilosophers. Rather, he is complaining that, as regards this widespread movement, most philosophers and culture critics are still generally behind, not ahead of events. In philosophy, he says, even after centuries of neglect, it is only just now that the

> non-metaphysical order of the body and language [in experience] is returning to consideration [and it] . . . is still spoken of only negatively, as what *dis*organizes a supposed system of rules, values, commonalities, similarities—generalities. Language had been explained as generalities, but how it works is not determined just by them. Generalities were also thought to be imposed on the human body as its only order. Indeed, all nature was thought to be just these. ("N," 300–301, 302)

Granted, along with Heidegger there have been a few nonmetaphysical pioneers like Merleau-Ponty, who (apropos of experience as "felt sensing") think of the human body as coming before concepts and language in a hermeneutically important way. Yet, so powerful is traditional teaching that such pioneers are still "bypassed" in favor of later luminaries like Foucault, who merely find new ways to recycle the old subordination of the body and its inner feelings to external forces (in Foucault's case, by conceiving of historical "events" which "totally imprint . . . and destroy" it). Such psychologizing demotion of bodily felt sense is nothing new. Feelings, Gendlin notes, were

> relegated to "tertiary" status in the eighteenth century. They appeared in the rear of philosophy books as "the passions," and had little or no role to play in the constitution of objects and objective reality. Humans were thought to be in touch with reality only in two ways: through perception and reason. . . . This view still structures most of our concepts, so that . . . "[f]eelings" are held to be internal, rather than a sensing ourselves living. It is then puzzling why there is so much implicit wisdom in feelings.[36]

This traditional interpretation of feelings, Gendlin continues, promotes hermeneutical ignorance in culture criticism just as in philosophy. One popular pseudo-explanation, e.g., makes "the very term 'narcissism' reactionary" and "denigrate[s] social change" by reducing any turn toward experiencing to a kind of "inward" preoccupation with "my [merely subjective, selfish, probably unsociable, maybe even irrational or pathological] feelings." For his part, Gendlin asserts sharply, he rejects

> the erroneous view that philosophical questions can be resolved by arguing from psychological factors, wrongly placed underneath as if they could determine philosophy. Freud, for example, thought he could give psychological reasons why philosophers say what they say. But when philosophy assumes Freudian underpinnings, it is no longer philosophy, for it omits at least the examination of Freud's kind of concepts and conceptual patterns.[37]

In short, Gendlin agrees that efforts such as Heidegger's historical critique have helped free us from the Western tradition's pinched picture of (bodily, felt, sensed) experiential intricacy and from its correspondingly inflated images of reason and conceptual generality; but he sees no evidence that his project needs to wait until a time when Heideggerian critique has more thoroughly prepared the ground. As proof, he can point to his own *Experiencing and the Creation of Meaning*—which he wrote before even reading Heidegger and which, though clearly informed about our metaphysical climate, appears to succeed without making this climate a central issue ("PNS," 408–9; "B," 70). Would Gendlin not be justified, then, in asking Heideggerians, with some confidence, if this question is rhetorical: Even though *Experiencing and the Creation of Meaning* explicitly privileges neither fundamental ontology nor historical deconstruction, is it not anyway a study of precisely the right "nonmetaphysical" kind to orient my project? The answer to this question is, I think, clearly yes. *Experiencing and the Creation of Meaning*—and also what I, at least, want to call his many other hermeneutical accomplishments—show that for *him*, the virtues of destructive critique are often already evident in a kind of project that does in fact carry Dilthey and Heidegger forward. If Gendlin's differences with Heidegger came to no more than this, one could easily let them be. *Sein und Zeit* certainly does not say that without a Daseinsanalysis no one can think like Gendlin. And we certainly need not construe Heidegger's historical critique "deconstructively," i.e., as explaining in advance why Gendlin's aim of "thinking with more than forms," of finding openness "implicit in anything," must be impossible.[38] But this is not all there is to the matter. When Gendlin says he pays homage to Heidegger by "really seeing" what Heidegger found but could not go on from, this is not just another case of genuine understanding always being to some extent "*Besserverstehen.*" Gendlin's carrying forward of *Sein und Zeit* includes an indictment of (let me call it for now) the *historical* strain in Heidegger, especially the middle Heidegger, on the grounds that *Sein und Zeit*'s more promising *hermeneutical* strain is actually at odds with it. I conclude by explaining why I find this criticism unpersuasive.

5. Conclusion: Historicity and Hermeneutics

For Gendlin, as I have noted, Heidegger's greatest contribution lies in his move toward hermeneutics. At the very least, this involves his radicalization of phenomenology with the explicit argument that, without exception,

> every statement, or truth, "stands in some kind of approach," and depends on it. That is to say, the world cannot be rendered as such, but only through some (historically developed) scheme.
>
> To get beyond this, Heidegger seeks "an approach that would not be again merely an approach." Rightly, he envisions that having gained perspective on the variety of possible schemes and approaches, and their historical development, we would not now simply settle for another scheme. But what else is possible? ("EP," 286)

Sometimes, as in this passage, Gendlin says Heidegger just "stopped" and could not answer this question—i.e., did not see that "thinking with more than forms" *everywhere* is precisely the needed "approach that is not an approach." But more often, he credits Heidegger with having actually stumbled upon this answer, which he was then unable to exploit.

> Heidegger called his terms "Existenziale," i.e., aspects of how we exist, and said that they were *not concepts*. They were explications (formed in and from) our *being-in* the world. But just in what way were they more than concepts? Heidegger called them "hermeneutical": they explicate a pre-explicit, pre-thematic understanding. But he did not go further into the *general notion of hermeneutics,* and later rejected even that notion. How could he have failed to pursue this opening he had made for a more-the-conceptual thinking? ("TBP," 30)

To Gendlin, the "general" hermeneutical implication of the Daseinsanaly-sis seems so promising that Heidegger's failure to follow it up calls for an explanation. How could he have missed the possibility of considering further the many ways of thinking that might "let the implicit understanding continue to function when we think on any topic"? The problem,

ROBERT C. SCHARFF

argues Gendlin, lies with Heidegger's project of historical destruction—
and specifically, with its way of treating the "always already determinate"
character of understanding. Unlike Husserl, "Heidegger did not assume
that experience can be described independently of our assumptions,
rather the full opposite" ("TBP," 30; my emphasis).[39] He "believed deeply
the dictum of his country and his period, that a genuine thinker can
only be the thinker of a particular nation and culture" ("TBP," 31). So,
after *Sein und Zeit*, instead of following out his deepest hermeneutical
discovery about all schemes and their relation to experiencing, he falls
back upon this old historicist notion of factual determination. As a result, he

> did not see in his "Existenziale" a more-than-conceptual way in which to
> carry on his further thinking. It seemed to him that what could be thought
> in them would still be determined within *Western* historical assumptions.
> How the historical determinants arise and how they could change seemed
> to him thinkable *only on an ultimate meta-philosophical level*. Therefore right
> after *Being and Time* Heidegger went on—*purely conceptually*—to look
> for an over-arching "*meta-ontology*" from which the "Existenziale" would
> be seen as derived. He discarded Husserl's renditions of experiential
> intricacy, and he also rejected his own precise more-than-conceptions. He
> merged all intricacy back into a single question: If anything *is* inherently
> historical, how do historical determinants arise? ("TBP," 30; author's
> emphasis)[40]

For Gendlin, then, whereas *Sein und Zeit* evinces a pioneering hermeneutical inspiration, there is in Heidegger's subsequent work a historical/
conceptual strain that frustrates it. In his middle period, when he turns
to the destruction of Western ontology, he knows only two ways of thinking
its "over-arching historically given assumptions," viz., either as "trapped
within them, or in a way that *reopens* the questions they closed, so as to
regain the openness which hides itself in them. In this way Heidegger
was able to provide a powerful critique . . . of Western philosophical concepts. He made them so visible and re-opened them so thoroughly that it
has become impossible any longer to just assume them and comfortably
argue from them" ("TBP," 31). Thus, on the good side, (1) Heidegger's
thinking contains elements of *both* hermeneutical insight about openness
and historical critique of entrapment. In this way, he stays a step ahead
of both relativists like Nietzsche (for whom "cultural forms are merely
imposed, and . . . aside from them there is only indeterminacy") and
deconstructionists like Derrida (in whom the very idea of openness is
"replaced by [the] assertion that new distinctions simply displace old

ones," but always in the same old impositional way). But alas, on the bad side, (2) Heidegger's thinking also *subordinates* hermeneutical insight *to* historical critique and as a result he is permanently diverted by his destructive project from making anything more than general gestures in the direction of openness itself. After his destructive work, the late Heidegger does come back to speak of *Sein und Zeit*'s new sense of openness—but only insofar as the destruction either "reopens" just precisely whatever the "over-arching" Western assumptions closed or, at this same excessively general level, somehow points beyond these assumptions. In the end, the pull of the destruction is so strong that,

> having left all but the ultimate determinants behind, Heidegger could not think how that which is more than form actually functions . . . in *each* situation and in *each* moment of thinking. He did not see how any bit of life and practice can talk back more intricately so as to change the determinants which are implicitly at work in it. So he could not investigate further just how the historical determinants actually work . . . *implicitly*, and how they change by *working-in a wider intricacy*. He could not further examine the role of *individual* humans in the coming new history. ("TBP," 31–32; author's emphasis)

For Gendlin, the moral of this story is plain enough. Rather than let Heidegger's critique sap the hermeneutic promise from his Daseinsanalysis, "we need a critique to limit [this historical way of thinking] the 'always already' and 'only within.' Anything human does indeed include implicit concepts and cultural forms, but . . . they do not work by a one-way [historical] determination." And once this correction is made, says Gendlin, we can also "read Heidegger in my way: The *openness is implicit in anything*—and *can function in our thinking further from anything*."[41] This insight, hermeneutically carried forward, not historical critique, conceptually imposed backward, will show us how "individual humans" can have a role "in the coming new history."

Let me repeat: I have only praise for what this reading of Heidegger's line of thinking inspires Gendlin himself to produce. Yet I do see problems with it as a piece of Heidegger interpretation. I am surprised, e.g., that Gendlin violates the spirit of his own project by judging Heidegger's "*Metontologie*" in purely *conceptual* terms. Why is there no consideration of what he might have been trying to *explicate* through it? And why no mention of the hermeneutically suggestive fact that Heidegger quickly "understood" that he could go no further with this strategy than a preliminary sketch of a "special problematic of questions" he worked out in a 1928 "Appendix"?[42]

Yet more generally, the most dubious feature of Gendlin's interpretation is its de*constructive*, or Derridian, conception of Heidegger's
middle period. To Gendlin, the historical critique turns Heidegger into
something like the "*full opposite*" of Husserl on historicity—i.e., into someone who, in his critical mode, even "*rejects*" the hermeneutical promise
of the Daseinsanalysis of *Sein und Zeit*. This view of the destruction—and
there are plenty of phrases like the two just quoted—is not only mistaken
but seems to me in Gendlin's case (and I will eventually close on this
point) to be directly connected with his adherence to a somewhat overly
optimistic picture of what it will take to widen the appeal—and empower
the practice—of just the sort of hermeneutical thinking he himself has
already begun.

Against Gendlin's interpretation itself, I would suggest that it is
not accurate to say that Heidegger only "knew two ways to think [the]
over-arching historically given assumptions" of the dominant Western
tradition; nor is it correct to say that his critique moves so much "within"
this tradition that he cannot contemplate change in its dominant assumptions. *Were* either of these characterizations right, *were* it true that
Heidegger, in his destructive mood, becomes like Derrida and "considers
philosophers *only* in terms of the single [metaphysical] linear progression, and . . . attacks *only* 'the' supposedly single Greek-Western 'logo-
centric' model" ("TBP," 140 n. 4; author's emphasis), I would not now
be defending him. But I think there is just too much evidence to the
contrary. Let me at least mention two items.

First, there are the newly available lecture courses from the pre–*Sein
und Zeit* period in which Heidegger already makes a "hermeneutics of
facticity"—one that is explicitly associated with Dilthey against the "un-
phenomenological" character of Husserlian phenomenology's starting
with consciousness—the necessary basis *both* for the general ontological
inquiry that will be the Daseinsanalysis *and* for the proper handling
the special problem of its originating within an inherited tradition of
metaphysics.[43]

Second, there is the evidence of the opening pages of *Sein und
Zeit* itself.[44] For when Heidegger introduces his task as a "retrieval" of
the Being-question, he depicts it in a thoroughly hermeneutical—and
at the same time "historical"—fashion. Given our present philosophical
situation, he says, in which the received epistemic ideal is that everything
must be justified and nothing presupposed, one tends to assume that
good questions are like shots in the dark, where whatever matters is
brought forth for the first time in (testable) answers. Yet in fact, even
the most casual questioning seeks *something*, and that something always
already guides ("structures") the search from the start; thus, when *Sein
und Zeit* (sec. 2) begins by "explicitly posing" its question so as to make

its structuring clear in advance, Heidegger understands himself to be exercising an option available to (but today mostly not taken up by) any inquirer. The point he must explain, of course, is why as a questioner of Being he should feel constrained to do this. His reply, we know, is in terms of a report (sec. 1) of what seems to occur when he tries to "simply ask" his question—and immediately finds that, in spite of himself, he tends to recreate a hostile atmosphere in which several "prejudices" continually reinforce the idea that there is really no reason to ask. In other words, reflecting on his initial situation, Heidegger notes that his very effort to retrieve what once was, after all, *the* philosophic question already evokes for him an "[implicit, intricate, functioning] felt sense" that Being must be—and at the same time cannot satisfactorily be—characterized as the most universal, or indefinable, or self-evident concept, and so in any case a matter one can safely ignore.

Unlike Gendlin, then, I find no basic tension between Heidegger's hermeneutics and his destruction—and not, I think, because I am more deterministically Western than Gendlin. To me, Heidegger's thinking, well before the opening Plato citation in *Sein und Zeit*, is already *hermeneutical in a historically determinate way*. *Sein und Zeit*'s recreation of the three standard prejudices "suggests," says Heidegger, the sort of understanding of Being that, already operating in our lives, dominates that aforementioned situation "out of which grows the explicit question *and the initial conceptual tendency with regards to it*." But for Heidegger (and for me), to find one is operating within a conceptual tendency—to tend continually to reenact a "vague and ordinary" understanding so thoroughly "pervaded by traditional theories and opinions about Being . . . that these theories, as the source of the dominant understanding, remain covered over" (*SZ*, 5–6; my emphases)—and to discover "being" so situated, is not to confront a forced option between historical entrapment and the need for a "new history." In other words, even before *Sein und Zeit*, Heidegger's talk about the "historical determinateness" of current understanding, far from staying *within* the traditional overarching assumptions about the Being-question and so operating *in tension with* a more inspired Daseinsanalysis, is already expressive of precisely the sort of "carrying forward" that shows how necessary it is to think both this analysis and the Being-question hermeneutically. As Heidegger reports in *Sein und Zeit*, he starts with ontological "perplexity," not just a casual question. He uncovers a pervasive "disincentive," not just some arguments, against doing anything about it. And yet *the very experiencing of this* opens up the possibility of a new sort of ontological asking.[45]

In short, I think that for fifty years Heidegger carries forward a project that has all the signs of one of Gendlin's uneasy cases. For Heidegger, the three initially deterring prejudices, far from offering "purely conceptual" grounds for abandoning his question or for explaining its incurable Westernness, function instead like the coming of "wrong words" when one is trying to say (in this case, ask) something. It is *in this functioning*, and not as part of any "metaphilosophical" problematic, that "historical" considerations first enter Heidegger's thinking. He *experiences* the three prejudices/assumptions as inherited, tradition-bound wrong words—i.e., standard explications that come easily but somehow will not do, even if for many others they still constitute obvious deflationary "theses." Given nothing more than this experience of "Perplexed, I ask again . . ." / "It is not worth asking . . . ," Heidegger already has enough. For just by explicating his sense of the way inherited prejudices deflate his question, he learns how to give it "ontological priority," to work toward thinking the meaning of Being in its "own proper way," and even—in light of the peculiar "relatedness back and forth" of question-posing and deterred questioning he *experiences in* these preliminary considerations— to begin by interrogating our lives, insofar as it is "there" where "one" already has an "unsuitably conceived relation between Being and human being" as a "distressing difficulty."[46]

On my reading, then, historical critique and hermeneutical inspiration—as a single project, already within but not trapped by the dominant Western assumptions—informs Heidegger's entire path of thinking, from perhaps 1919 on. To be sure, we have grown to know his historical/hermeneutical question-posing through the various Heideggeriana that have made him famous. In *Sein und Zeit*, e.g., there are phenomenological "science" and its "method," inauthentic and authentically "resolute" modes of existence, disclosures of Being as "transcendental truth," and a destruction of traditional ontology that is somehow linked with the uncovering of an "authentic meaning of Being." Yet, I recommend *thinking with* Heidegger here, rather than reading him *in terms of* these phrases. To focus on the story of his use and/or eventual rejection of various Heideggeriana is to put all the emphasis on discarded concepts and ignore what, precisely by using them, Heidegger came to see he did not mean and could not work out. For they are all—from "fundamental ontology" to Being, crossed out—in Gendlin's illuminating phrase, words working—and eventually not working well enough—in new ways.[47]

One of the eventually discarded vehicles is, of course, hermeneutics itself; and here I am of two minds. On the one hand, Gendlin's *Experiencing and the Creation of Meaning* (and later, when I found it, his MA Thesis) has served me for years as a model for what hermeneutics can become— once it loses the "scientific" tendencies it still has in Dilthey and was later, and counter to Dilthey's own deepest intentions, again presumed to have by so many others. On the other hand, precisely this widespread failure to take up the issue of Dilthey's "restiveness" makes me sympathetic with Heidegger's decision to give up the term. Yet it is, I believe, only the term he gave up.[48] I am unpersuaded that this terminological decision signals any counterhermeneutical tendency in Heidegger's historical critique.

Let me use this question of keeping/abandoning terminology to get to my final issue. There is a problem here, involving the possibility that one might become, let me call it, too easily attracted by the possibilities of Gendlin's experiential hermeneutics. This problem is nicely set up in *Sein und Zeit* (sec. 6) by Heidegger's seemingly innocent preliminary remark that in working out a more suitable conception of the relation between Being and human being, he will have to take seriously the fact that "Dasein *not only* has the inclination to have fallen into grip of the world [of implements and objects] in which it is and to interpret itself in terms of that world . . . [but] is *at the same time* in the grip of a tradition which it more or less explicitly grasps" (*SZ*, 21; my emphasis). Because it conceives human existence this doubled way, *Sein und Zeit* has often been read as leaving open the possibility that I, as individual, might deal with entrapment *first* factically (à la Division 1) and *then* historically (à la Division 2)—i.e., first in "my" authentic response to the anonymous press of daily affairs, and subsequently in relation to "our" entrapment in a larger sociohistorical context. Yet, this cannot be right. Had Heidegger actually fancied such a two-stage process—i.e., had he paused to contemplate an individualistic response to everyday fallenness, somehow to be worked out *before* considering the way the Being-question is now deterred by tradition—he would have turned his present asking of this question into one more event in the history of ontology, i.e., into one more choice to be made by a sufficiently self-possessed subject. In fact, however, this line of thinking runs counter to Heidegger's basic inspiration. Part 1, Division 2 of *Sein und Zeit*, is conceived from the start as a further interpretive "deepening" of Division 1's analysis of human facticity, and not as adding on another feature, or layer, called "historicity."

Yet, think of all those who did not appropriate *Sein und Zeit* in this "downwardly spiraling" way—from the existentialists content to privilege authentic over inauthentic "life" without taking up the matter of its "concrete" temporalizing (despite Heidegger's remark that explicating human *Zeitlichkeit* is "tantamount" to uncovering the "*Temporalität des Seins*"), to the current Anglo-American epistemologists who look to Division 1 alone for the means to rethink their inherited problem set.[49] Even Heidegger himself could "note only later" this weakness in *Sein und Zeit*'s treatment of history. In the meantime, he did at least project, if not actually pursue, such ahistorical notions as an "authentic sense of being" and a metontological analysis; and for a while, he did in fact imagine that metaphysics might be "overcome" in the experiences of art and poetry, and that a "people" or a "movement" might be uniquely situated to effect this overcoming. All of these efforts, taken in themselves, *could* be presumed to identify Heidegger's thinking as the "latest" in a linear series, as among the most recent "Western" philosophical strategies—and one all the more metaphysical for trying to be postmetaphysical. But this, I think, would be to measure his ideas from precisely the sort of spectator's standpoint which Heidegger avoided by making his line of thinking a hermeneutical "path" instead of the foundation for a "conceptual," or metaphilosophical, position. Yet, as Pöggeler puts it, Heidegger had to learn how to "critically distinguish between that which builds itself historically [i.e., metaphysical epochs] and that which, *also seen from a historical perspective*, is still more than, and different from, a historical becoming [viz., the "eventuation" of "clearing and Presence" together]."[50] My italics mark that "[hermeneutico-]historical perspective" which I believe Heidegger always had—one that does not fall out into a hermeneutical opening, on the one hand, and a "purely conceptual" survey of overarching determinants, on the other, but one that is nevertheless able to think how it is we *inherit* what has been "built up historically" and can thus empower us to carry it forward.

The issue here is important because, when Gendlin plays his own project off against Heidegger by criticizing the latter's "conceptual" handling of historical determination, out of a concern for "the role of individual humans in the coming of a new history," this appears to me to repeat an old and unfortunate contrast between history and individuals—one just like the "individualistic" contrast seemingly marked out when Division 1 analyzes facticity before historicity is even mentioned. Gendlin, I am sure, will object that he knows and often talks of the sad if not insurmountable effect of sociocultural constraints—e.g., on therapeutic practice, on ethical decision-making, on philosophical analysis, on our very bodiliness. Yet, to observe critico-sociologically the effects of cultural constraint is *not* to consider, *while thinking-with experiential intricacy*, "how" such constraints continue to operate. And in fact, Gendlin tends to talk *either* of constraints "on us" *or* of carrying forward "by individuals," one-on-one, between persons with good inclinations already willing to "process" objections/challenges.

The problem is that this double image of human life as involving "both" cultural imposition "and" creative processing—as possessing (say) Foucault's mechanisms of social control plus well-functioning experiential intricacy—is too neat. There is at work in this double image—if not for Gendlin then certainly for many of his readers—a deep and pervasively influential understanding that continues, silently and easily, to make everything Gendlin tries to do *seem* immediately unscientific, subjectivistic, a little too respectful of the process of conceptual change at the expense of the power of common schemes that resist it. The problem is not, I think, that most persons are still either unconsciously or willfully living out the culturally imposed norms, so that we can just look forward to a growing number of others who, once they have somehow found that Gendlin's kind of experiential processing involves "a deeper honesty than the usual kind, . . . [will] *soon prefer* the sincerity of living from that process."[51] Nor do I think Gendlin thinks so, even if he sometimes speaks of the future in this upbeat tone.

Gendlin's writings are full of acknowledgments that considerable traditional conceptualization stands in the way of seeing his points. Yet to foster a wider reception of his project, is it really right to speak, by turns, of a "historical critique" of overarching assumptions *and* of more and more "individuals" learning to think-with experiential processing? Or is there also the need for a more hermeneutical carrying forward of our Western inheritance—one that is more integral to the thinking-with process itself, i.e., one that does not wind up resembling the excessively "conceptual" critiques of Foucault or Habermas? Apropos Gendlin, I think this question is neither rhetorical nor merely a linguistic quibble. We agree that in thinking-with, something like a very nontraditional sort of "individualization" (*Vereinzelung*) opens up. Yet his "metaphilosophical" (or at other times Kantian, Derridian, or social-scientific) reading of Heidegger's destruction, and the manner in which he often turns from that "powerful critique" toward the possibility of you or I engaging in thinking-with, both make me nervous. As it stands, the previous sentence may be unfair to Gendlin's own practice. Yet it does, I believe, identify a recurring problem with his characterization of that practice. However successfully hermeneutical are his own studies, Gendlin seems to me to underinterpret the fact that, like Heidegger's retrieval of the Being-question in relation to the three metaphysical prejudices, any current practice of "thinking-with" takes place where "conceptual imposing" still predominates; hence, I have argued that, like this retrieval, it calls for the same sort of historico-hermeneutical carrying forward which Heidegger enacts, among other places, in the opening pages of *Sein und Zeit*.

Finally, however, it would be ungrateful to end on this accusatory note. Gendlin has found a way to universalize the hermeneutical promise of *Sein und Zeit*'s Daseinsanalysis—i.e., to think in detail *with* rather than *about* that endless, intricate, "finer experiential organization" which always functions in our conceptualizing/explicating process. After centuries of Epistemology, philosophy needs a good stiff dose of this thinking. It needs to take seriously the fact that in this process, as Gendlin says in one place, more always comes out than went in, and this is what makes

> human nature . . . a different sort of "is," an is-for developing into what (we later say) the person really "was." That development cannot be decided or directed by what a person now is, thinks, or wants, nor by anyone else. . . . If one's purposes were to determine the developmental process, one would be permanently stuck. Persons and situations are a single interlocking system. In [this] kind of process both person and facts turn out to "have been" more than they seemed.[52]

Dilthey and Heidegger have helped Gendlin say, as he goes on to do here, that this human process is no mere "assumption"—i.e., that "we observe it, we do it, we must face it." Yet, if he thus *carries forward* the experiential and hermeneutical spirit of their work, his writings make it clear that in finding this process everywhere—and not just in human scientific or Daseinsanalytic circumstances—Gendlin's project is one of the few today that may justifiably be said to come *after* Dilthey and Heidegger as well.

Reply to Scharff

I thank Professor Scharff for his rich and deep-going discussion, for bringing out so much of value in my work, and surely also for concluding that I "come justifiably after Heidegger." He says that I do not fall back from what Heidegger opened, and move a (highly conditioned) step further. He certainly gives me a wealth to reply to, concerning Heidegger, Dilthey, and my own work. I will take up two issues.

　　1. Scharff interprets my criticism of Heidegger as if I read him like the Derridians do, as leading to the current impasse. Scharff thinks I criticize Heidegger's beautiful "reevaluation of the concepts of the Western tradition" in *Being and Time*, especially part 2. But I do not criticize that at all, rather that during his middle period Heidegger *turned away* from *Being and Time*, thereby losing one of its crucial contributions. I will go into it below. Scharff dismisses the thirty years of the middle period with a sentence, telling us not to focus on it. But the whole subsequent development of "postmodern" philosophy has come from Heidegger's middle period. Not to deal with it means not dealing with the current issues. Of course I don't read Heidegger as Derrida does, but I see what

it is in Heidegger that has led to that reading. Instead of meeting my criticism of the middle period, Scharff defends *Being and Time* against my supposed criticism of its historical critique.

2. Scharff recognizes that I am not oblivious of how the tradition inheres in our language. What Heidegger did with the word "Being" I do with every word, he says. For many years I had to point to the old concepts inherent in peoples' words. I am thrilled that they now often turn in midst of a sentence, to recognize the old concepts. But this alone does not go far enough. We can go further because words can say something new. This is possible because more than concepts functions in speaking.

The history of philosophy and the reevaluation of concepts play a constant role in the construction of my sentences and in the . . . . . My kind of historical critique is not quite the usual one, since it stems *not only* from Heidegger, and since it often functions implicitly. At those times when we enter the intricacy, we are not *overtly* criticizing old concepts. This worries Scharff because surely an articulation of intricacy must *simultaneously* be at least an implicit critique of old concepts. I am glad he values the result, and I will be glad to reply on this issue.

Scharff awaits a great "sea-change," after which the old concepts would no longer obstruct us. Sometimes he sounds as if he advises us *only* to wait, as if our current thinking could not bring the change any closer. But in what other way could it come? In *Being and Time* Heidegger said that history moves through our "retrieving repetition," which need not be trapped in *mere* repetition. Gadamer has since brought this creative "repetition" to attention again. What counts is not only critique, but whether we *merely* repeat, or "repeat." The tradition is implicit in any thought and discussion, not only when it is overtly the topic. Nothing we say is merely individual. New saying is possible only because just these words with just this history say what they say when they come into new phrases in a new context. When that happens, we must allow them their new sense.

I agree with Scharff that the old assumptions cannot simply be overcome, because they inhere in the language. But for that very reason we cannot simply "await" a time when this won't be so. Heidegger did not come to such a conclusion. At the end he returned to a situated kind of thinking (although most readers have not followed him in this return). He called for a new thinking which he considered possible *now*. This "dwelling-thinking" (with which I have long been concerned) is not only overt critique, although that is implicitly involved.[1]

By a new beginning Heidegger did not mean something so far idealized that we should not begin it now.[2] The later Heidegger put more emphasis on *letting* something come, rather than *deciding*. He said that we come closer in those special moments when a further step "withholds itself" (*Beiträge*, 262).

I will discuss both issues, first my criticism of Heidegger, then the simultaneity of intricacy and historical critique.

Our disagreement comes near the end of the commentary, where Scharff turns to defend Heidegger. I criticize Heidegger for not employing the more-than-conceptual thinking with situatedness (*Befindlichkeit*), which he had developed in *Being and Time*:

> The possibilities of disclosure which belong to cognition reach far too short a way compared with the primordial disclosure belonging to moods. (*BT*, part 1, sec. 29, 134)

> Understanding is never free-floating, but always moody [*befindliche*, situated]. Having a mood brings Dasein face to face with its thrownness . . . not known as such, but disclosed far more primordially in 'how one is.'" (*BT*, part 2, sec. 68, 339–40)

In my criticism I asked: Since this moody (*befindliche*, situated, being-in) understanding "reaches further," don't we want to think with this superior, further-reaching kind of understanding in our philosophical thinking? But in Heidegger's long middle period he give no role to our situated "being-in." He considered all practice as merely derivative. Where earlier he had portrayed our being-in-situations (in practice, in the world) *as an understanding that exceeds cognition*, now he treated life and practice as *merely derived from* the overarching conceptions characteristic of each historical period ("from the top down," as I call it). Now it seemed useless to think from being-in. It offered no openness, only historical particularization.[3]

I argue that the current impasse, and why Heidegger now seems to have brought it on, rather than engendering the further thinking he intended, is due to the loss of the situated understanding of being-in, which could exceed the top-down constraint of any conceptions. Without this, there now seem to be only the old concepts, coupled with critique and contradiction.

Since Scharff does not see this (well-known) "top-down" determinacy in Heidegger, he thinks that what I refer to is the historical critique. He defends the critique in *Being and Time* by showing that it is not from the top down, but "*hermeneutical*." He applies this word also to my philosophy. This is not just wrong, but to be right we must let the old word acquire what it can mean, when it says how new uses let words acquire new meaning in new phrasings beyond the old conceptions. *Enabling the words to do this is the kind of "simultaneous critique" of the old concepts, which I require.* Such new emergence is just what Scharff first appreciates in my work, and then criticizes as seemingly without simultaneous critique. It is not without that, but we must understand and employ the capacity of language for new saying.

I studied McKeon's historical critique before Heidegger's. Knowing both, one cannot help thinking with and after both. Each immensely strengthens the other. What I write always moves with both of them. It is true that I do not constantly retrace their critiques as such. They *occur* in (they rearrange the language in the . . . . . which leads to) my sentences.

With Heidegger the strategies and assumptions are arrayed in a linear successive order; he deconstructs them moving backwards in history. But McKeon offers four strategies for doing history (each also variable in several other dimensions). Heidegger's way of doing history is only one. We always carry it with us, but we are now all aware that more than one treatment is possible on any topic, however small. And the history of Western thought is no small topic. It need not be understood only as Heidegger construed it. Perhaps my saying this sounded as if I reject Heidegger's "historical strand." But both critiques function ongoingly for me. After Heidegger we cannot lose the sense of living at a unique spot in a single historical development. We don't lose this just because McKeon lacked this point. And, after McKeon, we cannot fail to notice the philosophical strategies that compete contemporaneously throughout the history of philosophy. They also compete at every juncture of our own sentences, as they form.

When I began, it was McKeon who had shown that every treatment involves assumptions and strategies that could be otherwise. The now familiar accusations of relativism and nihilism were then aimed at him. Those of us who knew his work were alone in recognizing that every philosophy (in current terms) centers and cuts in ways that have equally good and equally unfounded alternatives. As with Heidegger and Derrida, the problem McKeon poses needs to be kept open; it does not need to be "solved." There is a way to go on with and from it. What is special about McKeon is the power that comes with the knowledge of alternative strategies. To be able to get out of one, and into another, is thrilling. For anything we say or read, alternative strategies and forms immediately suggest themselves. Once they are familiar, no one of them constrains. They are all implicitly at work in any . . . . . Historical critique happens as one thinks and speaks; now when we say just one, it brings its critique and also the others. In McKeon's time this was often thought to bring paralysis. But we can think forward from the . . . . . in which the alternatives are all implicit. Of course this happens only after much work with the concepts, but it lets us go *on*, rather than only retracing them.

Scharff sees how my work moves beyond relativism. Taken alone, different approaches are mutually exclusive, but our next step of thought can be *implicitly* protected by all the approaches we know. Then either we remain stuck with . . . . . , or the next step moves beyond those approaches.

I can hardly live my way into a sentence without calling its words into question. Take this very sentence: *I can hardly* say "I can hardly say . . . . ." without thinking "I? The agent subject?" (Then I turn inwardly to the *I* . . . . . from whom I spoke, who is of course still happening.) How about: A sentence hardly forms itself . . . . . ? "Hegel's dialectical movement? The distinctions march, he said—as if without us. Do sentences form without us?" How about: Each word brings alternate words . . . . . ? "Now we're in the atomic unit model." Next proposed comes: The context of thinking contains many traditional alternatives . . . . . ? "The scheme of contextual wholes and sub-wholes?" But all this happens without fully verbalized proposals. I write "I can hardly . . . . . ," and new phrases come from the . . . . . which has been carried forward by all those schemes, and protected from each by the others, so that it implies something beyond each, and may rearrange the implicit language. But even if I used an old phrase, now it would speak from . . . . .

Scharff says what he wants is a "thinking-with experiential intricacy about how the constraints (by the old concepts) continue to operate." I am concerned rather with how it is possible for the old concepts *not* to constrain. Both are possible only because concepts operate within the wider situational intricacy; it can open them, or they can reimpose themselves on it.

Scharff wants the old concepts always addressed *as such*. I find, on the contrary, that once we know them, we can open them only by articulating a further intricacy as such. The issue between us is itself intricate. To resolve it, let us enter into the intricacy of a situation, and then return to the question.

For example, in my class on "Theory Construction" the students come from many fields. I invite them to think of something in their field which they would like to articulate. From his research on Alcoholics Anonymous and from reading the current literature on "renarrating the past," a student has written a draft Ph.D. thesis in the current vocabulary, with a long section on the human subject as no fixed thing, "not like a chair." He says that a person is only "a changeable narration." Asked to find something he knows but has not yet articulated, he speaks about something unsatisfying that he did not even consider mentioning in his thesis. He says, "One's past is not like a chair, but . . . . ." When asked for an oddly phrased sentence, he writes: "One's past is not like a chair, but *one does butt up against something.*" Here he already has what Scharff worries about, the *overt* critique of the old objectivist concept of human events ("not like a chair"), and he also has an *implicit critique* of the current counterconcept of indeterminacy and arbitrary construction, no truth. Earlier he has read and written at length about the old concept as such, as Scharff wants, and so he will not be tempted to formulate the "butting up against" as entity-events. Nor should he concern himself with the new concept as such. Right now he must enter directly into the intricacy *of the narration situation* which exceeds what he can as yet formulate. He must let words make odd phrases from there. Without entering the intricacy, he only repeated what he had read.

When I invite students to attend to something not yet articulated, a few of them do reinvent Descartes, as Scharff fears. But many make quite un-Cartesian points that are more intricate than anything in the tradition. I will shortly show where Scharff is right, but he is wrong in this respect: *Humans do not need the critique of concepts in order to come up with more intricacy.* We live (act, think, speak . . . . .) from it all the time. *The old concepts do not even reach it, and so they do not constrain it. In practice the intricacy often eludes the concepts.* At such a point, I ask students to "write a sentence which cannot make any sense at all, unless it is understood as you mean it." After a few examples, the students can do it, because the new sense of the . . . . . has already implicitly rearranged the language.

The problem comes when students try to formulate theory. Then they lose hold of what they had, and often conclude something else— something Cartesian, because they cannot yet think about various kinds of concepts as such. *This is the respect in which Scharff is right.* But they need more than one line of critique. I must spend much of the course presenting typical conceptual forms (derived from Heidegger, McKeon, Merleau-Ponty, and myself). *But critiques are not enough.* They must learn to hold tenaciously to their . . . . ., and always to return to it, to insure that every step carries it forward. They must learn to notice when a formulation makes the . . . . . shrivel or disappear. And, even all this is not enough. I must show them how to form new concepts directly from the odd sentence, how such a sentence implicitly redefines the main words, how the new use can be explicated by other words, and how those also become redefined thereby.

Scharff is right to want *both* intricacy *and* overt critique, but he is not right to want the intricacy to be about the old concepts as such. With-out attending directly to intricacy, nothing would be new, and without letting new concepts emerge from language, there would be only the old concepts.

Scharff asks to hear about how the old concepts continue to constrain. Let us enter the intricacy to examine when they constrain, and when not: a concept works-in (has effects in, synthesizes, differentiates, lifts out something from . . . . .) *the intricacy.* Its effects *there* exceed what can follow from its conceptual structure. If we ignore its intricate effects, if our next step comes only from its conceptual structure, then it constrains. If we think and speak from its effect in intricacy, then the concept can contribute, but it cannot constrain.

Every sentence, and every aspect of a situation is an intricacy. We can override the intricacy, or dwell there.

I have written much overt historical critique (see "TBP," A1–2, and *ECM* on the reversal of the usual philosophical procedure, and on "reflexivity"). I track the traditional priority.

My essay "A Philosophical Critique of the Concept of Narcissism" was mainly on the social-historical level. Scharff quotes only an aside about one respect in which some people are ahead of most philosophers. He might have cited where I say that unemployed people cannot by experiential explication arrive at a critique of the tight money and scarce jobs policy of the Federal Reserve Bank. I argued that we need concepts about economics, and must overcome the current belief that it must be left to economists. I show how the personality types of successive age-cohorts derive in part from historical and macro-economic changes.

Yes, some problems can be found only on the social level. But that concerns the level of analysis, and social action. Individual experience is also always social, *although causation and influence can run in either direction.* A new sociology could investigate the conditions that make for either direction.

With the authors he quotes, Scharff is great and enjoyable as he pinpoints where they fall back in the very attempt to move ahead. But he gives them no credit for where they *do* move past the old traps. He is also unfair to Dilthey.[4] He cannot believe that our whole century has been a transition in which the "sea-change" *is happening,* and that Dilthey, Husserl, Wittgenstein, Heidegger, he and I and others are part of it.

Heidegger never stopped trying to go on. The poetic mode of his later writing was a way of going on. Over and over, he moves freshly from what he called an openness; he poetizes until the words and phrases seem to entrap him, then he shifts to what he called "pointing."[5]

In his last writings, Heidegger is sure that language opens more possibilities than it can foreclose. Dwelling goes beyond the forms. "Dwelling" is his late word for the "moody" (*befindlich*) situated thinking he had in *Being and Time*.[6]

Of course my reply had to deal with where we differ. I very much appreciate Scharff's appreciation of my work.

Language and Human Nature

Lawrence J. Hatab

In this essay I want to engage the question of human nature in a post-modern atmosphere, focusing on Eugene Gendlin's provocative contri-butions to this topic.[1] Gendlin presents a challenge to the postmodern movement and its approach to human nature inherited from Heidegger, which embraces differences and particulars in response to the collapse of traditional models of universals in the human condition. Gendlin is troubled by the fact that American scholars are advocating diversity in the spirit of a Heideggerian historicism, while not being mindful enough of the relation between that historical particularism and the horrors of the Nazi movement.[2] When Americans renounce the common in favor of the particular, we tend to imagine a tolerant celebration of differences. Gendlin, a Jewish refugee from Vienna, is less optimistic. He sees in particularism the danger of tribalism, namely the concentration on *one* people's language and culture at the expense of, or to the exclusion of, other groups. For Gendlin, such a development is certainly no less problematic than traditional assumptions of rational universals. When we postmodernists grope for a vocabulary to speak against the terrible ethnic conflicts in Eastern Europe and other regions, we should realize that Gendlin's admonition has great warrant. The abandonment of uni-versalism is an extremely dangerous course. We need to be reminded that belief in something universal, whether in ancient Greek thought or in the European Enlightenment, did not arise in the vacuum of mere academic musings, but in response to real, violent, fractious strife between different allegiances, each affirming their differences with great resolve.

What makes Gendlin's response so effective is that he does not ignore the legitimate critique of traditional universalism. He asks us to rethink what "universal" means or can mean. If we attend to human experience and language, he suggests, we can find a universality different from the notions of commonness, sameness, constancy, and the like. Surrendering these latter notions is the proper legacy of Heidegger's thinking, but surrendering any sense of universality is the danger facing postmodern thought. Gendlin thinks it is possible, and necessary, to discover a nonrationalistic universality in the human condition.

Gendlin believes that Heidegger's thought had the potential to develop a cross-differential sense of human nature (primarily in the early writings), but that his historical particularism led him not only to miss this opportunity but to inevitably fall into the trap of the German catastrophe. I have not yet been convinced that such failings are endemic to Heidegger's thinking. In fact, I have tried to work with Heidegger's deconstruction of traditional frameworks and forge out of this "void" a notion of ontological "negativity" that can speak against the abuses we deplore without slipping back into a kind of substantive universality.[3]

It is true that Heidegger's repudiation of Enlightenment universalism, rationalism, and individualism nourished an attraction for a folkish particularism, rustic primitivism, and authoritarianism—all of which brought on disaster. We should not forget that the Enlightenment project had an emancipatory effect in response to many abusive and constraining tendencies. But we should also heed the critique of that project fostered by thinkers like Heidegger. The Enlightenment ideal of a common human nature was generally a blend of scientific rationalism and Christian universalism, where the necessity of rational principles joined the spiritual transcendence of nature to produce a picture of humanity beyond the contingencies and differences in the physical domain. Such an ideal has been rightly criticized for its suppression of differences and its promotion of the assault upon nature in the manner of technicity.

In human affairs, a universalist ideal was in many ways bogus because it was a *disguised* ethnocentrism—in "we are all the same" read "be like us, or else!" Such a translation can decode the sincere paternalism of colonialists—"Our arrival will 'free' the native population from its primitive confinement"—to reveal the actual effect: cultural annihilation. But it is true that abandoning the Enlightenment project in favor of celebrating differences brings on the danger of tribalism—the movement from "we are not all the same" to "we have nothing in common" or, more subtly, to "you cannot understand our world"—something no less dangerous than universalism because the dehumanization of the Other can become almost effortless.

Cultural differences are natural, inevitable, and an enhancement of life. The problem, in my view, is not particularism, but reductionism—

the *grounding* of human nature in some definite condition or structure—whether particular or universal. Tribalism is no less reductive than traditional universals, it is simply a reduction to a particular group's characteristics. What we need is some general outlook on human nature that is based on openness, that is neither suppressive of differences nor limited to differences, and that can avoid the reductionism common to both tendencies.

I believe that the basis for such an outlook can be found in Heidegger's thought, especially in *Being and Time*. I am convinced that, for the most part, the Care configuration is universally valid. The existential analysis of a pretheoretical world organized around *Verstehen* (understanding), *Befindlichkeit* (disposition), and *Rede* (discourse) is the best candidate I know of for bridging cultural differences, because it precedes philosophical, scientific, and ideological constructions that are often not represented commonly across cultures. This is not to say that nothing needs to be added or modified in the Care structure, but I can think of no human culture that cannot fit into its contours. Heidegger himself proclaims that his existential analysis is general enough to encompass every worldview and ontical interpretation of Dasein.[4]

The Care structure, however, being "transcendental," does not prescribe the specific content of cultures. What is decisive for my thinking here is the "transcendence" of Dasein, which (as is made clear in the notions of Angst in "What Is Metaphysics?" and being-toward-death in *Being and Time*) means being held out into the Nothing. At the heart of Dasein is not a definable essence, but Nothing. What we have in common, then, is an "abyssal" dimension that shows the essential *finitude* of all constructs. And this dimension is what makes disclosure as such possible; the "negation" of beings illuminates the meaning of the Being of beings (that they are *not* nothing), a general notion that is given some concretion in the idea of disclosure as un-concealment. Disclosure out of the abyss lets our ontic differences be, because a common essence can not be presumed or discovered; but keeping the abyss in view *also* forbids reduction to these differences, and thus works against tribalism, which passes beyond cultural particularity to a myopic fixation that obscures or cancels out the dignity of the Other.

In my view, a "tragic" model of human existence—where the self dwells in the midst of an abyss—can protect against closure and oppression of all kinds by sensitizing us to our common finitude, by emphasizing the movements of life rather than fixed results, and by disrupting all the definitional references with which we promote ourselves and demote others. Since human beings cannot be fixed by any designation, all the categories of race, ethnicity, gender, class, and the like that fuel so much trouble can be intercepted by a negative correction. So the deconstruction of positive references that marks the postmodern condition need not mean the commission or permission of factional strife, as long as an abyssal limit is applied to any and all categories.

Gendlin is critical of talk such as this. He wants to go beyond talk of negativity and formlessness to find what is positive and generative in thinking beyond forms and structures. The rejection of fixed form in the tradition need not mean the rejection of any notion of form or the surrender to notions of formlessness, both of which are still caught up in the assumption that fixed form is the only kind, that the choice is between fixed form and no form. Gendlin, in my reading, wants to accomplish two things: first, to show that form and nonform, language and experience, are not opposites; and second, to draw from the first point the notion that linguistic forms are not an arbitrary imposition on some primal formlessness or undecidable process (a common trend in postmodern thought). What is important here for the question of human nature is that Gendlin maintains that an emphasis on negativity and formlessness generates or permits an ethnocentric segregation of particulars, since there is "nothing" between different cultural groups; difference is identity, and the "other" might not even count as "human."

It seems that Gendlin wants to restore the meaning of "nature" (in the Greek sense of *physis*) without ignoring the insights of postmodernism concerning the mistakes of the tradition. So we could talk about the "nature" of something without fixing it; nature need not be equivalent to a metaphysical concept of "essence." Consequently, we could say that a thing's nature *is* open and dynamic, getting us beyond the false choice between fixed description and indescribability. This is a view that I share. Gendlin also wants to use such a notion to challenge the unbridgeable particularism and historicism discussed previously, to work toward some sense of universality in human "nature." This is a view that gives me some pause.

Gendlin has found a way to work within a nonfoundationalist milieu without stumbling into a radical skepticism, anarchism, or nihilism.[5] His work on implicit intricacy, situation, and embodiment is a very rich articulation of the positive fullness of a decentered, ungrounded condition in human experience. But Gendlin speaks against a simplistic emphasis on nonform or loss of form that misses or underplays the process of form-in-the-making. What I have called negativity Gendlin wants to call implication or potentiality, the not-yet-form, which indicates not the absence of form but the elusive and yet palpable dynamics of form-ing.

In this way Gendlin takes issue with the polar opposition of experience and form that is common in both modern and postmodern philosophy. Such opposition stems from the assumption that the only valid model of form or structure is the constancy of logico-mathematical patterns, which the fluidity and particularity of experience do not or cannot match. For Gendlin, human experience has an order that is different from a rigid structure. Such an order can be read out by attending not only to what we experience, but to *how* we experience its unfolding. We can find, he suggests, that language and experience are not only not opposed to each other, they mutually inform each other in a single, reciprocal dynamic: "feelings, situations, and language are inherently involved in each other."[6] Such a correlation shows itself to be neither disorderly nor rigidly ordered: it is "nonnumerical, multischematic, and interschematizable," and the validity of such a scheme is not to be found in some theoretical justification but in its application to our practices.[7]

Experience and language are an open process of explication that is ever-fluid but not arbitrary, since situations and outcomes give us a sense of aptness, which forbids us just any description we want and which opens up the possibility of phenomenological truth.[8] What unfolds here is an "intricate order" that works with forms both implicit and explicit, but that is always more than form alone when we consider the process of our experience.[9]

An intricate order enables us to negotiate ways in which form and nonform interpenetrate each other, and to overcome the tendency to deny truth to human pursuits that do not fit the exactitude of scientific schemes. A crucial inheritance of modern philosophy has been the notion that human meanings are merely superimpositions upon experience that originate in the human subject and tell us nothing about the world.

> Currently people speak of "giving" meaning to events, or "adding" interpretation to experience, as if our situations were merely putty on which we could stamp whatever form we like. They rightly reject the simplistic notion that events have only a single formed meaning. But why turn to the opposite simplistic notion: that events have no meaning of their own at all? If that were so we would all put excellent meanings on our situations and life would be easy. No one seriously believes this. Then why is that said so often? It is because reality is assumed to be the spatial pattern-world. Human meanings seem to have no inherent connection to *that* reality. So they seem merely added on. There have not been concepts for the implicit intricacy that is more than patterns.[10]

The way is open to find truth in less exact conditions by rejecting a univocal model of truth in favor of a dynamic, pluralistic sense of truth. Such a move, of course, raises the question of the possibility of judgment, of how to recognize and discern better and worse outcomes, i.e., how we can differentiate truth and nontruth in an atmosphere without fixed references. Gendlin seems to take a pragmatic approach to this question, as when he addresses the open-ended process of explication:

> The method may seem as if it launches us on an endless progression, but even here there are methodic ways of knowing when a desirable stopping point is reached; again the stopping point is not a final statement *of* an experience, but rather a way of structuring words or situations adequately so that some living, some action, or some intellectual task may be carried out.[11]

This is a fruitful approach to the question of truth, although a crude and simplistic pragmatism that limits truth to what "works" must be avoided by elaborating on the contours of human practices and their correlations with environmental and social conditions.

Gendlin has also found a way around the so-called trap of circularity wherein the process of saying cannot be said because in being said, the saying is lost in the confines of verbal forms. He does a great service in showing how saying can be described by attending to our experiences and by renouncing the fetish of verbal closure and univocity.[12] A poet's experience of pregnant suspension, waiting for the right word in relation to words already composed or words to come—this moment, which is represented on the page by a slot (. . . . .), is not nonverbal or even preverbal, since it is caught up with the rest of a text and can recognize the right word when it comes. Gendlin calls it an implying, a potential that is neither a pure form nor a nonform, but a not-yet-form that nicely illustrates his contention about a unified relation between form and nonform, language and experience.

Such a dynamic of implying continues to function even within established forms and terms. We are given examples of words that can operate in surprisingly new ways beyond supposed root meanings, and yet with a kind of precision that works well. Notice the following passage that operates with the word "derive."

> We see that what words say is not just *derived* from the existing forms. ("Derived" usually means deducible.) We see that what words say is not constrained within existing forms. Rather, the forms work within a wider implying which functions to imply, demand, *and also to let the words say* something new and more precise than existed before.
>
> But, even though "derive" usually means deducible from extant forms, note what happens if I ask, "How does the poet *derive* the next line?"

> Coming here, the word "derive" means how the poet does it. But that happens with all the words, as they come into a new slot. Soon there are no words left to take back.
>
> None of this threatens the stability of truth. What "not derived" said earlier now *stays true*—although to say it we must *take* "derived" (or some other word) in that way. You can see from this, that how we *take* a word, (and how you take "take" here) depends on something that functions implicitly. The (new and old) ways in which words can make sense involve very precise *functions of implicit intricacy.*[13]

This provides relief from the tendency to see words as fixed meanings that cannot capture the fluidity of experience, a view that collapses if we listen to the movements of word-usage and relax an academic fixation on exactitude. Word-usage can be seen as flexible, creative, interactive, and looser than philosophical models of precision (e.g., Plato's) and yet quite workable and suitable for our experiences. In attending to actual occasions of language in *process* we are able to look beyond the products of language to a creative dynamic that is nevertheless not arbitrary, since it is guided by, and fitted to, situations. Words are implicitly connected to thousands of other words in an ever-fluctuating system of movements that works within the movements of experience.

As an aside, I think that contemporary discourse could benefit greatly from such a loosened approach to traditional philosophical words. Too often a kind of anti-essentialist fetish makes important words taboo or suspicious and generates a countervocabulary or obscure neologisms. Words like "truth," "reason," "ethics," "spirit," "technique," and such can still find a legitimate use after metaphysical constraints have been lifted. One reason is that, as Gendlin indicates, they can function in our talk in flexible but appropriate ways. Another reason is that such words were in fact pirated by the philosophical tradition and stripped of certain prephilosophical and pretechnical meanings that are disclosive in different ways. Heidegger's near obsession with etymology and the history of elemental words was an attempt at such a reorientation toward our philosophical vocabulary. *Being and Time,* for example, was trying to recast traditional terms so that we could apprehend their meaning and the world's meaning differently. He concluded, however, that this was not working; people were still pressing his efforts into the categories of academic schools and their agendas. The *Kehre,* announced in "Letter on Humanism," was related to the failure of Heidegger's *language* in *Being and Time* and its reception, not the matter for thought therein.[14] What followed was Heidegger's turn to more poetic discourse, which in many ways surmounted that failure but which also created additional problems of obscurity and mystification. The language of the early philosophical writings can still work, in my opinion, and Gendlin's attention to the implicit intricacy of word-usage helps sustain a more open attitude toward our intellectual inheritance.[15]

Gendlin maintains that with his approach we can discover a rich vocabulary to describe how language works beyond mere forms and conceptual distinctions. He offers several generalizations that express what he calls *ways* of thinking: (1) a "string" of words, or implicit multiple meanings and connections that operate in word-formation; (2) a "fan" of distinctions; (3) thinking an "instance," or the contextual shifts words can make; (4) self-instancing, where some words can say something about how they work; (5) letting a "pattern" be the concept, where pragmatic, fluid operations better describe how concepts work than do theoretical, more archival models of conceptual form. Gendlin adds to these thought-ways concepts such as implying, carrying forward, form change, and novelty, which also fit the way language works in contextual practices.[16] In this manner, I think, the Heideggerian notion of unconcealment is given a far richer and more tangible expression, a recognizable set of circumstances where what is concealed is almost yearning to open up, and does so in our verbal movements.

Gendlin adds an effective material dimension to his treatment by bringing in the body and how embodiment figures in our situations and linguistic dynamics.

> The old scheme is wrong, that only the five senses (separately or in sum) tell about a situation. In fact, one would be hard-put to describe any human situation just in bits of tactile roughness, color, sound and smell, put together by some rational unities. *Body-sense is a perception too,* but the word "perception" changes here. . . .
>
> Body-sense and situation carry each other forward. It is no wonder that something new and more realistic can come from the body-sense, since the body-sense *is* the bodily-implicit situation of that person.
>
> . . . attending in the body leads to statements about one's situation. . . . One begins where there is a bodily sense of confusion—but it is an implicitly intricate confusion and it may come into focus. A [. . . . .] may come. Then one finds that one's whole life-situation was *in* this at-first murky body-sense. We see: *The body-sense is not subjective, not just internal, not private; it is the implicit situation.*
>
> . . . the body has a truth about a situation.[17]

Our bodies tell us much about the meaning of circumstances and about how language works. Provocative parallels can be drawn between bodily and verbal occurrences to show that words come to us in much the same way that emotions, appetites, fatigue, and other bodily events come: in appropriate ways that can not be forced or fabricated.[18] This is a significant move that corrects the all too common bypassing of embodiment in philosophy. Altogether Gendlin's work is a masterful survey of the concrete ways in which human experience and language operate in co-creating our sense of the world.

In sum, Gendlin argues for an intrinsic correlation of experience, language, situation, and embodiment, to counter the notion that form is separate from experience, an imposition on a chaos or unsayable form-lessness, and to challenge the subsequent notion that forms are arbitrary or merely human constructions. Forms are not stable and separate from a fluid experience, and experience is not without its form(ing).

> Since human events do not consist of static things, why remain entirely within a theory of knowledge that assumes only a truth of static things? Then it seems that there is no truth of human events. But there is certainly a truth of the implying of situations. That is why we deliberate long and carefully.[19]

Gendlin moves thought in the direction of the prereflective richness and movements of experience and embodiment. There we see that thought is not a departure from, nor an imposition upon, nor absent in, this embodied experience. Consequently nature, whether human or otherwise, is neither a fixed form nor without form.

Attention to prereflective experience has been one of the great contributions of existential and phenomenological thought. This opens the door to resolving many philosophical problems that can be traced to what I call a praxocentrism: since the *practice* of philosophy requires a reflective pause from world involvement, philosophers have been naturally prone to interpret knowledge as a form of reflection that is distinct from the world (e.g., "ideas" versus "things"); such distinctions *create* perennial philosophical problems (e.g., How are ideas related to things in the world?). But here philosophers have been guilty of imposing a model of knowing that simply follows from the way *philosophers* think, and that misses or distorts other forms of engagement. In other words, philosophical reflection itself can lead to obfuscation of human experience and its circumstances—and it is for this reason that Wittgenstein called for a radical *limitation* of philosophical vocabulary, and Heidegger called for a radical *transformation* of philosophical discourse.[20]

Gendlin's analysis goes a long way toward overcoming the gap between philosophical reflection and human experience. Perhaps it is his working with real live human beings in psychotherapy that gives him an advantage over philosophers in such matters. (I don't think I mean to imply that philosophers are not real live human beings.) Such a milieu also gives him effective case data to illustrate the models he is proposing.[21] One question I have is whether Gendlin's model might itself be praxocentrically limited in scope, that is, limited to the psychotherapeutic milieu. Does such a model ignore or distort more stable forms of speech and experience? Does it ignore other forms of speech and experience that are *more* open than therapy, that are not aiming to "get at" something, such as a solution to a life problem? Aside from these questions, I do think that his model applies quite well to creative activities of all sorts[22] and could well evolve into a general model of human conversation, in the sense of those dynamic, interactive, open processes that are nevertheless "guided" by something.

Another question I have is regarding the phenomenology of language and the relation between language and experience. Gendlin insists upon a correlation of language and experience to counter the false dichotomy between the negativity of nonform and the positivity of linguistic form. This is important for avoiding a crude reduction to language (if there is nothing describable beyond linguistic forms) and a reduction of language to form-conditions (if there is no relation to nonform). But I remain wedded to a certain phenomenological priority of language that causes me to question even some of Gendlin's distinctions. If we talk of "experience" as distinct from linguistic form, or of "potential" linguistic form in the movements of language use, have we here identified anything even distinct from language? Are not "experience," "potential," even "nonform" words in our language that guide Gendlin's analysis? Is not *everything* informed by language in some way? Gendlin's "slot" seems like an ingenious device to represent something distinct from formed language, but even his . . . . . is, I think, parasitic on language, at least in a graphic sense. I am not suggesting some kind of linguistic idealism or skeptical separation of language from "reality" (Gendlin's work is an effective antidote to such positions). I only indicate that a phenomenological priority of language makes questionable *any* talk of the nonlinguistic, whether it be a chaotic "opposite" to language, or an experiential "correlate" to language, or even a pregnant "potential" in language-formation—since all these notions are themselves linguistic presentations. Here I travel with Heidegger and Wittgenstein, both of whom maintained that "language" and "world" are coextensive. For Heidegger, language cannot be captured by symbolification or signification or any explanatory theory, since such notions are defined in terms of something already given in language.[23] It is not that in a strict sense there is *only* language, but that in a strict sense nothing we "say," even in negative terms, is distinct from the disclosive function of language. Accordingly, Heidegger called language the "house of Being," or more dynamically the "advent of Being itself."[24] So the "other than form" that Heidegger's thought considers is not really properly rendered by something like "negativity" or "nonform." The "other" of language is, for Heidegger, a mystery, or *concealment.*[25]

My remaining questions return to the issue of human nature. Gendlin is challenging the idea of a disconnected, arbitrary particularism with his notion of a dynamic, pluralistic, but situated and embodied human condition that can admit some sense of universality.

> Most modern philosophers have utterly lost an order of nature, human nature, the person, practice, the body. They deny that anything could have an order of its own. All order is assumed to be *entirely* imposed by a history, a culture, or a conceptual interpretation that could as well be different. . . .
>
> When only imposed forms are assumed, then humans seem to have nothing in common. Few forms seem to hold across the different cultures. . . . The *forms of* language, religion, family, and the cultural understandings about the human body are so different, that very little universal meaning can be formulated. It is said that humans are not even one species.
>
> . . . to be human is to be entirely artificial, no human nature, no human subject, no truth or values—only the imposed forms. And that is also the dominant view today. To overthrow this view involves a whole reorientation.[26]

I am impressed by Gendlin's category called "crossing," an interactive, self-altering movement of reciprocal implications, and I am intrigued by his suggestion that this category can get at something cross-cultural in human nature that need not mean some kind of common form.[27] But this is still vaguely stated. What is a cross-cultural, universal humanity? Can it be described in terms of any content or structure or what? How would it be used to respond to the aforementioned problem of tribalism?

My guess is that Gendlin is some kind of postmetaphysical, Aristotelian realist. In "Thinking beyond Patterns," Aristotle's notion of self-development is mentioned,[28] as is the "ancient" notion that "nature and nurture are not separable in humans. Language and thought forms are not just added on; they reorganize the human animal."[29] The idea of living bodies as a "self-organizing process"[30] is reminiscent of Aristotle, and the configuration of "tripling"[31] suggests something like Aristotle's threefold structure of nutritive, sensitive, and rational soul. Aristotle's contention that the soul and the world are a unity, a dual actualization of thought and nature,[32] his belief in a telos to explain the forward driving dynamic of the lifeworld that a merely material account could not explain, and his general scheme of potentiality and actuality—these Aristotelian notions suggest themselves when I read Gendlin's work, especially the analysis of implication and carrying forward: "The [. . . . .] *implies* a carrying-forward step that has not yet been said."[33] Is Gendlin's proposal of a universality in the human condition anything like a modified Aristotelian realism?

I admit to being ambivalent about the whole question of the universal-particular distinction these days. Particularism has become an uncritical dogma in some circles, leading to significantly muddled and precipitous ideas about ethics and politics. But I also worry about the promotion of a discernible "human nature," for three reasons. First, I am suspicious of what would constitute a human universal. To return to the therapeutic milieu as an example, I can imagine a psychological problem being resolved in any number of ways that seem substantially different and that need not even fit familiar techniques in Gendlin's profession. I can imagine anxiety being resolved by uncovering early childhood traumas or relationships, by unmasking current oppressive regimes, by bootstrapping or coping skills, by the grace of Jesus, by Buddhist emptiness, or even by some success or a little good news. . . . What is universal here? What crosses? That humans know how to find solutions to their problems in different ways? That seems rather vacuous. Second, talk of universality is risky, because the less empty it is the greater the opportunity for exclusion or demotion (Is a fundamentalist Christian solution to anxiety something less authentic than an existential therapeutic solution?). Third, there is an inevitable tragic element in human existence in terms of death, loss, and limits, which from a phenomenological standpoint disrupts all "bases" and "attributes," and which moreover constitutes the meaning of our lives. I mean this in the Heideggerian sense of being-toward-death. For me, it is the openness to our finitude that illuminates why the world is meaningful to us, and that helps clear the brush of encrusted and inherited meanings so that appropriate individual meanings might show more clearly. In addition, although I am open to the possibility of some kind of ethical universal, *being* ethical usually requires compassion, which comes from sensitivity to finitude and suffering; it also requires risk and sacrifice, which demand release from our attachments; it also requires, in the end, *decision*, which as such is stripped of all external and cognitive supports—these are things that "embracing the abyss" can help foster, in my view.

As stated earlier, Gendlin believes that embracing negativity generates or supports the idea that there is *nothing* between human groups, which can inform a tribalistic ethnocentrism. But the negativity I am addressing here is an *existential* negativity, the *experience* of finitude, of the ultimate contingency of our lives, and not a conceptual negation beyond the borders of formed regions. From a Heideggerian standpoint, Angst names a genuine experience of a fundamental truth of existence (as opposed to a mood disorder calling for Prozac). Such existential negativity is something that can easily cross cultural differences without having to identify "something" that all cultures have in common. For example, human beings may have many different interests, but we all know what it means to *lose* our interests and to face our mortality (such could be the starting point for a cross-cultural ethics). Gendlin maintains that the more-than-form should be viewed in terms of potentiality and the movements of experience. But does this cover up radical finitude? We must also acknowledge and give voice to the tragic dimension in our lives.

Reply to Hatab

I thank Professor Hatab for the way in which he presents me. We agree on many issues. I will come to his provocative questions. First, I notice that he still says—with Heidegger—that there is "nothing" in humans other than the cultural forms. But Hatab *feels* what he says very differently than Heidegger did.

I always defend Heidegger when Heideggerians attack him for his early interest in the Nazi party (before 1935). He didn't vote for that party; he voted for an obscure small party. Victor Frankel says it is all nonsense; Heidegger is his friend. There is no personal issue, but there is a large philosophical one. American Heideggerians get this backwards. They blame him personally, but adopt his philosophy by splitting it off from him. They don't understand that his philosophy belongs to a century-long strand of thought—especially German thought—which held that humans are *nothing but* products of culture, so that German culture is the only sacred value. Not culture—*German* culture. This was the conviction not only of Heidegger, but also of Ranke, Hugo von Hofmannsthal, Rilke, Spengler, and Scheler.[1] Other countries had their version of it, for example Dostoyevsky and D'Annunzio. We have to grasp this strand of thought in all these thinkers. And let us not see it as *their* problem. If we do not share their conviction, then it is *our* problem to formulate ours. One cannot adopt their view, and then be shocked to discover that they meant it seriously.

Americans have trouble understanding that strand of thought. I don't say that we *cannot*, because that would instance the assumption that humans are *nothing* but culture. I think we *can* understand it, and I will try to explain it.

Hatab is correct in saying that this strand of thought rejects "Enlightenment universalism." But he says quite wrongly that it rejects this in favor of "celebrating differences," which he says brings "the danger of tribalism." No, not at all. Once there is a "celebration of differences," there is no danger of tribalism. To Hatab (and myself) the different cultures all seem roughly equal; but that is felt as offensive, a misunderstanding, or hopelessly superficial by those who hold *their* culture sacred. They feel we are lost creatures without any deep culture.

Heidegger did not *celebrate* differences. He thought that the destiny of the world lay in German culture. He seriously thought that philosophy could be carried on *only* in German or Greek.[2] Ranke said that to be a significant historian one had to be a German historian. Dostoyevsky thought that only Russians have any depth of soul. In his novels, all Poles, Jews, and Germans are portrayed as flat, soulless. The Italians who belonged to this strand of thought called it their "*sacred* selfishness."

Since the view that *only* one's own culture is sacred was held in each culture, an urban American easily takes this as if they had held that *each* culture is sacred and creates fully human beings. Not so!

Hatab thinks of that century-long rebellion against the Enlightenment as if it were a celebration of differences. It was rather a deep sense *that human nature is nothing, a gap, a void, so that those who lack my culture share nothing with me*; they are not the same species. An animal species has characteristic ways of living, nesting, and infant care. Humans share only the merest vegetative "biologism." A dog has a certain nature. You might think twice before killing a dog, but there is nothing at all in people of another culture except that other culture. And Americans? They don't even have *another* culture!

This conviction that there is no human nature led to the murder of millions of people (Armenians, Gypsies, Volga Germans, Jews, and many others—now Bosnians). But to call it "tribalism" is to look down on it without first understanding it. Some of the thinkers and poets we most value shared this assumption that the human being is purely a cultural creation. They found a deeper human being than the rational unity Kant had proposed. Of course we value the thinkers who went deeper. But their dreadful error was to think of humans as mere creations of culture, created out of nothingness, disclosed in the midst of an abyss.

Today in American philosophy and social science a *merely verbal* cultural particularism is dominant. I have long argued that one should not use this formulation if one does not mean it. I am now impatient when my Heideggerian friends are shocked at revelations of Heidegger's Nazism. It turns out that all along they *assumed*—while verbally denying—a real and valuable humanity in all cultures. That is the unstated basis of their outrage. Yet, they assert that nothing holds across. But taken seriously, it shocks them. Heidegger did not *think* beyond cultural particularism, but he also did not *feel* beyond it. If we feel beyond it, it is not his but *our problem* to think beyond it.

In the urban United States *the cross-cultural human being* is so obvious that its assumption is not even noticed. There has also been no way to state it. I argue that we should avow it, and I offer a use of words and concepts that can articulate it.

Hatab thinks we share "nothing" with another culture, only an abyss, but he means that it is nothing *formed*. He wants to be free of any final form. He assumes that the abyss brings compassion, but it can bring quite the opposite, as in Bosnia or with Dostoyevsky's Ivan. And compassion shows rather (as James Watson says) that the abyss is a lie. You feel the other people—isn't that what compassion is? We need to articulate what this compassion knows.

If besides cultural forms there were nothing, then our next step of speech or action would always be consistent with the given cultural forms. There being nothing else, nothing could open them. We could individualize this only in details subsumable *under* the cultural forms. Hatab does not mean this. His "nothing" is anything but nothing.

With and after culture, humans *are* for carrying forward. Humans are implicitly open for further steps that can alter all determinants. That explains how people can criticize their own culture from within it. It could be done only from another culture, if there were nothing in humans but what their culture gives them.

Kant and Hegel assumed that *nature* is only a machine. Hegel wrote before Darwin; nature seemed to consist only of repetitious patterns in Euclid's geometric space. For Hegel only humans change the essences and make real time—historical time, history. Therefore, humans have no nature. This view still underlies current thinking. Mechanistic logic depends on fixed units. It is graph paper. Machines are concretized graph paper. Nature was misunderstood as a machine.

Nature is intricate. It opens into all sorts of novelty. Single cells are vastly complex. Animals live complicated lives. Human sense-making is nature-emergent. We can use the word "nature" to say that nature is such that it could develop into animals and human beings. That seems obvious—since we are here. Nature's order is such that our own new sense-making can happen in it. Nature is not a machine.

If we take away what the cultures *variously* carry forward, very little is left. The cultures elaborate eating, sleep, procreation, and human relations differently, so it seems that human "nature" is autistic and lacking all these. No creature could have stayed alive with only such a nature. I call this the fallacy of the "remnant body" ("PCN"). Obviously human nature is not that, but what the cultures carry forward in various ways. So it cannot be a common form or content.

Hatab is right to oppose the old notion of a universal human form, pattern, or content, something a colonial administrator could try to impose on other cultures. What we all have in common exists only *as variously carried forward*, and always still open for further carrying forward. *The variety does not make a bridgeless difference, because further carrying forward is not determined by the present form.* The implicit intricacy can open all the forms.

That is the human nature which Hatab unconsciously assumes— what makes people of other cultures such that he can care about them in spite of their otherness. *That* human nature can be articulated, but only in terms that come from letting words work in that very kind of nature— in the implicit intricacy we share, which *is-for* carrying forward—always in various ways. The way to fashion such terms is just what I offer. If we can speak of what is not fixed-formed but can be *carried forward*, we can say how great is that which is shared—far greater than the differences. Then *we* can celebrate *our* differences.

Hatab wants to think of humans "beyond the realm of form." He worries that my assertion of a universal human nature might become something that some people could impose on others. We are in deep agreement, except on the important question how this should be articulated. We both see ways of saying it that could result in the opposite. He wonders what my universal human nature "really *is*," knowing that the very question invites some content, something it *is*. But *crossing* opens this "is." He invites me to say more exactly what I mean. Let the word define itself in use: forms cannot cross; if you put them together they yield only a contradiction. What can cross are unseparated multiplicities, for example the whole group of situations in which we use a certain word.

Hatab "travels with Heidegger's saying that 'the *disclosive* function of language' is 'the house of being.'" I say that language involves how words and situations *cross*: the word brings its many meanings (its use-situations), which are implicit in our knowing how to use the word. The present situation has its intricacy. In *this* situation *this* old word might *disclose* a new and sophisticated meaning, changing this situation in a subtle way that has *more new features* than one could have listed in advance either for the situation or the word. We see that crossing opens the "is" and—*discloses*—features that were not there before.

When crossing opens the constraints, what comes is not an unfocused plethora, but a finely precisioned *focal* implying.

In this example, "disclose" drops its old meaning of something that was already there, only covered. Now the word says what Heidegger means, as this also actually happens to the word, here. In *this* situation the word says how new features come—in a *crossing* of word and situation.

Now apply this to a person who has lived in two cultures, and is now "marginal" to both. The person cannot help but understand each culture better and more perceptively than people who have lived only in only place, because the situations of both cultures have crossed in the person's experiential mesh. Then each new situation *crosses* with all those. Many new, more precise meanings and perceptions arise, which did not exist in either culture.

Cultural particularism ignores what we know about such people. It would imply that they experience *less* meaning, are "decultured," since two cultures largely contradict each other and should cancel out. But contradictory meanings can implicitly *cross.* Marginality confers deeper perceptions, as we know from common observation. Europeans for whom cultural particularism is serious business think of us as lacking *any* real culture. I argue instead that the American (Hatab's) version of cultural particularism ("people of all cultures are valuable") is an unconscious universalism that needs to be articulated. It can be articulated if we have a concept like "crossing."

A *crossing* occurs also when we understand another person. The more different people we have known, the more easily we understand the next new person, although that one is again different. That is because understanding does not depend on a common content. Rather, the new thing *crosses* with our implicit experiential mesh. That is what makes us say, "Oh . . . I see. . . ."

Finally, see how terms in one of my strings *cross* when they all work-in the . . . . . at the end of the string. On any topic (including human nature) we can have (think, say, feel, be . . . . .) the . . . . . which comes after the variety. After the string each is implicit in our experiential mesh. Each is now implicit in our understanding of the others. In the . . . . . they all *cross* and open each other so that they do not confine, but help to shape our next-implied step of speech, thought, and action.

Hatab says "*We all* know what it means . . . to lose our interest," so that we no longer care about anything. I agree that this is universal, but someone might say that singling out interest (Hatab alludes to Heidegger's "care structure") shows Western drivenness rather than detachment or self-sacrifice. We can see the universal in human nature in how "anything human is in principle understandable," as Dilthey said. I would add: this is *because* to understand anything human, we need not already know or be it. Rather, it *crosses* (it informs and is informed by) what we already are and know.

Hatab asks "what crosses?" It might seem that an answer would have to define humans in terms of a *what*. I would rather answer: crossing opens any kind of *what*; it *shapes-and-is-shaped-by* what crosses with it. The universal human nature is the *can cross*. Crossing is a finely precise process. It cannot be spoken of as "less exact," "without fixed references," or as "flexible," "fluidity," or "looseness." Those mean *less* precision. They are only helpless negations of logic.

Certainly there was a time, Nietzsche's time, when inhibitory moralism needed to be exploded so as to free people. This is still needed in some provinces. But many of us are now tired of negative ways of saying that there is more. Abyss, rupture, tragedy, loss, nothingness, negativity, void, limbo, flux, fluidity, looseness—these deny what we try to affirm: that when the culture-forms and conceptual distinctions break, we find *more* precise meaning and order, not less.

I am not impatient with Heidegger, only with us. He has made his great contribution; let us make ours. Further steps of thought are needed. I think I provide them.

I love Hatab's list of what might alleviate anxiety, including "a little bit of good news." Yes, we also play freely without a . . . . . , and we can do mathematics where the answer is prefigured. No, I am not against "stable forms of speech." I am concerned with logic as well as with new word-uses and concepts.

Hatab sees signs of my thirty-year study of Aristotle, although crossed and changed by my own concerns and the implicit copresence of Plato, Leibniz, Hume, Kant, Hegel, and a great many others.

Yes, a . . . . . is created by the surrounding language (and the situations it brings). Of course the . . . . . also *contains* implicit language; that is why it can rephrase the old phrases and arrive at new ones. Nothing human is *without* implicit language. Of course I use language (and also conceptual patterns) when I let words show and say how they work. We need my way, or some way, to let our words do that. Hatab is right about the old error of wanting *to say* what is before or without language. Nothing is *separate from* language, but we must not overcorrect the error by saying that everything human is *created by* language (by cultural and historical determinants). Then there seems to be no human nature, no way to talk about ourselves.

Meaning Reflexivity: Gendlin's Contribution to Ethnomethodology

Kenneth Liberman

The Project

Summarizing phenomenology, Eugene Gendlin counsels practitioners to "seek to articulate experience as actually had, rather than laying some invented theoretical scheme on experience."[1] To acknowledge the place of schema and theoretical reflection, with all their (unavoidable) utility, while not permitting them to subvert experience beneath a mindless perpetuation of the formal order they supply, is one of the first tasks of thinking, whether it be philosophical or mundane.

Gendlin commences a recent volume[2] with this blunt announcement: "The project: thinking with more than forms." In the last century philosophical reflection has been stalled by the task of learning how to think without letting the formed ways of that thinking constitute an order that is less than the lived orders that compose our existence. Gendlin describes this historical moment: "The conceptual patterns are doubtful and always exceeded, but the excess seems unable to think itself. It seems to become patterns when we try to think it. This has been *the* problem of twentieth century philosophy."[3]

The abandonment of formal orders raises the terrors of indeterminacy and anarchy. Too much "openness" may lead to disorder and chaos, fears that some people think can legitimate the appropriateness of fascism as a response. Although "experience need not, and in fact does not, have the same character as logic, science, or knowledge,"[4] political practice in this century has compelled us to subvert experience in submission to logic, to science, and to formal knowledge while *at the same time* world civilization is learning ways to retain the creative fecundity of being-in-the-world within the world's practices of reasoning, i.e., to "think with more than forms."

Throughout his writings Eugene Gendlin takes up the activities of understanding and our ways of listening and speaking, in an effort to capture meaning as experience actually has it. In his best known work he writes, "*Meaning. . .* is not only a certain *logical* structure, but it also involves a *felt* experiencing,"[5] and Gendlin has stood by this topic—or more appropriately, task—with a nearly invincible tenacity. This felt experiencing is not derivative from a formal or theoretical order, and is originary; yet it does not live independent of formalization. It lives with, and beyond, theories, schema, forms, etc. It has been his principal effort to describe, develop, and demonstrate that there are lived orders that are orderly in more than formed ways. Gendlin addresses the basic phenomenological problem, "How does felt meaning function in cognition?"[6] While "philosophy usually asserts that the order, nature, rules, intelligibility of fully formed knowledge are properties of the raw material of knowledge,"[7] Gendlin speaks to us of a knowledge that formal schema do not know but with which we are very familiar, as with our life itself. He recognizes that logical schema have a proper role to fill, such as when one wishes to consider a given relationship between two orderly aspects, yet he is quick to warn us about the capacity of formal logic to deaden experience, *and to restrict our capacity to think.* Gendlin holds that, "Science is derived from life and cannot claim to explain and reduce life to the few thin patterns it uses."[8]

In ordinary life, the only life we live, the simultaneity of *many* orders soon exhausts what can be represented by a logical scheme,[9] and creativity may depend upon one's ability to let go of the constructs and interpretations one has in hand.[10] We should not be content only with subsuming ourselves, or others, under old categories of received notions. While we have heard this before, what is freshening is to observe how readily Gendlin practices it. This is certainly one of his principal achievements and comprises much of what he has to teach us.

Gendlin is not at all sanguine about the ease with which we can engage in such creative being. He observes the speed with which any fresh practice of thinking can become a trap that sets one's mind and practice in some narrow way. Even within an attack on overconceptualization we lapse quickly into a routinization of our own conceptualization. It is a cultural neurosis, or a human one. Gendlin observes that no sooner do we find a new practice of thinking than we become used to that "It is true that we may move from any *that* into fixed things."[11] While fixed concepts have their uses, we need to remain open to new possibilities of significance since "concepts and distinctions are not the main way language works."[12] Turning to the therapeutic relationship, an area to which Gendlin has devoted much of his career, he notes that it is possible to use the terms and concepts of an open, creative way of being, "and yet fall into a therapy that is only words, only arguing."[13] He does not underestimate our capability to deceive ourselves.

Language

Gendlin speaks a great deal about language, which, he explains, involves making sense beyond accounting in existing categories.[14] He argues that "Language use is wrongly thought to be governed by conceptual distinctions," in that "word-use has an order of its own, different in 'kind' from conceptual kinds, categories, constructs and distinctions."[15] These observations strike at the heart of how we use language to communicate.

Words work very intricately within the situations that they help to define, and frequently they can be made to work in novel ways that extend beyond customary paths;[16] words are in the habit of reinventing themselves. They are not limited by forms and rules because they must live beyond themselves, in the future to which every situation is addressed. Words abide within their logical meaning only when they operate within a well-formulated system, which guarantees its world in advance,[17] and not in new situations where the word's "meaning-making"[18] is always nonlogical. Our theoretical arts, including philosophy and the social sciences, give priority to fixated domains and view them as natural, real, and original; but this is an illusion, a "white mythology," i.e., the mythology of European thinkers.[19] In truth, "Rendering clean conceptual constructs that make logical steps is not word-use,"[20] or at least not word-use that is natural or original. Making logical steps has its place, Gendlin assures us of that, but only as one subset among our many modes of being human.

So how do words and concepts work, and how are we to think? Gendlin answers this Heideggerian question more by example than exegesis. He tells us that "words work, freshly,"[21] and then he displays for us words actually at work, words that invent their significance in, and as, their use. He calls such events "self-instancing,"[22] i.e., occasions when words mean their "saying," when they are the only source of authority for the work they are up to. "What I am trying to say is the saying."[23] We can better comprehend this "saying," perhaps, if we recall Levinas's distinction between the "saying" and the "said" when speaking about a similar theme:

> Thematization is inevitable, so that signification itself can show itself, but does so in the solipsism with which philosophy begins, in the betrayal which philosophy is called upon to reduce. This reduction always has to be attempted, because of the trace of sincerity which the words themselves bear and which they owe to saying as witness, even when the said dissimulates the saying in the correlation set up between the saying and the said.[24]

Gendlin inventories the perils of delivering over the "saying" to the "said" and warns us not to make static things out of experiences.[25] Turning to the therapeutic relationship, he observes, "It has long been known in all orientations that patients who 'intellectualize' or 'externalize' tend to fail in therapy."[26] Success, as a patient or a human, depends upon our ability to live beyond structures,[27] to mean beyond established schema, for that is what living and meaning demand of us.

Gendlin's Contribution

I came upon Gendlin's work early in my career, during my first year as a graduate student in 1970, working under Harold Garfinkel, the founder of ethnomethodology. Gendlin's book *Experiencing and the Creation of Meaning* was part of Garfinkel's reading list, along with other early introductions to phenomenology for social scientists, such as the texts of Marvin Farber and Aron Gurwitsch. Gendlin helped ethnomethodology formulate part of its initial agenda, and I wish to outline briefly this contribution here.

Gendlin helped to specify for us our inquiries into the reflexivity of social order, and he provided for us "an experiential version of the reflexive definition of 'meaning.'"[28] Instead of a causal theory of meaning, such as that in vogue among the symbolic interactionists, Gendlin recommended examining meaning as an experienceable fact, and this approach to social meaning subsequently figured, thanks in part to Gendlin's work, in much of the early research in ethnomethodology. Gendlin argued that "reflexivity refers to any case where something is an instance of itself."[29] That is, any intelligible matter has its sense and reference as a component of the world which it itself defines; it provides itself with its own reference, or in Gendlin's words, there is "an identity between what is asserted and one's procedure in asserting it." For example, "A metaphor happens only in so far as a word works in that slot, only if it makes sense. (*And that changes the slot as the word works.*)"[30] The world is continuously being redefined; order is not static, at least not without remarkable efforts. Words say how they work when they are used: "Words properly mean how they work, if we let 'properly' mean how the word works *here*, instancing how words work in use"[31] (and certainly not, for example, how "properly" works at an English tea party).

Gendlin corroborated ethnomethodology's turn away from the *what* of the social world to an investigation of the *how*, a turn that had baffled a generation of sociologists. We were captivated by what Gendlin called "process categories," because the more familiar content analyses of sociologists amounted, in Garfinkel's words, to nothing more than "detailing generalities" in which the theoretical schema held a certain hegemony. Gendlin argued that contents were made from processes: "Content categories would seem to be ineffectual, if the phenomena are more basically ordered by a process."[32] Capturing such processes, or social "praxis," was ethnomethodology's obsession. "Physics has succeeded in fashioning concepts other than Newtonian; the sciences of man can do likewise. The Newtonian concepts picture static, defined 'things' that exist in a space-time container."[33] The events we wanted to study were always processes: reality is always in flux. So when Gendlin told us, "Experienc*ing* is a process,"[34] and when he cautioned against "rendering people as concepts or as objects of techniques,"[35] we took note.

Gendlin's subsequent work took up the therapeutic relation, but he retained his phenomenological perspectives. He asserted, "We cannot explain personality changes with the sort of theory that considers experienc*es* as entities." Applying his phenomenological method within therapeutic practice, he came to the conclusion that "Early process studies usually analyzed verbal *content*. Classification systems were developed for content analysis of *what* the client said. Interviews were tape-recorded, statements were classified. An exemplary finding was: early in therapy there are more statements referring to other people;"[36] and Gendlin rejected such procedures, in favor of a search for more experiential practices. The contents, *especially the way they lend themselves easily to the-oretical respecification,* are not the proper object of inquiry; rather the lived process in which contents are endlessly generated and superseded ("without remedy" ethnomethodologists would say) is the phenomenon to be comprehended.

The Interactional Basis of Being

Phenomenology, in its philosophical and social scientific guises, was accused of being a subjectivism; but Gendlin rejected this accusation, recognizing that all the processes of understanding, listening, speaking, and being were interactionally based: "Experiencing is not 'subjective,' but interactional, not intrapsychic, but interactional. It is not inside, but inside-outside."[37] Above all, "A person is interaction."[38] Gendlin elucidated this well in his paper on anger, arguing that "activity is a certain organized pattern of change called for by the situation."[39] During my two years of fieldwork with traditionally oriented Aboriginal people in the central Australian desert, I observed that Aboriginal people provided an interactional system in which the self was minimized and self-assertion was poor social form. Not only did one not argue, but there were few places within the interactional structures for argumentation. Aboriginal social discourse provided for consensus, for congeniality, and for identification with group processes. Although I am a contentious urban American Jew, it was no effort at all for me to comply with these social constraints—I had no other choice. The person I was, with its new-found minimal selfhood, was a function of everyday Aboriginal social interaction.

After two years I became pleased, even proud (if being proud of humility is possible) with the new, agreeable person I had become; and I was eager to return to Los Angeles to see how it played. To my amazement, there was little space within urban American interaction for anything but egocentric, argumentative social being. My old self returned almost instantaneously, and that is because the self is interactionally produced. In our society self-assertiveness is necessary for survival, and if one lacks it, there are plenty of self-assertiveness training workshops available to take!

Upon my most recent return from fifteen months in India, the widespread use in the United States of anger as an interactional formatting device became apparent to me. For six months I lived in a house with thirty-five Tibetan monks who shared only one bathroom. During this entire time there was not one argument over whose right it was to use the bathroom. Imagine thirty-five, no let's say only five Americans sharing the same bathroom—contemplate all the arguments, appeals to justice, moral righteousness, etc., that would be heard. Across the country, in Denny's restaurants, in university hallways, at traffic corners, I have witnessed how Americans use anger to get what they want, but this anger is not an inherent part of these persons' being. It is compelled by interactional processes. As Gendlin advises, "You may have gotten angry on the basis of a situational pattern." Further, "The culture patterns our situations and only these can we then individualizedly pattern further."[40]

Gendlin perceptively observes, "What one feels is not 'stuff inside,' but the sentience *of* what is happening in one's living in the outside."[41] Although not "subjective," in that it is fully interactional and hence "objective" (in a Schutzian sense), there is nothing impersonal about it, and what we feel seems to come of its own and overtakes us. There is a problem for us here—How then can we change the "outside" by changing the "inside"? Anger is as good a point as any at which to experiment, and there is here a fresh meaning for us in Gendlin's invocation that we learn to live beyond structures.

Criticism of Derrida

Gendlin's tenacity in following up the lived orders that are orderly in more than formed ways is demonstrated by his unwillingness to accept the authority of deconstruction, which he believes misses the texture of these "more than formed ways." Recently, Gendlin has taken up a criticism of Derrida, from whom it is apparent that he has learned some things, although I suspect that the better part of what they share they learned independently, from their phenomenological forebears. Above all, Gendlin's observation that "Words mean as they work in moves"[42] finds common cause with Derrida's descriptions of the play of signification. As with Derrida, the meaning is not in the word, but without the word there is no meaning: "The new meaning is not without a word. The newly working word makes and says that meaning. So do the surrounding words, which also change." In this phrase I hear of the slippery *glissage* of signs. Each term delimits the others, and finds its own meaning as part of an ensemble: "All terms in a scheme are relative."[43] Of course, whether the signs "work" or "play" amounts to the same thing, so long as one is able to capture what is fresh about their meaning-making. In Gendlin's interpretation, and I suspect that he is correct, Derrida limits this play to conceptual distinctions, even though so many nonconceptual, poetic, emotional, and interpersonal channels of communication may be active. This is where Gendlin finds fault with Derrida. Gendlin finds him unwilling (not incapable, for Gendlin himself locates Derrida's fresh prose) to imagine language beyond the structures of conceptual distinctions. Not all "singing the world," to use Merleau-Ponty's words, is conceptual. In studies of "*différance*," there are concepts and distinctions, but what happened to the lifeworld, about which Husserl so richly informed us? Gendlin claims that Derrida misses many of the brilliant ways that humans are able to mean freshly.

Whatever this "fresh" meaning-making may be, it has something to do with the way words work with each other, how they transform each other and themselves, continuously and reflexively; and it has to do with how they work within each unique situation that they themselves settle. This is the matter to which Gendlin and Derrida address themselves, and I think it is more important for us to learn how to mean and how to think than to settle any differences between these two scholars.

Of Gendlin's critique of Derrida, I can say that it is suggestive, but I am unable to follow it all the way, or perhaps Gendlin has not yet said enough. His argument, if I have grasped it correctly, is basically that Derrida has become reified within his own conceptual apparatus for dereifying metaphysics. That deconstruction can become a reified strategy I am willing to grant right away. One only has to canvass one's students and colleagues for illustrative cases of this phenomenon. But that Derrida himself does so is a more difficult argument. Especially, I am disturbed by the vehemence with which Gendlin articulates it, which I believe comes from Gendlin's sense that he is waging a rear-guard battle on behalf of the commitments of phenomenological philosophy. The crux of the argument is that there is more to the "play" or "work" of words than conceptual distinctions. Gendlin writes, "Derrida thinks that word-use is governed only by distinctions . . . [but] the way words are used puts clean distinctions to shame."[44] While Gendlin approves of deconstructing old orders (and so his critique of Derrida is not a common one), he complains that Derrida "does not go on from his own words' new working," but remains stuck within the very concepts he rejects. What peeves Gendlin is that in avoiding the embrace of anything at all, Derrida "misses the texture of life and usage which the rejection opens."[45] Gendlin sees the routinization, and the need to deconstruct it, but if one does not then move on to some creative moment, the dialectic has ended: "His is a guerrilla warfare. Borrow the enemy's resources, steal the government's weapons, conquer and withdraw immediately. If you hold anything you become like them. No fresh thinking is possible, no line of thought either, only sporadic attacks and instant retractions." But what is it that we should hold? Gendlin is the first to admit that speaking conceptually about what is more-than-conceptual places one on very slippery terrain.

For myself, I recall here what seems to be a Buddhist critique of Derrida, a matter I have been considering, since Derrida's notions find a good deal of commonality with the Mahayana Buddhist philosophical school known as *prasangika madhyamika*. They share an interest in a practice of deconstruction that restricts itself to making self-contradiction visible, without making any positive assertions. Their styles of analysis are also similar—first a concept is presented, and then the contradictions are pointed out, but no new solution is proposed. Here, however, the parallels end, for the *madhyamika* philosophers recognize a fundamental reality, a suchness (Skr. *tathata*; "that way it is") and seek to make contact with "that." Conceptualization is only a covering that requires removal; remove everything and there is a "Buddha-nature," although interrogation of the term will lead one nowhere except to further conceptualization. The Buddhists concur with Derrida when the object of his criticism is any inherently existing nature that is associated with concepts. Gendlin: "Derrida's main preoccupation, always, is to reject the assumption that there is some given, some nature, some original to-be-specified, assumed before and without signifiers."[46] For a Buddhist there is some nature, some original, but it is not to be specified. Could this Buddhist witness find any common cause with Gendlin? He reflects, "Let us not say that there is no nature, just because nature is not a fixed category system. Let us not leave nature and words still surrendered to old categories after we reject these. Rather, nature *is* that way."[47]

So it seems that it is not what Derrida does that offends Gendlin, but what Derrida does not do. Gendlin's critique of Derrida amounts to this: Derrida applies his imagination to a range of cases that is too limited. If there is any nature at all, it must be for him the nature of names and forms, of metaphysics. But since there is no such inherent, metaphysical nature, any nature at all is rejected. Gendlin discusses Derrida and Foucault in a section he names "the tragic view."[48] He accuses Derrida's method of being in the end just another form of capitulation to metaphysics, whereas he is urging that we decisively go beyond metaphysics. For him there is "a texture of life" still to be made contact with, after deconstruction. In his opposition to the analyses of Derrida and Foucault, Gendlin is the humanist.

Unfortunately, we know little about what this "texture of life" is. Or, as the Buddhists suggest, do we rather know it very well? What does Gendlin say? It seems to be a moral space, because Gendlin speaks of authenticity and a sort of moral autonomy. What could "authenticity" be in a postphenomenological era? Gendlin tells us it is one's ownmost potentiality for being, which is not objectifiable, a "carrying forward" that is still in the process of changing. Can this Jewish humanist explain what place there is still for a Heideggerian authenticity? In what ways is our postmodern cynicism limited? Can Gendlin be more specific about the alternatives? At least, can we rid ourselves of bourgeois illusions of autonomy, to which, I fear, existential psychoanalysis carries us? How does "experiential phenomenology" avoid this? How can it take us to community, while steering us clear of fascism?

Gendlin's Critique of Formed Schema

Gendlin and Derrida are brothers-in-arms at least in regard to their assessments of the limitations of formal schema of understanding and their view that there are practices and knowledge that formed schema (patterned thinking, concepts, formal structures, etc.) do not know. Formal analyses of all sorts (lay and scientific) carry the assumption that only what is clear and consistent can exist and presume that every event must be derivable directly from the formal pattern,[49] when in fact these forms are idealized interpretations that are developed only after the fact. It is Gendlin's quest to capture the intricacy of understanding as it works with, and beyond, formed patterns. Since formal systems of analyses do not provide access to this intricacy, Gendlin must rely upon his own phenomenological methods. Formal analyses cannot even describe the intricacy of how they themselves work.

Logical forms and patterns are incapable of encompassing the intricacy of people and situations. Forms and distinctions cannot even define what forms and distinctions are. They are not clear about what clarity is: they cannot define their situation.[50] If we were to admit only reflections that are derivable (and therefore justified by) a formal logic of analysis, nothing new in the world could be thought. Understanding is capable of stepping beyond the grounds that its formed schema have laid down for it. In fact, this "stepping beyond" is more common than the formal aspects of thought—that is what is creative about thinking. "What anything *is* includes its implying of carrying-forward *steps*."[51] This is faithful to Heidegger's observation that every situation bears a future, which *is* that situation, and this implying addresses more than was already formed.

"Theory has kept silent about implicit intricacy, and has treated patterns as the only order,"[52] Gendlin tells us, and he is on the hunt for other orderings that work in complex, intricate ways. To preserve the clarity of its structure, formal analysis must simplify what is naturally extraordinarily complex, and Gendlin asks, "Why should we try to impose simplistic patterns? Let us permit ourselves to think and use the much more complex pattern which emerges. And why let even a complex pattern falsify the *implicit* way this intricacy functions?"[53] We must learn to use formal schema without capitulating to their idealized and simplistic respecifications of lived experience.

Not only are formal analyses simplistic, but their success depends upon separating the multiplicity of lived events with which natural understanding works in a preseparated form. "Logic works only with what has already been separated. But a situation is a preseparated multiplicity, and carrying it forward opens new possibilities that were not *separately* there before."[54] In order for any logical calculus to operate, a situation must be separated out into components that are wrongly thought to be foundational. Take, for instance, the debate over the approval of nutritional supplements sold at health food stores. The pharmaceutical testing required by the FDA relies upon isolating a single chemical compound and then administering randomized, double-blind, placebo-controlled clinical trials employing a physical measurement as the outcome variable. That is how scientific methodology knows how to test a compound. The difficulty is that, unlike synthetic drugs, natural herbs are not mono-substances, but contain hundreds of chemical compounds that are very difficult to isolate and may work synergetically with each other (rendering this scientific methodology mute). Natural substances provide too many confounding variables for a formal analytic strategy that must work on separated components. If validation depends upon scientific verification, and the formal system of verification lacks the capacity to handle the complexity, no approval can be provided.

It is not that the constructions of an objectivist and representational thinking cannot reduce the world to its own notions (e.g., witness the efforts of the FDA to ban nutritional supplements); however, success here is not provided by truth so much as politics. Conformity with the truth of a formal correctness is made compulsory by the political imposition of their formal interpretations. But even these formal interpretations must, according to Gendlin, work anew implicitly in their own intricate ways. This procedure of separating out performed by formal analysis is not nothing, it is an important event. It is part of the natural history of how humans think, yet there is more to thinking than that, and Gendlin extends his natural history to this "more-than."

Horizonal Phenomena

Gendlin's investigations are phenomenological throughout, and with impressive tenacity he keeps his analysis addressed to the living situation. He pays tribute to Husserl, who based his inquiries upon the lifeworld implicit in experience: "Husserl may be said to be the first to base philosophy, quite explicitly and deliberately, on an examination of experiencing as we actually live, have, and are, rather than regarding 'experience' as already imposed by the requirements of one view of science."[55]

Gendlin is especially faithful to Husserl's project in retaining in his analyses the horizonal character of understanding which Husserl describes. Understanding does not consist only of discrete items, but is drawn from the context of a situation. Orientation to possible synthetic operations that may be beheld at the fringe of one's awareness contribute to the sense of an event. Understanding is a temporal phenomenon because human beings are alive and are addressed to what is developing at the horizon of their experience. Analysis of separated items that are stabilized and allocated places within a formal order is not the usual analysis that human beings are called upon to perform in their mundane lives. The temporal view of living persons is addressed to the rush of oncoming events that bear a complexity for which formed schema are inadequate. The formed schema are part of the thinking, but only along with the horizons of meaning of any situation. The formed schema that humans work with are not isolated within an abstract universe but are in the world. A situation is not hindsight, Gendlin warns us, it is an embedded experience whose implicit intricacy is already addressed to a something further. Situations imply further steps.[56] It is this retention of the horizonal character of experience that commends Gendlin's investigations.

Gendlin's writings continue to inform ethnomethodologists, whose studies provide illustrations of how persons are able to provide for themselves a lived order that is indecisive yet fecund in ways that a formal order could never be. On occasion, the success parties have in developing and communicating a meaning depends upon the indecisiveness, as in the glossing practices of an Aboriginal translator who keeps the Aboriginal audience oriented toward possible contents of meaning of an English speaker without closing off any part of the potential vitality of the intent that is still developing.[57] In a recent study, Dusan Bjelic and Michael Lynch recommend that scientists pay close attention to the in-courseness of the production of the phenomenal field, an attention which may require a suspension of their theoretical categories.[58] In a similar vein Jeff Coulter argues that the practices of ordinary reasoning exceed the logic of theorems.[59] And Lena Jayyusi demonstrates that "the practical, the conceptual, and the moral are laminated together in the organization of situated action, and in their very intelligibility."[60] There is situated, practical activity that exceeds the deconstruction of formed/formal ways, and it is the aim of ethnomethodological studies to render this practical work accessible.

Gendlin speaks of this complex intricacy of practical knowing that is always implying its next step as "carrying forward." Although a knowing may not have defined its next step formally, it knows it with a precision that formal knowing does not have. It has its own kind of order from living. "Each step carries forward what was implied but was not simply there at the previous step."[61] This implying is already there but not in a way that a formal analysis addressed to distinct and static (non)events can gain access. Gendlin offers the example of a poet who is not quite able to write the next line. She knows what she does not want and has rejected several possible next lines, so it is not the case that she knows nothing. Rather, she knows *precisely* what is called for where the lines stop and the poem continues, but she does not have the words yet for this precise knowing.

> Many good lines offer themselves; they try to say, but do not say—*that.*
> The blank still *hangs there,* still implying something *more precise.* Or worse,
> the proposed line makes the . . . . . shrivel and nearly disappear. Quick,
> get that line out of the way. The poet rereads the written lines and ah . . . . .
> there it is again. Rather than that line, the poet prefers to stay stuck.[62]

There is a pregnant further implying that is precise but not complete. This is occasionally referred to as a vague or indeterminate understanding, but such negative terms do not capture the *positive* way in which it works in the experience of the poet. It is not just the absence of determinacy—that is the least of it. Such an emphasis only demonstrates how influenced even phenomenologists are by the very theories they reject. What Gendlin seeks to preserve with his "carrying forward" is something proactive. Consider, for instance, the way analysts of intercultural communication treat problems of understanding to be a puzzle regarding meanings we already have, when the massive work of understanding involves new meanings and new experiences.[63] The concepts, or the formal properties of a logical calculus, are not what drives the parties; they are compelled by the direction to which the situating is going and ways to take that next step. "The step is not only *the words* but also *what we want to say* to carry *the situation forward.*"[64]

Knowing with Schema

Although all practical knowing works by more than the pattern-relations that any knowing sets up, this "more-than" lives in a pattern-defined world. There is no question of getting rid of formed schema; not only do we not want to, we cannot: "We cannot think only with conceptual patterns, nor without them."[65] We think with, and also beyond, the present forms. Besides, "Our human capacity with patterns and our science vastly increase the scope of our lives."[66] Gendlin is not a romantic. It is silly to be against formal theories, he tells us, when the real question is when and how do we next think fully with them. That is, conceptual relations and assumptions are always involved, but it is false that everything follows directly from them.[67]

"Concepts do not limit. Rather, they carry forward. Such concepts function-in, and say, how implicit intricacy continues to function with them."[68] Again, the historical question is how to think with logic in a way that does not close us off to what is more than formed schema. Gendlin is not being an idealist, and he evinces a practical concern with the lived detail of knowing.

The More-Than-Formed

One of the foremost assumptions of formal analytics is that order can only be something that is imposed on experience. But formed schema do not dictate events; events always outstrip the formed schema, and what forms work-in, talks back.[69] Here is an update on reflexivity that bears important advice for ethnomethodologists. It may be presumed that nothing but disorder talks back from experience; but it is incorrect to assume that what is not form, or what is more-than-form, must be a disorder.[70] Rather, there are ways of human order to which formal analytics is blind.

The "more" here is not a fuzzy excess of form, it is very precise. Any word works in more than its formal semantic way. What is more-than-form is not a fleeting moment,[71] but, as Garfinkel once said of the etcetera that accompanies the meaning of all words—and all rules—this more-than is the inhabitant of the house. It is the source of what is creative about experience, an order more intricate than what formal analytic accounts of order know about. Such an intricate order is at work, but it is always superseding itself. The "there" that is familiar to us in our everyday activities is not always the same "there," but always new. It is a dynamic developing multiplicity that is always developing further, always more than what any formal schema can account for. "A situation does not consist of just static truths; it involves the implying of further situations, events and actions."[72] And yet has it not been the quest of Christian civilization to fix the world within static truths? Is civilization perhaps standing at the edge of a new paradigm of knowledge that can retain faith with the dynamic character of knowing?!

"Formed patterns are passive; they are observed but not observing, seen but not seeing,"[73] but *we* see in live ways. Wherever we find ourselves, we are always carrying ourselves forward to the step beyond, which supersedes what formed patterns have known. Do we have the capacity to keep faith with the intricacy that is our experiencing? This has been Gendlin's question from his earliest work to his most recent, and it is the guiding question of all phenomenological inquiry. "It seems complicated. Yes, familiar events are more intricate than most theoretical concepts."[74] But there is nothing so fecund, so originary, as our ordinary being in the world. Developing a method of analytic reflection—or more simply, a practice of knowing—that keeps faith with that originary being is one of the historical challenges of our era.

Reply to Liberman

Professor Liberman has me mostly right. What needs replying (or complaining) can seem small. I will come to it. There is one large issue: Liberman says culture "makes the self."

It is not that he believes in cultural determinism. He knows that we can go on in ways that do not follow from our culture. So, for example, he calls me a Jewish humanist, and then contrasts my work with "the quest of the Judeo-Christian-Islamic tradition to fix the world within static truths." He asks, contrary to humanism, whether Buddhism can "find common cause with Gendlin." He calls me a tenacious phenomenologist, but goes on to tell the many ways in which I differ from what is known under that name. I wouldn't want to deny my phenomenological heritage any more than my Jewish one, and I am glad that for him categories need not capture more than whatever they do capture. I do wish he would use them together. He tells what fits a category, and only many pages later what does not. It can sound like cultural determinism.

Liberman says that I am corroborated by his experience after living in another culture, when he found that here in the U.S. he could not be as he was there. That *does* corroborate my saying that we are interactional beings. But I do not believe that he has two just disparate cultural natures *and nothing else*. There is also the one who was "proud" of having been able to develop the other culture's self so well, the one who tells us about it. Liberman is the one who has both, and more. We are much more than culture.

By "self" Liberman means only our habitual way of reacting to others, and that does of course depend on them as well as us. I think his two cultures have "crossed" in him. I would ask him if he doesn't find that his second culture lets him understand his U.S. culture better than before. We get a crossing, when we have lived in two cultures, or when we know two philosophies, or when several words can make sense in the slot where one of them first appears. Then how we understand one is expanded by the implicit effects of the others. Considered just as forms they would exclude each other, but in experiential intricacy, they cross.

Liberman rightly has me saying that the intricacy of living is not subsumed *under* cultural traits; it is open to crossing.

I am happy that Liberman goes beyond the usual negatives. I might still carp at his saying that "creativity might depend upon one's ability to *let go* of the constructs," even though he is quoting me! I think I went on to say that mere letting go is not what brings something new. I wanted to replace that old negative theory of creativity. One can become creative by focusing on the (at first unclear) sense of something. We know what to attend to, not only what *not* to attend to.

Another accurate quotation worries me: I did not mean mere detail subsumed under categories, when I wrote: "The culture patterns our situations, and only these can we then individualizedly pattern further." I would add: in ways that need not be consistent with them.

Some years ago Liberman presented a paper along with a half page transcript of a native being questioned by a British colonial judge. The native knew that the true answer to several questions about what he had done was "no," but he nevertheless said the incriminating "yes." To show what happened in those few exchanges, Liberman formulated ten or fifteen specific facets, all valuable for understanding this sort of situation. He could never have derived those facets from generalizations. To find them, Liberman had to use the instance, his sense of that situation. So of course he knows—we all know—that in practice a situation has this sort of intricacy. We need to be guided by attending to our sense of the situation, not only by the few facets we can categorize.

Our sense of a situation is an intricate mesh of myriad never-separated facets. We *also* want the best possible generalizations and distinctions. Logical inference from them adds a power we need not do without; but we must often dip back into the directly sensed mesh. Otherwise generalizations mislead us.

Liberman asks this good question: "How can we change the 'outside' by changing the 'inside'?" Surely not alone or at once. Nor, as Liberman found, can we do it just by deciding to act as we choose, for example doing here as in Liberman's other culture. But we do discover that we can almost always act in one of a wild gamut of ways, as soon as we get past assuming that we must choose one of the obvious either/ors. In the texture of living are implications for totally unexpectable steps. But Liberman's deep question is better than these bits of an answer. Let the question stand.

I do not "warn" against falling into *the said.* I do not agree with Levinas that the said is formed and dead, and that the saying exists only for a wispy ephemeral moment, gone as soon as it happens. This assumes that the dead forms are real and can exist alone, as if we wish that the saying could be static, as if it were unfortunate that it cannot be. But if instead we dare to take the saying as the real, then we see that the forms do not exist alone. They mean the saying. The said goes right on saying. The said is still the endless and thick activity of the words.

The supposed falling seems to call for Derrida's method of "re-surrounding" his new metaphors with the old meanings (and with the old meaning of "metaphor"), to make them contradict themselves. It seems a good defensive strategy; the metaphorical novelty takes cover and leaves only the old forms—now in contradictions. But our words do not actually say the old schematic forms. They say the saying they mean in the implicit intricacy of their contexts. Words mean their saying. I deliberately allow them to do so.

Yes, I criticize Derrida "not for what he does but for what he does not do." Liberman is right that my criticism of Derrida is not the usual sort. I always defend Derrida against those. In the years before Derrida I was rarely understood. My work assumed that a variety of formulations (syntheses, cuts . . . . .) is possible at every point. Coming from McKeon, I recognized the traditional forms and how each can show the others breaking down. I went on from there. Derrida was right to see that this inherent breakdown of forms had first to be brought home. He says it will take three hundred years. He overestimates that a little. I think he has already done that, and superbly. It turns out that all along I was *post*-postmodern. It is well. Now that people are tired of both foundations and limbo, I am being heard and understood. I am ready with thirty years of work beyond those two oversimplifications.

The assertion-and-negation of distinctions and conceptual order makes it seem that there is nothing else. But breaking, rupture, *de*-centering and *de*-construction do not leave us in contradiction or aporia. Breaking the forms opens a realm we can enter. It is, as Liberman says, "very familiar, yet untouched by philosophy."

Liberman is not right that I accuse Derrida of becoming reified in his own apparatus. Nor am I "fighting a rear-guard action for phenomenology." I criticized phenomenology in 1963 for not attending to the variety of conceptual ways, and argued that "mere description" is impossible (*ECM*). I began where people stop today. I went on ahead, and now I turn and fight to pull them on. I am not fighting to go back from anything Derrida has done; I say "It is wrong to stop there; let us go on!"

Let us *enter* and speak from the realm that opens where all distinctions break down.

Where a distinction breaks down, there is not only the texture of earlier superimposed distinctions, as though our situations were nothing but results of old distinctions and philosophies, determined from the top down. Of course, there is no *separable* "other than language"; we cannot *talk* about something as it would be if it were not talked about, but living bodies and human life and language are much more than distinctions and comparisons. The Hegelian turn corrects an innocent empiricism, but at the price of making life and situations seem derived from comparison.

Liberman's quotation of the passage in which I laud Husserl could also have included where I differ (on the same page). This would show my arguments (since 1962) against the assumptions of the usual phenomenology ("EET," *ECM,* "WIT," "TPD," and "PNS"). I would say that I developed a way in which philosophy can go on further. Since my way has many sources, it is at once a way to go on from Husserl, from Heidegger, from Wittgenstein, from pragmatism, from Dilthey, Whitehead, McKeon, and others.

12

Carrying Forward: Gadamer and Gendlin on History, Language, and the Body

Jerald Wallulis

The contributions of Hans-Georg Gadamer and Eugene Gendlin on the subject of language do not lend themselves to simple and direct comparison. Rather, it is necessary from the very outset to bring into play Gadamer's philosophical hermeneutics of tradition and Gendlin's phenomenological description of bodily feeling. These descriptions are strongly interwoven into their respective accounts of language, so much so that its active and creative nature in each instance can be seen to flow directly from either the fusioning between past and future or the carrying forward of bodily feeling. The importance of these primary descriptions can, in my opinion, hardly be overestimated—either for their own sake, or for what may be broadly characterized as the phenomeno-logical hermeneutical understanding of language.

In this comparison between Gadamer and Gendlin, I present both the basic details of their accounts of historical understanding and bod-ily focaling, and how they intimately associate each account with the dynamism of the concrete unfolding of language. However, I also con-sider it crucial not to overlook the "other" description in each instance and its important fusioning or focaling as well. The desired goal, as I see it, may well be what Wilfrid Sellars spoke of first in a very dif-ferent but equally interesting context as "stereoscopic vision." It is the desire for such a synthetic viewpoint toward common understanding and lived bodily experience which prompts me at the end of this essay to pose certain questions concerning Gendlin's analysis of bodily felt meaning from the Gadamerian perspective of the language community, and then to question in a reciprocal manner the hermeneutical approach to bodily feeling from within the context of Gendlin's experiential phenomenology.

The Carrying Forward of Tradition

When Hans-Georg Gadamer first wrote *Truth and Method*, he was worried that it was appearing "too late" on the scene.[1] He was certain that the historical consciousness he wished to depict was still at work in the present. However, he also worried that historical consciousness in general was endangered by a growing hegemony of natural-scientific methods and, above all, by scientifically inspired, methodological approaches to history.

As a result, Gadamer's first characterization of philosophical hermeneutics is, from his own later admission,[2] more negative in character. It is advanced against any methodological approach to history which could distance one unnecessarily and erroneously from the present effects of tradition. Against any sense of separation between past and present, Gadamer chooses to follow the romantic tradition's sense of the present reality of classical and other historical texts. As a result, the articulation of historical consciousness in *Truth and Method* represents the reality of the past as the continual carrying forward of tradition into the present.

The translators of the new edition of *Truth and Method* capture both the active meaning of the German word for tradition, *Überlieferung*, and the negative challenge facing Gadamer when they write in their preface:

> English has no corresponding verb, nor any adjective that maintains the active verbal implication, nor any noun for what is carried down in "tradition." We have therefore admitted the neologism "traditionary text," and have sometimes used the phrase "what comes down to us from the past" or "handed down from the past" to convey the active sense of the German. We are likely to think of "tradition" as what lies merely behind us or as what we take over more or less automatically. On the contrary, for Gadamer "tradition" or "what is handed down from the past" confronts us as a task.[3]

The active meaning of the German term for "tradition" indicates how it is not in the first instance a formal or already completed entity, but rather is continually in the process of being carried forward as it is handed down and understood. As a true hermeneutical understanding of classic texts reveals, according to Gadamer, the transmission of tradition is anything but automatic or simply repetitive. Rather, it is historical in the sense that new meanings do emerge and necessarily emerge from the continuous handing down of the "same" classic. The active and changing carrying forward of tradition is expressed by Gadamer's justly famous words that to understand is always and not accidentally "to understand differently."

Hence, part of the "task" of the historical understanding of tradition is to recognize that there is no simple *text in itself* which must be understood, but rather an entire history of its being handed down, the history of its effects or, in Gadamer's terms, its *Wirkungsgeschichte.* However, this is only part of the task of *Wirkungsgeschichtliches Bewusstsein* or "effective-historical consciousness." Indeed, the new translators of *Truth and Method* choose to follow P. Christopher Smith's suggestion in translating this key concept as "historically effected consciousness."[4] The further task or additional dimension of this consciousness lies in recognizing that there is no interpreter "in herself" either. She or he is part of the effective history of the text, indeed "belongs" to this history, as Gadamer's very famous notion of the "fusion of horizons" makes clear.

Rather than the apparent separation between the traditionary text and the contemporary interpreter, a "fusion of horizons" is brought about in the very act or movement of understanding, and not through any conscious intention of the interpreter subsequent to the understanding of the text. In the encounter with the text, "the interpreter's horizon is already being stretched beyond itself, so that it is no longer the same horizon that it was independently of this encounter."[5] Similarly, "the horizon of the text has been caught up in this movement and only through it becomes accessible."[6]

The conclusion of this philosophical hermeneutical conception of tradition is elaborated by Joel Weinsheimer, when he writes, "There is a birth and growth of something reducible to neither the interpreter, nor the text, nor their conjunction."[7] This conception of a "resulting whole" that is clearly "greater than the sum of its parts" represents Gadamer's negative response to any methodological understanding of history that would see only parts. The "task" of the historical understanding of tradition just is to recognize oneself as part of a much larger event. The negative characterization of philosophical hermeneutics avoids at all costs any artificial separation from the past in favor of the skill "to let things speak which come to us in a fixed, petrified form, that of the text."[8]

The Life of the Language Community

Gadamer's description of a movement of birth and growth in an event that is larger than its principals is useful for understanding not only the handing down of tradition, but also, as the above brief characterization of philosophical hermeneutics already indicates, the movement of the coming into language. Indeed, the two are inextricably connected, as is seen in the way that part 3 follows part 2 of *Truth and Method*. Moreover, language rather than tradition is Gadamer's point of departure in more recent characterizations of philosophical hermeneutics. As he explains,

> I now begin where I ended in *Wahrheit und Methode*. I begin with language, the linguistic structure of experience, with art. In both cases I emphasize their role in the construction of the social, the forming of the social. . . . My argument has not become more political than it was, but it is more direct: I address the phenomena at issue rather than the science or theory of them.[9]

The beginning point of language allows for a positive characterization of philosophical hermeneutics, the characterization Gadamer now much prefers to the earlier characterization.

Language possesses its movement character for Gadamer precisely insofar as it is *not* seen as "a stock of words and phrases, of concepts, viewpoints and opinions."[10] Language is "not its elaborated conventionalism, nor the burden of pre-schematization with which it loads us, but the generative and creative power to unceasingly make this whole once again fluent."[11] Language possesses this generative and creative power "only in dialogue, in *coming to an understanding*."[12] Of this movement of coming to an understanding, Gadamer comments:

> This is not to be understood as if that were the purpose of language. Coming to an understanding is not a mere action, a purposeful activity, a setting up of signs through which I transmit my will to others. Coming to an understanding as such, rather, does not need any tools, in the proper sense of the word. It is a life process in which a community of life is lived out.[13]

The dialogue of the interpreter with the text—or perhaps better of the text with the interpreter—is no different from, indeed is inextricably connected with, the "conversation that we are." True conversation is described and understood by Gadamer not as an act between the separate conversation partners, but rather involves their coming together in a larger event or happening to which they belong. This event of conversation is not led by any of the partners, but rather by the subject matter (the *Sache*) of the conversation that "seizes" the conversation partners into the process of coming to an understanding. Just as play catches its participants up, so does conversation catch us up into its life-process. The resulting living out of a "community of life" is indeed "greater than the sum of its parts" and can be neither predicted nor imposed by any speaking member.

To analyze any statement, indeed any word or individual concept, in isolation from its larger linguistic context is to fail to do justice to the movement of coming to an understanding, the movement of solidarity in the community life-process. This movement never reaches finality, but such incompleteness is in no way a defect or a fault, but rather a, if not the, most important characteristic of the whole process. Any particular contribution to the conversation "brings a totality of meaning into play, without being able to express it totally."[14] Yet, this is precisely what most profoundly characterizes Gadamer's conception of experience. The truly experienced person is "one who, in acknowledging the ineluctability of experience and the limits of 'definitive knowledge,' has gained insight into the *finite* nature of his own existence."[15] It is crucial to realize that this finitude is best understood as an asset, if it leads to a true openness toward the subject matter and toward the carrying forward of the conversation. With such openness, all "human speaking is finite in such a way that there is laid up within it an infinity of meaning to be explicated and laid out."[16]

Dieter Misgeld expresses succinctly the most important aspects of this "positive characterization" of philosophical hermeneutics:

> We may believe, therefore, that for Gadamer dialogue and conversation, in their various forms, are constitutive of what the world is for people. And nothing is more important than having a world in common. Having a world in common means living in solidarity, and living in solidarity means openness to conversation and dialogue. The other becomes indispensable for us in this openness and for it.[17]

However, Misgeld, in his important essay, "Poetry, Dialogue, Negotiation," quickly adds that the positive value of this hermeneutical characterization is accompanied by a negative judgment by Gadamer. This judgment is no longer directed to a false methodological or scientific understanding, but rather toward the actual living circumstances of much of modern life: "these very same ideas underlie his skeptical attitude toward much of modern life, and his fear that the pace of technical, economic, and administrative progress (not to speak of the increase in military power) will overtake cultural resources contained in this tradition."[18] Gadamer judges modern life in terms of the anonymity of mass society and the employment of technical thinking to organize "habits of conduct not mediated by . . . the subtle forms of understanding of self and others achieved in intensive and searching forms of conversation."[19] Members of the modern community no longer exhibit the openness of dialogue, but rather adjust to such technical organization of life as "existing beyond their understanding and control."[20] Hence, Gadamer now seeks "to protect forms of intimate and deeply engaging conversation from the technologically reinforced invasion of culturally and intellectually still viable institutional spheres capable, in his view, of maintaining the mentioned forms of communication."[21]

The Movement of Bodily Feeling and Language

Eugene Gendlin's starting point for his conception of experiential phenomenology has much the same initial negative character as Gadamer's, only his target is the logical and conceptual analysis that is directed toward the human body. Against this most familiar and indeed dominant understanding of bodily awareness, Gendlin lodges an even stronger charge than Gadamer does:

> My proposed manner of using concepts can be contrasted with the more familiar one of speaking only about logical, conceptual relations. In that familiar mode, the bodily carrying forward of the situational mesh has been "dogmatically hidden away" so that it is underdeveloped, lacking an overt way to be thought.[22]

As with the active handing down of tradition that has been overlooked by methodological approaches to history according to Gadamer, so there is, for Gendlin, a "carrying forward" of the body that has been "dogmatically hidden" by conceptual thought. Its underdevelopment is above all evident in our inattentiveness toward the "felt meaning" of the body.

When Gendlin writes of bodily feeling, it is not with any momentary emotion in mind, but rather with a whole process of change and continuity. This process is best characterized as one of a "carrying forward" of feeling in the present and toward the future:

> What one feels implies certain further future interactional events with the environment: when something like that happens, it "carries forward" the body process which implied something like that. Something like that happening in the environment makes a continuation of interaction, and it is this continuation which is termed "carrying forward."[23]

Carrying forward thus indicates a relationship between the present and the future in which the future event carries out the implications of the present interaction without being a simple repetition. It involves a becoming clear about what may initially be an unclear bodily feeling. Gendlin is as interested in language within this situational mesh as Gadamer is in regard to community, but his avenue toward his understanding of it is not tradition, but the body: "What is the link between situations, the body, and language, such that *words* come to us to say in situations? And, how do *just the right* words come—the ones that might make the *situational* difference we need?"[24]

Gendlin's answer to the latter question is that the right words do not always come—*at least immediately*—but when they come it is because of a successful bodily sensing of one's situation. This sensing is itself the result of a movement that occurs in bodily feeling, and this movement is the subject of an analysis as nuanced as that of Gadamer's movement of tradition:

> How does one find these crucial carrying forward moves, acts, interactions, or words?
> What will carry the experiencing process forward is already *implicit* in it. However, it is often not implicit as word, as act, as interaction, as body move, but instead, is implicit as unclear feeling. When a specific feeling, word, or image is obtained, carrying forward has taken place.[25]

Of course, the right word may and often does not immediately emerge to carry forward the bodily experience. But even if the right word doesn't quickly come, the not yet articulated and explicated " . . . . ." (which Gendlin uses to characterizes the bodily sensed more-than-can-be-said at the present time) nonetheless represents a most significant movement forward. As Gendlin writes:

But sometimes no actual step forms. Perhaps at first there is confusion, but then a . . . . . can come. The confusion "jells." The coming of a . . . . . is a large change from the confused condition. We feel relief. Now in a way we "know" what to do, but words and actions have not actually formed as yet.[26]

Even though the words are not yet formed, a "focaling" has begun. The situational "mesh" among body, situation, and language represents an "implicit intricacy" in which none of the meshing phenomena are viewed or can be viewed in separation from one another. This implicit intricacy "focally implies" a further step. The further step will depend on a "bodily" coming of words: "The step is not only the *words* but also *what we want to say* to carry *the situation* forward, and that is bodily sentient. . . . you have (feel, sense, are . . . . .) the . . . . . *in a bodily-sensed way.*"[27]

The term "focaling" conveys a certain directionality that is implied by the bodily feeling and yet also given to the process of feeling through its explication in language. Its intricacy is implied by a whole bodily sense of the situation:

> If one lets oneself sense the *whole* feel of now, a sense of direction emerges, if it is sought. . . . It is not just any release from any pressure, but a *whole* body sense of one's life or specific situation which is used implicitly, without having to separate out all its many facets. . . . It is the whole of one's living, which shapes this direction.[28]

Yet, at the same time, this whole bodily sense "comes" only when the right word "comes" to explicate it as well:

> One cannot design such steps. They come. They happen. All one can do deliberately is to *focus* attention on the body's sense of more than can be said. We could not have predicted the next step from the earlier steps. Each step makes sense retroactively, but only as we go back and *alter* what had seemed so true at the previous step. The [bodily sensed more than can be said] . . . . . has *new* implicit speech which has not yet formed. . . . the *new* saying is not yet *in* the unclear sense—obviously not, since a *body-change* comes physically only when the saying forms. . . . One does not design new phrases or actions. They "come" physically—the body produces them if we attend to the body-sense of what cannot be said or done.[29]

Such sensitive phenomenological attention to an implicit speech which is "not yet formed" is precisely what is precluded by standard conceptual thinking about the body. Its emphasis upon pregiven patterns serves to analyze away any whole body sense of life and its potential "focaling" effects. Even more crucial to its unintended hiding away is the analytical separation among body, situation, and language. It is this neglect of the "implicit intricacy" of the situational mesh of the whole which is Gendlin's major basis for the charge of dogmatism. To make overt what is hidden in this manner is to act in a directly analogous way to Gadamer when he seeks to let speak the "fixed, petrified form" of the text. Gendlin's experiential phenomenology uncovers the felt meaning of "what comes to us" otherwise only as undynamic, indeed, dead conceptual patterns of a most limited, if indeed most familiar, analysis of the body. As David Michael Levin elucidates, "This . . . . . is a priceless hermeneutical gift, because it lets us think (into) a spacing, an openness, that is both vague and precise, both more determinate and less determinate than the conceptual structures which, on paper, appear to surround and control it."[30]

The Life of the Community and the Life of the Body

Hans-Georg Gadamer and Eugene Gendlin are clearly similar in regard to what may be termed, following Gadamer, as the negative characterizations of their endeavors. Both object strenuously to the limitations of a methodological or conceptual approach to historical understanding and bodily feeling, respectively. Both offer phenomenologically sensitive and compelling descriptions of play and conversation, on the one hand, and of bodily felt meaning, on the other, to reveal or uncover what is so often overlooked or intentionally understated by other thinkers and rival approaches.

Moreover, there is also an equally important similarity in regard to the positive characterizations of philosophical hermeneutics and experiential phenomenology. Gadamer's and Gendlin's descriptions of tradition and bodily feeling are quite comparable in regard to the movements they depict. Each description is most definitely a nonmomentary analysis: there is no text in itself or feeling in itself, but a carrying forward of feeling and a history of textual effects. For Gadamer, language is the medium within which a fusion of horizons happens between past and present and within which a solidarity happens in coming to an understanding. For Gendlin, language is itself caught up in a situational mesh of body and situation, a part of a "fusion" of bodily experiencing between present and future. Indeed, the fundamental similarities in the temporal movements of these two descriptions as resulting wholes that are clearly "greater than their parts" confirms, in my opinion, both the basic accuracy and the power of both descriptions.

While to focus on the movements and their dynamic character is to ascertain a great deal of similarity between Gadamer and Gendlin, there is at the same time a noteworthy difference in the way language is situated in both cases. For Gadamer, the generative and creative power of language is evident in the process of coming to an understanding. The description of a conversation as a larger event that catches its participants up into its subject matter indicates how language is situated in a community of life, indeed, is the way that this community of life is "lived out." For Gendlin, too, language has a generative and creative power in making explicit an "implicit intricacy." However, Gendlin attributes this power to a situational mesh that he describes as obtaining between body, language, and situation. Thus, whereas Gadamer locates the carrying forward of language first and foremost within a life community and emphasizes the sense of having a world in common, Gendlin situates language with the body, and points toward a focaling of whole bodily feeling in new felt meaning.

While I take this to be an important difference, I also believe it essential that this difference in accentuation between community meaning and bodily felt meaning not be used in an oppositional manner. My evaluation of this difference in accentuation is that it is indicative of a span of varying emphases within a common philosophical approach. Within this philosophical approach, whose allegiance I share, there may be widely divergent views about the relative importances of phenomenological analysis, above all in regard to the body, and of the ontological role of hermeneutical understanding, especially in regard to tradition and community. What is apparent to me is that it is extremely difficult to do justice to the "other" of the pair of the ontological role of coming to an understanding and the carrying forward of bodily feeling, when the primary explication of either the hermeneutic understanding of tradition or the phenomenological description of lived experience is being given.

Gendlin's characterization of experiential phenomenology shares a great deal with Gadamer's earlier, "negative" characterization of philosophical hermeneutics. For both thinkers the opponent is a patterned or schematic way of thinking that abstracts from the situational mesh or historical context. What is more interesting is to compare this negative characterization of experiential phenomenology with the more recent, positive characterization of Gadamer's hermeneutics. Crucial to that characterization is the emphasis on language precisely not as a conceptually patterned or conventionally schematized phenomenon. Rather, the phenomenological description of conversation and the emphasis on coming to a social understanding describe directly a dynamic process of potentially infinite participation:

> To say that the language in which we become immersed as we grow up is more than just a set of symbols serving the needs of a civilizing apparatus should not be misinterpreted as a romantic idolization of a mother tongue. It is indisputable that every language has a tendency toward schematization. As a language is learned, it creates a view of the world which conforms to the character of the speech conventions that have been established in the language. . . . Nevertheless, it seems to me that in contrast to every artifically devised system of signs, the living aspect of language perfects and develops itself in association with the living traditions that encompass historical humanity. This secures for the life of every language an inner infinity.[31]

My first line of questioning concerns the "living aspect of language" for both Gadamer and Gendlin. For Gadamer, this aspect is intimately associated with community and participation in a continually unfolding dialogue that has a potential "inner infinity." Gendlin's living aspect involves its own linguistic unfolding of unpatterned, potentially continuous explication of initially unclear bodily feeling. Do not both these patterns indicate in different and legitimate ways how language as it is concretely spoken is "beyond patterns"? Does not the first process of coming to an understanding even assist in the explication of felt meaning by promoting—and not opposing as do "more conceptual approaches"—the articulation in common of the bodily more-than-can-be-said? In other words, is it possible to formulate a more positive characterization of experiential phenomenology and its relationship of body to language parallel to the more recent positive characterization by Gadamer of philosophical hermeneutics?

The second line of questioning is prompted by the still more recent pronouncements by Gadamer concerning modern difficulties in regard to conversation and dialogue. Unlike the earlier characterization that opposed false or highly limited methods of historical understanding, the object of Gadamer's criticisms now appears to be aspects of modern life itself. Indeed, it appears that the greatest danger to the carrying forward of tradition and the coming to understanding of conversation now lies not in inadequate methodological understandings of these phenomena, but rather in actual historical conditions of "routinized and automatically unfolding forms of behavior."[32] True conversation and intimate dialogue appear to be in need of protection from what was earlier described as the "technologically reinforced invasion" of advertising, mass media, and other sources.

Gadamer's criticisms of modern patterns of behavior are of course not original, but only part of an almost Gadamerian-like tradition of continental thinking beginning with Weber and the early Frankfurt School and proceeding to Foucault and Habermas. Such an emphasis on routinized behavioral patterns and the reference to the larger critique of instrumental reason do, however, bring into focus several questions that can be posed in regard to Gendlin's experiential phenomenology of bodily felt meaning. Does Gendlin's main target for criticism continue to be a conceptually patterned understanding of the body, or does criticism also extend to patterns of behavior and their effects on bodily carrying forward? Does he have a view—or feel that he has to have a view—in regard to the technical organization of human conduct and its penetration, as Foucault has so conclusively demonstrated, into the smallest aspects of bodily movement and feeling? Finally, does the "carrying forward" and "focaling" of bodily feeling need *protection*, as it appears to be the case with Gadamer in regard to conversation, from such "routinized" and "automatically unfolding" habits of conduct, or can it also offer in any way *resistance* to such behavioral patterns?

As I pose this series of questions, I want to avoid at all costs the impression that the questioning is all one-sided. As excellent as Gadamer's descriptions of tradition and dialogue are, they may still be queried with regard to their adequacy to the richness of the wide breadth of bodily experiencing. In particular, it may be asked whether the phenomenological descriptions most associated with the Gadamerian movement privilege the coming to an understanding in regard to subject matter to the neglect of the focaling of bodily experience as it is phenomenologically described by Gendlin.

Encapsulated within Gendlin's important conception of "focaling" is a view toward lived experience which attributes to it itself—and not to any external factor or even to the linguistic medium—a considerable capacity for coherence. There is a *wholeness* to the body sense even in regard to the present, nonmomentary feeling which one has in her or his bodily situation. To become conscious of this wholeness is to recognize a sense of direction to the carrying forward of bodily feeling. This directionality allows one to gain insight into the larger body sense of one's living or even into the bodily coherence of one's whole life.

Such directionality, coherence, and wholeness of course does not occur out of historical context and must be expressed in the medium of language. However, to consider it solely, as Gadamer considers consciousness, as "historically effect*ed*" is to fail to do justice to the "focaling" achieved within the experiencing itself. Gadamer's conception of experience is oriented, above all, to the experience of human finitude. This conception is certainly accurate in its own way and faithful to the results of phenomenological analysis. It is also powerful in its implications. These implications are not only and not primarily about limitation, but rather point toward the much greater positive aspect of openness toward a still uncompleted historical process.

But it would then appear that Gadamer is arguing for and emphasizing the importance of the ontological role of understanding in a way that undervalues the full role of experiential coherence. Gendlin is correct to insist that focaling is implied by the process of lived experience itself, is indeed its most prominent and important feature. Hence, Gadamer's hermeneutically oriented conception of experience is certainly not false, but may be incomplete with respect to the processual character and the richness and coherence of finite human experience.

If this brief reciprocal questioning of Gadamer and Gendlin is at all appropriate, then there may be a larger lesson within it concerning the nature and breadth of their common enterprise. Phenomenological hermeneutics is best represented as a dynamic and contextual approach to philosophizing, as Gadamer's analysis of coming to an understanding and Gendlin's description of the articulation of felt meaning well illustrate. However, to describe one of these processes with complete phenomenological detail and sensitivity is to open oneself to an almost inevitable incompleteness with regard to the other. Thus, phenomenological hermeneutics must probably always deal with both the lived experience of the body and the life of the language community, and it must seek to interweave comparisons between them from the standpoint of multiple contributions such as those of Hans-Georg Gadamer and Eugene Gendlin.

Reply to Wallulis

I am grateful to Professor Wallulis for his careful discussion of the parallels and differences between myself and Gadamer. I can agree with most of them. I am especially glad that he saw that my emphasis on the body is "not oppositional" to Gadamer's emphasis on tradition. They would be oppositional if the body were construed as usual. Wallulis saw that I "oppose the analytical separation among body, situation, and language." He understood that of course what Gadamer means by "the tradition" is implicit in how we live in situations. He saw that I agree with Gadamer that speaking occurs *within* tradition in a particular way, namely that it can move the tradition forward; we are not within it in the sense of being caught in it. Much of what I say is what Gadamer has long been saying.

I speak of "situations" (in the U.S. tradition) rather than of "world" and "tradition" (as one does in the German situation). Heidegger's "*Befindlichkeit*" is translated "situatedness." We can move both of these traditions forward. I see language not as the ultimate source, but as carrying *life* forward, and I see human life as a carrying forward. The body is neither a bundle of mere needs and emotions, nor a mere precondition (as Merleau-Ponty sometimes has it). The body is *now* what we act and speak from. If I may address my reader: without your body-sense of the situation now obtaining, you would be disoriented and could not read this, nor think, speak, or act. Of course, your situation is never yours alone; every situation involves (present or absent) people with whom you share a long history in which *such a* situation developed, nearly always in part by using words. Situations and language developed together, and they continue to develop together.

The current emphasis on "the tradition" (history, language, culture . . . . .) sounds as if human life floats about, separated from our bodies and from practice. This view would not be defended, if faced flatly. I think it is an overcorrection of an earlier overvaluing of the individual, as if society had been created by adult individuals meeting together on a large lawn, or as if the objects of science were the product of a single mind's connectives, as with Kant and Piaget, or as if *Being and Time* came out of one person's inspired individual mind. Now it is said that there is "*no* author," and we seem unable to speak of "the human subject" (ourselves) at all, because we use the words "human subject" only to name an old view we deny. Let us carry the tradition forward by regaining the words to say what we mean, rather than only to deny the old mistakes.

I agree with Gadamer that our situations, our world, and our human nature are still being constitutively carried further. I say that our human nature is a "V" at bottom resting in body-life, but its arms moving always further apart.

I think our real difference is my drive to a new way of speaking and using philosophical terms. Of course, it "belongs" to the tradition and the world. We can take our own bodily sensing into our philosophical thinking, and let our terms work newly from how situation-body-and-language imply and invite new precision. Deliberately using words in this way seems to be my main difference with Gadamer. While I recognize and agree with much of what he says, I have great trouble with how he says it, leading to implications with which I deeply disagree, such as that there can be no exact understanding, no standards, no better or worse understanding either. Of course, this is not what Gadamer says, but there has been no way to avoid these implications, and he is often read with them. Wallulis manages *not* to imply them, but at least partly by means of using my kind of terms. He refers (five times) to Gadamer's view of tradition as a "carrying forward" of tradition. I think he is right; what Gadamer means requires such a term, and not only a term but the precision that demands the term. Words like "to understand *differently*" and "*fusion*" must be read in this more precise way. I will try to show it here.

Gadamer always points to creativity and fresh thinking beyond existing patterns; let us enter there, and let us speak precisely from where patterns and distinctions break down. That is where we all think and speak from, but customarily one pretends to speak from outside this realm, even to be unable to speak from within it. We can enter it deliberately. We can allow the words newly to say what they mean *in it* and *about it.*

Let us enter Gadamer's "arriving at an understanding," and see exactly how it involves a "common world" to which we belong. Let us first consider Gadamer's dictum "to understand means to understand *differently.*" I think it loses something vital from what Dilthey had said: "To understand means to understand *better.*" Both statements reject the assumption that understanding is mere reception of fixed messages that we only copy. But where Gadamer has only "same" or "different," Dilthey had another kind of relation: he said that one *can* understand *exactly* only if one understands *better.* Better, but notice: still *exactly.* Let me tell a story to bring *this* kind of "exactly" home.

Suppose you tell me something you are excited about, perhaps something personal or a new point in philosophy. Now you are eager to hear from me. Suppose I say only your own words back to you, over and over, with no indication that I have grasped their meaning, and without saying anything further. You would be angry. You want to hear what your point makes me think, how I would move on from it.

Now I oblige you and begin telling you what I think, but you notice that I have not grasped your point *exactly.* Now you stop me. "Wait," you say. "That wasn't my point." *You do not want to hear my reaction to a misunderstanding of your point.* Now suppose I am very stupid. I might object: "You don't like it if I say what you said, and you don't want something different either. Well then, what *do* you want?"

But if I am not stupid, I stop the moment you tell me that I have not understood exactly. You say "Let me say what I mean more exactly." Then you say more, or put the point differently, and soon I say "Oh, I see." *Now* you are again eager to hear what I will say, and perhaps this time you see that what I say is *what your exact point* makes me think.

What does the story show? Understanding is more intricate than either a copy or something different. *We need more terms than "same" or "different"! We can generate the needed terms from the intricacy of the story.* You are not eager to hear how I go on from something *different* that you did not say, nor do you want the *same* thing back. You want to hear how I *move from* your point, because *I* will move in a way you cannot imagine without me, yet may be able to follow as being from your point; if so, you may then move on still further.

From the story we find that two people can both have an exact understanding of a point, and yet not the same one. We see that they are not the same, since the first person cannot alone generate how the other will move from it.

We must augment Gadamer's dictum by insisting that to understand is to understand *exactly, although differently*. It must be possible for understanding to be *both* exact *and* different, since our familiar story is possible. Like other familiar situations, it is more intricate than our concepts. If asked to explain how both are possible, we may first stick to our story: What can "*both* exact and different" mean? It means *exactly* the sense in which you want to hear comments only when both obtain. We can use *that* meaning from now on.

We can use the story's sense of "exactly" as a concept, and apply it in many instances. As long as we keep the story with us, we can find many ways and schemes to say what exactly means. None are final, nor is this relativism; we can always return to let the words tell and mean the story.

We can also enter further into the intricacy of the story, in which the three terms ("understanding," "a point," and "to move on from") work and are interconnected. *To understand* (to get the point) is to be able to move on from the point. *To move on from* is to say something that shows this understanding. And *a point* is what one can move on from only if one stays with it exactly. These terms define each other by how they work in the intricacy of the story's situation. From this one can devise a system of mutually defining terms, redundant unless we expand it. We could add to it arbitrarily, but why do that? Let us expand it by finding more in the implicit intricacy.

We find that we cannot even paraphrase what we don't understand. So paraphrases can be included in "moving on." We can repeat the words without getting the point, so the point is not the words.

But a point is not without words. So, with or without words is not the point. What is the point? What happens when we "get the point"? Aha!—when we get the point, it is a flood of many unseparated things. A point affects *many* things at once; we cannot say them all . . . . . The point *is* the change it makes in the many other things. It makes many more changes than we can think, one by one. (If we didn't already have the term "unseparated multiplicity," we can use it from here.)

Now we can look to see if our argument makes sense. Aha, yes! If *to understand is* many effects at once, then you might well tell me one I didn't think of explicitly, or even one that was not implicit for me. Yet, I could recognize them as one of those that *was* my point. And, aha, yes! Many *different* changes could be effects of exactly that point. *To move on from* a point is to find some of those, but to find them one has to stay with the point. So it makes sense that *a point* is what one can move on from, while staying exactly with it.

Understanding is said of individuals, whereas the point makes more differences in the language and the world than one person can find.

Doesn't one have to have the building blocks, the same shared public meanings out of which to construct the point? No, not in advance. As Gadamer shows, the dialogue first *makes* the new shared meanings; it is not composed of old ones. If you spend enough hours or years slowly building my experiential mesh, I will become able to follow any point you make. That is what Dilthey meant by "anything human is understandable in principle." If our experiences were units, and if they were just different, then we would always understand just differently. But meaning is not composed of units, as in mathematics and logic. Therefore, Gadamer calls it "fusion." When two people (or text and interpreter) enter a dialogue, they have already *changed* each other. But to say this exactly, the word "changed" (or any other word that comes here) has to change in just this way (the way it is changed by coming to us to say here).

When my old meanings cross with your point, the result is more precise and includes more requirements than before. So it is a better understanding of both my own meanings *and* yours. So I argue that what Gadamer means by "understanding differently" is both exact and better.

So I do not deny Gadamer's "coming to a social understanding." But let "social" and "individual" (or "public" and "private") change as they say this. Social and private are each both wider and narrower than the other. No person can implicitly sense all the differences a point makes. But a seemingly private point of yours rearranges and expands the implicit language, even if it remains a . . . . . and you never speak from it. And, the more unique your point, the more universally significant the changes will be to all of us, if we come to cross with it (see *ECM*).

Many metaphors can cross with (let us understand, say, make, go on from . . . . .) the same point exactly, but differently. We see this because we can go on differently from each. A point can cross with almost anything else, yet its crossing will always be exact, if it makes sense at all. If it is not exact, it makes a different point.

Today it is said that no exact understanding is possible; one can "deconstruct" a text without understanding it very far. But Derrida understands a text very exactly before he arrives at the spot where he begins to deconstruct it. Yet, he has no way to say what he does, or what "exact" could mean if we reject the old correspondence criteria. To say it, we need more terms, and terms of a new kind. We can let the terms emerge from letting the words speak from their working, as the working happens. A whole vocabulary of such terms can speak from the happening of what they are about.

My "primary opponent" (to use Wallulis's term) is not conceptual patterns. It seems less than serious to want to do without those. I devise new concepts that can link logically as well as experientially. My opponent is rather the assumption that conceptual patterns or distinctions consti- tute the only order. Today this assumption is the silent second premise in the view that, *since* conceptual patterns and distinctions break down (and since they are the only order), *therefore* there is no order at all.

I need to reply to Wallulis's question about "resistance" to oppres- sion. One main power of situated thinking is that its intricacy "offers resistance" to the imposed routines of action and thought. It resists them if we enter into what we are already living, but this is always at first a . . . . . It is at first inarticulate because it exceeds and differs with the official views which largely shape the public language. To tell people that any saying must inevitably fail, that it cannot help but fall into the old dead forms, is just another mode of silencing that in them which needs to speak, and can come to speak. The existing language comes from the activity of speaking. It is not a system of dead forms into which our saying must inevitably fall.

This is false about personal as well as philosophical thinking, since they are always implicit in each other. We do not find only the old forms and assumptions when we enter what is at first inarticulate. For example, when a person directly discovers from a . . . . . —"Oh, it's that sense— from my mother—that it's bad and selfish ever to *want* anything"—the re-jection of a personal and cultural code is inherent in the experiencing. One does not first unearth one's early training and invasive events, merely coming to know them, as if one must then separately appeal to some external value code to reject them. Rather, the rejection arises in the very experiencing that comes upon it, in which new and more intricate ways of being are implied (. . . . .) and sometimes arise. But, even if no further steps come, even if the bodily felt sense remains only a . . . . . , its very coming frees the person from the imposed thoughts and routines which alienate us from how we are already living in our situations, and from what we can soon say if we enter the implicit intricacy as we read and think.

13

Intricacy: A Metaphysical Idea

Graeme Nicholson

Eugene Gendlin has worked out an approach to language that deserves the close attention of all philosophers. It turns upon the saying in connection with the said. This is not a speech-act theory, nor is it really a new distinction that he is proposing. Rather he opens up a different *dimension* of language. In "Thinking beyond Patterns," Gendlin has identified, under the common name of "patterns," a myriad of forms, distinctions, and models that seem to guide us in our utterances and in our understanding. Words are supposedly governed, in a thoroughgoing way, by these delimitations. What Gendlin is referring to, first and foremost, are all the distinctions and patterns that constitute the discourse of special disciplines like psychoanalysis, and this science and that science. There are further structures and differentiations, too, that supposedly determine the nature of language as such. They include the differential character of language in the Saussurean sense, whereby the determinateness of a given word can be expressed as its exclusion of all the other words. There are the syntactic forms that supposedly guide all our speech, and along with them the associative or metaphorical connections. All this is referred to as the determined, the determinate, or the form.[1] As his title announces, Gendlin in this essay wants to propel our thinking beyond these forms or patterns.

What is his point? Why should we seek to transcend the forms and patterns presented by language? Our colleagues in linguistics devote their lives precisely to the explanation of them. Is it just a magical metaphysical flight beyond structures and forms? No. Gendlin insists that in our speaking and in our saying we enter into a different order of things that lies before and above these "patterns." "The very practice which *seemed* founded on certain concepts was actually responded to by much more intricacy than could derive from the concepts."[2] Or, as he said in a 1987 paper, "Language and life work in ways that are not assimilable to distinctions or forms."[3] In particular, as far as language is concerned, Gendlin will comprehend linguistic patterns and forms as being true of the said. But they do not suffice to bring before us the saying. The saying exhibits a type of order of its own that cannot be assimilated to the patterns of the said. And this remains central for any thinking about language, because the saying does not pass away and vanish in favor of the said, but continues in the said.

The present paper will focus on the account Gendlin gives of this duality—of the saying and the said and their connection. I hope to make it clear, moreover, that his treatment of language does not close it off from other strata of our experience—the practical, the therapeutic, and so on. Language is the spinal cord of our whole being. When we look at how Gendlin comments on poems and the making of poems, we see that he does not divide them off from experience. When we examine his transcripts from psychotherapy sessions, we cannot doubt their concreteness, their closeness to life as it is lived. So we shall be able to see that the linguistic difference I have been speaking of has a deeper echo in the structure of human life itself.

In the first part of this paper, devoted to the saying and the said, I'll discuss the kind of order that prevails within saying—it is what Gendlin calls "intricacy." Then I shall add here and there a few supplementary points of my own about the interpretation of poems, and about difficulties that can arise in our attempt to think about saying. These comments will only offer further confirmation of Gendlin's ideas. In the second part of the paper, I want to try to show that the duality of the saying and the said is really one case of an ancient principle of philosophy—a metaphysical principle I call it, not with the slightest polemical interest but as a testimony to the seriousness and truth of Gendlin's thought. I'll try to do that by showing parallels to Gendlin's thought in such authors of metaphysics as Aristotle and Schelling. If this parallel holds, we shall have to recognize that Gendlin's philosophy of language and his existential therapy both proceed out of the deepest necessity of Western thought. The metaphysical dimension as such is a vital part of his philosophy, and makes the study of his work valuable for philosophers. Metaphysics is also, I submit, the atmosphere that endows his whole life project with its humanity and wisdom: Eugene Gendlin surprises us and refreshes us, when we have become weary of the barbaric jargons of contemporary philosophy, and suspicious of the research projects of modern psychology.

GRAEME NICHOLSON

1. Formative Energy

One might have the fear that any effort of thought to pull us "beyond patterns" would leave us in a void. And, indeed, when one starts out from all the accepted forms and distinctions known in experience, looking for the saying itself, there certainly has to be some degree of negation: without some degree of ascetic negation there can never be transcendence. We have to put ourselves beyond the expressed forms and patterns if we are to approach their source. Now a great deal of current philosophy, especially the philosophy after Heidegger, is doubtful, skeptical, and even anxious about such a procedure. Several inhibitions can come into play to stop us from the project of going beyond and behind the forms and patterns of language and science. Gendlin refers to several of these obstacles both in "Thinking beyond Patterns" and in earlier papers. In "Thinking beyond Patterns," he writes:

> The Deconstructionists would argue that the "*act of saying*" falls instantly into the *said*. The process of crea*ting* seems to turn instantly into crea*ted* forms. New distinctions arise, but the aris*ing* seems to disappear, leaving only what ar*ose*. So *saying* seems unsayable—supposedly it becomes the *said*—and they take the said to be just distinctions and forms.[4]

We might think, thus, that we confront an impossible task. We might persuade ourselves in advance that such an undertaking would be self-defeating. To speak about saying is, after all, to make it an object of speech, thereby bestowing on this process the articulations and patterns that hold for the said. We'd fall into the danger of objectifying it. Or, if we succeed in avoiding that danger, wouldn't we just get lost in a void? Wouldn't everything here be indeterminate, shapeless, and slip through our fingers like the wind?

Gendlin says no. He shows us instead that this saying is the home of another type of order. Distinctions, patterns, and forms do not constitute the only variety of order: the other variety is what he calls "intricacy," and what he symbolizes consistently with the device . . . . .

At many points in his "Thinking beyond Patterns," Gendlin deals with the experience of poetry composition; where there are the lines that have already been written, each of them exhibits its form and its pattern. But how does the poet go on? How to continue and complete the poem? We recognize here the presence and operation of some wellspring and power. "The poet stops in midst of an unfinished poem. How to go on? Perhaps there is only confusion. No leads. The poet reads and re-reads the lines. Where they end something *does* come! The poet hears (knows, reads, senses . . . . .) what these lines need, want, demand, *imply*."[5]

That is one of the illustrations of the principle of intricacy. Another is to be found in Gendlin's practice of psychotherapy and his transcripts of it. In his own practice of writing and therapy, Gendlin proceeds into the saying, the saying of the other person, the source of that which the other has said. It is signified by his mark: . . . . . The therapeutic dialogues that he offers us in "Thinking beyond Patterns" show again and again that the people he was speaking with made their own entry into the source of their forms and their distinctions, the source of what they were able to feel and to express.[6] At the point of their entry into the source, they become able to bring forth a new form, a new pattern, to make sense anew, a new kind of sense. Gendlin's device . . . . . which he includes in the therapy transcripts, signifies not just silence or pausing, but the interlocutor's entry into the dimension of saying, and it communicates to us, the readers, that Gendlin too had been able to follow his interlocutors into the dimension, and come back out of it with them, and then to express the journey to us in the transcription. This is an Orpheus-Euridice journey into the underworld with a successful return!

Saying is the source of the said, and thinking is the source of a thought. But how could we in our thinking and saying study our own source? It is certainly an important question of *philosophy* whether and how a discourse can encompass the possibility of discourse. What kind of thinking can it be which turns its attention upon the thinking itself, rather than what is thought? What kind of saying can it be which seeks to express, not something said, but rather the very saying itself? Gendlin's work sketches a number of features of discourse that permit this recursion. I would like to amplify his discussion by offering one or two other cases that resemble his cases.

Gendlin dealt with poetry composition. Let me offer a supplement, referring to the reading and interpretation of poems. This will tend to show, I think, that his "thinking beyond patterns" is not relevant only to creativity, but is a phenomenon of human language as such. To read and to speak is already to be pushed beyond patterns. In the interpretation of a written text, such as a poem, it is a central fact that I can interpret only where I grant that I could read and understand the poem in the *absence* of interpretation. Perhaps that point may seem too difficult to accept without longer proof, but it is easy enough to see that my interpretation of the poem is unthinkable except on the hypothesis that *someone* (whether myself or another) could read and understand the poem in the absence of interpretation. Nothing can be a poem unless, for example, its author could read it and understand it.

Therefore, to interpret a poem, I must comprehend it as proceeding from the formative energy of an intelligence. The interpretation not only seeks to comprehend the poem, it also seeks to let the poem be. It does that by granting the role of the author, granting that the wellspring of the work lies in another intelligence. It is a *formative energy* that we've encountered here, the intricacy that brought the poem forth.

My purpose here is not to pursue these questions about poetics and hermeneutics any further—though the anti-authorial orthodoxy of our times could be challenged by these points. I have been speaking of "mind" and "intelligence," and suggesting at points that we have an *intuition* of such a source. It is quite clear that Heidegger, for one, did not care to approach poetry and interpretation in that way. And yet he too was invariably led beyond and behind the forms and patterns of the said, toward a living wellspring of the said, and he identified it, for the most part, as the language, *die Sprache*, or as the speaking of language, *das Sprechen der Sprache*, or as saying and saga, *die Sage*. Gendlin's way of proceeding is exactly in line with Heidegger's. My terminology might involve some difference and contention with Heidegger. But rather than exploring issues here about "mind," "language," and their relation, I want merely to confirm that *all* cases of hearing and interpretation, however they are analyzed in detail, are as fully committed to Gendlin's twofold as is the case of poetic composition. We shall have to concede Gendlin his intricacy.

Gendlin also offered us transcripts of psychotherapeutic dialogues to illustrate the intricacy that dwells within saying. Let me point out that an equivalent analysis might reveal the same point about every case of dialogue. I am able to understand you and interpret what you say in a dialogue (let's call what you say p) only under three conditions: (1) if I grant that it was you and not I who said p; (2) if I am able to entertain p as a thought on my own behalf; and (3) if I am able to grasp p, and the fact of your saying it, as proceeding from some source or wellspring of which I have some intuition: your mind, your intention. If one of these three things is lacking, I cannot interpret what you say. Lacking (1), I am a person completely incapable of dialogue. Lacking (2), I cannot even understand you. Lacking (3), I cannot interpret what you say, but only agree or disagree with you. Only if there is that which prompts and yields the utterance, and only given some sort of access to that wellspring (intuitive, perhaps), can there be interpretation. A formative energy brought p forth.

I posed the question, above, how we were able to think the source of our thoughts, and speak about the source of what we say: think the thinking, say the saying. It is indeed a profound problem. Is it not impossible to probe into the dimension that sustains us and what we say and think? The plant cannot uproot itself to examine its own soil. Could I examine my face in advance of the mirror-reflection so as to verify the mirror's work? Could I be in attendance at my own birth? Gendlin's recursions into the intricacy, the formative energy, might be further illustrated by some similar experiences.

Consider a dancer at the theater. As we sit watching the movements of a ballet dancer, we may both be thrilled at the beauty of the dance, and indeed equally thrilled. But you might be a dancer, a choreographer, or a ballet scholar, and I not. You, therefore, may admire this dancer's execution of a certain solo as an exceptional performance, implicitly comparing it to performances of other dancers, whereas I, no less sensitive to the beauty, may fail to distinguish between the solo that was performed and the performance of it. For me, every movement of this wonderful dancer was like spontaneous play, and it was her finger movements that called forth music from the orchestra pit. Later on, you may help me learn to separate the dancer from the dance, but you will not downgrade that evening's performance or pretend that the choreographer's scribbles are the true dance and that a performance is only an imitation. It is the leap of the dancer's body, really, that *discloses* the trajectory or form of the dance itself. True, one dancer may do the solo better than another, yet the solo itself, appearing behind the dancer's movements, only appears with them, not apart from them.

And of course you too can perform some parts of this dance yourself in your living room, and, watching you, I begin to see that there are movements, trajectories, that are the dance itself. Last night's performance was the enactment of it. Still better, you may begin to coach me in those movements. It is when I seek to execute them myself that the dance becomes most distinct from the dancer, and most distinct from Tuesday night's performance. And now I am prepared to enjoy a performance as the revelation of the dance, of its fullest possibilities. The gestures of the dancer *reveal* an intricacy that is a repeatable formation in space and time, a possibility for the female or the male body, and a conjunction of music, color, and movement.

It is in a somewhat similar way that a reflection, an interpretation, can reveal the saying and the thinking, the source and the wellspring of what we articulate. The source has an intricacy. Somebody can return upon an earlier awareness, and then undertake the leap of thought that will reveal the moving power behind that thought, reveal the intricacy just as the dancer's leap revealed the dance. We can turn back behind the beginning of one of our awarenesses. In philosophy, we are all the dancers, but some of our movements of thought can *reveal* what sustains thought and the said. Our language permits us to go to the intricacy.

You do not merely look on at the dancer, but, in trying the leap yourself, you move into the source and wellspring of her art. And, in thought, you move into the very saying and thinking, the source of the said. The thought that seeks to capture, recapitulate, and express the . . . . . has a further aspect of reflection, of course, beyond what the patient experienced in the therapy session. The patient entered the dimension, but was not concerned with the philosophical problem of defining the dimension and probing the possibility of gaining access to it. The reflection that we are attempting has to have exactly the same degree of living access to the dimension as the patient does, and in addition the reflective awareness that there is such a dimension, that we are seeking entry to it, that philosophy needs to explain why there is such a dimension and why we can gain access to it; and all of the above has to be communicated philosophically to a public. We participate in the awareness that we reveal, and if we reflect on it even as we participate in it, what is it that permits this reflection? We have to be equipped somewhat differently than one who has an awareness without the reflection. The philosopher's question, or the psychoanalyst's question, permits us to *reveal* the wellspring, the source. We too follow the contours of the source and the wellspring that first gave the awareness its life, but equipped with some questions. It is like a trip that we make on a three-lane freeway, following the lane dividing lines just like everyone else. But in this case, we are differently equipped, with paint and brushes—for we are driving the vehicle that repaints the lane dividers every decade or so. It is thus that we are immersed in an awareness even as we reveal it.

2. The Ontological Difference

Study of the saying, the thinking, leads into the dimension that sustains what is thought, what is said. But how to think and speak about this dimension? As I said above, there is a negative movement of thought needed as we surmount the patterns of the said, but it is not a pure negation, a pure asceticism, and we are right to refuse an ascesis that will deny us all form, all determination. The surmounting of the forms and pattern of the said is only the first movement, and it will open then into the exploration of intricacy itself.

A child playing in the sand by the side of the sea may pick up a stick and draw a line—one that is either straight or curvy, and perhaps about a meter long. The line may last for a day or so. While it lasts, it lies in an indeterminate extent of sand. Often the line, determinate in length as it is, may also serve to reveal to us, bring before us, the character of this sand, this beach, so vast, so old, and so much older and vaster than all the marks that this child and all other creatures have left here since time immemorial. Marks of all kind, of many specific shapes, can sometimes open up for us something bigger lying beyond patterns. The words that Shakespeare wrote for Antony evoke Egypt. A child's mark or a poet's words can disclose something vast, such as a beach and a type of sand, or a medium for marks, or Egypt, the first great empire of our tradition. The qualities of the sand that are revealed by the mark also enabled the mark to be made. But, besides that, they even invited the mark!

This is where the post-Heidegger philosophy tends all too often to yield to anxieties about the indeterminate, the void. Of course, these philosophical developments are centered on the question of Being. Heidegger's life was devoted to that question, and to the *difference* between Being and beings: things, entities, structures—a difference that he called in the 1920s the ontological difference. To introduce into thought the difference between Being and beings was the decisive rebuke to an ancient prejudice that Being itself, i. e., the Being of beings, that whereby each being is a being, is itself only formless and indeterminate. That is the meaning of Heidegger's work in history. Now my point has been, and will be, that the difference, and the connection, which Eugene Gendlin discerns between the saying and the said is one embodiment, one concrete case, of Heidegger's ontological difference. A good deal of post-Heideggerian thought tries to free itself from thinking of Being—they have been turning away from Being toward language or toward praxis or science or human relations. They have been dismissing Being as a mere ghost, the evanescent breath exhaled by a dying metaphysics, trying to turn instead to something real (language, etc.). They are leaping *across* the ontological difference, from Being towards beings. But anyone who makes that leap, fleeing from Being towards the real, has only understood the ontological difference in an abstract way. The result will be that their treatments of language and praxis and human relations will go astray. Now Gendlin corrects this. He is not the victim of an abstract interpretation of the ontological difference. Rather, he has looked within language itself for a concrete embodiment of the ontological difference—the duality of the saying and the said. And he looks within experience itself for another concrete embodiment of it, and he finds it—the interplay between our effort of being and all the specific social arrangements and devices we have set up.

Gendlin has shown us the order, the intricacy, that inhabits the saying itself. The point I want to make now is that the dimension of this intricacy has an *enabling* character. The forms and patterns that are familiar to us are not merely "surpassed" and "negated" by the intricacy, but have been brought forth out of the intricacy. Where Gendlin uses the term "pattern" to mean forms and structures that are brought into being, he sees intricacy not as having-been-constituted, but as the formative power. In "Thinking after Patterns," he sometimes called the patterns "formed forms,"[7] and this led me to refashion his words after the manner of Spinoza: form that has been constituted can be called *forma formata*, but Gendlin's point is that every such form proceeds out of a creative power which is another kind of form, the intricacy, which I might call the *forma formans*. With respect to speech and writings, poems and dialogues, we have to grant that the *source* of the "pattern," *forma formata*, is formal in a still higher degree, an intricacy that brings forth. To approach this in thought is by no means easy, but it is this which deserves the name of formative energy, *forma formans*.

There are various responses Gendlin sees in contemporary thought to the surmise or fear that, beyond the patterns, *forma formata*, there is only the formless: various kind of nihilism or deconstruction or dialectic arise at the rim of the world of pattern. They stem from blindness to the intricacy. "There is something more precise and determinate than distinctions or forms."[8] "The blank [i. e., the intricacy] is *vague, but it is also more precise.*"[9] Formative energy.

I would like to link this point to Gendlin's lifelong study of Aristotle and to the great authors of metaphysics, such as Maimonides, who amplified the thought of Aristotle. And I would like to appeal to their metaphysical thought as offering the evidence that the intricacy, *forma formans*, does lie behind and above the formed patterns of everyday life. It was the common teaching of the Aristotelian tradition that form is not found only in the concrete substances that now exist in the world. Order has already been at work in the *genesis* of each concrete substance, whether in the reproduction of animals and plants or in the *poiesis* of the technician. The form of health is the medical art.[10] Aristotle saw that the form, or intricacy, had a preexistence—not of the Platonic type in a separate abode above the heavens, but in whatever was creative and formative: the reproductive organs, for instance, or the deliberations of the producer. More than that, a truly metaphysical thinking can proceed beyond these instances of a creator entity, these organs and technicians, toward that very form itself which is the creative power per se. Then we see that the form is not something different when it is present in the creator entity and present in the created entity, but rather one and the same. But if it is one and the same, then metaphysical thinking will be able to identify, even in the created entity, just what is formal, what is identical to form in the creator. The climax of Aristotle's *Metaphysics* teaches us not only that true being is substance, not only that a substance must have form, but that the substance of an entity is the form of the entity. And here we must not take form in a commonsense way as a perceptual form or shape discerned in or on the entity. It is the inner form, the penetrating essence and constitution, the governing law and inner principle of development, the driving power of its being and its growth, in short as *energy, energeia*, formative energy, *forma formans*. It is different from the ontic presence of the substance, yet only because of it is there an ontic presence.

I have been using the word "form" here from time to time, to signify the intricacy that precedes the formed entity, though Gendlin, for his part, usually reserves the word "form" for the created and ontic pattern. The point I am making is not at all confined to Aristotle, even though his thought is the great prototype for all systems of metaphysics. The point is one which pertains to metaphysical thinking as such, and would appear clearly enough in a study devoted to any author, such as Augustine or Spinoza, any of the great Western philosophers. No doubt, it is contentious in Heideggerian circles to speak of these principles as cases of the ontological difference. Many texts of Heidegger speak of the oblivion of Being running through the Western tradition, and clearly imply the neglect or absence of the ontological difference in metaphysical systems. I grant that my account runs against many of the remarks of Heidegger, but it could be that a review of his writings on metaphysics would show considerable nuance, subtlety, ambiguity over this very point of contention.

Let me refer to another embodiment of the ontological difference—in F. W. J. Schelling. I'll draw upon his 1809 essay *On Human Freedom*, because that work, as its title indicates, is searching for the essence of humanity and freedom, rather than being confined to nature and the essences displayed there for our thought.[11] It is hence able to come into contact with our thinking and our saying, just the domain that is important to Gendlin. In the context at hand, Schelling was dealing, to be sure, with the philosophy of nature. But his concern was to try to rescue the domain of nature from a deterministic and mechanical mode of science, by showing that natural things have their deepest root in an *Urgrund* that lies even prior to the being of God: both God, on the one hand, and nature, on the other, have their ground in a primordial abyss of lack. He shows that that same abyss is what grounds the possibility of human freedom. But this is not an abyss that is empty and sterile, merely deprived of determination and form.

> The current philosophy of nature first established in science the distinction between a being insofar as it exists, and a being insofar as it is merely

the ground of existence. This distinction is as old as its first scientific presentation [i.e., in earlier writings of Schelling]. . . . And although it is this very distinction that yields the most definite distinction between nature and God, yet this did not prevent its being accused of mingling God with nature.

Schelling now proceeds to exhibit this distinction even within God himself, and he offers an analogy whereby the *gravity* in nature would be parallel to the ground of God's being, and the *light* in nature would be parallel to God's actual being or existence. Light proceeds from the depth of the darkness of primordial gravity. But Schelling then returns to an account of natural entities.

The view that proceeds from things also leads to this same distinction. First the concept of immanence must be discarded altogether insofar as it is supposed to express a dead comprehension of things in God. Instead we recognize that the concept of becoming is the only one commensurate to the nature of things. But they cannot become in God viewed absolutely, since they are entirely, or, to say it more concretely, infinitely different from God. In order to be divided from God, they must become in a ground that is different from him. But since nothing can have being outside of God, this contradiction can be resolved only by things having their ground in that which is in God, but *is not God himself*, i.e., in that which is the ground of his existence. If we wish to speak of this being in terms more accessible to man, then we can say that it is the longing felt by the eternal one to give birth to itself. . . . Following the eternal act of self-revelation, all is rule, order and form in the world as we now see it. But the unruly lies ever in the depths as though it might again break through, and order and form nowhere appear to have been original, but it seems as though what had initially been unruly had been brought to order. . . . All birth is a birth from darkness into light; the seed must be buried in the earth and die in darkness, so that the lovelier figure of light might arise and unfold itself in the rays of the sun. Man is formed in his mother's womb, and from the darkness of non-understanding (from feeling, longing, the glorious mother of knowledge) lucid thoughts first grow. Thus we must represent original longing to ourselves in this manner: it directs itself towards the understanding, which it does not yet know, as we in our longing desire an unknown, nameless good, and it moves presentiently like an undulating, surging sea, similar to Plato's matter, following a dark, uncertain law, incapable of forming something lasting by itself. But this longing, which as the still dark ground is the first rousing of divine existence, has as its counterpart a reflexive representation engendered in God, through which, since it can have no other object but God, God beholds himself in his own image.

Schelling's account of the formative surge of energy did not by any means define it as a formless void; but, as this passage shows, Schelling was able to see in the creative surge a kind of darkness that was divine.

Gendlin, I suspect, is more likely to invoke the name of Aristotle than that of Schelling. And perhaps he would accept the Spinoza-like formula, the *forma formans*, because he could see how profoundly formal and intricate it was, being the wellspring of everything that deserves the name of form. Yet, I myself would want to linger over Schelling at this point: it could be that the intricacy which inhabits the saying is actually closer to Schelling's vision of the formative unruly darkness. In particular, if the intricacy that informs saying itself is truly formative and generative, able to yield the said and all its patterns, such a formativeness must have the attribute of the unruly surge, the longing. If it were not a longing, it would yield nothing.

I doubt whether Gendlin would want to accept a view so romantic. Perhaps he is enough of an Aristotelian to insist that that which brings forth the ordered patterns and forms in speech and life must be yet more formal, more orderly, in every way, marked by no privations such as we hear about in Schelling. But I suppose my question to him is whether he can quite bypass the incompleteness, the anxiety, the ignorance and fear, that afflict us in our life and that affect our utterances. Is there not an unruly surge in the soul when it utters or outers itself in the said? Doesn't some unruly surge even put its mark on the intricacy?

Reply to Nicholson

Professor Nicholson knowingly uses some of my favorite words just the way I oppose, and I will reply first to that. He also invites me to differentiate myself from romanticism. I like his really large questions and I will certainly respond to them.

I don't agree that "the said" is only the formed. That view inclines people to surrender what is said to the ossified forms. Then it seems that the intricate live "saying" is only momentary, ephemeral, helpless, as if it disappeared as soon as there is a said. People *may* take a said (or a saying) as reinstancing old forms, but I strongly reject the assumption that this is what *saying* inherently is. That is just one more oppression of that in us which lives and speaks. Do not surrender speech to the forms

from the start and in principle. Do not reduce the living process to a
vanishing wisp. If we see how the forms *can seem* to substitute themselves
for the saying that creates them, then we are "rescued," Heidegger said.
Yes, and I go further: we can do this by letting the words mean what
they do in the context, how they change a situation, how they carry the
discussion forward. Then the said is still always also the saying, however
anciently written.

But since we know what Nicholson means, does it still matter how
he uses the words? Most philosophers would say yes, most people no. I
say the question is more intricate. From the intricacy we can do much
better than just yes and/or no.

I agree with much of what Nicholson said in the opposite words.
How is this possible? It would not be possible if what he *said* were just
the dead forms. But what he *said* is still also the saying. Therefore, I can
grasp *how his words work here*, in this context, what they do to our situation.
And I can do this from the printed page, not from some wispy long-gone
process. So yes, I can let him have his use of "saying versus said," but only
because the said is still also the saying.

The ordinary person is right this far: If we care only about one
moment, then if I understand and agree, why quibble about the words?
But it may matter *at the next moment* and this depends on how he moves
on. It is not true that he *must* be misled by the old forms in his words.
If he moves from the intricacy (the more-than-formed, experienced,
situational, open, the carried-forward . . . . .), if he moves on from what
we just now called "we know what he means," then I go with him. But if
he goes on from the formed forms and schemes, then I will regret that
I let his opposite words pass. So when it comes to the next moment, the
philosophers are right: we are right to care about the old forms brought
by the words, because those may lead to different *further* steps.

Nicholson does say that "Gendlin usually reserves the word 'form'
for the created and ontic pattern." But he makes me nervous when he
calls intricacy "*forma formans*," although I understand the point. He means
the actual living activity of forming, but will he then move on from the
living activity? Or will he move from the old concept? It can lead to paths
I would not want to travel. *Forma formans* had sometimes meant a forming
that exhausts itself in its product. Nicholson is saying something far larger
than the production of forms. But later *both* formata and formans have
become just "form." Now the dance is form.

I would say to Nicholson: You cannot tease dancer and dance
apart, but why do you want to do that? It's the old distinction, the old
hankering to capture both sides, to distinguish and define them both
with just form. It ends you up saying what you didn't want to say. What

you want to say can't be said with the old distinction. Now we understand about the saying falling into the said—it falls if and only if one stays with the old distinctions! That is not inherent in all saying; it is *not* the fault of the words. You can let them enter the intricacy—enter your *forma formans* right there. From actually attending there we can carry your . . . . . forward and then also still keep it with us. Let us speak and *dance* from there.

Specifics: I don't agree that *the dance* is what the different performers do in the same way. That is only the general formula, the scheme that works in the intricacy to open possibilities for a dance. We don't go to see Hamlet just to see the play we know. The play is only a formula, an outline, an opportunity for something living to emerge. Crease (*The Play of Nature*, 70–71) calls a successful performance "a phenomenon that appears." As we go to all the effort of getting there at 8:30, we wonder: Will this production of Hamlet be a phenomenon? We know Bruckner's Fourth Symphony, but will this performance be a brooding infinity, or a sparkling sun dance—or only a pointless repetition of the score? It is disappointing when a technically perfect performance is only the score.

That is so also in logic, theory, and philosophy. We appreciate well-developed theory because it can be so exciting when it takes us deep into something, thirty-nine steps of logic cutting into the intricacy, and then—so far in!—*then* it lets us think freshly *from there*! A good score or choreography also goes far in; it gives the performer the opportunity to live newly—*from there.*

But is the performer's contribution not also prepared and rehearsed? Soloists ponder their accents, and develop novel phrasing. These decisions are also only detailed formulas. To succeed, the performance must livingly arise—that night. Performers "warm up," but they know not to practice the piece just before the concert. If practiced now, it will *come from underneath*, upward through the music, wholly alive—but it cannot do that over again, immediately. It will come out cut-and-dried in the concert.

Is it wrong to say "from underneath"? Will it make for some scheme of layers imputed to the human person? Here it said a coming we invite, but do not control, like the coming of tears, sleep, anger, love, appetite, orgasm, ideas, funny remarks, and new phrasing. Dancers know how to invite this coming of the dance. It must *take* them, Nicholson said, but this shows that the dance is not the form. His "take them" says what my "coming from underneath" said.

Do these phrases say what the dance is? Not likely! But they carry the question forward by entering the intricacy and speaking from that deeper place. Let us keep carrying the question forward, but never lose the question. Not to lose the question doesn't mean that we don't answer it, just that we don't stop answering it.

I like Nicholson's question about the source. He senses it here somewhere, implicit in the " . . . . ." and in all this talk of steps coming, and "intricacy." I love the question—let us answer it and keep answering it.

 I cannot just agree with Nicholson that the source is a "longing," because someone will take that back to the old dialectical "lack," which attributes everything new to negativity and nothingness. But I agree it is a "longing . . . . ."

Must it be a source? That is only a single metaphor. Let us rather think of it as a source . . . . . The "it" can also be a destination, or the ground that holds us up where we already are, or an overarching sky, or an endless depth . . . . . Anything might be a metaphor with which to answer what Nicholson asks here. The openness doesn't mean that we fail to answer: Is intricacy the same as, or different from Heidegger's source and openness? But is his source the same as his openness and the holy he talks about? But intricacy is already more than same or different. None of them are the same. We would lose a lot if they were.

But each of us can say only what each knows (is, ...), and this differs greatly among us. The harmonies one person hears are lost on another; one person has timeless states that seem impossible to others; what opens through the intricacy is a territory of territories . . . . . ; no one of us can cover it. The various words that go before the . . . . . are not to be identified. Each carries the . . . . . forward and becomes implicit in it.

Of course, we know to counter the old schemes and associations here. If "intricacy" means distinctions, then we lose the place where a thousand distinctions are possible and not made. If "holy" brings the old scheme and associations that make people feel small and helpless, then "unholy . . . . ." would be better. If "open" means indeterminate, then let us call it "more than open . . . . ." or some other phrase that makes no sense without the . . . . . A windy place . . . . . , we might say.

We also want to feel-grasp . . . . . the different convictions or felt positions, for exmaple the life-recognizing pragmatist's contempt for what seems mere abstraction-mongering, or the contempt which a horizon-grasping thinker feels for what looks like unphilosophical empirics. If we think with the felt sense . . . . . , we soon find our own biases (deepest apprehensions . . . . .). Since these play such a great role, of course we want to think into those, and not just our own. Let us not disdain *any* that we come across! Instead, we can demand and work to understand what it is about these felt positions, that can so deeply speak for a human being.

That is never nothing, and when someone gives us the time, patience, and expressiveness that allows us to grasp it (to cross with it . . . . .), more will function implicitly in our thinking than before.

For example, we limit our thinking if we remain only serious. Between Heidegger's open and Derrida's denial of it, I side with Heidgger, but I prefer both! Derrida's play saves us from a constant seriousness which would defeat life, while Heidegger's openness saves Derrida's play from being trivial and makes it High Play. Without work, play is nothing, but if there is work, play is higher than work.

Similarly, seriousness is one point of view, humor requires at least two. With and after the tragedies, comedy is more. That doesn't mean we mix them, only that we bring them both to our understanding of each, and of everything else.

I seem to know a lot about the open, since I argue that it is not only at the outer edge of what can be thought, but everywhere, in any little thing and any specific aspect of anything. Do I really know this about *the* open? I had better say there is *an* open which I do know, which is everywhere and in any little thing. These large edge-notions about a source sound too good. That prevents people from finding it.

Let me return to what is new here: the intricacy in a felt sense, and the little steps. They are not yet widely known. It is not widely known that one can let a . . . . . come, and that it is a space in which one can expect a small next step to come. If it doesn't come immediately, one can keep still and wait. If one loses hold of the . . . . . , one can let it come again and return to it again and again, checking back with it, sensing that it gradually becomes a focal implying, a sense for what has not yet come. Little steps come there, after a while a large one too.

In the last two decades we have developed ways to teach people how to do this. It begins by attending within the body in a very ordinary way. (It can become extraordinary once through this little door.) Any aspect of living can give rise to a bodily sensed version of it, a . . . . . from which finely fashioned next steps come.

All this is new as something that most people can fairly easily find. I can show how new it is by contrasting it with a movement Nicholson mentions. The romantics I have read did not find the intricacy. They emphasized emotion, not the intricate felt sense. Most of them saw humans as created by culture. They searched for a freedom from the usual forms. We can see that they didn't find the intricacy if we notice where they searched. It was assumed that almost everything had to be surrendered to rationalism and science. The only way out was art, the only viable exception in a world of mechanics. Other than art, they searched into the primitive, the archetypes. Like Bakhtin and Bataille still do, they searched for an openness in the exceptional or the exaggerated. This entrapment would have been removed instantly, had they found the intricacy which opens any closed thing.

The intricacy is a discovery of our century. It begins with Freud's "pathology of everyday life," Dilthey's "experiencing-understanding," and the plethora that Husserl attempted to explicate. I do not mean to denigrate romanticism or any of our tradition. Dilthey drew inspiration from Schleiermacher, and I from Dilthey. I thank Nicholson for these lovely questions.

14

Alterity and the Dynamics of Metaphor

Véronique M. Fóti

1

In "White Mythology: Metaphor in the Text of Philosophy," Derrida notes the pervasive metaphoricity of philosophical discourse and argues that the very notion of metaphor is metaphysical as well as intrinsically metaphoric, leaving philosophy, no less than its "outside," deprived of any pristine avenue of access to the issue of metaphor.[1] Metaphoricity, he finds, does not submit to the metaphor of domination that is the key metaphor of (Western) philosophical discourse, but veers, rather, toward multiplicity, syntactical articulation, and textuality, that is to say, toward an unauthorized proliferation. Derrida indicates two philosophical avenues that remain open for coming to terms with metaphoricity: the avenue of an effacing sublation or *Aufhebung* that guards the "restricted economy" of metaphysics against irretrievable loss, and the deconstructive avenue that subverts the "metaphysical" opposition between the metaphoric and the proper by wresting from philosophemes their "borders of propriety."[2]

Gendlin, though certainly no advocate of *Aufhebung* and its whitening out or effacement of metaphor, is critical of Derrida's deconstructive moves. He praises deconstruction for its fastidious attention to words, and for its willingness to let them work in new ways; but at the same time he problematizes Derrida's (metaphoric) identification of the "flower of rhetoric" with the heliotrope, turned toward an unfindable original, a withdrawn sun. Although Derrida relinquishes this fictive original, which is said to be "*mis*represented by metaphor," he does not, Gendlin finds, relinquish the notion that metaphors are meant to (but fail to) represent. He focuses instead on the requirement of an unattainable original, on the "usury" metaphor perpetrates in its "wear" (in keeping with the double meaning of *usure*) by making exorbitant profits on an elusive investment.[3]

Gendlin, by contrast, seeks to understand the working of metaphor in a way that steers clear of the Scylla of "metaphysics" as well as of the Charybdis of deconstruction. Instead of treating metaphor as something to be designated, spoken of, and theorized about, he seeks to speak from out of the metaphorizing itself, which, as he notes, exceeds concepts. The excess in question negates the "metaphysical" structure of the withdrawn original and its always inadequate representation, in that it is devoid of any positivity, being no more than a blank or lacuna of the sort one may encounter in writing poetry: one does not know the words; but one knows what it would mean to know the words; and the words, when they come, do not represent but "carry forward" the tension of the blank.[4] The blank calls for words which it does not render available.

The intrinsic difficulty which Gendlin marks in Derrida's thought on metaphor is probably inalienable from the basic "strategy" of deconstruction: its repetition or redoubling of the structural articulation of texts, so as to subvert their governing philosophemes and undo their closure. Deconstruction *must* repeat the metaphysical quest for the original and proper meaning. Given its inherent "parasitism," it can hardly advance Gendlin's own original insights into "how words work" to generate meaning by "nonlogical moves." This work of words is particularly evident in the metaphoricity that permeates the text(s) of philosophy only because it already traverses language in its entirety.

The question of the generation of linguistic meaning, and in particular the theory of metaphor, is today a focal concern on which important lines of work in both the continental and the analytic traditions of philosophy converge. Gendlin investigates these issues in dialogue not only with the Derridian theory of metaphor and the paleonym, but also with Heidegger's meditations on language and poetics, with Merleau-Ponty's painstaking studies of the preconceptual and prelinguistic origination of meaning in the "anonymity and generality" of our bodily participation in the world, with speech-act theory, and with Peirce's distinction between symbol and icon. He could also, with equal justice, have entered into dialogue with Max Black's "interactionist" theory of metaphor, with Donald Davidson's "pragmatic" (rather than semantic) analysis, with Nelson Goodman's view that metaphors "remake" reality and alter experience, or with Mark Johnson's work on the "elusive irreducibility of metaphoric insight to conceptual rules."[5]

This rare convergence of traditions is not, of course, accidental. It is motivated, first of all, by Kant's pathbreaking insights, in the *Critique of Judgment*, into the irreducibility of aesthetic ideas to conceptual determinations or rules, and into the creative role of imagination.[6] Furthermore, Ricoeur, in his seminal work on metaphor, brings the continental and analytic traditions to bear on one another, while drawing on Kant's schematism of the productive imagination.[7]

Kant's view that "it is properly the art of poetry in which the power [*das Vermögen*] of aesthetic ideas can reveal itself in full measure"[8] is echoed by Ricoeur's statement that "every metaphor is a poem in miniature." The poem, conversely, constitutes in its entirety a metaphor; for "it carries the whole discourse from its apparently descriptive position into an elsewhere which comes to the fore as the converging point of innovation and heuristic."[9] Gendlin remarks that poetry "would not be poetic" (it would lack creativity), if it were governed by "the philosophical concept of metaphor" (that is, the understanding of metaphor as an elliptical simile of a—possible or impossible—original), even if that concept is placed *sous rature.*[10]

Poetry emerges, in these discussions, as a nexus of the problems of truth, creativity, and transformation, opened up by the metaphoric power of language. The present paper is a contribution to the exploration of this nexus, with a focus on lyric poetry, rather than on dramatic poetry which Ricoeur (like Aristotle) tends to privilege.

2

The little word "is" (*ist*) in the verses "Über allen Gipfeln / Ist Ruh" from Goethe's poem "Ein Gleiches," which, as Heidegger shows, and as M. D. Levin explains, eludes paraphrase, can hardly lay claim to the status of metaphor.[11] Its basic function, according to Kant, is to posit existence or to serve as a copula in judgment, so that it cannot be regarded as a predicate that would genuinely enrich the concept of the subject.[12] One may, regrettably, find it difficult to convince one's banker that a hundred imaginary thalers (Kant's example) are not inherently different from an equal sum actually deposited in one's account; yet—bankers' reactions notwithstanding—the view that the notion of Being is devoid of any significant content is widely shared. At the outset of *Being and Time*, as well as in *An Introduction to Metaphysics*, Heidegger identifies this view as a philosophical prejudice, pointing out that the notion of Being is taken to be utterly general and indefinable, but also self-evident, so that it seems neither to call for nor to be capable of rewarding analysis or inquiry. One tends, therefore, to turn immediately from Being's supposed vacuity to the presence and ontological plenitude of beings.[13] In this turning, however, one forgets, according to Heidegger, that one's very attraction to beings as such already presupposes a certain understanding of Being. Without such an understanding, he points out, language itself, and therefore Dasein's disclosive existence, would not be possible.[14] This initial pre-understanding seems to be, for him, devoid of any metaphoric contamination.

If language is, however, inherently metaphorical (as de Man claims), or is at least importantly so,[15] the humble assertion of Being must—appearance and the Kantian analysis notwithstanding—be accorded a primary metaphoric force; for it trans-ports (*metapherei*) Being's emptiness into the compelling plenitude of phenomenal manifestation. The metaphoricity of this trans-port conceals itself, so that beings or phenomena seem to be imbued with intrinsic and unquestionable reality. Language is then cast into the role of representation (complemented by expressive and communicative functions), so that it becomes relatively easy, at least in principle, to distinguish straightforward linguistic representation from metaphoric transpositions.

Goethe's brief poem "Ein Gleiches," which occasioned this entire reflection—a poem original pencilled, as Heidegger remarks, unto the mullion in a log cabin—appears, at first hearing, to be so plainly spoken as to verge on the simplistic:

> Über allen Gipfel
> Ist Ruh.
> In allen Wipfeln
> Spürest du
> Kaum einen Hauch;
> Die Vögelein schweigen im Walde,
> Warte nur, balde
> Ruhest du auch.

> Over all the summits
> There is calm.
> In all the treetops
> You sense
> Scarcely a breath;
> The little birds are silent in the forest,
> Only wait, soon
> You also shall rest.[16]

Not a single metaphor is in evidence; yet the title, promising a sameness or equality, suggests the metaphoric process as traditionally conceived: a perception or creation of similarity between what, on the face of it, is dissimilar. The peaceful repose that is settling down over the summits and into the treetops at dusk, leaving "scarcely a breath" still to be sensed, and the birds' falling silent, bring not only the anticipation of a restful night, but also an intimation of the cutting of the breath of life that will inevitably and "soon" befall both poet and listener. The breathless calm and the birds' silence are both soothing and ominous, or, to echo Heidegger's favored term, uncanny, indicating the unfindable boundary that would seal life off from death or give death a graspable identity, whether peaceful or terrifying. The poem as a whole has a metaphoric force that brings about the "unsettling" (*entsetzen*) that Heidegger, in his discussion of Trakl's poetry in "Language in the Poem," considers to be of the essence of spirit (*Geist*); "for spirit transposes into what is alien."[17]

Gendlin suggests that, in metaphor, the customary "use-family" of a word "crosses" with an unexpected situation—a situation, one might say, that is not governed by the literality of the word—so that the metaphorizing unsettles facile assurances and opens up dimensions of "intricacy." In Goethe's poem, moreover, the fact that different "use-families" may lay claim to the same quite ordinary word (a complexity here tied to the euphemistic ways in which one can speak about death), makes for a still more intricate crossing: in crossing with a particular situation, "use-families" in tension may also intercross. As Gendlin points out, metaphoric crossovers involve not mere logical patterns, but rich "experiential intricacies:"

> When experiential intricacies cross, the result can be new, and not logically consistent with how each seemed to be, alone. In crossing neither functions as it was. Rather, *each functions as already cross-affected by the other.* Each is determined by, and also *determines* the other. If they functioned as logical patterns, they would limit each other down to a much smaller overlap. But: *In crossing each opens the other to a carrying forward which makes new possibilities.* The more determinants cross, the more novelty is possible.[18]

The function of the "is" in Goethe's poem shows the justice of Ricoeur's remarks that even the verb "to be" is made into a metaphor by poetry, "insofar as it says in a single breath: this is, this is not, this is like . . . ," and that the locus of metaphor as well as the key to its tensional truth is the metaphorized "is."[19] It must, however, be kept in mind that metaphoric power accrues to the simple "is" of the poem only in the context of a certain textual articulation. A singularized word or expression does not work as a metaphor—although Heidegger suggests otherwise by his fragmenting of poetry, his insistent etymologizing, and his sustained focus on single words. His assertation, in *An Introduction to Metaphysics*, that "the word 'Being' has an essentially different relation to Being itself than do other words to the beings [*dem Seienden*] that they say,"[20] is problematic not only because it disregards the textual and situational complexity in which, as Gendlin stresses, words work, but also because, against Heidegger's own better insight, it drives a wedge between Being and beings. If the sheer assertation of Being can, at least in poetry, be said to exercise a primary metaphoric force, it does so not in virtue of any intrinsic privilege of Being apart from beings, but rather by releasing the metaphoric workings of the poetic text in it entirety, while also keeping it tied to reality or to what Wallace Stevens calls "the world in which we live," and its necessities.[21]

Gendlin points out that *every* use of a word has, in fact, a certain metaphoric force because, whenever a word is brought to speak, its sedimented meaning and connotation intercross with the speaker's sense of the particular context or situation.[22] What sets explicit metaphorizing apart from this general metaphoricity of language may well be the more complex intercrossing that brings different, and seemingly incompatible, "use-families" to "cross" with the same context or situation, as well as with one another. In the case of the poetic text, the issues are further complicated by its heightened metaphoricity, even where it lacks actual metaphors (as just seen in Goethe's poem). The question of how the poetic text can carry one beyond (*metapherein*) what Gendlin calls "existing categories" or merely logical moves, how it allows words, in his terms, to carry meaning forward, rather than conforming to established patterns of meaning,[23] will here be explored with reference to the poetry and poetics of Wallace Stevens. Stevens, to be sure, is not much concerned with Heidegger, nor is he himself of any concern to the philosopher; yet he is preoccupied with the questions of Being, fiction, and poetic metaphoricity in a way that intercrosses with Heidegger's own preoccupations.

Whereas Heidegger diagnoses, in the oblivion of Being, a dread of its emptiness, and a consequent turn toward beings, Stevens, by contrast, articulates the poet's dread of plenitude and fixity, her suspicion of any pretense to final and evident truth. As Alan D. Perlis writes, the Stevensian poet "explodes the myopic search for an ultimate, imperishable truth into a fragmentary and fleeting panoply of images," preferring the twighlight of metaphor, metamorphosis, or metonymic displacements to the natural light, as Descartes calls it, of reason.[24] It is immediately clear that the function of metaphor, in a Stevensian poetic context, is far removed from the "metaphysical" function that both Heidegger and Derrida criticize.[25] In "The Motive for Metaphor," for example, the "you" addressed (who may be the poet's self, or, as Eleanor Cook thinks, metaphor personified[26]) is said to "like it" under the autumn trees for a reason that would cause the literal-minded discomfort: "[b]ecause everything is half dead," and the wind repeats "words without meaning." The "you" also enjoys "spring's half-colors of quarter-things" and desires "the exhilaration of changes"; it shrinks from "[t]he weight of primary noon," the arrogance of ideologies, from any "X" that is both "vital" and "fatal."[27]

Metaphor, for the poet, is not "degeneration" or the displacement of some original; but rather makes certain, as Stevens writes in "Metaphor as Degeneration," that and "how being / Includes death and the imagination."[28] This ascertaining is not a matter of philosophical analysis (which, as already seen, tends to devalue metaphor), but of a modality of experience that is finely attuned to the complexity of everyday things. To the map reader, for instance, it might be certain that the river he sees is in fact Swatara; and it is tautologously certain that oceans are water; but to the poet:

> It is certain that the river
> Is not Swatara. The swarthy water
> That flows round the earth and through the skies,
> Twisting among the universal spaces,
> Is not Swatara. It is being.
> That is the flock-flecked river, the water,
> The blown sheen—or is it air?
> How, then, is metaphor degeneration,
> When Swatara becomes this undulant river
> And the river becomes the landless, waterless ocean?[29]

What poetic metaphor, in its care for ordinary things, brings to awareness or trans-ports one to is the alien character of the familiar or, as Heidegger likes to call it, the enigmatic withdrawal in all presencing. The trans-port does not terminate in transcendence, but rather restores one to the things and restores the things themselves, divested of positivity (or, in Stevens's terms, traversed by "death and the imagination"). The river, in Steven's poem, becomes a bearer of commemoration.

In Stevens's "The Woman in Sunshine"—a poem which immediately follows "Metaphor as Degeneration" in the 1950 collection *The Auroras of Autumn*—metaphoricity affects the sun itself, the Platonic symbol of the origin of presence, as well as of phenomenality and knowledge. The metaphoric transmutation of sunshine to "a woman in threadless gold" does not come about through any resembling image, but in virtue of sheer "warmth and movement." The poem articulates a progression from "It is only" to "It is not" to "It is empty" to the "dissociated abundance of being" possessed by the woman in sunshine precisely in that she is "disembodied," metaphoric, and without any positive or graspable identity.[30]

Whereas Paul de Man ascribes a "totalizing stability" to metaphoric processes (in that they depend on the "necessary link" of resemblance, or on the part/whole relation),[31] Stevens stresses the fortuitous character of metaphor, its work of ceaseless alteration. Resemblance belongs, for him, to "the text of life," which is, to be sure, reality; but a reality that is text cannot function as what he ironically calls "the they," *alias* the transcendental signified. Lest this elimination of a transcendental signified be condemned as textual narcissism, it is worth pointing out that Stevens concurs with Gendlin's critique of the psychoanalytic dogma that narcissistic regression "is the only alternative to full identification with prevailing forms."[32] According to Gendlin, these forms are themselves crude when compared with experiential, let alone poetic, intricacy.[33] Stevens, unlike Gendlin, engages in an indirect rather than an up-front critique: he interprets narcissism as a love of one's self-displacements, rather than of one's self grasped in identity; and on this basis, he embraces narcissism. Narcissus, he points out, "did not expect, when he looked in the stream, to find in his hair a serpent coiled to strike . . . nor, in general, to discover himself at the center of an inexplicable ugliness . . . [rather,] as we seek out our resemblance, we expect to find pleasure . . . so strong is this expectation that we find nothing else."[34]

The pleasure Narcissus takes in his found image is not a pleasure in self-identity; for he finds and loves his image in the mutability of water, which is to say, in difference or metaphoric displacement; such displacement and diversification are, *pace* Plato, experienced compellingly as beauty.

Metaphoric inscription in mutability is, in the end, appropriate to "the unaccomplished, / the finally human, / natives of a dwindled sphere," whose indigence, nonetheless, is "an indigence of light."[35] For Stevens, the impulse toward ideal totalization that troubles de Man's reflection on metaphor is held in check not only by unrelenting metaphoric displacement, but also by irony, which is itself a form of the metaphoric process of redescription. Irony blocks the escape routes to the various guises of the transcendental sublime.

Poetic language which, as Stevens points out, springs from the source of metaphor, heightens the experience of reality by revealing its pervasive strangeness that is recalcitrant to interpretive systems. It brings one up not only against what Heidegger calls the uncanniness or enigma of Being, but also against the enigmatic dignity and "height" (as Levinas calls it) of the human as well as nonhuman other in its particularity.

Poetic metaphor, for Stevens, is ultimately anagogic in the sense of accomplishing an elevation to alterity. This is shown with particular clarity in his "last"[36] poem which bears the ironically Heideggerian title "Of Mere Being":

> The palm at the end of the mind,
> Beyond the last thought, rises
> In the bronze distance,
>
> A gold-feathered bird
> Sings in the palm, without human meaning,
> Without human feeling, a foreign song.
>
> You know then that it is not the reason
> That makes us happy or unhappy
> The bird sings. Its feathers shine.
>
> The palm stands at the edge of space.
> The wind moves slowly in the branches.
> The bird's fire-fangled feathers dangle down.[37]

The poem does not explicitly speak of metaphor, but of "mere" (sheer, bare)[38] Being, and of the fictive artifice of poetry. The mythical phoenix rising out of life's ashes is also, and at once, the palm with its wind-waved fronds (leaves or sheets of texts?), and the "bird or golden handiwork" of Yeats's Byzantium poems,[39] a self-figuration of poetry. As concerns the understanding of poetry, an instructive parallel can be found in one of Stevens's much earlier poems, "Nuances on a Theme by Williams," which first appeared in the 1923 collection *Harmonium*: "Shine alone, shine nakedly, shine like bronze / that reflects neither my face nor any inner part / of my being, shine like fire, that mirrors nothing."[40]

Poetry rises "beyond the last thought" in that it transcends not only the poet's subjectivity, but also the entire edifice of "human meaning," of explanatory and purposive reasoning; it sings a "foreign song"; and its radiance is that of an empty mirror, rather than of an image of life. Nevertheless, poetry does not just move, as Yeats puts it, "out of nature"; it is not a writing in league with death; but rather, and especially by its metaphoricity, it introduces alterity into the fabric of everyday experience, redirecting one's gaze from the transcendent to the concrete particular. In "Of Mere Being," the bird's "fire-fangled feathers" do not, for all their splendor, carry it aloft to abscond into transcendence, but rather, in a countermovement to the rising emphasized in the first strophe, they "dangle down," allowing the radiance of alterity to reach into and move through the dense opacity of ordinary existence.

3

It needs to be noted that the countermovement of "rising" to alterity and descending again to the concrete other carries ethical import. Stevens does not develop this import, since he assimilates the ethical to "social obligation," which the poet "is bound to resist or avoid today."[41] The poet's task, as he understands it, is to discover "the possible work of art in the real world" (rather than in escape from it), and to give to life "the supreme fictions without which we are unable to conceive of it."[42] The difficulty that menaces this view is obviously that all sorts of fictions can be made "supreme" and rhetorically compelling; ideological and totalitarian thought is certainly not lacking in fictions. Such fictions, however, tend to be reductive; they negate or simplify the "intricacy" that Gendlin emphasizes throughout his studies of language and metaphor. Conversely, "intricacy" counteracts the claim of any fiction to supremacy, so that Gendlin's analyses of "intricacy" function as a corrective to a rhetoric of "supreme fictions."

Heidegger opens up a way for thinking the ethical import of poetic alterity by his recognition that thinking itself is originary action, and that neither art nor theory can be separated from praxis;[43] but he does not follow out this way. Ricoeur approaches the question by a meditation on the notion of *ergon* in Aristotle's *Poetics*; he develops its implications as follows: "If there is a moment in our experience in which a living expression expresses living experience, it is the one in which we, ascending by a movement contrary in direction to the entropy of language, meet up with the movement by which we take back the distinction between realization (act), action, making, and meaning."[44] The ascent envisaged here approximates what has been called an elevation to alterity; and it "encounters" or converges with a recusation of the conceptual distinctions that have heretofore governed the relation of thinking to agency. In other words, the ascent to alterity demands a restructuring of the ethical domain. Ricoeur, however, is not explicit about this restructuring, or about its connection to poetic articulation.

On this last point, Gendlin's work, informed, as it is by his psychoanalytic and therapeutic experience, and by his deep interest in social transformation, makes a particular contribution. He illumines the dynamic interrelation between the articulation of "experiential intricacy" and conceptual structures or linguistic and social forms. He shows how these modalities of order enable articulation, yet are exceeded and "carried forward" by it, emphasizing that the patterns redouble their logical import by their own "carrying-forward effect, which is vastly more than they, and not enclosed by them."[45] This effect, though characterized by a "demanding exactitude" (the sort of precision that governs the saying of poetry), is not simply reducible to making finer logical distinctions; but rather, its precision exceeds logic.[46] Although patterns are continually revised and retracted, their break-up and retraction does not bring about inarticulate confusion, but rather refines articulation through a "crossing" of the retracted pattern with subsequent patternings:

> all order is pattern, yet all patterns break. We can think how what breaks them is not chaos; indeed, we think that with patterns—with how they are inherently doubled, how they carry forward an intricacy that includes a vast crossing of doubled sequences. . . .
>
> There is no way to take the intricacy along. But this is no disorganizing "excess"; it is not that the pattern works-and-fails-to-work—it is the pattern's working.[47]

Gendlin shows that such crossings, with their innovative charge, can bring about genuine interpersonal and intercultural understanding—an understanding that cannot be conformed to a representational model of meaning and articulation. Neither is it just a matter of creating compelling fictions, but of giving oneself over—without abandoning the enabling patterns and forms—to the concrete other in its demanding alterity. This willingness to extend oneself to the other without reserve, yet not in the manner of a *tabula rasa*, is ethically crucial.

If (poetic) articulation needs to be analyzed dynamically, this is particularly true of metaphor. It is refractory to the static schema of substitution or of the proper and improper. Both Gendlin and Ricoeur emphasize this point. They also concur in noting critically that Derrida's deconstruction of metaphor in the text of philosophy (as well as Heidegger's relegating metaphor to "metaphysics") presupposes a substitution theory.[48] Ricoeur's basic critique of the substitution schema is that a wearing down or effacement of metaphor in the interest of thought is not tantamount to *thought*, that the dynamic moment of creation needs to be respected.[49] Worn metaphors (analyzable in terms of substitution) are metaphors only in name; the process of wearing down has given them a new literality which can no longer be contrasted with a supposedly primitive *etymon*. A focus on the singularized word is basic to the substitution theory; but both Gendlin and Ricoeur reject the idea that words as such could have any proper or literal meaning which can then be metaphorized; words, as Gendlin puts it, "work in use." Although he proposes that the meaning of a word be identified with "what the word does," this doing cannot simply be equated with usage; for it belongs, in every instance, to a situation and participates in creation, even if it is not conspicuously innovative or arresting. Metaphoric power, far from being invested in singularized words, is ultimately invested in the text; to speak of the working of words is to speak metonymically.

Within the structure of metaphor one can, following Ricoeur, distinguish the dynamic moments of a *dissociation* from a received context of meaning, and a *transfer* to a new domain. This twofold dynamics brings into play the powers of both domains. The domain of received meaning furnishes what Ricoeur, following Ladrière, calls "a principle of induction," a guiding thread for expansion and transformation.[50] The new domain, far from being indeterminate and inert, exerts an energy of its own that annexes, refines, and heightens certain meanings, while repudiating others. The intentionality at work here guides and informs creation from the outset, while also depending on creation for its own realization. It draws on prethematic experience as well as on sedimented meanings to open up new semantic possibilities and dimensions of experience, so that, as Ricoeur points out, creation becomes inseparable from discovery.[51]

Gendlin carries this dynamics still further in that he does not recognize any domain of inert, received meanings in the working of the metaphoric process. The words, he argues, immediately say something new in the context or situation in which they are brought into play. They are not drawn from some pristine fund, as if the alterity released by metaphor were merely supervenient upon an initial purity. Alterity traverses and contaminates them from the outset, due, on Gendlin's analysis, to the complex "crossings" that inform the working of words.

The dynamics of metaphor, finally, opens up new ways of thinking the tensional yet intimate relationship of philosophy to poetry. Poetic articulation runs counter to what Ricoeur calls the entropy of language, its tendency to obliterate its own creation of meaning and its opening up of a space for phenomenal presencing, in favor of a panorama of supposedly stable and self-existent entities. The entropy of language is tied to a representational model of meaning and truth which, as has been seen, is disabled by a grasp of the metaphoric complexities of language, which are concentrated in and enowned by poetic articulation. While Ricoeur thinks that "the final sense of poetic saying is articulated only in speculative thought,"[52] Gendlin holds that, as soon as philosophy, and psychotherapy in its theoretical aspect, enter into "intricacy," their relationship to poetry becomes mutually enhancing, without any need for subordination or subsumption.[53] Just how this mutual furthering can occur is a question that deserves further study in the wake of Gendlin's researches.

As the Hölderlinian "flower of the mouth," language is not a heliotrope turned toward a philosophical (quasi-Platonic) sun. It draws its nourishment from a rhizomatous network of complex ramifications and intercrossings. Hölderlin's metaphor indicates not only that language cannot adequately grasp itself in abstract self-identity (the flower blooms presumably when the season is right); it also calls attention to its poetic freshness and its beauty, which Hölderlin himself thinks of in Heraclitean terms as a unity that is always at variance with itself.

Reply to Fóti

I admire Professor Fóti's great theme that a whole poem may be a metaphor. It is beautiful and thrilling when Heidegger's assertions about Being and the withdrawal of presencing become the metaphors that are the poems of Goethe and Stevens. I will support her criticism of Heidegger for setting "is" up alone.

Fóti finds my concepts useful to say that what a poem says does not come from a store of existing meanings; it speaks rather from life, which is always more-than-defined, always more intricate, a "plenitude of phenomenal manifestation" into which the poem "trans-ports (*metapherei*)" any "emptiness of Being." The metaphoricity of this transport can always transcend the existing meanings again, no matter how many meanings have already been created at any point.

We agree that all talk of "Being," for example, Heidegger's, must be mistaken if it is "devoid of metaphoric contamination," not only because all talk is language, but also because Being cannot be split away from beings, that is to say from life and practice. It is well to say this, but Fóti *shows* it. The two poems she chose are instances par excellence of how Being metaphorizes in the world.

Fóti sometimes describes my work in the vocabulary of deconstruction, which can speak only negatively—for example, of metaphor as *the lack* of a "proper" assertion. First she rightly says that I "speak from out of the metaphorizing," but then she adds what she intends as a complement, that for me "the excess is always inadequate representation in that it is devoid of any positivity." Read here: "Gendlin does not make the usual representational mistake; does not assert objective givens that we have to get right." Another instance: when she says that my . . . . . is "*no more than* a blank or lacuna of the sort one encounters when writing poetry," she does not mean that it is nothing; only that it is no *thing*. Terms that only negate the old concepts cannot say what I am saying, for instance, how a metaphor is *more precise* than determinate distinctions. Fortunately Foti does not limit herself to the negating vocabulary; she speaks from, with, and through the poems!

Fóti comments on my criticism of Derrida. She says that due to his deconstructive project, he "*must* repeat the metaphysical quest" in order to "subvert it" by a contradictory doubling. Rather than remaining with the juxtaposition (aporia) of contradictory notions of the old type, she recognizes that metaphorical crossing goes further: rather than coupling two opposites, the metaphor creates something new.

Fóti does not find self-contradiction, but a metaphorical crossing through which something ordinary is *transported* to become something new in its own realm. She agrees with me that if this were not possible, poems would not be possible. There could only be concepts and their contradiction.

From and with the poems, she fashions a critique of Derrida and Heidegger, which broadly supports mine. She shows how Stevens's metaphors transport the ordinary, so that it lets Being become visible, and it is done *quite without similarity, difference, or subsumption*. To argue that Being cannot be separated from metaphoricity, she shows that even when Being is taken as utterly other, the ordinary is transported even there—a realm "without human meaning," "beyond the last thought," "shining *like* fire that mirrors nothing." She lets the poem instantiate how *by metaphor* it brings *not similarities or alterity*; rather, it lets "*the radiance of* alterity . . . move through the dense opacity of ordinary existence."

Heidegger discusses Goethe's poem in relation to Being. Fóti knows that her critique of him touches his deepest themes. It also supports what I have said about metaphor.

Of course, we cannot deal quickly with Heidegger's question of Being, but we can disagree with what he is looking for in his discussion of this poem. Where Goethe says "silence *is* over all the summits," Heidegger tries out various words in the slot of the word "is." I think he is wrong when he thinks he finds "*a strand of common meaning*" which he says "*does run through them all.*" Nor is he right to say that "is" is superior here; those other words "*won't do.*" Rather, when another word is put instead of "silence *is* over all the summits," when he tries "silence abides" or "prevails" or "lies" over the summits, I argue that the different words *do* each time *say* a way in which silence *is*. Some sense can always be made by each of many words, if we let them work in the slot that is already made by a word in a sentence (in this case by "is"). Can we say the stillness "philosophizes" over the summits? Then it *is* a cosmic *nous*. Instead of "silence lies" we could even say "silence *stands* over all the summits," or "silence screams over all the summits" (see "CD" and *ECM* 4, characteristics 7 and 8). Anything crossing with anything might make new sense. Traditionally, metaphor is based on *preexisting* similarities. I argue that they are generated *after and from the metaphor*. *First* we sense how a silence *can* be a screaming; *then* we can derive what they have in common. For example, silence and screaming can have in common not a sound but an intense quality, also an insistent, piercing quality, also a spreading out, and also a threatening quality and also . . . . . When a word makes sense in another's slot, it is not because they always did have something in common. Rather, *first* it makes *immediate* sense, if it makes sense at all. *Only* then—slowly—can we generate a long chain of commonalities and differences to say what it does and does not mean. Those are not the metaphor. *Making sense is an implicit function.*

Each word brings its own meanings into the slot, but *there* it may mean something more intricate. If, like Heidegger here, we don't accept what *more* each new word brings into the slot of "is," then we will not find what "is" means. Here each *crosses* with what is already implicit in the slot. If it makes sense here, it makes sense in and about *is*. Each word that has worked here, remains implicit and crosses with any other word that makes sense in the slot.

If we *try* to prohibit the crossing (which happens anyway), if we think we must limit words to their distinctions, then "stands" would cancel "lies." Each would cancel the preceding. That would leave very little, just Heidegger's thin "common strand." But it is a mistake to think of them as generating a commonality. Instead, each crosses with the work of the previous ones, and thickens the "is." Being is not one thing, for which other things are metaphors. Each is also Being.

Each word and thing is intricate and never just the form it seems to have. It is not true that a definite thing excludes everything else. Actually it is a crossed mesh of many situations, an intricacy, not only something distinguished by divisions or classifying concepts. Such concepts are powerful, but they are not the only order, not the order of situations and language.

Heidegger rejected classification concepts, but then still thought of "gatherings." As so often, he brilliantly opens an old assumption, but may then go on with it nevertheless. Pioneers would not be possible if they had to supply well-developed alternatives. Heidegger says we must not take Being as one thing among others. Yet this happens if "is" has a strand of meaning in common with other things.

Heidegger should not look for what "does run through," and drop out what the other words bring. He should let a thousand words work and cross in that slot, to say how *is* is.

Heidegger said "humans are the shepherd of Being." He said that Being "rapes," and that it "gives." He also spoke of it as a "source," like the spot just above a brook where there is no brook. It would be an error to look for a strand of common meaning. Rather, let these *and many others* cross; then our sense of Being becomes very thick. It turns out that anything is being, and not another thing that shares a strand with Being. Each thing *is* (rapes, needs shepherding, screams, gives . . . . .). Each can cross with anything and yet it *is* special.

How anything *is*, is intricate, and like the source of a brook, it can open out into an irreplaceable ontology, if we take it as an instance (an access, a crossing, a possibility, a giving . . . . .) to be shepherded. This explains, for example, how it is possible for Levin in his lovely way to develop an ontology of breathing, of seeing, hearing, listening, gesturing, and moving. An ontology is not a description of breathing, and certainly not what Being and breathing have in common. He finds an understanding of Being opening out from the bodily intricacy of how breathing is. We could try to enter anything in this way.

Anything *is* always already crossed, always an unseparated multiplicity, a metaphor we grasp. Situations do come in kinds (love, for instance), but *that* kind of kind is a crossed mesh. We do not lose logic and patterns if we recognize that they come with a crossed intricacy. For example, a chair, or the new moon can be the patterned thing over there, but only if we do the implicit work of *taking* them as the patterned things. The chair *is* still always inviting and ready to receive us, or to unburden us of our packages, or to help the decor, and "chair" can tell about academic honors or running a meeting, or even more: the mountains can be a chair for the silence.

New phrases involve listening into an open realm, as the poet Henry Rago said. Heidegger constantly affirmed this openness, and I argue that it inheres in each situation, in each thing and each small aspect of anything, and not only in poetry.

Anything is a crossed intricacy. That is where and why words can speak in new and intricate ways. The new moon is not just the absence of the monthly patterned thing. The new moon is the silence over the mountains.

15

Language as Lingual

Joseph Margolis

1

I begin rather brusquely. I cannot be quite sure I understand Eugene Gendlin.[1] What I think I understand, I agree with—at least partly. But I cannot use Gendlin's insight by way of the verbal strategies he favors. I find he disables the analytic powers of his own idiom. He succeeds, I think, in directing us to the profound question he has in mind. He does this by making the familiar world seem most strange. He works with a technique of estrangement that is something of an analogue of what the Russian formalists claimed to have found to be the distinction of literature— "literariness," the estrangement of the ordinary (*literaturnost'*). He draws it out of his professional work as a therapist and a reflective reader of poetry. I don't deny that it sensitizes readers to what they might otherwise miss. But the language seems to me to exhaust itself by that achievement. It subverts its own incipient analytic contribution.

Philosophically, I find Gendlin's remarks akin to labile versions of phenomenology (say, in Heidegger, possibly also in Merleau-Ponty, as opposed to Husserl) and of pragmatism (say, in Dewey more than in Peirce, though the theme is in Peirce as well, perhaps more rigorously than in Dewey). There's also a touch of Bergson in what Gendlin says, though not quite the same suspicion of the conceptual; also, a touch of Polanyi, whose account of the "tacit" is similarly impossible to unpack. Be that as it may, I find that Gendlin exhausts his contribution in bringing us to consider his puzzle. Beyond that, the terminological inventions threaten to be singularly unhelpful—philosophically, but perhaps not therapeutically. I therefore find no way of *discussing* the matter *with*

Gendlin: I can only offer him my version of a related concern and ask him if he finds the world "to be like that"! Perhaps it is enough. So I begin abruptly, so as not to appear merely sly.

My point is an extremely simple one; it is also remarkably frustrating at the level of theory. It is this: although analysis is, by its very nature, the conceptual dissection of some ordered world, *a strictly holist idiom cannot be perspicuously reconciled with an analytic idiom at any particular point of analysis.* This is as true of Wittgenstein's or Quine's holism as it is of Bergson's or Gendlin's. One is tempted to assume a God's-eye view or at least a view *not yet infected* by language: Levinas, I should say, is the great exemplar of the utter incoherence of that way of proceeding, dreaming that there *is* a *cognitive* correction that brings the analytic into closer accord with the holistic or the verbally ineffable. But it is a sham. There is a great fear here, noticeable in Levinas—also in Heidegger and Bergson—that ordinary referential and predicative resources somehow threaten the humanity and uniqueness of the human being. I oppose the idea.

The corrective persuades us *linguistically* as well; linguistically, *we* speak of the part/whole relation, and in that way the "whole" *is* part of our analytic resources: hence, abstracted from a tacit, unfathomable, undifferentiated "whole" that may support alternative analyses and never bring us closer to the *origin* from which (we conjecture) they must have been generated. There is no escape, although, certainly, eating and making love are not, as such, forms of linguistic analysis.

The sense that, by analysis, we are violating some deeper continuum of life is itself (if it means anything at all) an instrument *of* language. Gendlin, I think, is always on the edge of failing to believe that that is so—or, of respecting the fact that it is so—in his own discourse. That is what I sense in the palpable charm of his prose. And yet, of course, he does succeed in conveying the sense that "there is" a whole world violated by our analyses. The mistake lies in thinking that the perceived "disorder" is any different from the perceived "correction." I find the evidence, as I say, already in Bergson's verbal skills.

As I make it out, Gendlin is talking about the process of talking and thinking and living as an ongoing holistic process that cannot be captured by what is, so to say, deposited on the way. Gendlin opposes treating the products as equivalent to the process (which is Bergson's point); but he is also persuaded that the posits *can* be informed by the process (which comes out of his appreciation of Heidegger, applied, I should say, to both therapy and poetry—and philosophy if possible). Fine. But what more? Beyond that, I have difficulty with Gendlin's idiom. I think it insists on an obtuseness in philosophy that I don't find necessary. I don't deny that many a philosophy *is* obtuse in just the way he suggests. But then Gendlin also believes that Freud was ultimately obtuse in the same way, and yet Gendlin is not obtuse in Freud's way.

In short, it's not that reason must "listen" to appetite or feeling: there is no separate cognitive resource by way of such "faculties." It's rather that speaking and thinking exercise, *holistically*, whatever, on reflection, may be discerned, discursively, as rationally and emotionally and appetitively distinct. The impoverished quality of my way of viewing the world as opposed to yours is not due to my ignoring the additional "language" of feeling or the linguistically ineffable "communication" of my emotional resources; it is simply the impoverished quality of my entire life. Therapy may perhaps redeem my life from *that* (the latter) disorder, but there is no separable or deeper idiom of thought or perception or knowledge that, as a speaker "confined" to mere language, I have somehow deprived myself of.

The continuity and complexity of anyone's life *is implicit* in one's speech, but it is implicit, *indifferently*, in every utterance. There is no way of speaking that fails to implicate such holist features; there is no generic way of speaking that captures them better than another; and there certainly is no separable or higher cognitive channel that is in touch with continuity and complexity that technical analysis *could* fail to address.

No, the resources of our language are already collective, holist, emergent, enabled, perfected, practiced individually, by having (tacitly) learned to share our society's *lebensformlich* habits. We cannot fail if we succeed in speaking. But we may fail, as anyone may fail, to speak in a gifted way. We may learn to enrich our experience and speech, but we cannot learn a privileged way of being in touch with the holistic nature of life's "communications." There are no such channels.

The holist aspect of life never functions criterially, and where it "corrects" the discursively separated elements of our picture of the world, it is already part of that same world. We never get back to the origin of experience but forever construct our picture of what it "must" be like. Our appraisal of the match is internal to our picture.

2

Consider the following. There is no reasonably apt account of language that does not make provision for reference and predication. The standard view is that reference and predication are "dependent" speech acts, speech acts that cannot stand alone, that must be embedded in such primary acts as those of making assertions and asking questions. I agree.

On my own account, this means: (1) that reference and predication cannot be analyzed solely in terms of the *sentences* that are the "products," let us say, of the primary speech *acts* in which they are embedded; (2) that there is no rule or algorithm ranging over sentences by which to capture what is informative about reference and predication; (3) that there is no rule or algorithm ranging over referential and predicative acts in virtue of which their effectiveness can be determinately confirmed or discerned; and (4) that the communicative effectiveness of reference and predication does indeed depend on the context of use in which they obtain, which cannot itself be satisfactorily analyzed in any closed or formal linguistic way.

Constraint (1) is the point of Strawson's well-known criticism of Russell's "On Denoting"[2] and constraint (4) is more or less in accord with Wittgenstein's notions of a "form of life" within which all human behavior, linguistic and nonlinguistic alike, makes sense.[3] Strawson does not discuss the Wittgensteinian theme; but neither he nor Austin (as opposed, say, to Searle) appears to oppose constraints (2)–(4).[4]

Searle believes, mistakenly, that the necessary and sufficient conditions for the linguistic success of speech acts can actually be determinately stated. Austin treats the analysis of (what amount to) speech acts as inherently informal and ad hoc. He approaches Wittgenstein's theme from the side of ordinary language analysis, but he never fills out our sense of its social space. Wittgenstein multiplies cases that confirm the inherent informality of the linguistic and the interlocking continuum of linguistic and nonlinguistic processes. But his philosophical taste forbids his venturing an actual theory of language.

The decisive finding is this: although it is true that "context of use" *is* holistic with respect to punctuated referential acts, it is not the case that context is ineffable even if is (taken to be) verbally inexhaustible or residually indeterminate. The first theme is very close to Popper's claim about the unfathomable depth of nature that Popper (inconsistently) proceeds to fathom and, by fathoming which, to go on to measure our progress in having done so. The second is Peirce's profounder claim (which Popper may have misread), namely, that verbal precision—the initial conceptual interpretation, the precise demarcation, of a relatively indeterminate subspace—always succeeds against the backdrop of a further or more inclusive subspace not yet thus determined, and that there is no end to that process.

I offer an even more radical thesis. I claim flatly that it is impossible for mere humans to *fix* reference, except in a "story-relative" sense.[5] And yet, they succeed in making reference. Certainly, reference cannot be retired, as Quine seems to believe possible, by only predicative resources.[6]

The speculation was originally Leibniz's, though Leibniz believed that nothing like Quine's project could be achieved on merely logically disciplined grounds. (Leibniz made the favorable solution depend on God's benevolence.) It is not convincing to suppose that humans could distinguish everything "there is" by way of uniquely satisfied predicates or know that they were doing that. To meet the condition (if possible at all: Leibniz doubts that it is possible), one would need to be God. The conclusion I draw is that success in referring to this or that—communicative success, success regarding speaker's intentions and hearer's understanding (to speak informally, though not inaccurately)—requires our aggregatively sharing the *lebensformlich* practices through which we *first* learn to refer and predicate and through the mastery of which we learn to interpret *what to count* as success and failure.

My point is that reference is: (1) inherently informal in the logical sense; (2) *lebensformlich* in origin and effectiveness; and (3) successful only in virtue of the work of an aggregate of human agents sharing certain collective practices that include but go beyond the narrowly linguistic. Reference is not linguistically autonomous, cannot be satisfactorily analyzed in any punctual or particulate way, and entails the seamless continuity of the linguistic and the nonverbal practices of a viable society. I don't deny *that*: I insist on it. There's much more to be said on that score: I shall come to it in a moment. But I cannot see how, if anything like this is true, it can be denied that a familiar part of the theory of language is already committed to much of what Gendlin requires, *and* that that theory has already shaped a fairly standard vocabulary to that same end. What can be said about predication goes even deeper and, if I am not mistaken, captures nearly everything else (perhaps *everything* else) Gendlin has in mind to say about *language*—philosophically—except for the threatening ineffabilism. I put this provocatively, because (not knowing Gendlin personally) I mean to draw him out. Let me hint at what else is needed. I shall risk only a few strokes.

3

Before I do that, I must say again: it's the analysis *of* language that is at stake, not a reminder or analysis of a relationship *between* language and some other cognitive sources. There are none. Human thought is "languaged" through and through, even where it seems otherwise; ditto for perception, feeling, memory, intention, desire, and action when viewed in cognitively pertinent ways. My thesis is quite simple in this regard:

language is not merely linguistic. It is itself a biologically grounded and bio-logically effective competence. What misleads us is that, on the evidence we have (*pace* Chomsky), its actual structure is not initially biological but culturally evolved. We become the competent creatures we are by growing up among the apt speakers of a shared natural language (and "lingual" culture). We may misperceive what that competence involves. I claim that that is already apparent in the puzzles of reference and predication. But reclaiming what is needed need make no concession in the direction of the ineffable.

I don't deny that the ineffable may obtain: I only insist that we not be quite so garrulous about it! The difference between my model and Gendlin's is this: by drawing all our discursive differences out of the *lebensformlich* (which functions holistically), I do not presume that there is a complex order of things already in place apart from the symbiosis of our intelligible world—*which* we somehow *recover.* I think Gendlin is committed to that, but it cannot be confirmed: confirmation is itself part of the *lebensformlich* world. Put another way: profundity about the human can only be found in the history of our linguistic practices (which, as I say, are lingual). There is no reservoir of profundity that language cannot reach, or can reach only by a special effort. There is nothing of that sort.

To understand predication aright, you must understand how "real generals" (Peirce) or "divided reference" (Quine) is possible.[7] The classic story is a dismal failure, not for the reasons Gendlin favors but simply because: (1) "universals" don't exist; (2) we have no way of pretending to apply universals criterially in predicative contexts; and (3) universals could not in any case capture what does obtain *in* predicative contexts. The entire medieval world seems to have been obsessed with universals, possibly because of a pious concern regarding God's providential plan. But the only solution to the problem is to construe predication in a way akin to reference.

On the argument: first of all, random speakers must be able to *extend* spontaneously the use of general predicates to new cases that could never have been party to any original or continuing convention about what *to regard as* instantiating those predicates; second, random hearers must be able to grasp the extension spontaneously and smoothly, on the strength of their own linguistic history; and third, speakers and hearers must succeed communicatively without reference to any supposed exemplars, conventions, or the like agreed upon in advance of such discourse. Once again, the only way that that is possible requires that, whatever inexplicit, indeterminate, or inchoate similarity may be deemed favorable to dis-course on the basis of our "common" biology *must be consensually deter-minate,* linguistically, by our sharing the collective interpretive tolerance and interpreted specificities that our *lebensformlich* practices can and do sustain. *There is no ulterior court of appeal apart from language.*

In short, we do not make our verbal powers sufficiently determinate by mere or narrow linguistic resources alone, but we do not do so by nonverbal means either. There is a habituated and rehabituating practice *of* speech within the terms of which our intentions as speakers and the tolerance of hearers are effectively mediated: the informalities of context and the generality of speech itself are *recognized and overcome* piecemeal, serially, openendedly, within whatever limits are acceptable for ongoing life at the moment. Similarly, we do not *find* the general predicables our predicates intend. We constantly improvise new instantiations of our general terms, and the same accommodating society (to which, as apt speakers, we belong) implicitly (behaviorally) confirms its tolerance of every particular such extension. There are no other pertinent resources. The success of reference and predication depends on the embedding of our specifically linguistic resources *in* the deeper collective habits of our "form of life," which is not itself free of the linguistic.

In my own idiom, language is not autonomous; it is "lingual," successful against a backdrop of the habits of life of socially (in particular, linguistically) organized creatures (ourselves). Our nonlinguistic practices are the practices of creatures who *are* linguistically apt. Speech acts are at once linguistic and lingual in this sense: performed by individual agents, they are also *lebensformlich*, already collectively structured, though certainly not fixed or frozen in any way. Wittgenstein makes the point by remarking that, in natural languages, one is not bound by rules:[8] whatever we may suppose the rules are, they are retrospectively formulated, ad hoc, by the same apt speakers who are free to improvise beyond them, who have a sense of how "to go on." There *is* no determinately correct way to refer or predicate, but there are determinate ways of failing. Success is interpretive, then: collective, consensual, tacit, confirmed by the absence of a breakdown in communication. If language is an artifact of a deeper strategy of life, so be it. But confirmation is an artifact of that artifact.

In a word, the determinateness of language is *not* the determinateness of names or predicates or terms or sentences. It is the determinateness of the human use of these. That is the deeper sense of Wittgenstein's instruction—that "meaning is use." It is *not* the distributed use *of* terms and sentences: that is, it is not a *further* linguistic factor (speaker's intentions, say, captured by linguistic utterance or not); it is rather the *lebensformlich* or lingual embedding *of* the narrowly linguistic, however the linguistic may be supposed to be defined by way of terms and sentences and speech acts. For example, Searle's treatment of speech acts is hardly different from his treatment of terms and sentences (though they are obviously different). Searle is committed to the autonomy of language every bit as much as Russell, except that Searle follows Strawson and Grice rather than Russell and Quine. Wittgenstein outflanks both, I say, by drawing our attention to the enormously important fact that the linguistic is itself *not analyzable in terms of its merely linguistic "parts"* and that what must be "added" *cannot be added as so many further nonlinguistic "parts."*

My own way of putting this is to say that the linguistic—the cultural in general, what I call the "Intentional" (by way of a term of art)—is *incarnate* in our physical and biological processes.[9] The linguistic is an "abstraction" from the complex real phenomenon of living speech. The linguistic (all the forms of cultural life) *emerges*, by some culturally apt process, among biologically apt creatures (Homo sapiens). *We* emerge thereby as *persons*. Persons (or selves: linguistically and lingually apt agents) are (I say) indissolubly *embodied* in the members of Homo sapiens insofar as their linguistic, lingual, cultural, Intentional attributes are *incarnate* in their biological and physical powers.

We *abstract* the significative or semiotic or culturally meaningful features of our life (the Intentional, as I say) from the physical and biological; but they cannot stand apart, simply because there *are* no persons that are not embedded (embodied) in biological organisms and because there *are* no linguistic aptitudes that are not embedded (incarnate) in biological aptitudes. Both (cultural) entities and (cultural) attributes are indissolubly complex—emergent in a way that is fundamentally different from what is emergent in the physical and biological world.[10]

The merit of putting matters this way is twofold: first of all, it provides a conceptual space for everything Gendlin could possibly want to say, but not by giving aid and comfort to the partisans of the ineffable; and second, it does this at the same time it affords a clue as to what we should mean by the determinateness and indeterminacy of language. The crisp demarcation of term, sentence, and speech act is itself an artifact of the conditions under which language functions as a meaningful instrument of life; *and* the determinateness of the meaning of actual speech is a function of the *lebensformlich* consensus by which the first demarcation is itself sustained. There is no determinateness of meaning apart from the "form of life" we share, and every conceded form of determinate meaning is contextually set in a wider milieu of indeterminacy. But the *lebensformlich* has no criterial function of its own. If it did, it would be privileged with respect to the holistic.

There you have a marriage between Peirce's and Wittgenstein's great insights. You cannot *find* the meaning of what is said. You "find" it by actively determining it (*not* by deciding on it) in the process of linguistic communication. It is seen *to be* (or to have been made) determinate in the interpretive tolerance shared by the apt members of a speaking community: one says that "*this*" is what is being referred to and that "*that*" linguistic act confirms, collectively, that its sense is sufficiently determinate for what follows. Every effort to make that consensus more precise is another episode of the same sort—subject to the same process. That is what Wittgenstein means when he says: "If language is to be a means of communication there must be agreement not only in definitions but also (queer as this may sound) in judgments. This seems to abolish logic, but does not do so."[11]

4

My point in all this is not to say that the questions that arise in the philosophy of language are all resolved. No, the point is rather that there is no need to assign language, thought, experience, perception, desire, and the like a *profoundeur* that "effs" the "ineffable." That's all. Discourse obtains only in the midst of life. We conjecture that language itself has emerged from a deeper stratum, but that conjecture is itself an artifact of that "late" emergent. Philosophy is the reconciliation of these two intuitions. There are many possible resolutions, but none requires the privilege of some original concatenation of the elements of the world— only our conjectures of what that must be (or have been) like.

We ourselves, the palpable sites of such conjecturing, are forever reflexively defined to match whatever we suppose is true of our discerned world. Our knowledge of ourselves is just as superficial as the world we picture. There is no deeper or more reliable *subjectivity* that our linguistic habits have somehow obscured. The phenomenologists are mistaken in this regard: they penetrate no further than the "objectivists" (to use Husserl's damaging epithet). Or, better: there is no difference between the two as far as their cognitive resources are concerned.

Phenomenology is naturalized and naturalism, phenomenologized; and both are subject to the opposed intuitions just mentioned. The human world, we say, must have evolved from the inanimate and prehuman world; but then evolution itself is a retrospective posit made only at the level at which *we* already entertain that possibility. That is why reductionism must fail and why cognitive privilege ignores the contingency of the work of understanding. It is true that you cannot reconstruct the processes of life and behavior from the discrete qualities assigned to sensation. Empiricism hopelessly impoverishes explanatory theories. And yet, the "improvement" which embeds sensation in a congeries of living and behavioral processes is as abstract as the other—perhaps not impoverished in quite the same way as far as explanation is concerned, but a discrete posit nonetheless. The link between visual sensation and behavior is an analogue of that between either of them and sentence or speech act. Only the holistic "world" escapes, but it does so at the cost of being nondiscursible. There is no approximation to the holistic by way of the discursive. That was Popper's folly just as much as F. H. Bradley's. Now, I am inclined to think there is a touch of it in Gendlin. I admit I cannot be entirely sure.

The point again is that language is not a disorder. There's no better way to be in touch with the human. Sharing a wine or intercourse and caring for the sick are not counterinstances. Language is the sole, the generic instrument by which we understand the world, just as clearly *in* the lingual as in the linguistic. That is the meaning of the notationality of music, for instance. We know that discrete sound cannot capture the melodic or harmonic lines of a string of sounds: it is only by our languaged skills that we comprehend that fact. This also holds for listening to music without analyzing scores. If we say that the melody is "implicated" in some sense in the discrete notes, we confirm two findings: first, that the notes (or sounds) are not notes (at all or merely) except in the context of the melody (which is *not* a deeper or linguistically ineffable stratum of musical understanding); and second, that their distinction and the "implicative" connection is itself an artifact of the theory in terms of which they are thus discerned (which, at some level of reflection, may be fully articulated and challenged by another theory).

My point is that all this is already conceded by the most hardnosed of the atomistically inclined: that is, by those who suppose it *is* possible to build a complex world out of discrete elements—bottom-up thinkers, logical atomists. Thus, no theorist of language neglects to admit *somewhere* that speech requires speakers; and no empiricists neglect to admit that sensation requires sentient creatures. I concede that both sorts of theorist impoverish our understanding. But the correction does not entail deeper cognizing resources—only a better theorizing sense at the same level of understanding as the other. It is for this reason that I say—somewhat against Gendlin, if I understand him correctly—that *there is no supplementing discourse by nondiscursive knowledge, and there is no asymptotic progress leading from the discursive to the holistic.* (It may be, I admit, that we agree in this. In a brief note, he says we do. I can only fall back to admitting a slim familiarity with his texts and the impression produced by those I've read.)

Within these limits we may quarrel as we please. From my own vantage, I cannot see how, if *any* "fragment" of an (impossibly) completed or final account is reasonably valid, there can fail to be indefinitely many alternative (and competing) accounts that cannot be reconciled in a single theory. Only the doctrine of cognitive privilege could ensure the intended advantage.

Finally, as I say, I take the cultural world to be fundamentally different from the biological and the physical. It is not alien, however, in the sense (which I favor) that the entities of cultural space *are* indissolubly embodied in the biological (possibly in the physically inanimate, as may obtain with smart computers raised to a suitable level of interaction with the human) and in the sense that the attributes peculiar to the cultural world are indissolubly incarnate in the physical and biological.

But the evolution or emergence of the cultural is utterly unlike anything that occurs in the (animate) prehuman world. Everything other than what is cognitively competent *in* the *lebensformlich* way in which humans are competent (linguistically and lingually), or other than what is directly cognizable at the emergent level in terms of what humans do or make (speech and art), are "anthropomorphized" one way or another, that is, brought within the terms of the reflexively intelligible world of humans. That is what I mean to signify by the *Intentional*: the culturally potent or culturally meaningful phenomena of the real world of specifically human life.

In that sense, for instance, no matter how gifted prelinguistic infants are, *they* are "anthropomorphized" as capable of discriminating "facts" (as Gendlin says): characterized as discerning *that* this or that is so. The attribution is not unreasonable, but it is a posit that depends on the same Intentional order of things in terms of which *we* conjecture that we must have evolved from some original cosmic soup. What I am saying is this: every bottom-up conjecture is a top-down posit; every compositional account of how things start is controlled by some factorial analysis of what functions already at the emergent level to be explained. The perceived complexities of the world, therefore, are utterly unlike the idea of an undifferentiated "whole."

Holism is simply discourse's way of reminding us of the historicity of our conjectures (that we alter and build upon prior conjectures that are already discursive) and of the inherent incompleteness of our conceptual schemes (that there is no sense in which we could ever be justified in supposing our categories ever catch any "originary" conceptual distinction, known or barred from being discovered by what we now pretend is known).

Perhaps it will be useful to put some of my claims in a tabular form without further comment:

1. The real world is symbiotized: we cannot segregate the world we discern and the categories by which we come to understand it.
2. There are no forms of privileged access to reality, and there are no nondiscursive cognitive resources, except those that are anthropomorphized.
3. All thought and talk are contexted and inexhaustible for that reason; but context is not itself criterial or distinguished by particular cognitive resources.
4. The linguistic is itself lingual and *lebensformlich*, but the *lebensformlich* has no criterial function of its own.
5. Human life is Intentional and historicized, and the Intentional world (= the cultural) is as real as physical nature; in fact, the natural is an abstraction from the Intentional.
6. The holistic is nondiscursible; but then it does not afford any cognitive privilege, it functions only as the vacuous context of all contexts.
7. The real world is artifactual, but that is compatible with real things' actually existing independent of the conditions under which we discern and understand them.
8. There is no difference in any cognitive sense between thought, feeling, emotion, desire, memory, perception, sensation, or the like; all are distinguished within the same general cognitive and practical competence that, as apt members of a human society, we are and have become.

I take these eight findings (at least) to be reasonably defensible philosophical characterizations of the human condition and to make provision for whatever else we may care to claim without any presumption of doubtful sources of understanding or questionable views of the nature of reality. In this sense, I cannot see that Gendlin's own recommendations are, where reasonable, incompatible with what I am affirming or, where they appear to go beyond the constraints I offer, defensible on their own. But perhaps I have not understood him well. I should like to believe that we differ primarily in emphasis and idiosyncrasies of idiom. That may be the simple truth.

Reply to Margolis

Professor Margolis is in far-reaching agreement with me. Both here and in his own work he has with great clarity laid out the problems that make for the current dead end in philosophy, and he understands them very much as I do—up to where I go on. I sometimes refer people to his work because how he understands the problems includes much of what enables me to go further. He does this in the language of the analytic community. The divisions among different philosophical groups are currently disappearing, which helps me since I cut across them.

Margolis rightly limits what analytic thinking can do, and then still defends it, also rightly. Like me he recognizes how impossible it is to give up on logic and science. He notices that I don't have Bergson's "suspicion of the conceptual."

But while we agree about the limits of logic and conceptual analysis, and also agree to honor and retain it, we differ insofar as he still wants "analytic resources" to be the exclusive and only way we can make sense. He does not notice that what he says about analysis already invokes more than analytic resources, and he does not wonder what resources enable him to say what he says about life and the "lingual." Therefore, he rejects those who do ask how they are able to say these things. He misunderstands us as proposing the "ineffable." He thinks that we are unaware of speaking in language about what exceeds language. For this reason he rejects the work of Wittgenstein and Heidegger along with mine. But what Margolis calls "lingual" is precisely what he calls "ineffable" when others speak of it. I think he attacks them only from habit, since his work resembles theirs much more than it differs. He drastically limits analysis and discusses how language is embedded in life and situations. He constantly implies the conclusions of Wittgenstein, Heidegger, and many of mine. Margolis could draw many of their conclusions from what he says.

I agree with Margolis about the lingual. In the language of the analysts he makes many of my points. But he does not see how one can go on, and sees no need to move further. He is satisfied that his statements "provide everything Gendlin provides." I will list some of his points both because his agreement is valuable to me, and because I want to show that he is far from providing what we need. Let me compare and contrast his version with mine.

1. When I deliberately employ the more-than-analytic ways in which language can make sense, he criticizes me for "exhausting the analytic resources of language." In his argument he wants to identify the lingual with language, and then think of the sense-making powers of language as "analytic resources," but simultaneously he moves in the opposite direction: analysis is "*exceeded*" by language, and language "*depends*" for its meanings on how it is embedded in the lingual. So in fact *he agrees that the implicit contexts exceed the resources of analysis.*

2. Margolis points out that I am "persuasive" by linguistic means. He sees that I am conscious of this, but he is used to arguing with people

who don't know it, so he wants to read me as being "always on the edge of failing to believe that this is so." He does not respond to my emphasis *and employment* of this very point: the wider (persuasive, sense-making) powers of language (his "lingual") can be spoken about only because speaking about them is itself *an instance of them.* How language is embedded in our interactional life can be spoken about, because we speak of, in, and from that embeddedness, and not merely about it. And *he agrees that language exceeds any formal analytical system, and that it has the more than analytical powers he sees me employing.*

3. The words "corrective" and "holism" are his, not mine, and they name straw men. His argument is only against a "corrective" of language that would be without language, separate, not "already infected by language." So he thinks we cannot study the corrective function of what is wider than language, although not separate from it. Language is constantly corrected and precisioned by the *implicit* context in which it occurs, and which we *can* have (be, live, feel, speak in . . . . .) only because language is always already implicit in human life and human bodies. Except for not drawing the conclusion that this constantly corrects and precisions what we say, *Margolis agrees with the bodily "biological" function of language.*

4. He argues rightly against someone who would seek to correct language by appeal to an "external" "correspondence" with an independent picture, not realizing that "the match is internal to the picture." I am glad he says this so clearly, since it is still a hard point to grasp. He also agrees with me that statements like mine about what functions implicitly have (only) *the same sort of* confirmation as other statements (which is quite enough). But he thinks of "confirmation" as if it came only from other speakers who understand our messages (which he attributes to "tolerating" ambiguity), rather than from the way in which speaking *is* inherently an altering of situations. *But he agrees with me to reject both the correspondence and the coherence theory.*

5. He differs with me utterly when he insists that what exceeds language has no *differential* import that could *specifically* correct or precison speech. He agrees that life and the lingual are always "implicit," but he thinks of this as a general presence that makes no specific differences. He writes: "life . . . is implicit *indifferently* in every utterance." This is the very crux of our argument. I think he does not see that what he says involves a specific and always newly different precisioning effect on what we say and mean. But I am glad that he agrees that "speech acts cannot stand alone," but "must be embedded," and that "there is no rule or algorithm ranging over sentences by which to capture what is informative," and that "the communicative effectiveness of reference and predication does indeed

depend on the context . . . which cannot itself be satisfactorily analyzed in any closed or formal linguistic way." *He agrees "flatly, that it is impossible for mere humans to fix reference except in a 'story-relative' sense."* Doesn't he see that each *specific* situational story determines much of what we are moved to say in a situation, as well as what it means to the others? That is much more than "tolerance."

6. *Margolis agrees that the process exceeds its products, and that "the posits can be informed by the process,"* although he implies that this does not amount to much. He comments: "Fine. But what more?" His agreement would be important if he saw that the process is always more precise and determinative, not something general, "indifferent," and always the same.

7. He adopts Wittgenstein's forms of life, but says that what is "*lebensförmlich* . . . functions holistically" and is *not* "a complex order . . . *apart* from the symbiosis of our intelligible world" (my italics). Again here he argues only against a *separate* realm apart, but thinks of the *inseparable* order as "holistic," so that he misses how it *specifically* informs and augments his own and everyone's speech. So he also misses that the implicit can function in different ways at a given point, and that we may have choices about how to let it function.

8. He says that "universals don't exist," and sees God as the only reason for their invention. But when he asserts that "the only solution . . . is to construe predication in a way akin to reference," does this not assume that each context *specifically* precisions what our words mean, since he agrees that they are not universals? He says that "Reference . . . entails the seamless continuity of the linguistic and the nonverbal practices." Doesn't "seamless continuity" merely hide the fact that the two always inform each other in *specific* ways? If we enter into this, how it functions changes, and we can sometimes chose among alternative ways. But I am glad *he agrees that language does not consist just of universals and rules.*

9. He says that "eating and making love are not language," but insists that "Language is the *sole* . . . instrument by which we understand the world" (my italics). According to this view, a rabbit does not know whether it is eating or making love. But not only what rabbits understand is at stake, rather the bodily way in which we live, act, and have something to say from (with, at, in . . . . .) the *human complexity* of our situations and interactions which always exceeds and specifies our use of language. Of course, language vastly precisions our biological processes, but it is also still embedded with, and informed *by* our more complex bodily living. Margolis does not draw the conclusion that language is specifically augmented by it, and certainly not that we can devise various ways of employing this, but I am glad that *he agrees that "language is itself a biologically grounded and biologically effective competence."*

10. Margolis agrees with me that words acquire new meaning in new contexts: "Speakers . . . extend spontaneously the use of general predicates to new cases that could never have been party to any . . . convention about what to regard as instantiating those predicates" and hearers are "able to grasp the extension spontaneously and smoothly *on the strength of their own linguistic history*" (my italics). He seems not to see that the extension arises each time from the specific intricacy of each situation, and that there are various ways in which this may happen. For example, the structure of a sentence may ensure it. He does not understand how I employ it, but I am glad that *he agrees about this "spontaneous extension" of the meaning of words beyond any antecedent "conventions."*

With "seamless continuity," "symbiosis," and "tolerance," Margolis wants to escape the *specific* determinacy of the implicit contexts in which he lives. He thinks of their role as general and always the same "indifferently." He speaks of "embeddedness" and "forms of life" without recognizing their always specific roles.

I wish Margolis would notice that this "lingual" which he delineates can augment and precision his speech in many different ways. He could then join me in entering and examining these functions. I argue that we *can* examine them just because—as he says—they are not something separate without language. They happen in our speech acts; they determine what words come to us, and what the words will mean in the situation.

Margolis's commentary lets me answer those of my readers who ask why I have to wrestle with these problems. Why not go directly to the deep and beautiful things we want to say? Why must Gendlin first be so concerned with language? Margolis's commentary can stand for my answer to this question. We must not fall back from the insights he states, which are making for the current stoppage. Someone is sure to lead a return to partial blindness on these topics, which would make doing philosophy much easier. Let us not accept it. These problems open avenues on which we can go further.

If Margolis joined me, he could go further in his own terms. But we can use his terms to draw the conclusions which he does not draw: lingual situations specifically inform what we say and hear. The lingual is never arbitrary, always what the specific situation *is*, but situations have an "is" that various statements might differently carry forward, although even one such statement may be hard to devise. A situational intricacy is partly shaped by previous speech, but it contains implicit possibilities that do not yet exist. Here the meaning of "implicit" changes *spontaneously* and *smoothly* to say something more intricate than either formed events or arbitrary construction. We cannot escape it, but we can employ its role in many different ways.

For example, what will Margolis do when he reads my reply? He might recall his ready positions, but he might also lean back and think. If he does, he might pursue some ready line of thought for a telling reply. But there is another possibility: he might first invite an *implicit* sense of how my reply leaves this philosophical situation. Of course, the situation always plays *some* implicit role even without any direct sense of it, but when such a sense comes, it brings more than was in play before, and it can function in many different ways. If Margolis first lets such a sense come, it will now "correct" (reject) one of his thoughts after another, until he finds one that carries this sense of the situation forward. If he notices it, he can examine this and other implicit functions, and carry them further by articulating them. Thereby he would provide a new and promising role for what he calls "analysis."

Of course, it is not a *separate* reality that corrects us; it is how we are already alive-in a situation. Our past speaking, reading, and thinking is implicit in our sense of a situation, yet it implies more. Its intricacy far exceeds cognitions and emotions. If Margolis enters it, he might find steps of carrying the situation forward beyond my conclusions.

How does one have (live, feel, think, say, be . . . . .) the intricacy of a situation? It is *with the body*, but not the reduced, *merely* "biological" body, rather this one, our biological and interactional body that senses the specificity of each situation, and comes up with specific phrases to change it as we need it changed. Culture and history are surely implicit in the body, but from them alone we cannot derive what Margolis will say. Only his *further* bodily living-in the situation can bring that.

Postmodernism errs in attributing the multiple possibilities to "interpretation." Human events are not interpretations, nor are they entities to which interpretations are added. We are always already *bodily* in action in the situations we create. Human events *are* inherently "post-modern" because they exceed conceptual forms and rules, as Margolis recognizes, but they *are* also inherently beyond the impasse of postmodernism because our bodies have always already made intricate sense in situations. The sense-making always functions in some way, but we can open and employ it deliberately, and we can study it in self-instantiating ways.

Conceptual analysis never could have done more than Margolis now credits it with being able to do. It could never produce final formulations that are utterly consistent or equivalent to a separate correspondent reality. But where analysis breaks down, something functions as its context which analysis could not encompass, but which it *could* often carry forward. We need no final list of implicit functions. We let them continue along with various formulations. The great project is to open this arena.

Carrying forward is not more modest than representation; it has far greater possibilities. Analytic thinking is one (only one) irreplaceable way to carry a context forward. But it becomes much more powerful and honest when it enters a specific implicit intricacy, moves *from* it, and returns and reissues from there in a continual zig-zag to check if it is carrying the context forward, or if it is only weaving a thin substitute, as if in the absence of what is being concretely lived.

We can do much more than reject the mind/body distinction. We can actively enter into that which is undividedly both, and let its many functions enable us to speak about them.

It cannot be right to stop where Margolis and the postmodernists stop—as if we could not go on without the kind of criteria now recognized as impossible. There never were criteria of that kind, so there will be some account of how people do think and work, as well as more powerful ways to go on by knowingly employing the body as it functions in thought and language, since language is a bodily-situational interaction, not mere aboutness.

Works Cited

Black, Max. *Models and Metaphors*. Ithaca: Cornell University Press, 1962.

Bordo, Susan. *Unbearable Weight*. Berkeley: University of California Press, 1993.

Crease, Robert P. *The Play of Nature*. Bloomington: Indiana University Press, 1993.

Depestelle, F. "A Primary Bibliography of Eugene Gendlin." *Tijdschrift voor Psychotherapie* 22, no. 1 (1996).

Derrida, J. "Violence and Metaphysics." In *Writing and Difference*. University of Chicago Press, 1978.

Dilthey, Wilhelm. *Gesammelte Schriften*. Vol. 7. Stuttgart: Teubner, 1958.

Gendlin, E. T. *Experiencing and the Creation of Meaning*. New York: Free Press, Macmillan, 1962, reprinted 1970. Japanese Translation 1994. Paper Edition, Northwestern University Press, 1997. Abbreviated as *ECM*.

———. "What Are the Grounds of Explication Statements? A Problem in Linguistic Analysis and Phenomenology." *The Monist* 49, no. 1 (1965). Reprinted with French translation in *The Human Context* 5, no. 3 (1973). Reprinted in *Analytic Philosophy and Phenomenology*. Edited by H. A. Durfee. The Hague: Martinus Nijhoff, 1976.

———. "Experiential Explication and Truth." *Journal of Existentialism* (1965/66). Reprinted in *The Sources of Existentialism as Philosophy*. Edited by I. R. Molina. Englewood Cliffs: Prentice Hall, 1969. Abbreviated as "EET."

———. "Values and the Process of Experiencing." In *The Goals of Psychotherapy*. Edited by J. A. Mahrer. New York: Appleton-Century Crofts, 1967.

———. "Neurosis and Human Nature in the Experiential Method of Thought." *Humanitas* 3, no. 2 (1967).

———. "Analysis." In Martin Heidegger, *What Is a Thing?* Chicago: Regnery, 1968. Abbreviated as *WIT*.

———. "A Phenomenology of Emotions: Anger." In *Explorations in Phenomenology*. Edited by D. Carr and E. Casey. The Hague, Martinus Nijhoff, 1971.

———. "Two Ways of Reading a Philosophy—and Their Pitfalls." Unpublished manuscript, 1972. Abbreviated as "TWRP."

———. "Experiential Phenomenology." In *Phenomenology and the Social Sciences*. Edited by M. Natanson. Evanston: Northwestern University Press, 1973.

———. "Befindlichkeit." *Review of Existential Psychology and Psychiatry* 16, nos. 1–3 (1978/79).

———. *Focusing*. 2d edition. New York: Bantam Books, 1981. Translations in Danish, Dutch, French, German, Hungarian, Japanese, Spanish, and Swedish. Abbreviated as *F*.

————. "Two Phenomenologists Do Not Disagree." In *Phenomenology: Dialogues and Bridges*. Edited by R. Bruzina and B. Wilshire. Albany: State University of New York Press, 1982. Abbreviated as "TPD."

————. "Dwelling." In *Proceedings* of the Heidegger Conference. Edited by R. Scharff. University of New Hampshire, 1983. Also in *The Horizons of Continental Philosophy: Essays on Husserl, Heidegger and Merleau-Ponty*. Edited by H. Silverman, et al. Dordrecht: Kluwer, 1988.

————. "Time's Dependence on Space: Kant's Statements and Their Misconstrual by Heidegger." In *Kant and Phenomenology*. Edited by T. M. Seebohm and J. J. Kockelmans. St. Louis: Center for Advanced Research in Phenomenology, 1984.

————. "The Politics of Giving Therapy Away." In *Teaching Psychological Skills: Models for Giving Therapy Away*. Edited by D. Larson. Monterey: Brooks/Cole, 1984.

————. "Process Ethics, and the Political Question." In *Analecta Husserliana* 20. Edited by A-T. Tymieniecka. Boston: Reidel, 1986. Reprinted in *The Focusing Folio* 5, no. 2 (1986). Abbreviated as "PEP."

————. "What Comes after Traditional Psychotherapy Research?" *American Psychologist* 41, no. 2 (1986).

————. "A Philosophical Critique of the Concept of Narcissism." In *Pathologies of The Modern Self*. Edited by D. Levin. New York University Press, 1987. Abbreviated as "PCN."

————. "Phenomenology as Non-logical Steps." (Autobiography.) In *Analecta Husserliana* 26: *American Phenomenology: Origins and Developments*. Edited by E. F. Kaelin and C. O. Schrag. Dordrecht: Kluwer, 1989. Abbreviated as "PNS."

————. "Crossing and Dipping: Some Terms for Approaching the Interface between Natural Understanding and Logical Formation." In *Subjectivity and the Debate over Computational Cognitive Science*. Edited by M. Galbraith and W. J. Rapaport. New York: Center for Cognitive Science, 1991. Also in *Minds and Machines* 5, no. 4 (1995). Abbreviated as "CD."

————. "Thinking beyond Patterns: Body, Language and Situations." In *The Presence of Feeling in Thought*. Edited by B. den Ouden and M. Moen. New York: Peter Lang, 1992. Abbreviated as "TBP."

————. The Primacy of the Body, Not the Primacy of Perception. *Man and World* 25, nos. 3–4 (1992). Abbreviated as "PB."

————. "Meaning Prior to the Separation of the Five Senses." In *Current Issues in Linguistic Theory: Current Advances in Semantic Theory*. Edited by M. Stamenov. Philadelphia: Benjamin Publishing Co., 1992.

————. "The Wider Role of Bodily Sense in Thought and Language." In *Giving the Body Its Due*. Edited by M. Sheets-Johnstone. Albany: SUNY Press, 1992. German translation: *Deutsche Zeitschrift für Philosophie* 41, no. 4 (1993).

————. "Human Nature and Concepts." In *Psychological Aspects of Modernity*. Edited by J. Braun. London: Praeger, 1993.

———. *Körperbezogenes Philosophieren*. Focusing Bibliothek. Vol. 5. Wurzburg: DAF, 1994.

———. *Focusing-Oriented Psychotherapy*. New York: Guilford, 1996. Abbreviated as *FOP*.

———. "Words Can Say How They Work." *Synthesis Philosophica* 10, nos. 1–2. Zagreb, 1996. Abbreviated as "WCS."

———. "What Happens When Wittgenstein Asks: 'What Happens When . . . ?'" Paper given at University of Potsdam Seminar entitled: "Zur Sprache Kommen: Die Ordnungen und das Offene nach Wittgenstein." November 1996. *The Philosophical Forum*, vol. 28, no. 3 (Spring 1997)

———. *Collected Works* in Spanish. Translated and edited by C. Alemany. Madrid: Brouwer, 1997.

———. "The Repressive Order." *Man and World* (in press 1997).

———. *A Process Model*, unpublished manuscript available on Internet http://www.focusing.org/postmod.htm, 1996 and Focusing Institute, N.Y., N.Y. Abbreviated as *PM*.

———, with J. Lemke. "A Critique of Relativity and Localization." *Mathematical Modeling* 4 (1983).

———, with D. Grindler and M. McGuire. "Imagery, Body, and Space." In *Imagination and Healing*. Edited by A. A. Sheikh. New York, Baywood, 1984.

Goldfarb, M. "Making the Unknown Known: Art as the Speech of the Body." In *Giving the Body Its Due*. Edited by M. Sheets-Johnstone. Albany: SUNY Press, 1992.

Heidegger, M. *Being and Time*. New York: Harper and Row, 1962. Abbreviated as *BT*.

———. *Metaphysische Anfangsgründe der Logik*. 1928. Reprinted in *Gesamtausgabe*. Vol. 26. Frankfurt: Klostermann, 1978.

Kohn, Hans. *The Mind of Germany*. New York: Scribner, 1960.

Levin, D. *The Body's Recollection of Being*. London: Routledge, 1985.

McKeon, Richard P. *Thought, Action and Passion*. Chicago: University of Chicago Press, 1954.

———. *Freedom and History and Other Essays*. Chicago: University of Chicago Press, 1990.

———. *On Knowing*. Chicago: University of Chicago Press, 1994.

———. *Selected Writings*. Chicago: University of Chicago Press, 1997.

Nagel, T. *Mortal Questions*. Cambridge: Cambridge University Press, 1979. Abbreviated as *MQ*.

———. *The View from Nowhere*. Oxford: Oxford University Press, 1986. Abbreviated as *VFN*.

Perl, S. "A Writer's Way of Knowing: Guidelines for Composing." In *A Writer's Way of Knowing: Writing and the Domain Beyond the Cognitive*. Edited by A. Brand and R. Graves. Portsmouth: Boynton-Cook Press, 1994.

Putnam, Hilary. *Realism with a Human Face*. Cambridge: Harvard University Press, 1990.

Rogers, C. R. *On Becoming a Person*. Boston: Houghton Mifflin, 1961.

Schneider, H. J. *Phantasie und Kalkül.* Frankfurt: Suhrkamp, 1992.

Warren, Mark. "Democratic Theory and Self-Transformation." *American Political Science Review* 86, no. 1 (1992).

Williams, Bernard. *Ethics and the Limits of Philosophy.* Cambridge: Harvard University Press, 1985.

Wittgenstein, L. *Philsosophical Investigations.* Oxford: Blackwell, 1974. Abbreviated as *PI.*

Notes

Chapter 1

Eugene Gendlin, How Philosophy Cannot Appeal to Experience, and How It Can

I wish to thank John D. Bailiff, David Crownfield, Frank Edler, Wayne J. Froman, David M. Levin, Richard E. Palmer, and William J. Richardson for their helpful reading and suggestions.

Chapter 2
David Michael Levin, Gendlin's Use of Language

1. Rainer Maria Rilke, *Rilke on Love and Other Difficulties* (New York: W. W. Norton, 1975), 74–75.

2. Gilles Deleuze and Félix Guattari, *What Is Philosophy?* (New York: Columbia University Press, 1994), 2.

3. Jacques Derrida, *Circumfession,* and Geoffrey Bennington, *Derridabase* (Chicago: The University of Chicago Press, 1993). Approximately translated, Derrida could be taken as saying that, "As soon as the concept is in the grasp of writing, it is cooked." By which I understand him to mean that the concept is subject to dissemination, deconstruction, and disintegration.

4. Jacques Derrida, "Violence and Metaphysics," *Writing and Difference* (Chicago: The University of Chicago Press, 1980), 147–48.

5. Ibid., 117. Also see my essay, "Cinders, Traces, Shadows on the Page: The Holocaust in Derrida's Writing," in *Postmodernism and the Holocaust,* ed. Alan Milchman and Alan Rosenberg (Atlanta and Amsterdam: Rodopi, 1996).

6. Gendlin thus defies a long tradition of thinking. In the preface to his *Remarques sur la langue française,* published in 1647, Claude Favre de la Vaugelas wrote: "Usage is that to which we must subject ourselves entirely in our language."

7. Eugene Gendlin, "Thinking beyond Patterns: Body, Language and Situations," in *The Presence of Feeling in Thought,* ed. B. Den Ouden and M. Moen (New York: Peter Lang, 1992), 27–28. Hereafter references to this text will be indicated by the abbreviation "TBP."

8. A typical example of how most philosophers of today approach this problem, even when their argument reaches the conclusion that meaning-formation

343

is of the utmost importance, is the statement by Charles Taylor, at the end of his impressive historical narrative in *Sources of the Self: The Making of the Modern Identity* (Cambridge: Harvard University Press, 1989), that, "As our public traditions of family, ecology, even *polis*, are undermined or swept away, we need new languages of personal resonance to make crucial human goods alive for us again" (513). I can think of no one other than Gendlin who has actually contributed more to our understanding of what this involves; nor can I think of anyone who has done more to demonstrate in practice the way(s) in which such "new languages of personal resonance" can actually work—and how they can indeed "make crucial human goods alive for us again." What Taylor can only dream of, as a desirable possibility, in the poetic language of metaphor, Gendlin theorizes in detail and puts into practice.

9. Eugene Gendlin, "Process Ethics and the Political Question," in *Analecta Husserliana*, vol. 20, ed. A. T. Tymieniecka (Boston: Reidel, 1986), 265–75. Also published in *The Focusing Folio*, vol. 5, no. 2, 69–87. Hereafter "PE." See also my discussion of Gendlin's paper in *The Listening Self: Personal Growth, Social Change, and the Closure of Metaphysics* (New York: Routledge, 1989).

10. I have argued this criticism of Husserl in "Phenomenology in America," *Philosophy and Social Criticism* 17, no. 2 (1991), 103–19. As for my criticism of Merleau-Ponty, I have argued for it in greater detail in "The Poetic Function of Phenomenology," in *Phenomenology in a Pluralistic Context*, ed. William McBride and Calvin Schrag (Albany: SUNY Press, 1983), 216–34.

11. Eugene Gendlin, "On Emotion in Therapy," in *Emotion, Psychotherapy and Change*, ed. J. D. Safran and L. S. Greenberg (New York and London: Guilford Press, 1991), 255–79. Hereafter "OET."

12. Blaise Pascal, *Pensées* (New York: E. P. Dutton, 1958), 78.

13. See Frederick C. Beiser, *The Fate of Reason: German Philosophy from Kant to Fichte* (Cambridge: Harvard University Press, 1987). Jacobi argued against the separation of reason from desire and instinct, and that reason is a function of our needs and functions as living beings.

14. See ibid. Herder argued for a naturalism without supernaturalism and without mechanism and reductive materialism. He also argued against mind-body dualism in the Cartesian and Kantian philosophies.

15. Michel Foucault, "The Subject and Power," in H. Dreyfus and P. Rabinow, *Michel Foucault: Beyond Structuralism and Hermeneutics* (Chicago: The University of Chicago, 1982), 216. See also my study, "The Body Politic: The Embodiment of Praxis in Foucault and Habermas," in *Praxis International* 9, nos. 1, 2 (April and July, 1989), 112–32.

16. See Martin Heidegger, *What Is Called Thinking?* (New York: Harper and Row, 1968). To the extent that theoretical elaboration of reflexivity makes a practical difference in the formation of meaning, it can be shown that, in comparison with Gendlin's use of words, Heidegger's "poetizing" leaves the reflexivity-potential of (his) language insufficiently elaborated. In this connection, also see my "The Poetic Function of Phenomenology."

17. See Theodor Adorno, *Negative Dialectics* (New York: Continuum, 1977). Adorno mounts a strong theoretical argument against identitarian thinking, the reduction which equates the conceptual and the nonconceptual; but he does

not demonstrate, with his own use of language, how to work with the implicit dimensions of meaning to form new conceptual constellations. On Adorno, see also my study, "Making Sense: The Work of Eugene Gendlin," *Human Studies* 17, no. 3 (July 1994), 343–53. In this study, I discuss meaning-formation in Merleau-Ponty and Heidegger as well.

18. See Herbert Marcuse, *One Dimensional Man: Studies in the Ideology of Advanced Industrial Society* (Boston: Beacon Press, 1964). Marcuse articulates a useful critique of one-dimensional language; but his discussion of the alternative(s) remains highly abstract.

19. Eugene Gendlin, "A Philosophical Critique of the Concept of Narcissism," in *Pathologies of the Modern Self,* ed. D. Levin (New York: New York University Press, 1987), 251–304. Hereafter "PCN."

20. Theodor Adorno, "Subject and Object," in *The Essential Frankfurt School Reader,* ed. Andrew Arato and Eike Gebhardt (New York: Continuum, 1987), 505.

21. Adorno, *Negative Dialectics,* 10. For the German, see *Negative Dialektik* (Frankfurt am Main: Suhrkamp Verlag, 1973), 21: "Die Utopie der Erkenntnis wäre, das Begriffslose mit Begriffen aufzutun, ohne es ihnen gleichzumachen."

22. See Thomas McCarthy's review of Richard Bernstein's *The New Constellation: The Ethical-Political Horizons of Modernity/Postmodernity,* forthcoming in *Philosophy and Phenomenological Research,* some time in 1997.

23. See my essays on "Moral Education: The Body's Felt Sense of Value," *Teachers College Record* 84, no. 2 (Winter, 1982), 283–300; "Justice in the Flesh," in *Ontology and Alterity in Merleau-Ponty,* ed. G. Johnson and M. Smith (Albany: The State University of New York Press, 1990), 35–44; and "Visions of Narcissism: Intersubjectivity and the Reversals of Reflection," in *Merleau-Ponty Vivant,* ed. M. Dillon (Albany: The State University of New York Press, 1991), 47–90. My thinking in these papers is deeply indebted to the work of Eugene Gendlin.

24. Max Horkheimer and Theodor Adorno, *Dialectic of Enlightenment* (New York: Seabury Press, 1972), 101.

25. Adorno, *Negative Dialektik,* 358. Italics added. For an English translation different from mine, see *Negative Dialectics,* 365.

26. Hans-Georg Gadamer, *Truth and Method* (New York: Seabury Press, 1975), supplement 2, 494.

27. Ibid. 498.

28. Ibid. 426.

29. Ibid. 416.

Chapter 3
David Kolb, Filling in the Blanks

1. Gendlin's writings are cited using the following abbreviations:

"TAD": "Thinking after Distinctions," unpublished essay.
ECM: *Experiencing and the Creation of Meaning: A Philosophical and Psychological Approach to the Subjective* (New York: Macmillan, 1962).

"TBP":   Thinking beyond Patterns: Body, Language, and Situations," in *The Presence of Feeling in Thought,* ed. B. den Ouden and M. Moen (Peter Lang, 1992).

"WCS":   "Words Can Say How They Work," *Proceedings of the Heidegger Conference* (1992), 29–35.

"TPD":   "Two Phenomenologists Do Not Disagree," in *Phenomenology: Dialogue and Bridges,* ed. R. Bruzina and B. Wilshire (Albany: SUNY Press, 1982), 321–35.

"NLM":   "Nonlogical Moves and Nature Metaphors," *Analecta Husserliana,* vol. 19 (1985), 383–400.

2. The quotation is from "TAD," 2. However, the sixth, seventh, and twelfth sentences were added from the largely identical description of the case in "WCS," 31.

3. "When the right phrases come, they don't copy the blank" ("WCS," 33). This denial that the poet has in experience some latent but definite propositional content waiting to be expressed moves Gendlin's appeals to felt experience and thick situations out of the direct line of fire from Sellars's attack on the myth of the given and Wittgensteinian worries about private language. But, as I suggest later, he may not be totally out of range.

4. "There is, then, very good reason to conclude that there is no clear meaning to the idea of comparing our beliefs with reality or confronting our hypothesis with observation. This is not, of course, to deny that there is an ordinary sense in which we perform experiments and note the results, or discover in our everyday pursuits that some of our beliefs are true and others false. What should be denied is that these mundane events are to be analyzed as involving evidence which is not propositional in character—evidence which is not some sort of belief" (Donald Davidson, "Empirical Content," in *Truth and Interpretation,* ed. Ernest LePore [London: Blackwell, 1986], 324).

5. See, for instance, the essays collected in Rorty's *Contingency, Irony, and Solidarity* (Cambridge: Cambridge University Press, 1989).

6. This tendency has been reinforced by the current scientific hope of finding physical brain states that will "be" the occurrence of a color, or the perception of a square, or the belief that the square is red. For this research program it is very helpful if each intentional item be distinct and carry its own functional role. However, such an atomized analysis of the intentional sphere is unnecessary even for strict physicalists. If one gives up Cartesian dualism, it is not necessary to adopt a strict token identity theory that demands that to each described mental (intentional, experienced, conscious) item there should correspond one item in physical theory. Token identity theories seemed necessary when the goal was ultimately to reduce intentional descriptions to physical ones. After Quine it became clearer that a physicalist could admit that the two kinds of descriptions individuated their objects in different ways. If one then gives up token identity, the field is open to holistic descriptions such as Davidson's, and to descriptions such as Gendlin's, for which experience is more complex than a holistic set of beliefs and desires.

7. Rorty discusses these issues in *Contingency, Irony, and Solidarity.*

8. This does not mean that the pragmatist story is committed to "the assumption that order can only be something imposed on experience" ("TBP," 24). The pragmatist story allows that successful innovations put us in touch with real patterns in nature. If one accepts any of several modern theories of metaphor, including Davidson's or Ricoeur's, this is true of the poem as well. The pragmatist story does, however, accept the assumption Gendlin criticizes "that forms, distinctions, rules, and concepts are the only possible kind of order— so that there is nothing else, no 'other,' and hence no possible interplay between the forms and something more" ("TBP," 24). It is not correct, however, to say as Gendlin does that according to such theories "nothing but disorder talks back!"

9. Gendlin links his discussion to Heidegger's notions of *Befindlichkeit* and *Wohnen* ("WCS," 2). The case of the poet raises the Heideggerian question of thrown project, where the relation of project and facticity is not the relation of eye to object.

10. In this case, the example of the poet would touch on the difficult problem of subjective aim in Whitehead's ontology.

11. Is there a difference between thinking of meaning as a set of inference moves and thinking of it as a set of structural contrasts? If one reduces the content of experience to sets of beliefs and desires there will be little difference, but otherwise the kind of "absence" involved in each case will be different.

12. Putting the matter this way recalls Wittgenstein's discussions about continuing a series of numbers, but what he has to say about that problem does not help Gendlin's poet, since in contemporary poetry there is no settled practice that will help the poet know that a "correct" line has been formed.

13. Gendlin says, "The said is not formed forms we must cross out, to return to openness or indeterminacy. The said is that more precise saying which is indeterminate in form, and more determined more precisely than form-deter- minations" ("TAD," 11). Again, "For Derrida a word can only mean distinctions. Since anything is thus denied-and-affirmed, Derrida ends in 'undecidability,' limbo" ("NLM," 385). "Derrida thinks that word-use is governed only by distinc- tions (schemes, kinds, logical constructs). . . . He remains in the old tradition for which concepts are the only order. He rightly denies that events (including linguistic ones) instance the concepts, but he says this denial leaves only disorder, decentering, limbo. So after all, the concepts are the only order" ("NLM," 387f.).

However, Derrida denies that he ever sponsored total indeterminacy (see, for example, *Limited Inc* [Evanston: Northwestern University Press, 1989], 115f.). Furthermore, while Derrida would challenge the definiteness of the poet's cur- rent lines and the blank, he also speaks about an "event" or "gift" that would be prior to the interaction Gendlin discusses. Derrida's ideas about the gift (a descendant of Heidegger's *Ereignis*) imply that to arrive at the situation the poet faces there must already have been an event that set up a regime of meaning. That event cannot itself be an interaction of symbolic and felt meaning; the event makes such interaction possible. The event sets up an order by which we can see anything at all, including possibilities. Some deconstructionists describe that event as a repressive selection among systems of signification. But the event cannot be a selection or powerful choice exercised on an array of possibilities. The act of setting up the economy is not a cutting of a form out of an indefinite soup (which would, after all, be another definite kind of object; an indefinite flow is an object, not a pre-object). Pre-object, there is only the general economy of difference or Heidegger's forest darkness.

There is a tension between the almost transcendental priority of the Heideggerian-Derridian event and the pragmatic story mentioned earlier, where what sets the terms for current interpretation is the result of earlier interpretations. Does the kind of activity described in the pragmatic story presuppose a Derridian-Heideggerian event of this prior kind, or is the event only the result of an earlier stage of pragmatic interaction? This question opens into the debate about transcendental versus genetic explanation. It might be helpful to relate Gendlin's ideas more precisely to that debate.

14. About constitutive relations of contrast, Gendlin has said, "I do deny the assumption that anything is a comparedness (samenesses, differences, distinctions). I think that assumption is Idealism—everything is only for (and the passive result of) someone's comparing" (from a letter). This objection contains another remnant of the logical empiricism that Gendlin attacked: the idea that there are only two alternatives, intrinsic meaningfulness or subjectively imposed similarities and differences. To treat this objection fairly would require another long paper discussing the status of relations and the way contrasts and traces of the absent can be active because of the operation of systems that are without conscious intentional control, as well as being implicit in forms of life that have no self-conscious author.

15. I suspect that Gendlin might find unexpected support in Derrida's attempts to show that while concepts and propositions get their individuality and meaning through systems of contrasts, they always exceed such systems even on the level of syntax and signifiers. This is not the same as what Gendlin has to say about the way situations exceed conceptual definition, but Derrida might help Gendlin loosen up the overly tight view of the conceptual and logical connections he contrasts with his own proposals.

Reply to Kolb

1. Currently, when people say "distinctions," what they think includes forms, rules, and conceptual structures as well. The current use would be more properly written (in my terms) as "distinctions (forms, rules . . . . .)." For a discussion of this, see n. 9 in "Thinking beyond Patterns."

2. *ECM* is a critique of the whole tradition of symbolization as merely "about," merely representational. I used the word "represent" about others. Here is the spot he cites: Traditionally, "definitions and schemes . . . *represent* something, but are not *in themselves* something. On the other hand, experiencing (any aspect of it) is a physically felt "this" (*ECM*, 27; original italics).

3. Professor Kolb and other current philosophers do not mean that our situations depend only on words. Life would be easy if we could determine our situations simply by saying how we want them. What these thinkers *mean* is that anything human has words (language) implicit in it. What they *say* is an overcorrection of an error. The earlier error was to use language to discuss something (things, experience, the body) as if before or separate from language. This is impossible, but *with and after language* a situation (a felt sense) has a familiar (but philosophically odd) determinative power that exceeds language. Kolb meant this determinative power when he said: "If anything, the relation (of a . . . . . to a next line) is *more* causal than evidential, but neither of Davidson's relations quite fit."

Chapter 4
William James Earle, Tacit Knowledge and Implicit Intricacy

1. William Empson, *The Structure of Complex Words* (Ann Arbor: University of Michigan Press, 1967), 40.
2. Actually a character in a story by Gordon Lish, "What Is Left to Link Us," in *What I Know So Far* (New York: Holt, Rinehart and Winston, 1984), 16.
3. See Bruno Latour and Steve Woolgar, *Laboratory Life: The Construction of Scientific Facts*, 2d ed. (Princeton: Princeton University Press, 1986).
4. See Michael Lynch, *Art and Artifact in Laboratory Science: A Study of Shop Work and Shop Talk in a Research Laboratory* (London: Routledge and Kegan Paul, 1985).
5. See, e.g., Peter Galison, *How Experiments End* (Chicago: University of Chicago Press, 1987); Allan Franklin, *The Neglect of Experiment* (Cambridge: Cambridge University Press, 1986), and *Experiment Right or Wrong* (Cambridge: Cambridge University Press, 1990); and *The Uses of Experiment: Studies in the Natural Sciences*, ed. Gooding, Pinch, and Schaffer (Cambridge: Cambridge University Press, 1989).
6. Ludwig Wittgenstein, *Philosophical Investigations*, 2d ed., trans. G.E.M. Anscombe (New York: Macmillan, 1958), 8e/8: "And to imagine a language means to imagine a form of life."
7. Ludwig Wittgenstein, *Tractatus Logico-Philosophicus*, trans. D. F. Pears and B. F. McGuinness (London: Routledge and Kegan Paul, 1963), 3.
8. Eugene Gendlin, "Crossing and Dipping: Some Terms for Approaching the Interface between Natural Understanding and Logical Formation," in *Subjectivity and the Debate over Computational Cognitive Science*, ed. Mary Galbraith and William J. Rapaport (Buffalo: SUNY Press, 1991), 48.
9. Wittgenstein, *Philosophical Investigations*, 26e/26: "But first we must learn to understand what it is that opposes such an examination of details in philosophy."
10. See Eugene Gendlin, *Focusing*, 10th printing (New York: Bantam New Age Books, 1988 [originally, 1978]), 80: "The inward complexity, which can stop

us but can also make us better, more effective, interesting, and creative, is often not welcome."

11. Rodney Needham, *Belief, Language, and Experience* (Chicago: University of Chicago Press, 1972), 3.

12. Paul Veyne, *Did the Greeks Believe in Their Myths? An Essay on the Constitutive Imagination* (Chicago: University of Chicago Press, 1988), xi; *Les grecs ont-ils cru à leurs mythes? Essai sur l'imagination constituante* (Paris: Seuil, 1983), 11.

13. Serge Leclaire, *Psychanalyser* (Paris: Seuil, 1968), 14–15.

14. C. S. Peirce, *Chance, Love, and Logic*, ed. Morris R. Cohen (New York: George Braziller, 1956), 2.

15. I am thinking, here, of Norbert Elias's concept of *Handlungsspielraum* or *scope for action* or *marge de manoeuvre*. See his *Die höfische Gesellschaft* (Frankfurt am Main: Suhrkamp, 1983), 30; *The Court Society* (New York: Pantheon, 1983), 15.

16. Pierre Bourdieu, *Questions de Sociologie* (Paris: Minuit, 1984), 47.

17. Wittgenstein, *Tractatus Logico-Philosophicus*, 151 (6.53).

18. Eugene Gendlin, *Let Your Body Interpret Your Dreams* (Wilmette: Chiron Publications, 1986).

19. Gendlin, *Focusing*, 79.

20. Ibid., 83.

21. Gendlin, *Let Your Body Interpret Your Dreams*, 144.

22. Recourse, here, is to Roland Barthes's sense of *doxa*. See *Roland Barthes par Roland Barthes* (Paris: Seuil, 1975), 51: "*La doxa . . .* c'est l'Opinion publique, l'Esprit majoritaire, le Consensus petit-bourgeois, la Voix du Naturel, la Violence du Préjugé."

23. Willard Van Orman Quine, *Elementary Logic* (Cambridge: Harvard University Press, 1980), 5: "The words 'I,' 'he,' 'Jones,' 'here,' 'remote,' and 'good' have the effect, in these examples [e.g. 'he is ill'], of allowing the truth value of a sentence to vary with the speaker or scene or context. Words which have this effect must be supplanted by unambiguous words or phrases before we can accept a declarative sentence or a statement."

24. Willard Van Orman Quine, *Word and Object* (Cambridge: MIT Press, 1960), 193.

25. See Michel Foucault, *Les mots et les choses* (Paris: Gallimard, 1966), 79: "A partir de l'age classique, le signe c'est la *représentativité* de la représentation en tant qu'elle est *représentable*,"; *The Order of Things* (New York: Pantheon Books, 1970), 65.

26. Of course, sentences have effects by being said or heard or written or read and, above all, by being believed to be true or false. One further remark: ordinarily, we needn't distinguish, for example, believing that it is raining and believing that "It is raining" is true, but the beliefs are not identical and this may sometimes matter.

27. Gendlin, *Focusing*, 7.

28. "Tacit knowledge" is associated, above all, with the work of Michael Polanyi, another serious non-Cartesian. See his *The Tacit Dimension* (New York: Doubleday Books, 1966), x: "all thought contains a component of which we are subsidiarily aware in the focal content of our thinking and . . . all thought dwells

in its subsidiaries, as if they were parts of our body." Most simply put, qualifying knowledge as "tacit" reminds us that *"we can know more than we can tell"* (italics in original).

29. "Implicit intricacy," is, of course, one of Gendlin's key terms: he uses it to point to the complexity and detail of cases and instances which do not reduce to the concepts or rules or generalizations they are taken to fall under or be governed by. Appreciable (experienced and felt) intricacy can inform, or be implicit in, our use of language. See, e.g., "Thinking beyond Patterns: Body, Language, and Situations," in *The Presence of Feeling in Thought,* ed. B. den Ouden and M. Moen (New York: Peter Lang, 1992), 59: "We let words be defined by how they worked in an instance. If a word made *new* sense, we let that be the meaning of the word. Most people do the opposite. They lose the intricacy of an actual situation as soon as they use words. If they have a hold of something implicit, pregnant, still vague because it is new and more precise, they lose it as soon as they apply a word."

30. See Gendlin, *Focusing,* 66: "Try to pass up all the glib, familiar answers that come very fast."

31. Richard Rorty, "Putnam and the Relativist Menace," *Journal of Philosophy* 90, no. 9 (September 1993), 447–48.

32. This (partly) paraphrases Rorty, "Putnam and the Relativist Menace," 458: "What he [Putnam] has in mind is the idea that we are constructed by evolution so as to be capable of tracking truth—that nature has cleverly contrived an organism that represents it accurately, as opposed to merely coping with it cleverly."

33. Gendlin, "Thinking beyond Patterns," 88.

34. Ibid.

35. Reference is to Mark Ptashne, a microbiologist who did pioneering work at the Harvard Biological Laboratories on recombinant DNA. See Philip J. Hilts, *Scientific Temperaments: Three Lives in Contemporary Science* (Robert Wilson, Mark Ptashne, John McCarthy) (New York: Simon and Schuster, 1984).

36. Institutions develop *ethoi.* See Ed Regis, *Who Got Einstein's Office? Eccentricity and Genius at the Institute for Advanced Study* (New York: Addison-Wesley, 1987).

37. See, e.g., Dominique Pestre and John Krige, "Some Thoughts on the Early History of CERN," in *Big Science: The Growth of Large-Scale Research,* ed. Peter Galison and Bruce Hevly (Stanford: Stanford University Press, 1992).

38. "Over-correction" is, of course, a Gendlinian term of art. See, e.g., "Thinking beyond Patterns," 24.

39. *Feeling,* though given cognitive weight, remains epistemically inconclusive; so we can at least half-agree with Hegel, *Phenomenology of Spirit* (New York: Oxford University Press, 1977), 43:

> Since the man of common sense makes his appeal to feeling, to an oracle within his breast, he is finished and done with anyone who does not agree; he only has to explain that he has nothing more to say to anyone who does not find and feel the same within himself. In other words, he tramples underfoot the roots

of humanity. For it is the nature of humanity to press onward to agreement with others; human nature only really exists in an achieved community of minds. The anti-human, the merely animal, consists in staying within the sphere of feeling, and being able to communicate only at that level. (*Phänomenologie des Geistes* [Frankfurt am Main: Suhrkamp Verlag, 1970], 65)

40. Foucault's remark (part of his discussion of Velasquez's *Las Meninas*) seems just about right; see *The Order of Things*, 9: "But the relation of language to painting is an infinite relation. It is not that words are imperfect, or that, when confronted by the visible, they prove insuperably inadequate. Neither can be reduced to the other's terms; it is in vain that we say what we see; what we see never resides in what we say" (*Les mots et les choses*, 25).

41. Gendlin, "Thinking beyond Patterns," 89; see also, 24–25: "Most modern philosophers have utterly lost an order of nature, human nature, the person, practice, the body. They deny that anything could have an order of its own. All order is assumed to be *entirely* imposed by a history, a culture, or a conceptual interpretation that could as well be different."

42. Foucault, *The Order of Things*, xx; *Les mots et les choses*, 12.

43. This is not influence or correction, but the convergence of independent research projects.

44. Gendlin, *Focusing*, 28.

45. Ibid., 55.

46. "Raw" is suggested by the following from Foucault, *The Order of Things*: "the empirical and murmuring resemblance of things, that unreacting similitude lies beneath thought and furnishes the infinite raw material for divisions and distributions" (*Les mots et les choses*, 72).

Reply to Earle

1. Kolb put it this way: "If anything, the relation is more causal than evidential, but neither of Davidson's relations quite fit."

Chapter 5
Hans Julius Schneider, The Situatedness of Thinking, Knowing, and Speaking

Most of this material has appeared in German as "Die Situiertheit des Denkens, Wissens und Sprechens im Handeln," *Deutsche Zeitschrift für Philosophie* 41, no. 3 (June 1993), 727–39. I would like to thank Maja Grell and John Granrose for helping me with the English translation and the editor of this volume for many stylistic improvements.

1. Hubert Dreyfus, *What Computers Can't Do: A Critique of Artificial Reason* (New York: Harper and Row, 1972; 2d ed., 1979). New ed., *What Computers Still Can't Do* (Cambridge: The MIT Press, 1992).

2. Cf. Fergus Kerr, *Theology after Wittgenstein* (Oxford: Blackwell, 1986).

3. Ludwig Wittgenstein, *Philosophische Untersuchungen (Philosophical Investigations)* (New York: Macmillan, 1953), part 1, sec. 206. In the following text this book will be quoted as *PI*, followed by the number of the paragraph.

4. My main reference is Eugene Gendlin, "The Wider Role of Bodily Sense in Thought and Language," in *Giving the Body Its Due*, ed. Maxine Sheets-Johnstone (Albany: SUNY Press, 1992), 192–208.

5. Strictly speaking, to learn a foreign language also means more, of course, than to learn new sounds. The model Wittgenstein is criticizing fits more to the case where a secret code for written marks has to be learned, in which a one-by-one deciphering is possible.

6. Cf. Wittgenstein, *PI*, 661.

7. For a much more detailed discussion of these points (and many others related to Gendlin's philosophy of language), cf. my *Phantasie und Kalkül* (Frankfurt: Suhrkamp, 1992), esp. chap. 3. Concerning my interpretation of Wittgenstein's philosophy of mind, I found that it agrees in many points with Michel Ter Hark, *Beyond the Inner and the Outer: Wittgenstein's Philosophy of Psychology* (Dordrecht: Kluwer Academic Publishers, 1990).

8. The concept (image) of an originally correct act of meaning to which a speaker can refer back seems to be unknown in some cultures; cf. Alessandro Duranti, "Intentions, Language, and Social Action in a Samoan Context," *Journal of Pragmatics* 12, no. 1 (February 1988), 13–33.

9. Leonard Bloomfield, *Language* (Chicago: University of Chicago Press, 1984).

10. The view that the realm of the mental can always be treated in terms of a processing of cognitions is convincingly criticized, e.g., in Jerome Bruner, *Acts of Meaning* (Cambridge: Harvard University Press, 1990).

11. John R. Searle, *Speech Acts: An Essay in the Philosophy of Language* (Cambridge: Cambridge University Press, 1970). For a detailed critique, see my paper "Die sprachphilosophischen Annahmen der Sprechakttheorie," in *Sprachphilosophie: Ein internationales Handbuch zeitgenössischer Forschung*, vol. 1, ed. M. Dascal, D. Gerhardus, K. Lorenz, G. Meggle (Berlin: de Gruyter, 1992), 761–75.

12. Cf. Ludwig Wittgenstein, *On Certainty* (Oxford: Blackwell, 1969).

13. This is one of the reasons why the term "*thick* description" is a good choice. Cf. Clifford Geertz, "Thick Description: Toward an Interpretive Theory of Culture," in *The Interpretation of Cultures: Selected Essays* (New York: Basic Books, 1973), 3–30.

14. Cf. Wittgenstein's remark: "If a lion could talk, we could not understand him" (*PI*, part 2, 223).

Reply to Schneider

1. I have written about how the internal/external distinction arises. See "A Philosophical Critique of the Concept of Narcissism," and *A Process Model.*

Chapter 6
Meredith Williams, The Implicit Intricacy of Mind and Situation

1. Eugene Gendlin, "Thinking beyond Patterns" in *The Presence of Feeling in Thought*, ed. B. den Ouden and M. Moen (New York: Peter Lang, 1992). All in-text references to this work will be identified as "TBP," followed by page number.
2. Ludwig Wittgenstein, *Philosophical Investigations* (Oxford: Basil Blackwell, 1953), secs. 151–52.
3. With work as complex and rich as Gendlin's "TBP," any discussion and critical evaluation runs the risk of distorting or in some ways misrepresenting the content of that work. I try to present some of Gendlin's ideas as accurately and clearly as I can—indeed, doing so is one of the main goals of the paper. However, any failure to achieve this will provide, I trust, the basis for a fruitful discussion of these important issues.
4. Ludwig Wittgenstein, *Tractatus Logico-Philosophicus*, trans. D. F. Pears and B. F. McGuinness (London: Routlege and Kegan Paul, 1961).
5. It might be objected that assigning this methodological role to the cases of poetry and therapy misdescribes their function in Gendlin's thought. If they play this methodological role (as paradigmatic for all speech situations), then what is discovered about concept- and belief-formation and change would apply in general to all speech situations. In other words, these two cases play an evidential role in supporting the intricacy thesis. This is the way in which I am treating the use of these two cases. The objection to this states that the two cases do not provide evidence for the intricacy thesis, but are examples that make intricacy salient. For this objection to hold, we must assume the acceptability of the intricacy thesis. On this interpretation, intricacy is always at work and the two cases in which the significant silences occur make that intricacy salient. These cases are illustrations of intricacy, then, and not evidence for intricacy. Gendlin then is not under the burden of extrapolating from the two cases to ordinary cases, for it is simply assumed that all situations are structured by intricacy. I take it that that is a substantive claim that needs to be established, and so prefer to interpret the two cases as playing an important methodological role in establishing the truth of the intricacy thesis.
6. This description is far too simple. Gendlin uses the " . . . . ." to indicate implicit intricacy ("TBP," 48), implicit change ("TBP," 56), implicit form or pattern ("TBP," 57–58). This makes it difficult to assess the claims he makes, as there is such wide discretion in the interpretation of the text. In my discussion, I shall treat the " . . . . ." as primarily marking an implicit intricacy, though there may well be an indeterminacy in the identity conditions for that intricacy.
7. Rene Descartes, *Meditations on First Philosophy*, trans. Donald A. Cross (Indianapolis: Hackett Publishing Co., 1980), meditation 5.
8. Karl Popper, *Objective Knowledge* (Oxford: Clarendon Press, 1972).
9. See esp. *Philosophical Investigations*, secs. 183–98.
10. Ibid., sec. 196.
11. This is Wittgenstein's central objection to the use of phenomenological markers in explaining rule-following. See *Philosophical Investigations*, esp. secs.

139–97. In these passages, Wittgenstein attacks the idea that some kind of sensation or experience marks our being guided by something: "We imagine that a feeling enables us to perceive as it were a connecting mechanism between the look of a word and the sound that we utter" (sec. 170). Equally, we can say of Gendlin that he imagines that the poet can perceive a connecting mechanism (an implying) between the silence and the words written. Rather than assimilating this connection to a causal mechanism, Gendlin assimilates it to logical derivability.

12. David Hume, *Dialogues concerning Natural Religion*, esp. part 3.

13. I shall discuss this in sec. 3, below.

14. This example does not really support a strong reading of the incompleteness of identity for the reasons given earlier for holding that the range of a bird's possible situations is limited. It is used as an illustration only and not as evidence for the claim.

15. Wittgenstein, *Philosophical Investigations*, sec. 92.

16. See my "Transcendence and Return: The Overcoming of Philosophy in Nietzsche and Wittgenstein," *International Philosophical Quarterly* 13 (December 1988), for a fuller discussion of Wittgenstein's metaphilosophical views.

17. The similarity to Berkeley's critique of matter is striking. He condemns matter as a passive, insensible stuff incapable of being the cause of anything. See, e.g., *Principles of Human Understanding*, in *Berkeley's Philosophical Writings*, ed. David M. Armstrong (New York: Collier Press, 1965).

18. It is interesting to note that some forms of theory building in cognitive science also reject these two traditional forms of explanation in favor of searching for the correct "functional analysis" of cognitive capacities. These functional analyses provide abstract descriptions of the psychological "microstructure" of cognitive capacities. See, e.g., Robert Cummins, *The Nature of Psychological Explanation* (Cambridge: MIT Press, 1983).

19. Formally, the argument is structured as follows:

P1   Behavior is orderly.
P2   There are only two forms of orderly behavior: rule-obeying and law-instantiating.
P3   Behavior is not rule-obeying.
P4   Behavior is not law-instantiating.
C   Therefore, behavior is not orderly.

The argument is a reductio ad absurdum. The question is: Which premise is false? Gendlin holds that P2 is the faulty premise, and so he maintains that there is a kind of self-ordering behavior that is utterly different from either rule-obeying behavior or law-instantiating behavior.

20. This is a filling in of an argument not explicitly given by Gendlin. But I think that this is the only way he can claim that the ethological studies support his intricacy thesis.

21. See Wilfrid Sellars, "Some Reflections on Language Games," in his *Science, Perception and Reality* (London: Routledge and Kegan Paul, 1963).

Chapter 7
Mark Johnson, Embodied Meaning and Cognitive Science

1. Much of the relevant literature is summarized in George Lakoff, *Women, Fire, and Dangerous Things: What Our Categories Reveal about the Mind* (Chicago: University of Chicago Press, 1987), and in Mark Turner, *Reading Minds: The Study of English in the Age of Cognitive Science* (Princeton: Princeton University Press, 1991).

2. Raymond Gibbs, "Psycholinguistic Studies on the Conceptual Basis of Idiomaticity," *Cognitive Linguistics* 1, no. 4 (1990), 417–62. See also Raymond Gibbs, *The Poetics of Mind* (Cambridge: Cambridge University Press, 1994).

3. Maxine Sheets-Johnstone, *The Roots of Thinking* (Philadelphia: Temple Univeristy Press, 1990).

4. Mark Johnson, *The Body in the Mind: The Bodily Basis of Meaning, Imagination, and Reasoning* (Chicago: University of Chicago Press, 1987).

5. F. Varela, E. Thompson, and E. Rosch, *The Embodied Mind: Cognitive Science and Human Experience* (Cambridge: MIT Press, 1991); Gerald Edelman, *Bright Air, Brilliant Fire* (New York: Basic Books, 1992).

6. Eugene Gendlin, *Thinking beyond Patterns: Body, Language, and Situations*, unpublished manuscript. A version of this appeared in *The Presence of Feeling in Thought*, ed. B. den Ouden and M. Moen (New York: Peter Lang, 1992).

7. Lakoff, *Women, Fire, and Dangerous Things*, and Johnson, *The Body in the Mind.*

8. Eugene Gendlin, "Crossing and Dipping: Some Terms for Approaching the Interface between Natural Understanding and Logical Formation" (unpublished manuscript, University of Chicago, 1991).

9. Ibid., 38.

10. R. Levins and R. Lewontin, *The Dialectical Biologist* (Cambridge: Harvard University Press, 1985), 89.

11. Most of the first half of *Thinking beyond Patterns* is devoted to this task of being very precise about what lies in our experience. I make no pretense of capturing his elegant and nuanced formulations.

12. The term "idealized cognitive model" is coined by Lakoff in *Women, Fire, and Dangerous Things*, which provides an extensive taxonomy of types of cognitive models that we use to understand situations.

13. Charles Fillmore, "Frame Semantics," in *Linguistics in the Morning Calm*, ed. Linguistic Society of Korea (Seoul: Hanshin, 1982).

14. George Lakoff, "The Invariance Hypothesis: Is Abstract Reason Based on Image Schemas?" *Cognitive Linguistics* 1, no. 1 (1990), 39–74; Turner, *Reading Minds*, 172–82.

15. Some of this evidence is surveyed in Lakoff, *Women, Fire, and Dangerous Things*, 456–59.

16. George Lakoff and Mark Johnson, *Metaphors We Live By* (Chicago: University of Chicago Press, 1980).

17. Gendlin, "Crossing and Dipping," 47.

NOTES TO PAGES 158 - 69

18. Ibid., 47–48.

19. Ibid., 48; parentheses mine.

20. Ibid., 51.

21. Ibid.

22. Fillmore, "Frame Semantics."

23. Gendlin, "Crossing and Dipping," 52.

24. Lakoff and Johnson, *Metaphors We Live By*, 147–55.

25. Gendlin, "Crossing and Dipping," 52.

26. One primary constraint on metaphors, for example, appears to be what George Lakoff has named the "Invariance Constraint" (Lakoff, "The Invariance Hypothesis."). This constraint can be expressed as follows: In any metaphorical mapping the image-schematic structure of the source domain is mapped onto the target domain, but only insofar as it does not conflict with any preexisting structure in the target domain. This is an empirical hypothesis that is subject to disconfirmation by examples. So far, the constraint appears to hold in all of the cases we have examined.

27. Gendlin, "Crossing and Dipping," 54.

28. George Lakoff and Mark Turner, *More Than Cool Reason: A Field Guide to Poetic Metaphor* (Chicago: University of Chicago Press, 1991).

29. Gilles Fauconnier, *Mental Spaces: Aspects of Meaning Construction in Natural Language* (Cambridge: MIT Press, 1985).

30. Steven Fesmire, "Aerating the Mind: The Metaphor of Mental Functioning as Bodily Functioning," *Metaphor and Symbolic Activity* 9, no. 1 (1994), 31–44.

31. Eve Sweetser, *From Etymology to Pragmatics* (Cambridge: Cambridge University Press, 1991).

32. Frederick Perls, R. F. Heferline, and P. Goodman, *Gestalt Therapy: Excitement and Growth in the Human Personality* (New York: Julian Press, 1951), 118.

Reply to Johnson

1. A succession of research studies shows that psychotherapy clients who are successful (by many criteria) engage in significantly more reference to directly felt events during their tape-recorded therapy hours, as measured by reliably recognizable linguistic turns. See my "What Comes After Traditional Psychotherapy Research," *American Psychologist* 41, no. 2, 131–36.

2. One strand in our tradition assumes that reality (events, situations, whatever we study . . . . .) consists *first and primarily* of mere space-and-time fillers, things that move in logic-like mathematical patterns. They have meaning "given" to them only *secondarily*. If we recognize it, we need not make this assumption. "The pile rises" and "the ball goes up" do not mean pure Newtonian motion just literally. Every word brings many uses, and we must grasp what it says here. When "the pile rises" we know that it is because more was added; it didn't rise like dough. And, when "the ball goes up" we know it did not walk. Those are just as

dependent on the metaphorical crossing, as when our love relationship is "really going." There is no uncrossed event (experience, situation . . . . .), but there is always an openness for further crossing.

3. In etymology words often move to neighborly realms rather than by correspondence. "Journey" is a move of the word "*jour*," and used to mean *a day's* work *or* travel. It is an extension, not a similarity-correlation. "Drive" came from driving cattle, and before that from the driven snow. It meant agitated movement, and did not contain Johnson's concept of "starting location; final location; motion." Nor does this concept fit how the word has moved today, when many people feel "driven," always in motion, precisely without starting and final locations. Only after a word has moved can we see the "concept" or correlations.

4. A situation is inherently *the crossing* of *many* possible further actions and sayings. What it is now consists of many implicit relations to other (real and possible) moments and places. For example, giving someone money *is now* a change in a great many (some unforeseeable) possibilities at other times and places. The situation *is* these possibilities. A situation is a cluster of stories that might further ensue. I say that the stories are *implicitly crossed* because any one that actually happens will change whether and how the others could still ensue. Whatever happens will implicitly change all the others. (See *ECM* and *Thinking beyond Patterns*, A5.)

5. See my discussion of Max Black's theory in "Dwelling."

Chapter 8
J. N. Mohanty, Experience and Meaning

1. Eugene Gendlin, *Experiencing and the Creation of Meaning: A Philosophical and Psychological Approach to the Subjective* (New York: Macmillan, 1962), 2. Henceforth referred to in-text as *ECM*.

2. E. Husserl, *Ideas Pertaining to a Pure Phenomenology and Phenomenological Philosophy*, vol. 1, trans. Boyce Gibson (New York: Macmillan, 1931), sec. 124.

3. W. Wundt, *Kleine Schriften*, vol. 1 (Leipzig: W. Engelmann, 1910), 573–74.

Chapter 9
Robert C. Scharff, After Dilthey and Heidegger

1. "A Philosophical Critique of Narcissism: The Significance of the Awareness Movement" (hereafter, "N"), in *Pathologies of the Modern Self: Postmodern Studies on Narcissism, Schizophrenia, and Depression*, ed. David M. Levin (New York: New York University Press, 1987), 268.

2. See, e.g., "Thinking beyond Patterns: Body, Language, and Situations" (hereafter, "TBP"), in *The Presence of Feeling in Thought*, ed. B. den Ouden and M. Moen (New York: Peter Lang, 1992), 24; cf., *Experiencing and the Creation of Meaning* (hereafter, *ECM*) (New York: Free Press, 1962), 146–47; and "Experiential Phenomenology" (hereafter, "EP"), in *Phenomenology and the Social Sciences*,

2 vols., ed. Maurice Natanson (Evanston: Northwestern University Press, 1973), vol. 1, 282.

3. "The Wider Role of Bodily Sense in Thought and Language," in *Giving the Body Its Due*, ed. Maxine Sheets-Johnstone (Albany: SUNY Press, 1992), 197; emphases altered.

4. "Phenomenology as Non-Logical Steps" (hereafter, "PNS"), in *American Phenomenology: Origins and Developments, Analecta Husserliana*, vol. 26, ed. Eugene F. Kaelin and Calvin O. Schrag (Dordrecht: Kluwer, 1989), 409.

5. Gendlin's best summary account of his project is, I think, "EP," 281–306. See also, *ECM*, 47–62.

6. Gendlin, *ECM*, 140–48 (quoted from 146; my emphasis); see also, 219–25.

7. For Gendlin's own recent summary of his philosophical sources, see "PNS," 404–10.

8. Leibniz and Hume, e.g., accept this image and then radicalize philosophy's denial of experience—by giving accounts of why we were ever silly enough to take such experience seriously in the first place.

9. P. L. Heath, "Experience," in *Encyclopedia of Philosophy*, 8 vols., ed. Paul Edwards (New York: Macmillan, 1967), vol. 3, 156–57. In German (and French), an *Empiriker* (*Empirique*) may be either an empiric or a quack. On the other hand, a quick survey of the *OED* shows that both prephilosophical speech and now obsolete English usages tend to stay close to the word's Latin origins (viz., the present participle of *experiri*: to try, to learn by trying, to put to the test).

10. Hilary Putnam, "Why Is a Philosopher?" in *Realism with a Human Face* (Cambridge: Harvard University Press, 1990), 118.

11. Hilary Putnam, *Renewing Philosophy* (Cambridge: Harvard University Press, 1992), 197; and Preface, *Realism with a Human Face*, ix. In Putnam's recent accounts of philosophy's proper task, he stresses Wittgenstein's "constant effort to understand sympathetically forms of life he did not share"; Dewey's "reflections on democracy [that] never degenerate into propaganda for the status quo" (*Renewing Philosophy*, 198); and (with Ruth Anna Putnam) James's Radical Empiricism. See, e.g., his "James' Theory of Perception," *Realism with a Human Face*, 232–51; "Reply to John McDowell," *Philosophical Topics* 20, no. 1 (1992), 358–61; *Pragmatism: An Open Question* (Oxford: Basil Blackwell, 1995); and her "Weaving Seamless Webs," *Philosophy* 62 (1987), 207–20.

12. Charles Taylor, "Self-Interpreting Animals," in *Philosophical Papers*, vol. 1: *Human Agency and Language* (Cambridge: Cambridge University Press, 1985), 74–75 (for "philosophical anthropology," 1–12). Cf. Hilary Putnam, "Why Functionalism Didn't Work," in *Words and Life* (Cambridge: Harvard University Press, 1994), 441–59.

13. Taylor, "Self-Interpreting Animals," 50–51; and "Interpretation and the Sciences of Man," in *Philosophical Papers*, vol. 2: *Philosophy and the Human Sciences* (Cambridge: Cambridge University Press, 1985), 15–57.

14. Charles Taylor, "Overcoming Epistemology," in *After Philosophy: End or Transformation?*, ed. Kenneth Baynes, James Bohman, and Thomas McCarthy (Cambridge: MIT Press, 1987), 483–84; my emphasis. I must add that this is

not entirely fair to Taylor; elsewhere, he insists that part of what it means to abandon epistemology is to see the mistake in treating every dispute as if it were between "extra-terrestrials" in need of a common criterion; so, he argues, in deep disputes between, say, two cultures, commonality will have to be "developed" by their "growing together" as cultures. See "Philosophy and Its History," in *Philosophy in History: Essays on the Historiography of Philosophy*, ed. Richard Rorty, J. B. Schneewind, and Quentin Skinner (Cambridge: Cambridge University Press, 1984), 28–30.

15. Eugene Gendlin, "Process Ethics and the Political Question," in *The Moral Sense in the Communal Significance of Life*, in *Analecta Husserliana*, vol. 20, ed. Anna-Teresa Tymieniecka (Dordrecht: Reidel, 1986), 265.

16. Eugene Gendlin, "Values and the Process of Experiencing," in *The Goals of Psychotherapy*, ed. Alvin R. Mahrer (New York: Appleton-Century-Crofts, 1967), esp. 187–89, quoted from 198; see also, "Process Ethics," 266–70. In fact, Gendlin argues, one such experiential process (re)creates the ancient virtues!

17. Eugene Gendlin, "Two Phenomenologists Do Not Disagree," in *Phenomenology: Dialogues and Bridges*, ed. Ronald Bruzina and Bruce Wilshire (New York: State University of New York Press, 1982), 323. Medard Boss tells of an accommodating client who changed dream languages every time he changed therapists. See *Psychoanalysis and Daseinsanalysis*, trans. Ludwig B. Lefebvre (New York: Basic Books, 1963), 273–83. Boss's point is that it was not the Freudian and Jungian concepts that made the first two therapies unsuccessful, but the Freudian and Jungian analysts' pressing their patient to impose their concepts on his dreams.

18. E.g., Wilhelm Dilthey, *Gesammelte Schriften* (hereafter, *GS*), 20 vols. (Stuttgart: B. G. Teubner; and Göttingen: Vandenhoeck and Ruprecht, 1913–), vol. 1, 359–73; Wilhelm Dilthey, *Selected Works*, vol. 1: *Introduction to the Human Sciences* (hereafter *SW* 1), trans. Rudolf A. Makkreel, et al. (Princeton: Princeton University Press, 1989), 192–206.

19. *GS* 6, 313–14; *Selected Works*, vol. 5: *Poetry and Experience*, trans. Rudolf A. Makkreel, et al. (Princeton: Princeton University Press, 1985), 223–24; my emphasis, trans. slightly altered.

20. Dilthey, *GS* 1, xviii; *SW* 1, 50–51; my emphasis.

21. For the former, see, *GS* 5, 139–240; in Dilthey, *Descriptive Psychology and Historical Understanding*, trans. Richard Zantes (The Hague: Martinus Nijhoff, 1977), 23–120. For the latter, see *GS* 7, 191–291 (a complete translation of *GS* 7 is forthcoming). For "The Understanding of Other Persons and Their Expressions of Life" (*GS* 7, 205–27), trans. Kenneth L. Heiges, see *Descriptive Psychology*, 123–44.

22. Dilthey, *GS* 5, 200–201; *Descriptive Psychology*, 82.

23. Dilthey, *GS* 7, 86. In one place, Dilthey even says one should "assume the attitude of understanding [expressions] with respect to our own life as well as other people's" (*GS* 7, 196).

24. This way of reading Dilthey still has famous adherents—e.g., Karl-Otto Apel (*Understanding and Explanation: A Transcendental-Pragmatic Perspective*, trans. Georgia Warnke [Cambridge: MIT Press, 1984], 3–6, 12–14) and Jürgen

Habermas (*Knowledge and Human Interests*, trans. Jeremy J. Shapiro [Boston: Beacon Press, 1971], 145–46, 177–81). For a more judicious treatment of the issues, together with a discussion of Dilthey's important analysis of "objective apprehension" in knowledge (from 1905, in *GS* 7, 24–44), see Rudolf A. Makkreel, *Dilthey: Philosopher of the Human Studies*, 2d ed. (Princeton: Princeton University Press, 1992), 207–9, 274–88.

25. Gendlin's conception of experiencing is thus to be traced, not to his association with Carl Rogers, but to his earlier MA thesis, "Wilhelm Dilthey and the Problem of Comprehending Human Significance in the Science of Man" (Department of Philosophy, University of Chicago, 1950), where *Erlebnis* is discussed at length, primarily with reference to *GS* 7. See also, e.g., *ECM*, 11, 14–15, 32–33; and "A Theory of Personality Change," in *Personality Change*, ed. Philip Worchel and Donn Byrne (New York: John Wiley and Sons, 1964), 111, 115, 123–26.

26. Gendlin did not in fact work out his view in critical response to Dilthey (personal communication); but he does think "Dilthey did not go very far into how what is more than shared forms functions" ("TBP," 34), and many passages read as if the *Ideas* and *Critique* have just been juxtaposed.

27. Gendlin, "EP," 291; also *ECM*, 18–19; and, summarizing *ECM*, "*Befindlichkeit*: Heidegger and the Philosophy of Psychology" (hereafter, "B"), *Review of Existential Psychology and Psychiatry* 16 (1978), 70.

28. The recent publication of some early drafts of Dilthey's unfinished *Introduction to the Human Sciences* (*GS* 19, 58ff. [*SW* 1, 245ff.]) has made this promising direction much easier to trace. See Makkreel, *Dilthey*, 441–46. That there is a "hermeneutical philosophy" implicit in Dilthey's work was already my view (without benefit of the early drafts) in "Non-Analytical, Unspeculative Philosophy of History: The Legacy of Wilhelm Dilthey," *Cultural Hermeneutics* 3, no. 3 (1976), esp. 311–16.

29. Martin Heidegger, *Sein und Zeit* (hereafter *SZ*), 10th ed. (Tübingen: Max Niemeyer, 1963), 398; *Being and Time*, trans. John Macquarrie and Edward Robinson (New York: Harper and Row, 1962), translation slightly altered; page references not given, since German pagination is in the margins. I chose "restiveness" rather than "restlessness" for "*Unruhe*" because restiveness more strongly implies "resistance to something that constrains"—specifically here, as I argue in a moment, the constraint of residual loyalty to an epistemological ("spectatorlike") orientation.

30. From, respectively, *SZ*, 46 and 398; and *Prolegomena zur Geschichte des Zeitbegriffs* (*Gesamtausgabe*, vol. 20) (Frankfurt: Vittorio Klostermann, 1979), 164; *History and the Concept of Time: Prolegomena*, trans. Theodore Kisiel (Bloomington: Indiana University Press, 1985), 118–19.

31. For a more detailed analysis of Heidegger's Dilthey-interpretation, with extensive references to Heidegger's recently published early Freiburg lecture courses, see my "Heidegger's 'Appropriation' of Dilthey before *Being and Time*," *Journal of the History of Philosophy*, 35/1 (1997), 99–121.

32. See, e.g., *ECM*, 226–68; "EP," 307–17; "A Theory of Personality Change,"

100–148; "Experiential Psychotherapy," in *Current Psychotherapies*, ed. Raymond Corsini (Itasca: F. E. Peacock, 1973), 317–52; and "What Comes after Traditional Psychotherapy Research," *American Psychologist* 41, no. 2 (1986), 131–36 (for application to psychological theory and research). Also see *Focusing*, 2d ed. (New York: Bantam Books, 1981), esp. 43–109, and *Let Your Body Interpret Your Dreams* (Wilmette: Chiron/Open Court, 1986) (for psychotherapeutic practice); the works cited in notes 16 and 17 (for ethics); "A Critique of Relativity and Localization," *Mathematical Modelling* 4 (1983), 61–72 (for physics); and *A Process Model*, 8 parts, unpublished manuscript (for the life and behavioral sciences).

33. See, e.g., his MA thesis, 3, 55.

34. It is not only *SZ* that Gendlin construes this way. See also, e.g., his "Dwelling," in *The Horizons of Continental Philosophy: Essays on Husserl, Heidegger, and Merleau-Ponty*, ed. Hugh J. Silverman, et al. (Dordrecht: Kluwer, 1988), 133–52 (on *Vorträge und Aufsätze*, among others); and his "Analysis" of *What Is A Thing?* (*Die Frage nach dem Ding*), trans. W. B. Barton and Vera Deutsch (Chicago: Henry Regnery, 1967), 247–96. The general idea is that "[h]omage to a great philosopher is best done by *really seeing* what the philosophy points to, and by going on further" ("B," 55; my emphasis). The parallel between this attitude and Heidegger's own toward Husserl and phenomenology is of course striking.

35. Eugene Gendlin, "Words Can Say How They Work," presented at the 27th Annual Heidegger Conference, State University of New York at Stony Brook, 4 June 1993.

36. Gendlin, "B," 67. That the "greater intricacy" of experiencing, since it is always something "felt," must be bodily not just cerebral is a point Gendlin develops in, e.g., "The Primacy of the Body, Not the Primacy of Perception," *Man and World* 25 (1992), 341–53; "The Wider Role of Bodily Sense in Thought and Language," 192–207; and "TBP," 102–6. The Foucault citation is to "Nietzsche, Genealogy, History," in *Language, Counter-Memory, Practice: Selected Essays and Interviews*, trans. Donald F. Bouchard and Sherry Simon (Ithaca: Cornell University Press, 1977), esp. 147–48.

37. "B," 67; also "N," 302. Neither Foucault nor Habermas are mentioned here by name.

38. "Currently it seems impossible to think or speak about what is more than form, because . . . [w]hat is not clear and distinct is said to be simply indeterminate, a limbo, undecidability, merely a negation of determined form. Now Heidegger's great openness [that is neither 'a form nor a formed thing'] seems mere indeterminacy. Derrida can lop off this great openness. He says honestly that he just does not find it. We can conclude that it could be important to find it. . . . I will show how we can find it everywhere and in anything" ("Words Can Say How They Work," *1993 Heidegger Conference Proceedings*, 29; corrected as read).

39. See also, e.g., "TBP," 32, where Gendlin claims that Heidegger, like Kant, "assumed that experience has *always already* been organized by certain determinants *so that no change in the determinants can come from it*. Experience can happen *only within* the determinants" (second emphasis mine).

40. Gendlin's reference to "met[a-]ontology" is *Metaphysische Anfangsgründe der Logik im Ausgang von Leibniz* (*Gesamtausgabe*, vol. 26) (Frankfurt: Vittorio Klostermann, 1978), 196–202; *The Metaphysical Foundations of Logic*, trans. Michael Heim (Bloomington: Indiana University Press, 1984), 154–59.

41. Gendlin, "TBP," 32; emphasis altered. Gendlin cites his "*Befindlichkeit*" and "Dwelling" pieces at this point.

42. "It would be superficial and pedantic to believe that once fundamental ontology is founded as a discipline, a further ontology with a new title would be adjoined to it. Fundamental ontology, further, is not a fixed discipline which, once the baby is named, should now for good occupy the previously empty place reserved for it in some putative philosophical system. . . . In fact, that 'place' is, in every philosophy, an occupied place, and it is in each case transformed" (*Metaphysische Anfangsgründe*, 200/157).

43. See my "Heidegger's 'Appropriation' of Dilthey," and the discussions of this period in the three recent volumes by Theodore Kisiel, *The Genesis of Heidegger's "Being and Time"* (Berkeley: University of California Press, 1993); John Van Buren, *The Young Heidegger: Rumor of the Hidden King* (Bloomington: Indiana University Press, 1994); and *Reading Heidegger from the Start: Essays in His Earliest Thought*, ed. Kisiel and Van Buren, (Albany: SUNY Press, 1994).

44. For details, see my "Repeating Heidegger's Question," in *American Phenomenology*, 369–73.

45. Moreover, as one sees from his remark that raising the Being question offers "the possibility of a most focused *individualization* [*Vereinzelung*] of inquiry for any given Dasein," these reports of initial perplexity and disincentive are no abstract observations meant for other inquirers (*SZ*, 39; my emphasis); cf. 38, 187–88, 263–66, 307.

46. From the "Addendum" (1956) to *Der Ursprung des Kunstwerkes* (Stuttgart: Philipp Reclam, 1960), 100; trans. Albert Hofstadter, in *Poetry, Language, and Thought* (New York: Harper and Row, 1971), 86; reprinted in *Basic Writings*, 2d ed. (New York: HarperCollins, 1993), 211.

47. Elucidating the Being question, *SZ* concludes, "is a matter of finding a *way* to *go*. Whether it is the *only* or in general the *right* way can only be decided *from the process of going along it*" (*SZ*, 437).

48. Gendlin and I apparently read Heidegger's "Dialogue" with a Japanese quite differently. When Heidegger says his abandonment of the term signals an effort to think further into the "nearest nearness we constantly rush ahead of," I hear a continuing following out of the path opened up in the first pages of *SZ*—a reaffirmation of its initially "felt sense," now under the conditions of some thirty years of effort at carrying forward just such notions as a hermeneutics that (thanks to Dilthey) was never understood as a methodology, that (thanks to *SZ*) was thought from the start as interpret*ing* itself, and that (since then) has finally stretched beyond appropriateness in the effort to "think back" to its meaning as "that exposition which brings tidings because it can listen to a message." See *Unterwegs zur Sprache* (Pfullingen: Neske, 1959), 98–99, 121–22; *On the Way to Language*, trans. Peter Hertz (Harper and Row, 1971), 11–12, 28–29. All the talk

in the "Dialogue" about representational thinking and European habits of mind should, I think, be read in this same spirit.

49. The existentialist reading of *SZ* is, of course, not dead. See, e.g., my "Habermas on Heidegger's *Being and Time*," *International Philosophical Quarterly* 31 (1991), 189–201. On the Anglo-American misreading, see my "Rorty and Analytic Heideggerian Epistemology—and Heidegger," *Man and World* 25 (1992), 483–504.

50. Otto Pöggeler, "'Historicity' in Heidegger's Late Work," *Southwestern Journal of Philosophy* 4 (1973), 72.

51. Gendlin, "Process Ethics," 270; my emphasis.

52. Ibid., 266.

Reply to Scharff

1. Richardson reports that Heidegger in his last years once told him: "Until now I wrote about others, but now at last I am saying what I myself have to say." He surely thought it possible to do something other than direct historical critique.

2. Heidegger wrote about a "procedure which, within certain limits, at first always meets ordinary thinking halfway and accompanies it a certain distance in order to require at the right moment a sudden turn in that thinking, *but under the power of the same word.* For example *'decision'* [*Entscheidung*] can and should at first be used to signify an 'act' of man . . . until it suddenly means the essence of being. . . . man is placed back into the essence of being and the shackles of anthropology are torn away" (GA 65, 83–84). Cited in H. W. Edler, "Retreat from Radicality: Pöggeler on Heidegger's Politics," *Graduate Faculty Philosophy Journal* 14, no. 2, and 15, no. 1 (1991).

3. In his dialogue with the Japanese scholar, Heidegger says they share only the featureless source, and can communicate about nothing else; it is all culturally shaped. In this period Heidegger denies that openness inheres in situations. All they are, and all that one can make of them is derivative.

4. Instead of telling us Dilthey's great advance, Scharff says only that Dilthey could not provide a good general description of his new moves. But this is not surprising! Innovation comes first; only from it, can new general concepts develop. In terms of old concepts he had to sound either "subjective" or "objective," and had to correct both. I thank Scharff for pointing out that I carry Dilthey forward, but let us mention what I carried forward:

Dilthey said that experiencing is always also an understanding and an expression (explication), and conversely, that they are always each a further experiencing.

To explicate experience does not represent or interpret; it is itself a further experiencing. The old question of accuracy becomes rather a question of a certain continuity (*Zusammenhang*) or lack of it, between experiencing and further experiencing.

This overcomes the whole problematic of interpretation and perception. It does not fall into Nietzsche's (again current) conundrum of "There are only interpretations." Experiencing *is* always also an understanding. Then, *further* understanding is not an added interpretation, but a sense-making continuation, a further experiencing. If one enters deeply into the equation of these three, not only does "carrying forward" follow, but also a thoroughgoing overthrow of the tradition.

5. Heidegger often speaks *from*, but does *not return to* the "mooded" understanding from which he moved, so as to notice and enter the effects of his saying (to see if it carried forward), and from that again to say more, a zig-zag movement that I developed. My pointing this out was a friendly criticism which I first made of Husserl, Sartre, and Merleau-Ponty.

6. Stambaugh (personal communication) quotes the aged Heidegger saying that "situatedness" (*Befindlichkeit*) "is now called 'dwelling.'"

Chapter 10
Lawrence J. Hatab, Language and Human Nature

1. The present essay is a revised and expanded version of an article published in *Human Studies*.

2. Eugene Gendlin, "Heidegger and Forty Years of Silence," in *Proceedings of the 20th Annual Heidegger Conference*, ed. Manfred Frings (DePaul University, 1986), 48–56.

3. See, e.g., "Nietzsche, Nihilism, and Meaning," *The Personalist Forum* 3, no. 2 (Fall 1987), esp. 101–11; and "Rejoining Aletheia and Truth," *International Philosophical Quarterly* 30, no. 4 (December 1990), 431–47. See also my article in *International Philosophical Quarterly* (December 1995), "Ethics and Finitude: Heideggerian Contributions to Moral Philosophy."

4. Martin Heidegger, *Being and Time*, trans. John Macquarrie and Edward Robinson (New York: Harper and Row, 1962), 244.

5. Two writings to which I am referring are: "Experiential Phenomenology," in *Phenomenology and the Social Sciences*, ed. M. Natanson (Evanston: Northwestern University Press, 1973); and "Thinking beyond Patterns: Body, Language, and Situations," in *The Presence of Feeling in Thought*, ed. B. den Ouden and M. Moen (New York: Peter Lang, 1992).

6. Gendlin, "Experiential Phenomenology," 291.

7. Ibid., p. 299.

8. Ibid., pp. 302–3, 305, 319.

9. Gendlin, "Thinking beyond Patterns," 21–23. An effective summary of how the opposition of form and experience arose in modern philosophy and led to the notion of arbitrary imposition of form on experience is given on 42–45. An account of how Heidegger's thought avoided this outcome but did not follow through in detailing the full range of an intricate order is given on 30–32.

10. Ibid., 96.

11. Gendlin, "Experiential Phenomenology," 305.

12. Gendlin, "Thinking beyond Patterns," 46ff.

13. Ibid., 54.

14. Martin Heidegger, *Basic Writings*, ed. David F. Krell (New York: Harper and Row, 1977), 235.

15. Heidegger himself indicated that there is in fact positive phenomenological content in terms such as subject, soul, consciousness, spirit, and person, but the traditional presumption of ontological reification has concealed such content, and so such terms must be avoided (*Being and Time*, 72).

16. Gendlin, "Thinking beyond Patterns," 58–65.

17. Ibid., 81–83.

18. Ibid., 104–5.

19. Ibid., 95–96.

20. Lawrence J. Hatab, *Myth and Philosophy: A Contest of Truths* (La Salle, Illinois: Open Court Publishing Co., 1990), 361.

21. See, e.g., Gendlin, "Thinking beyond Patterns," 66–77.

22. This is effectively illustrated by the discussion of poetry in ibid., 51–57.

23. Heidegger, "Letter on Humanism," 206. See also the collection *On the Way to Language*, trans. Peter D. Hertz (New York: Harper and Row, 1971). For references from Wittgenstein, see *Tractatus Logico-Philosophicus*, trans. D. F. Pears and B. F. McGuinness (London: Routledge and Kegan Paul, 1961), 3.3 and 5.6, and *Philosophical Investigations*, trans. G.E.M. Anscombe (New York: Macmillan, 1953), secs. 13–15, 49, 257, 261, 353–56. For an analysis, see Lawrence J. Hatab and William Brenner, "Heidegger and Wittgenstein on Language and Mystery," *International Studies in Philosophy* 15, no. 3 (1984), 25–43.

24. Heidegger, "Letter on Humanism," 206.

25. Even this, of course, does not release us from the linguistic "circle." Perhaps this is why Wittgenstein insisted on keeping silent about such matters.

26. Gendlin, "Thinking beyond Patterns," 24–26; see also, 41 and 98.

27. See ibid., 144–45.

28. Ibid., 85.

29. Ibid., 41.

30. Ibid., 110.

31. Ibid., 121–31.

32. See, e.g., *Physics* III.3, and *De Anima* III.1–8.

33. Gendlin, "Thinking beyond Patterns," 78.

Reply to Hatab

1. For a history of this strand, see Hans Kohn, *The Mind of Germany* (New York: Scribner, 1960).

2. Heidegger said that the Greeks created a new way of being human, and he wanted the Germans to do that too. He thought this required going *through* the Greek creation backwards, so as to re-emerge not only with a new way, but a special one that would remain aware of how human ways emerge. To him the German language had the perfectly serious advantage that one did not have to work back through Latin to think the Greek beginnings. And it is true the Latin in our English words *is* a barrier when we want to understand something Greek, for example, Aristotle.

Chapter 11
Kenneth Liberman, Meaning Reflexivity

1. Eugene Gendlin, "Experiential Psychotherapy," in *Current Psychotherapies*, ed. Raymond Corsini (Itasca: F. E. Peacock, 1973), 317.

2. Eugene Gendlin, "Thinking beyond Patterns: Body, Language, and Situations," in *The Presence of Feeling in Thought*, ed. B. den Ouden and M. Moen (New York: Peter Lang, 1992).

3. Eugene Gendlin, "Words Can Say How They Work," in *Proceedings, Heidegger Conference*, ed. Robert P. Crease (Stony Brook: SUNY Press, 1993), 29.

4. Eugene Gendlin, "Experiential Phenomenology," in *Phenomenology and the Social Sciences*, ed. M. Natanson (Evanston: Northwestern University Press, 1973), 282.

5. Eugene Gendlin, *Experiencing and the Creation of Meaning* (Glencoe: Free Press, 1962), 1.

6. Ibid., 44.

7. Ibid., 146.

8. Ibid., 313.

9. Ibid., 26.

10. Eugene Gendlin, with J. Reebe, J. Cassens, M. Klein, and M. Oberlander, "Focusing Ability in Psychotherapy, Personality, and Creativity," in *Research in Psychotherapy* 3 (1968), 233.

11. Eugene Gendlin, "Nonlogical Moves and Nature Metaphors," in *Analecta Husserliana*, vol. 19, ed. A. T. Tyminiecka (1985), 397.

12. Ibid., 384.

13. Gendlin, *Experiencing*, 321.

14. Gendlin, "Nonlogical Moves," 392.

15. Ibid., 385, 388.

16. Gendlin, "Thinking beyond Patterns," 98.

17. Edmund Husserl, *The Crisis of European Sciences and Transcendental Phenomenology* (Evanston: Northwestern University Press, 1970).

18. Gendlin, "Nonlogical Moves," 385.

19. Jacques Derrida, *Margins of Philosophy* (Chicago: University of Chicago Press, 1982), 213.

20. Gendlin, "Nonlogical Moves," 392.

21. Ibid., 384.

22. Ibid., 388.

23. Gendlin, "Thinking beyond Patterns," 46.

24. Emmanuel Levinas, *Otherwise than Being, Or Beyond Essence*, trans. A. Lingis (The Hague: Martinus Nijhoff, 1981), 152.

25. Gendlin, *Experiencing*, 326.

26. Gendlin, et al., "Focusing Ability," vol. 3 (1968), pp. 217.

27. Gendlin, *Experiencing*, 313.

28. Ibid., 186.

29. Ibid., 201–2.

30. Ibid., 392; italics mine.

31. Ibid., 396.

32. Ibid., 32.

33. Ibid., 29.

34. Gendlin, et al., "Focusing Ability," 219.

35. Gendlin, *Experiencing*, 329.

36. Gendlin, et al., "Focusing Ability," 222.

37. Gendlin, *Experiencing*, 324.

38. Ibid., 323.

39. Eugene Gendlin, "A Phenomenology of Emotions: Anger," in *Explorations in Phenomenology*, ed. D. Carr and E. Çasey (The Hague: Martinus Nijhoff, 1973), 367–98.

40. Ibid., 387, 390.

41. Gendlin, *Experiencing*, 323.

42. Gendlin, "Nonlogical Moves," 397.

43. Gendlin, *Experiencing*, 213.

44. Gendlin, "Nonlogical Moves," 387.

45. Ibid., 391, 393, 395.

46. Gendlin, "Nonlogical Moves," 389.

47. Ibid., 399–400.

48. Gendlin, "Thinking beyond Patterns," 31–35.

49. Ibid., 111.

50. Ibid., 21.

51. Ibid., 83.

52. Ibid., 100.

53. Ibid., 91.

54. Ibid., 92.

55. Gendlin, "Experiential Phenomenology," 286–87.

56. Ibid., 287.

57. Kenneth Liberman, *Understanding Interaction in Central Australia: An Ethnomethodology of Australian Aboriginal People* (London: Routledge, 1985), 186–87. Also, see the discussions of "the necessity of indeterminacy" and "the global nature of communication," in Kenneth Liberman, "The Economy of Central Australian Aboriginal Expression: An Inspection from the Vantage of Merleau-Ponty and Derrida," *Semiotica* 40, nos. 3/4 (1982), 267–346.

58. Dusan Bjelic and Michael Lynch, "The Work of a (Scientific) Demonstration: Respecifying Newton's and Goethe's Theories of Prismatic Color," in *Text in Context: Contributions to Ethnomethodology*, ed. Graham Watson and Robert M. Seiler (Newbury Park: Sage, 1992), 52–78.

59. Jeff Coulter, "Logic: Ethnomethodology and the Logic of Language," in *Ethnomethodology and the Human Sciences*, ed. Graham Button (Cambridge: Cambridge University Press, 1991), 20–50.

60. Lena Jayyusi, "Values and Moral Judgement: Communicative Praxis as Moral Order," in Ibid., 227–51.

61. Gendlin, "Thinking beyond Patterns," 77.

62. Gendlin, "Words Can Say How They Work," 31.

63. Cf. Kenneth Liberman, "An Ethnomethodological Agenda in the Study of Intercultural Communication," in *Cultural Communication and Intercultural Contact*, ed. Donal Carbaugh (Hillsdale: Lawrence Erlbaum Associates, 1990), 185–92.

64. Gendlin, "Thinking beyond Patterns," 102.

65. Gendlin, "Words Can Say How They Work," 34.

66. Gendlin, "Thinking beyond Patterns," 118.

67. Ibid., 125.

68. Ibid., 139.

69. Gendlin, "Thinking beyond Patterns," 23–24.

70. Ibid., 125.

71. Ibid., 35.

72. Ibid., 93.

73. Ibid., 111.

74. Ibid., 98.

Chapter 12
Jerald Wallulis, Carrying Forward

1. Hans-Georg Gadamer, *Truth and Method*, 2d ed., revised, trans. Joel Weinsheimer and Donald G. Marshall (New York: Crossroad, 1991), 551.

2. Hans-Georg Gadamer, *Hans-Georg Gadamer on Education, Poetry, and History: Applied Hermeneutics*, ed. Dieter Misgeld and Graeme Nicholson, trans. Lawrence Schmidt and Monica Reuss (Albany: SUNY Press, 1992), 150.

3. Gadamer, *Truth and Method*, xvi.

4. Ibid., xv.

5. Joseph Dunne, *Back to the Rough Ground: 'Phronesis' and 'Techne' in Modern Philosophy in Aristotle* (Notre Dame: University of Notre Dame Press, 1993), 121.

6. Ibid.

7. Joel Weinsheimer, *Gadamer's Hermeneutics: A Reading of Truth and Method* (New Haven: Yale University Press, 1985), 251.

8. Gadamer, *Hans-Georg Gadamer on Education, Poetry, and History*, 65.

9. Ibid.

10. Gadamer, *Truth and Method*, 549.

11. Ibid.

12. Ibid., 446. This is only one instance where the revised edition is clearly superior to the original.

13. Ibid.

14. Ibid., 458.

15. Dunne, *Back to the Rough Ground*, 131.

16. Gadamer, *Truth and Method*, 458.

17. Dieter Misgeld, "Poetry, Dialogue, and Negotiation: Liberal Culture and Conservative Politics in Hans-Georg Gadamer's Thought," in *Festivals of Interpretation*, ed. Kathleen Wright (Albany: SUNY Press, 1990), 166.

18. Ibid.

19. Ibid., 167.

20. Ibid.

21. Ibid., 162.

22. Eugene Gendlin, "Human Nature and Concepts," in *Psychological Aspects of Modernity*, ed. Jerome Braun (Westport: Praeger, 1993), 10.

23. Eugene Gendlin, "Experiential Psychotherapy," in *Current Psychotherapies*, ed. Raymond J. Corsini (Itasca: F. E. Peacock, 1973), 325.

24. Eugene Gendlin, "Thinking beyond Patterns: Body, Language, and Situations," in *The Presence of Feeling in Thought*, ed. B. den Ouden and M. Moen (New York: Peter Lang, 1992), 87.

25. Gendlin, "Experiential Psychotherapy," 336.

26. Gendlin, "Thinking beyond Patterns," 100.

27. Ibid., 102, 103.

28. Gendlin, "Experiential Psychotherapy," 327.

29. Eugene Gendlin, "A Philosophical Critique of the Concept of Narcissim," in *Pathologies of the Modern Self*, ed. David Michael Levin (New York: New York University Press), 283, 290.

30. David Michael Levin, "Making Sense: The Work of Eugene Gendlin," *Human Studies*, 17, no. 3 (July 1994), 344–45.

31. Gadamer, *Hans-Georg Gadamer on Education, Poetry, and History*, 177–78.

32. Misgeld, "Poetry, Dialogue, and Negotiation," 167.

Chapter 13
Graeme Nicholson, Intricacy: A Metaphysical Idea

1. Eugene Gendlin, "Thinking beyond Patterns: Body, Language and Situations," in *The Presence of Feeling in Thought*, ed. B. den Ouden and M. Moen (New York: Peter Lang, 1992), 22–23.

2. Ibid., 35f.

3. Eugene Gendlin, "Thinking after Patterns," Heidegger Conference, 1987, 2.

4. Gendlin, "Thinking beyond Patterns," 46.

5. Ibid., 47.

6. Ibid., 67–78.

7. Eugene Gendlin, "Thinking after Patterns," 11–12.

8. Ibid., 2.

9. Gendlin, "Thinking beyond Patterns," 48.

10. Aristotle, *Metaphysics*, Zeta, chap. 7, 1032b5–14.

11. I quote (with one or two small alterations) from the translation *Philosophical Investigations into the Essence of Human Freedom and Related Matters*, trans. Priscilla Hayden-Roy, in *Philosophy of German Idealism*, ed. Ernst Behler (New York: Continuum, 1987), 236–39.

Chapter 14
Véronique M. Fóti, Alterity and the Dynamics of Metaphor

1. Jacques Derrida, "White Mythology: Metaphor in the Text of Philosophy," in *Margins of Philosophy*, trans. Alan Bass (Chicago: University of Chicago Press, 1972), 207–71.

2. See Derrida, "La métaphysique—relève de la métaphor," the last section of "White Mythology."

3. Eugene Gendlin, "Nonlogical Moves and Nature Metaphors," in *Analecta Husserliana*, vol. 19, ed. A. T. Tyminiecka, (Dordrecht: D. Reidel, 1985), 383–400.

4. Eugene Gendlin, "Thinking beyond Patterns: Body, Language, and Situations," in *The Presence of Feeling in Thought*, ed. B. den Ouden and M. Moen (New York: Peter Lang, 1992), 47–49.

5. For a selection of texts and discussion of the authors and perspectives mentioned, see *Philosophical Perspectives on Metaphor*, ed. Mark Johnson (Minneapolis: University of Minnesota Press, 1981).

6. Immanuel Kant, *Kritik der Urteilskraft* (Hamburg: Felix Meiner Verlag, 1959), sec. 49; see also, sec. 59.

7. Paul Ricoeur, *Die lebendige Metapher* (hereafter *LM*) (German translation of *La métaphor vive*), trans. Rainer Rochlitz, (Munich: Wilhelm Fink Verlag, 1986); see also, Ricoeur, "The Metaphorical Process as Cognition, Imagination, and Feeling," in *Philosophical Perspectives on Metaphor*, 228–47.

8. Kant, *Kritik der Urteilskraft*, 179.

9. Ricoeur, *LM*. Since both the French original and the English translation are not available to me at the times of this writing, I translate Rochlitz's German into English.

10. Gendlin, "Nonlogical Moves and Nature Metaphors," 376.

11. See Martin Heidegger, *Einführung in die Metaphysik* (Tübingen: Niemeyer, 1976), 68–70, and David M. Levin, "Making Sense: On the Work of Eugene Gendlin," *Human Studies* 27, no. 3 (July 1994), 343–53.

12. Immanuel Kant, *Kritik der reinen Vernunft* (Transcendental Dialectic, part 3, sec. 4).

13. Besides Heidegger's *Einführung in die Metaphysik* (especially part 1), see his *Sein und Zeit*, 12th ed. (Tübingen: Niemeyer, 1972), chap. 1, sec. 1, 2–4.

14. See Heidegger, *Einführung*, part 3, 57–70.

15. Paul de Man, "Epistemologie der Metapher," trans. Werner Hamacher, in *Theorie der Metapher*, ed. Anselm Haverkamp (Darmstadt: Wissenschaftliche Buchgesellschaft, 1983), 414–37. This article first appeared in *Critical Inquiry* 5 (1978), 12–30, in English.

16. The poem is cited from *Johann Wolfgang Goethe: Sämtliche Werke*, vol. 2, ed. Hartmut Reinhardt (Munich: Carl Hauser, 1987), 53, where, however, it is given under its alternative title, "Wanderers Nachtgesang."

17. Martin Heidegger, "Die Sprache im Gedicht," *Unterwegs zur Sprache* (Pfullingen: Neske, 1975), 37–82; see 60.

18. Gendlin, "Nonlogical Moves and Nature Metaphors."

19. Gendlin, "Crossing and Dipping: Some Terms for Approaching the Interface between Natural Understanding and Logical Formation," in *Subjectivity and the Debate over Computational Cognitive Science*, ed. M. Galbraith and W. J. Rapaport, published as a Technical Report of the Center for Cognitive Science, State University of New York at Buffalo, May 1991, 53.

20. Heidegger, *Einführung*, 67.

21. Wallace Stevens, "The Noble Rider and the Sound of Words," in *The Necessary Angel* (New York: Knopf, 1951), 31.

22. Gendlin, "Crossing and Dipping," 51, 54–56. I am greatly indebted to Professor Gendlin for his generosity in discussing the issues in personal correspondence.

23. See Gendlin, "Nonlogical Moves and Nature Metaphors."

24. Alan D. Perlis, "Wallace Stevens' Reader Poems and the Effacement of Metaphor," *The Wallace Stevens Journal* 10, no. 2 (Fall 1986), 67–75.

25. Heidegger's critique appears in *Der Satz vom Grund* (Pfullingen: Neske, 1958), 89.

26. Eleanor Cook, *Poetry, Word-Play, and Word-War in Wallace Stevens* (Princeton: Princeton University Press, 1988), 183.

27. Stevens's poems are cited from *The Collected Poems of Wallace Stevens* (New York: Knopf, 1965), hereafter referred to as *CP*. See *CP*, 288.

28. Stevens, *CP*, 444.

29. Ibid.

30. Ibid., 445.

31. Paul de Man, "Semiology and Rhetoric," in *Allegories of Reading* (New Haven: Yale University Press, 1979), 14. See also his "Reading (Proust)," in the same volume.

32. See Eugene Gendlin, "A Philosophical Critique of the Concept of Narcissism: The Significance of the Awareness Movement," in *Pathologies of the Modern Self: Postmodern Studies on Narcissism, Schizophrenia, and Depression*, ed. David Michael Levin (New York: New York University Press, 1987), and *Experiencing and the Creation of Meaning* (New York: Free Press, 1978), 253.

33. Gendlin, "Thinking beyond Patterns," 46–65.

34. Stevens, "Three Academic Pieces," in *The Necessary Angel*, 79f.

35. Stevens, "Lebensweisheitsspielerei," *CP*, 504f.

36. Although "Of Mere Being" is known as Stevens's last poem, there is no conclusive reason to regard it as such. See Tim Armstrong's discussion in his "Stevens's 'Last Poem' Again," *The Wallace Stevens Journal* 12, no. 1 (Spring 1988), 35–43.

37. The poem is cited from *Opus Posthumous by Wallace Stevens*, ed. Milton J. Bates (New York: Knopf, 1989), 141; but I have retained "distance" in place of "decor" in the third verse, in keeping with S. F. Moore's first edition of the *Opus Posthumous* (New York: Knopf, 1957). The reasons for such a choice are discussed in Armstrong, "Stevens's 'Last Poem.'" The poem survives only in a single typewritten manuscript, which does show "decor"; but it is not certain that this manuscript constitutes Stevens's final version.

38. Harold Bloom, in *Wallace Stevens: The Poems of Our Climate* (Ithaca: Cornell University Press, 1976), writes: "The 'mere' in the title is both a litotes and a play on the archaic meaning, which is 'pure,' and perhaps even carries a hint of the root, which means 'flickering.' But 'mere' has a special force in the late Stevens anyway" (371).

39. See W. B. Yeats, "Sailing to Byzantium," and "Byzantium," in *The Collected Poems of W. B. Yeats* (New York: Macmillan, 1956), 191f. and 243f.

40. Stevens, *CP*, 18.

41. Stevens, *The Necessary Angel*, 28.

42. Ibid., 31.

43. For a discussion of these issues in Heidegger, see Reiner Schürmann, *Heidegger on Being and Acting: From Principles to Anarchy*, trans. Christine-Marie Gros (Bloomington: Indiana University Press, 1987).

44. Ricoeur, *LM*, 295.

45. Gendlin, "Thinking beyond Patterns," 126.

46. Ibid., 57.

47. Ibid.

48. See Ricoeur, *LM*, 254–73, and Heidegger, *Der Satz vom Grund* 89.

49. Ricoeur, *LM*, 270.

50. Ibid., 278.

51. Ibid., 289.

52. Ibid., 291.

53. My formulation refers to Gendlin's summary of these points in personal correspondence.

Chapter 15
Joseph Margolis, Language as Lingual

1. What follows is a reflection on reading Eugene Gendlin, "Thinking beyond Patterns: Body, Language, and Situations," in *The Presence of Feeling in Thought*, ed. B. den Ouden and M. Moen (New York: Peter Lang, 1992).

2. See P. F. Strawson, "On Referring," *Mind* 59 (1950); also Bertrand Russell, "On Denoting," *Mind* 14 (1905).

3. See Ludwig Wittgenstein, *Philosophical Investigations*, trans. G.E.M. Anscombe (New York: Macmillan, 1953).

4. See J. L. Austin, *How to do Things with Words* (Oxford: Clarendon, 1962); and John R. Searle, *Speech Acts: An Essay in the Philosophy of Language* (Cambridge: Cambridge University Press, 1969).

5. See P. F. Strawson, *Individuals: An Essay in Descriptive Metaphysics* (London: Methuen, 1959), 18.

6. See W. V. Quine, *Word and Object* (Cambridge: MIT Press, 1960), sec. 37.

7. See *The Complete Papers of Charles Sanders Peirce*, 8 vols., ed. Charles Hartshorne, Paul Weiss, and Arthur W. Burks (Cambridge: Harvard University Press, 1931–58).

8. For a general account of Wittgenstein's position, see Joseph Margolis, "Wittgenstein's 'Forms of Life': A Cultural Template for Psychology," in *Meaning and the Growth of Understanding: Wittgenstein's Significance for Developmental Psychology*, ed. Michael Chapman and Roger A. Dixon (Berlin: Springer-Verlag, 1987).

9. See Joseph Margolis, "Constraints on the Metaphysics of Culture," *Texts without Reference: Reconciling Science and Narrative* (Oxford: Basil Blackwell, 1989).

10. See Joseph Margolis, "Emergence and the Unity of Science," in *Science without Unity: Reconciling the Human and the Natural Sciences* (Oxford: Basil Blackwell, 1987).

11. Wittgenstein, *Philosophical Investigations*, part 1, sec. 242.

Contributors

William James Earle is Professor of Philosophy at Baruch College and the Graduate Center of the City University of New York and member of the Executive Committee of the Center for Cultural Studies at the Graduate Center. A former Woodrow Wilson and National Endowment for the Humanities Fellow, Dr. Earle is the author of many scholarly papers, *Introduction to Philosophy*, a guide-book to contemporary analytic philosophy, and the entry on William James in the *Encyclopedia of Philosophy*. He is currently Associate Editor of *Philosophical Forum*.

Véronique M. Fóti is Associate Professor in the Department of Philosophy at Pennsylvania State University, University Park. Dr. Foti is the author of *Heidegger and the Poets: Poiesis, Sophia, Techne,* and the editor of *Merleau-Ponty: Difference, Materiality, Painting.* She has also written numerous articles for journals and edited collections.

Eugene Gendlin received a Ph.D. in Philosophy from the University of Chicago and, in 1963, he accepted a joint appointment to teach there in the Department of Philosophy and the Department of Psychology. Gendlin is the author of numerous papers in philosophy, psychology, and psychotherapy, as well as four books: *Experiencing and the Creation of Meaning, Focusing, Let Your Body Interpret Your Dreams,* and *Body, Experiencing, Language.* He is currently finishing a book entitled *Focusing-Oriented Psychotherapy.* In 1963, he founded *Psychotherapy: Theory, Research and Practice,* the journal of the Psychotherapy Division of the American Psychological Association, and served until 1976 as its first editor. Since 1995, he directs the International Focusing Institute of Chicago, where social and psychological applications of his philosophy are researched and taught.

Lawrence Hatab is Professor in the Department of Philosophy at Old Dominion University, Norfolk, Virginia. Dr. Hatab is the author of *Nietzsche and Eternal Recurrence, Myth and Philosophy: A Contest of Truths,* and *A Nietzschean Defense of Democracy.*

Mark Johnson is Professor and Chair in the Department of Philosophy at the University of Oregon. Dr. Johnson is co-author, with George Lakoff, of *Metaphors We Live By*, editor of *Philosophical Perspectives on Metaphor,* and author of *The Body in the Mind: The Bodily Basis of Meaning, Imagination and Reason* and *Moral Imagination: Implications of Cognitive Science for Ethics.*

David Kolb is Professor in the Department of Philosophy and Religion, Bates College, Lewiston, Maine. Dr. Kolb is the author of *The Critique of Pure Modernity: Hegel, Heidegger and After,* as well as *Postmodern Sophistications: Philosophy, Architecture and Tradition* and *Socrates in the Labyrinth,* a collection of hypertext essays. He has also edited *New Perspectives on Hegel's Philosophy of Religion.*

David Michael Levin is Professor in the Department of Philosophy at Northwestern University, Evanston, Illinois. He is the author of *Reason and Evidence in Husserl's Phenomenology* and a trilogy, *The Body's Recollection of Being, The Opening of Vision: Nihilism and the Postmodern Situation,* and *The Listening Self: Personal Growth, Social Change, and the Closure of Metaphysics,* as well as numerous scholarly studies in hermeneutical phenomenology, art criticism, cultural studies, ethics, and sociopolitical philosophy. He has also edited *Pathologies of the Modern Self: Postmodern Studies on Narcissism, Schizophrenia and Depression* and, more recently, *Modernity and the Hegemony of Vision.* A second edited collection on vision, *Sites of Vision,* has just been published.

Kenneth Liberman is Associate Professor in the Department of Sociology at the University of Oregon, Eugene. He is the author of *Understanding Interaction in Central Australia: An Ethnomethodology of Australian Aborigines,* and numerous journal publications using phenomenology and hermeneutics to discuss problems of meaning and understanding in sociology, philosophical anthropology, and ethnomethodology. Dr. Liberman is currently Co-Director of the Society for Phenomenology and the Human Sciences.

Joseph Margolis is Laura H. Carnell Professor of Philosophy in the Department of Philosophy, Temple University, Philadelphia. Dr. Margolis is the author of many books, including *The Persistence of Reality* (4 volumes), *The Truth about Relativism, The Flux of History and the Flux of Science,* and *Interpretation Radical but not Unruly: The New Puzzle of the Arts and History.*

J. N. Mohanty is Professor in the Department of Philosophy at Temple University, Philadelphia. He is the author of numerous journal studies in phenomenology, the philosophy of mind, and the philosophy of language, including studies on Indian philosophy. His books include *Edmund*

Husserl's Theory of Meaning, Husserl and Frege, Phenomenology and Ontology, and *Transcendental Phenomenology: An Analytic Account,* and an edited volume on *Phenomenology and the Human Sciences: Readings on Husserl's Logical Investigations.* His two most recent publications are *Reason and Tradition in Indian Thought* and *Essays on Indian Philosophy, Traditional and Modern.* Dr. Mohanty is a past President of the Indian Philosophical Congress, was a Visiting Fellow at All Souls College, Oxford University, and is currently a member of the Institut Internationale de Philosophie, Paris. In 1992, he was awarded a Humboldt-Forschungspreis for research in Germany.

Graeme Nicholson is Professor in the Department of Philosophy at Trinity College, University of Toronto. He is the author of *Seeing and Reading* and *Illustrations of Being,* co-author, with Louis Greenspan, of *Fackenheim: German Philosophy and Jewish Thought,* and co-author, with Dieter Misgeld, of *Hans-Georg Gadamer on Education, Poetry and History.*

Robert C. Scharff is Professor in the Department of Philosophy at the University of New Hampshire, Durham. His main interests are the philosophy of the history of philosophy and the epistemological significance of belonging to a tradition. His publications are mostly on nineteenth- and twentieth-century continental philosophy (especially Dilthey, Nietzsche, and Heidegger) and nineteenth-century positivism (especially Comte and Mill). He is the author of *Comte After Positivism: Rethinking Philosophy's Past for Current Practice,* recently published by Cambridge University Press, and is editor of *Man and World: An International Philosophical Review.*

Hans Julius Schneider, formerly Professor of Philosophy in the Interdisziplinäres Institut für Wissenschaftstheorie und Wissenschaftsgeschichte at the University of Erlangen-Nürnberg, is currently Professor of Philosophy in the Institut für Philosophie at the Universität Potsdam, Germany. Dr. Schneider is the author of two books, *Pragmatik als Basis von Semantik und Syntax* and *Phantasie und Kalkül: Über die Polarität von Handlung und Struktur in der Sprache,* as well as numerous journal studies in philosophy of language, philosophy of science, and hermeneutics. Publications in English include: "Syntactic Metaphor: Frege, Wittgenstein, and the Limits of a Theory of Meaning" (*Philosophical Investigations* 13, [1990]); and "Objectivism in Pragmatics as a Hindrance to Intercultural Communication," in *The Pragmatics of Intercultural and International Communication,* ed. J. Blommaert and J. Verschueren, vol. 3: *Selected Papers of the International Pragmatics Conference,* Antwerp, 1987.

Jerald Wallulis is Associate Professor in the Department of Philosophy at the University of South Carolina, Columbia. He is the author of *The Hermeneutics of Life History: Personal Achievement and History in Gadamer,*

Habermas and Erikson, as well as a number of journal studies. He is also co-editor of *Changing Social Science: Critical Theory and Other Critical Perspectives.*

Meredith Williams is Associate Professor in the Department of Philosophy at Northwestern University. She is the author of numerous journal studies in cognitive psychology, the philosophy of mind, and the philosophy of language. In particular, there are some important essays, among these publications, on Wittgenstein and Vigotsky.